McGINNESS

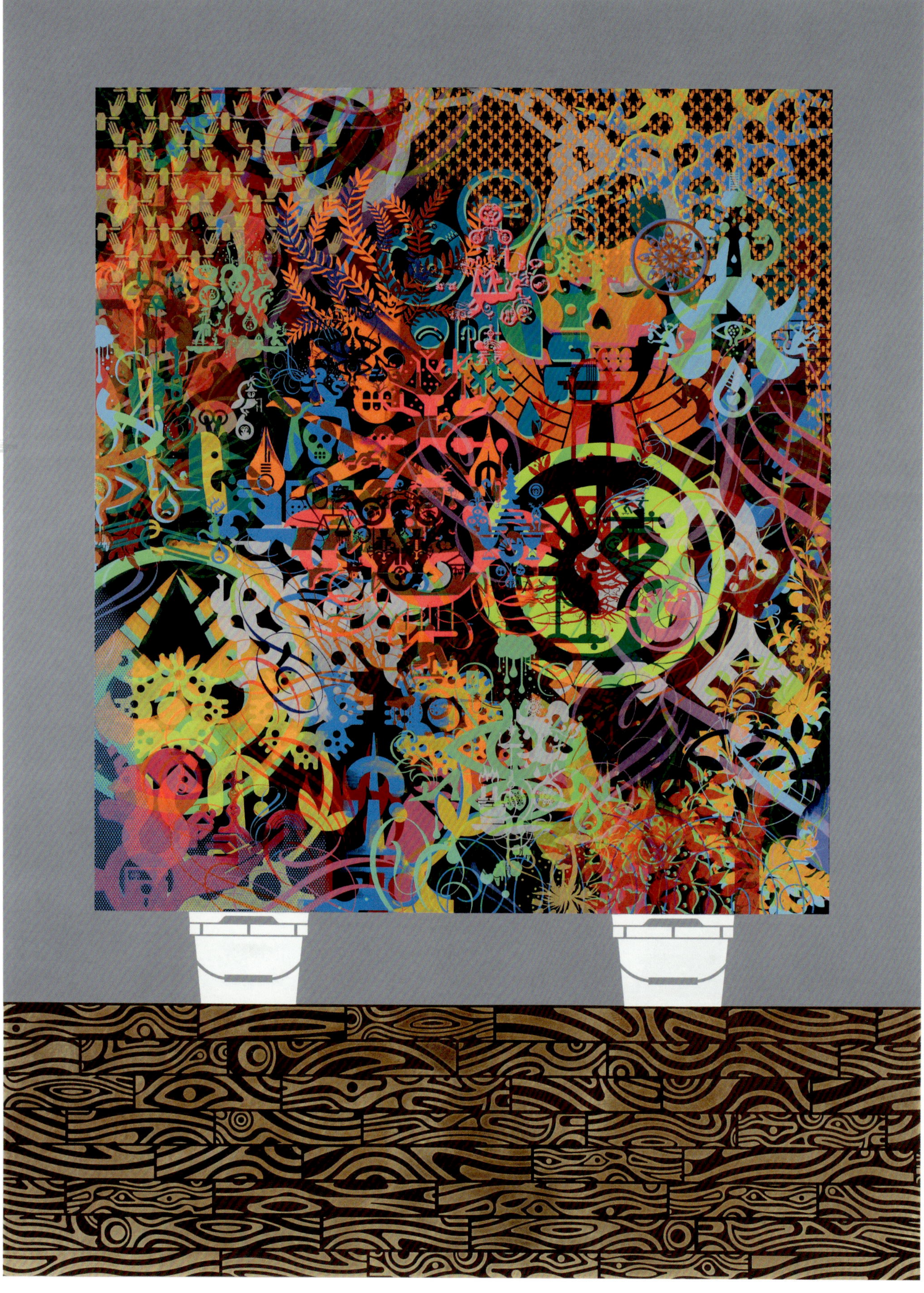

MᶜGINNESS

#metadata

Essays by

Dieter Buchhart
Andrew Blauvelt
Ben Sutton
Carlo McCormick
Bill Powers

DAMIANI

Front Cover & Frontispiece:
A Pigmented Purpose,
2015, acrylic and metal
leaf on linen, 84 x 60 in.
(213.5 x 152.4 cm)

Back Cover:
*Something About the Collapse
of Art and Language*
(Detail with color calibration
chart held by photographer),
2013, acrylic on canvas,
8 x 8 ft. (243.8 x 243.8 cm)

Ryan McGinness
#metadata

Published in Italy in 2018
by Damiani srl
info@damianieditore.com
damianieditore.com

Published in an edition
of 1,500 copies.

This book is typeset in
Baskerville and Univers.

Printed and bound in Italy
by Grafiche Damiani—
Faenza Group SpA, Italy

International Standard
Book Number:
978-88-6208-572-4

© 2018 Damiani

All works by Ryan McGinness:
© 2018 Ryan McGinness
Artists Rights Society (ARS),
New York

Ryan McGinness Studios, Inc.
ryanmcginness.com
@McGinnessWorks

Contents

Photograph taken in 2013 of primed wood panel (48 x 48 in. (121.9 x 121.9 cm)) in kraft paper on two plastic gallon-sized paint containers in the studio, used as source image for *Blank Painting* (2017)

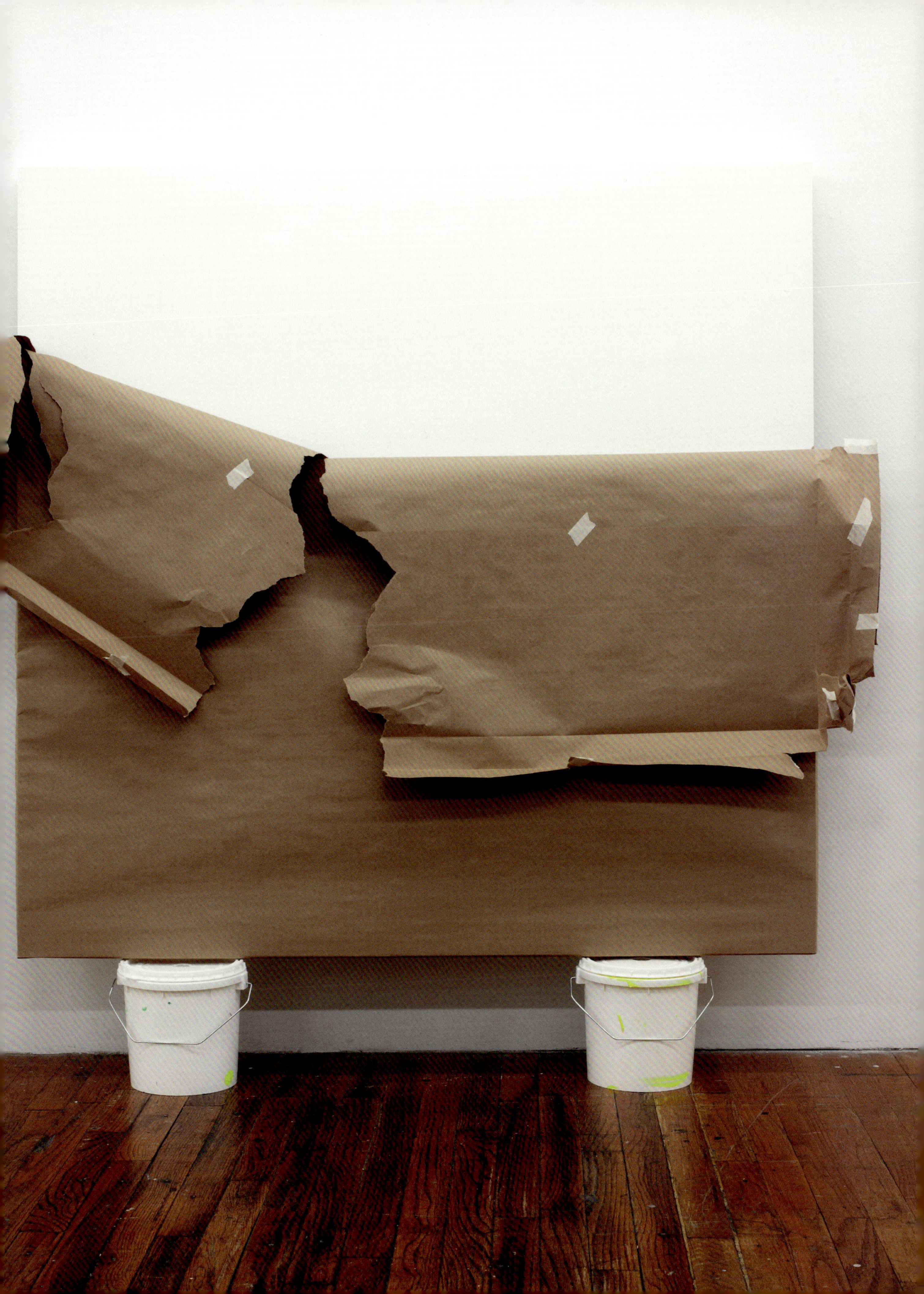

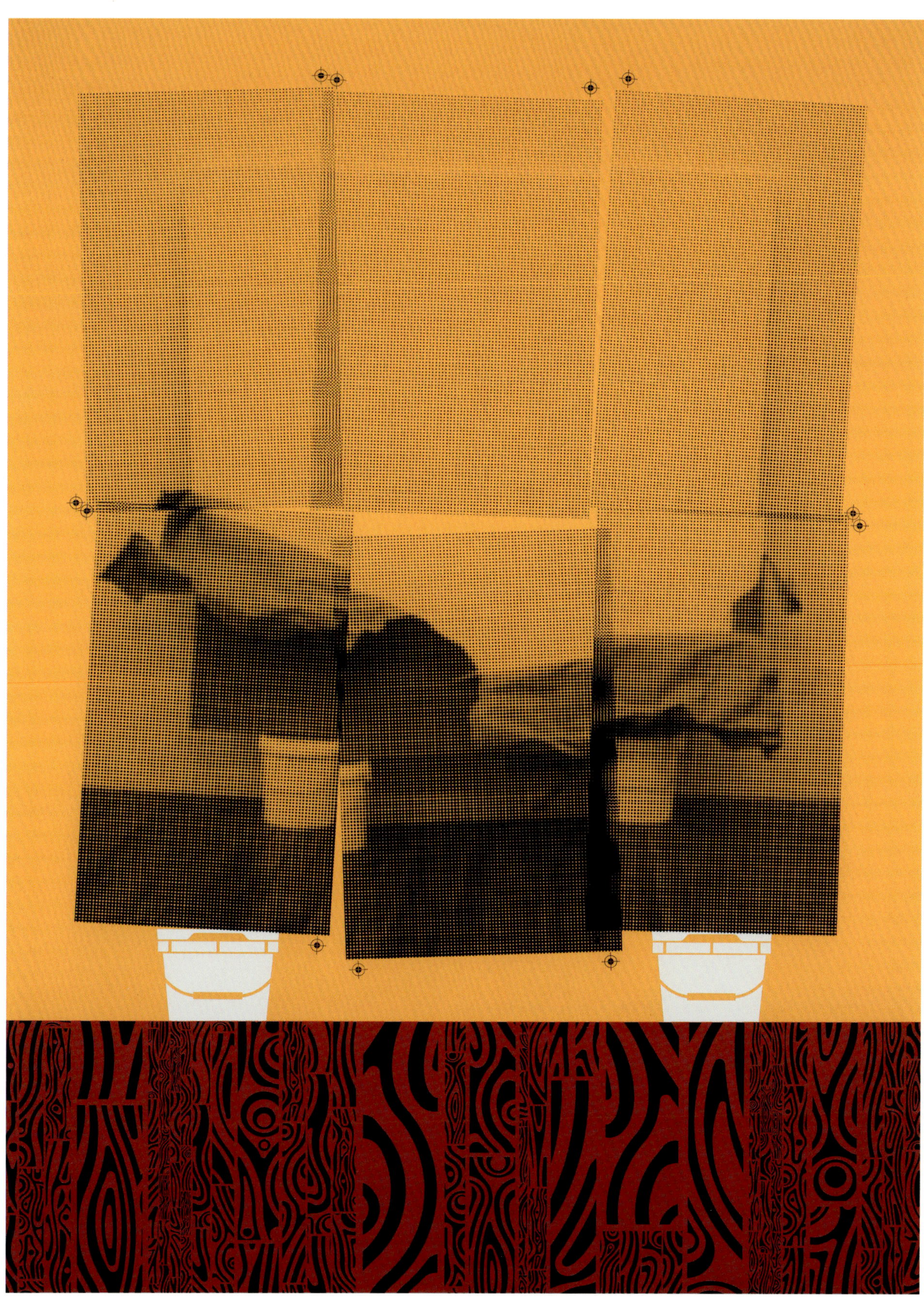

Blank Painting (Yellow), 2017, acrylic on linen, 84 x 60 in.
(213.4 x 152.4 cm); Opposite Page: Detail

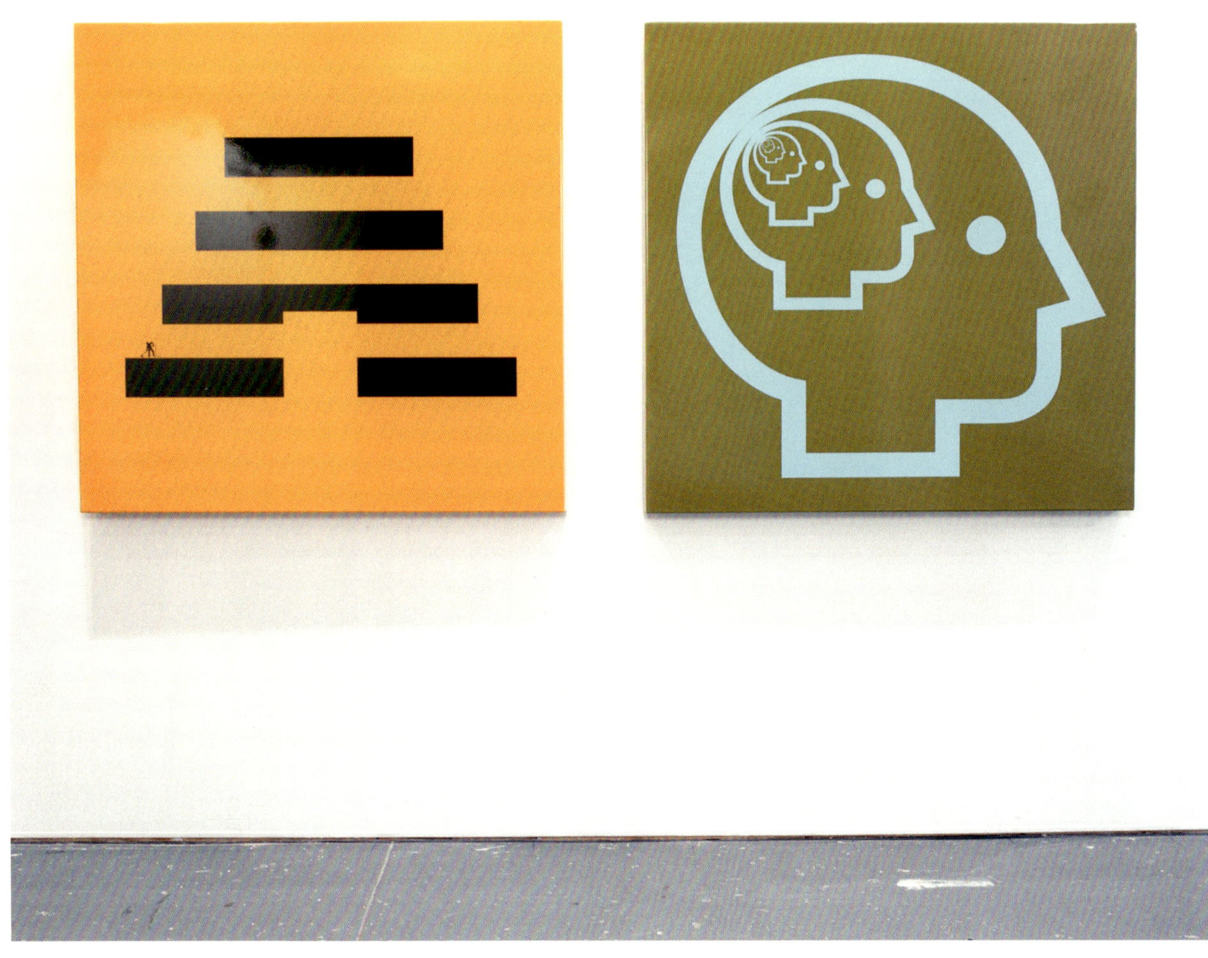

Left: *Cleanliness and Godliness*, 2001, porcelain-baked enamel on steel panel, 48 x 48 in. (121.9 x 121.9 cm)
Right: *I Am a Living Sign*, 2001, porcelain-baked enamel on steel panel, 48 x 48 in. (121.9 x 121.9 cm)

The Fragmentary Quality of
Ryan McGinness' Periodic System

Dieter Buchhart

Whether in communication, advertising, design, or art: emoji have become a self-evident part of our everyday lives. Day in, day out, we exchange up to six billion emoji in our global village using our smart phones and other devices. But the emoji aesthetic has also found its way into our lives by way of kitschy design articles like glassware, pillows, or clothing and through everyday advertising. As Marcel Danesi, a semiotician and linguistic anthropologist, maintains: "Emoji are products of an increasingly expanding global culture, where a common ground of symbolism is developing and spreading throughout the culture. Emoji usage fits in particularly well with many popular trends that characterize the global village." For these "picture words"—the word *emoji* is the English adaptation of the Japanese "e" for "picture" and "moji" for "letter, character"—promise a global legibility that leads some linguists to the enthusiastic conjecture that this could be a "new universal language."

According to Emojipedia, the impressive number of 2,666 emoji were in existence by June 2017. Taking his inspiration from manga comics, Japanese telecommunications employee Shigetaka Kurita created the very first emoji symbols in 1998. At around the same time, Ryan McGinness began developing a comprehensive system of symbols that by now has grown to include several thousand symbols. In the process, McGinness referred to the reduced visual language of graphic design of the twentieth century and its attempt to create "legible universal images" and to traffic signs, whose immediate legibility is of decisive importance. For due to the dominance of imagery, the meaning of objects, images, and symbols is clear within nanoseconds, while reading a word involves a much more complex cognitive process. Like emoji, McGinness' symbols can be read as picture words that he mixes as basic elements in comprehensive compositions with and literally on top of one another. But what fundamental meaning is assigned to his picture words? What importance does the artist assign to his artistic process of development? And what role does language play as a local or universal system of communication in his art? In a sketchbook, McGinness noted: "At the essence of our being are the need to know and the need to understand…our need to read into and interpret—to make sense of chaos and give meaning to seemingly abstract forms." He emphasizes the human striving toward legibility, the desire to understand. In the process, he alludes to the concept of "ordering" that he emphasizes elsewhere in a sketchbook: "All art is an ordering." And ordering and systematicity is in turn the foundation of every complex abstract, communication system based on an alphabet and that of public traffic signs. "The Order of Things," the objectification of language and knowledge about this order, differences, and characteristics are the points of departure for McGinness' symbolic system. Here the artist understands his signs as elements in a periodic system that take on a highly different significance, like the differing masses of the chemical elements. This introduces three fundamental concepts of McGinness' artistic system: *legibility*, *order*, and *element*. The various complexity of the elements of his periodic system are based on their process of emergence and abstraction, for like the development of our abstract linguistic alphabet, as picture words, McGinness' elements are based on real-world living beings or objects that are more or less rigidly schematized and abstracted in their reproduction. Like the chemical elements that as pure substances can no longer be separated into other substances using chemical methods, McGinness' signs form the smallest indivisible units.

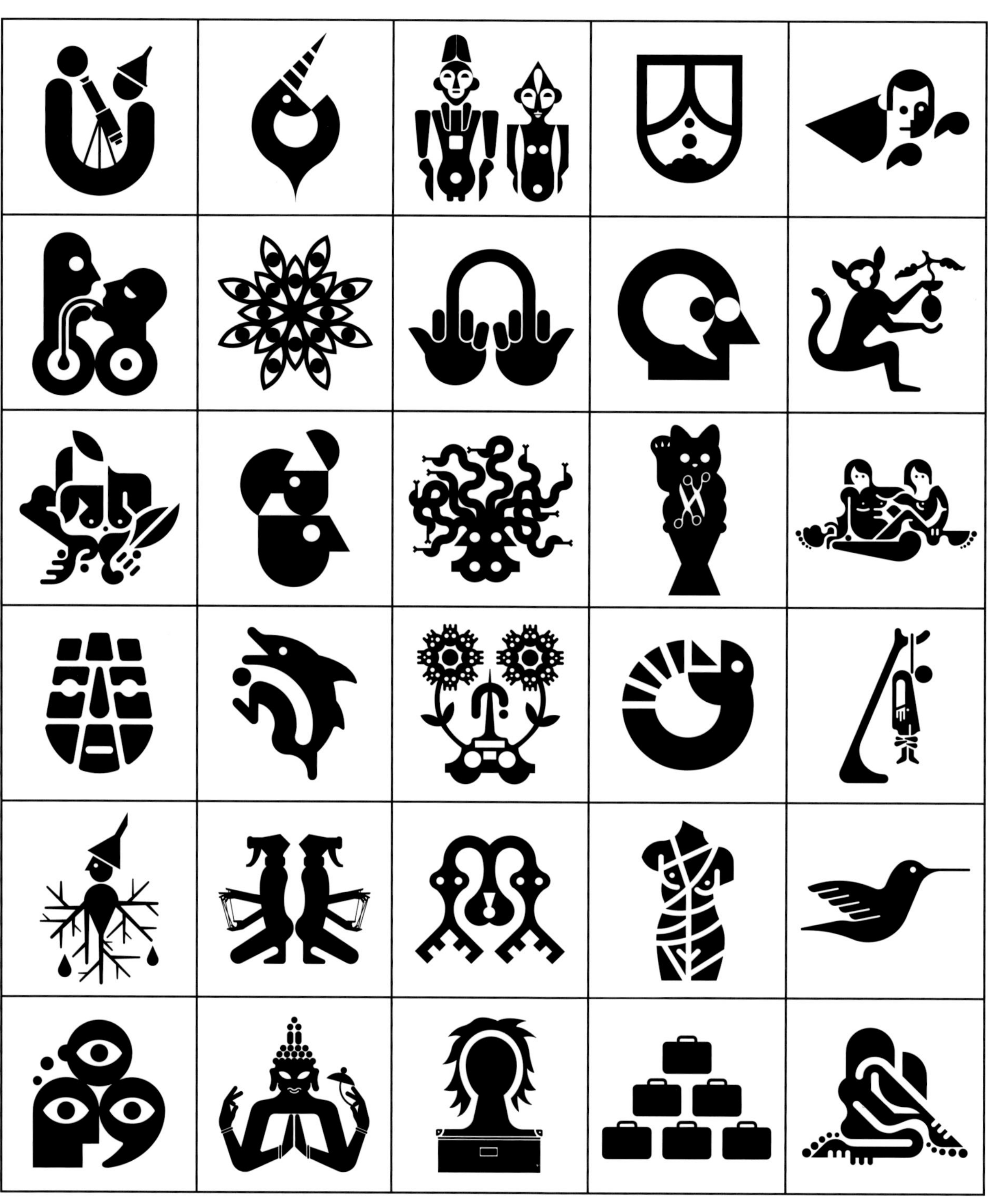

A selection of various drawings, 1997-2017, digital vector files

But it is only in combination with other elements that they form the molecules that blended together define McGinness' artworks. His elements have developed in a process of drawing, or as McGinness sums up his artistic creed, "It's about a drawing of a drawing." Thus, the foundation of his elements legibility, order, and the drawing are like the atomic nucleus and the electrons of the atom.

The working process always begins with a free sketch of real world objects or living beings like a female nude, an historical painting, or something else from his and our lifeworld. This drawing then serves as the model for the following drawing of the drawing, which in turn can serve as a basis for the next drawing, and so on, until the artist has approached a "visually logical geometry" that enables a translation to a digital drawing. Then, the relevant drawing is scanned and translated to a digital drawing of geometric shapes using a digital drawing tool. The final version of his element is a vector graphic that can be randomly scaled without a loss of quality and refers to "a new and truly contemporary method of image-making." Like letters and words, a uniqueness inheres in a vector graphic that can be varied in size without loss of information, as Ed Ruscha comments on his word paintings: "The words have these abstract shapes, they live in a world of no size: you can make them any size, and what's the real size? Nobody knows." With the vector graphic, McGinness withdraws all proportions from his elements, and the dependence and lack of focus of a photographic depiction of an object that always depends on resolution. His elements can be reproduced from microscopic dimensions to theoretically infinite sizes, although his standardized visual formats are 7 by 5 feet and 30 by 22 inches, for always the (infinite) legibility of the order is provided for, guaranteed by way of fixed standardizations. The artist thus not only defines the most minute detail of both his artistic procedure and all his studio processes in his *Studio Manual*, but also makes them transparent. He draws a striking image of the transparent individual of the Internet and the post-Internet age, where computer algorithms know more about us than we know ourselves. His *Studio Manual* becomes a manifest, an expression of an automated, technified world where computer algorithms not only influence public opinion, elec-

tions, revolutions, and consumer behavior, but also recognize our needs and manipulate our consumption and lifeworld. Like our digital trails online and in the world, his artistic development and the anatomy of his works can be followed step by step and can always be reconstructed.

After the vector graphics are created, they are transferred to a silkscreen and can be transferred to paper and canvas in various colors. In that very moment, McGinness counters the order and standardization a second time, as in the free drawing at the start, by applying intuition in the sense of a "metaphysical experience" to his artistic practice, like Kurt Schwitters' collages and assemblages of trash. Like Schwitters, McGinness collages his various elements first to form molecules and then clusters and assemblages entirely in Schwitters' sense: "These artworks are thus consistent for they emerge in the artist in the moment of artistic intuition. Intuition and creation of the artwork are here one and the same thing." In so doing, McGinness mixes up his elements, legibility and strict order, with intuition, thus questioning them. His intuitive visual spaces that emerge over months culminate increasingly in picture words that open new spaces of association in their unique combination for the beholders. With his strict "studio manual," that pushes the pain of "over control" and detailedness, he takes our bureaucracy, the strict norms of our society, and the computer algorithmic illumination and control of today's human being to the point of absurdity.

The studio itself, the means of production, and the products become the focal point of his artistic engagement. In a series of works, McGinness tries to show the tragic absurdity of the ordering of things and people by way of the fetishization of his work tools like the squeegees or silkscreens that he combines to form assemblages or even uses as the foundation for his paintings. The means of production are not just made visible, but as in Jasper Johns' practice become a part of the work itself.

His *Studio Views* from 2015-2017 seem on first glance to be classical depictions of artist studios: the wooden floor, objects, the buckets on which the paintings are placed, and the paintings themselves. And yet, those who suspect the reproduction of an

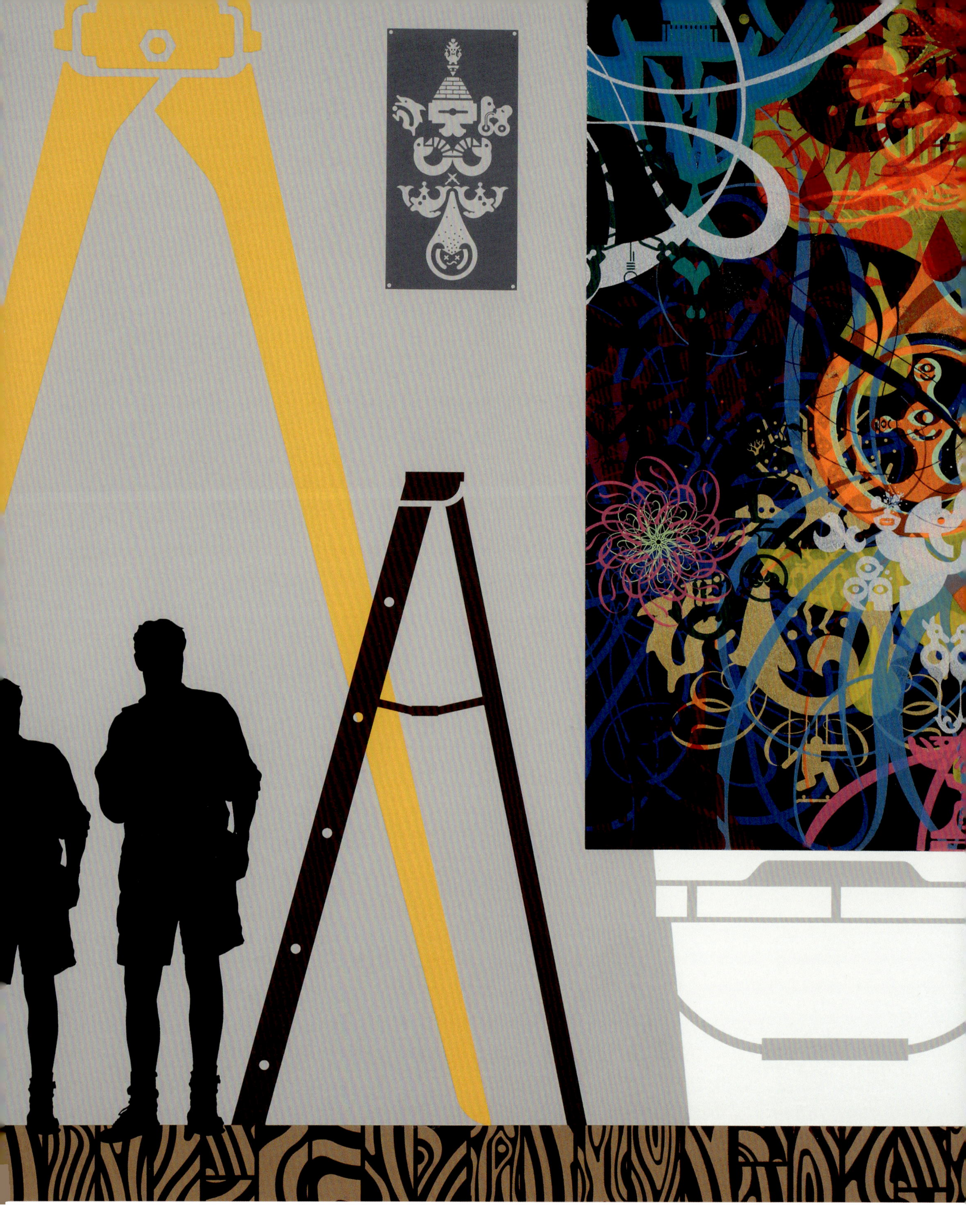

The Logic of this Work Is Stronger than the Logic of the World in which it Exists (Detail), 2016, quadriptych, acrylic on linen, 84 x 60 in. (213.4 x 152.4 cm) each, 84 x 240 in. (213.4 x 609.6 cm) total

existing painting in the work are quite mistaken. Rather, McGinness creates the works presented in the image anew with artistic intuition. Photographs served as the inspiration for his drawings of the studio floor and the buckets. He plays virtuosically with the proportions, since his vector graphics are able to take on any random size, he turns everything upside down and puts our perception to the test: the human silhouette is only somewhat larger than the paint buckets, the skateboards blown up to immense shapes, extending over the edge of the canvas, cut off by the trestles and table tops. Or an entire spatial ensemble is turned 90 degrees as a painting on a bucket.

McGinness creates his studio reality anew: reality reloaded—with a virtually surreal absurdity. It is the fragmentary quality that he generates in his apparently perfect paintings with artistic intuition: apparently unintentionally, doubled, slightly staggered painted elements or poorly inked picture words. For the fragmentary quality of the system can always be read in the detail. Just as a small computer error can lead to the total crash of our financial system, a small manipulation of our identity could destroy our lives, McGinness opens the gaze for the danger of orders and systems. His elements, molecules, clusters, and mixtures open new gazes and contexts and open new spaces for thought. Nothing is a given, nothing lasts forever. The fragmentary quality in the order, the tear in the system, evokes Michel Foucault's outlook at the end of *The Order of Things*: "If those arrangements were to disappear as they appeared, if some event of which we can at the moment do no more than sense the possibility…were to cause them to crumble…then one can certainly wager that man would be erased, like a face drawn in sand at the edge of the sea."

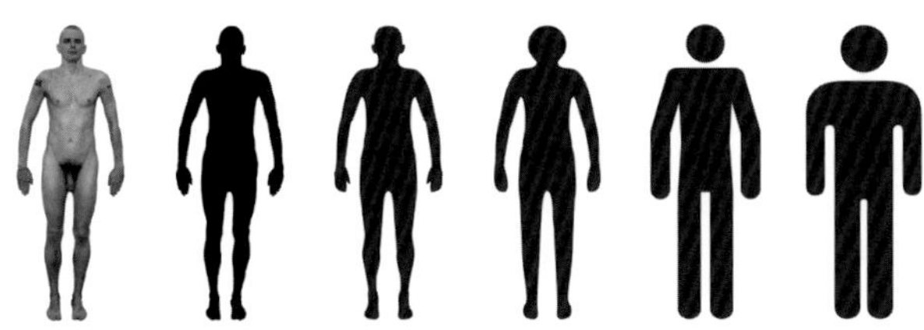

Untitled, 2001, digital files, self-portrait that is transformed over five stages into a universal icon for a man

The I Love You Machine Is Unplugged (Detail with color calibration
chart held by photographer), 2016, cyanotype on Saunders
Waterford paper, 60 x 40 in. (152.4 x 101.6 cm)

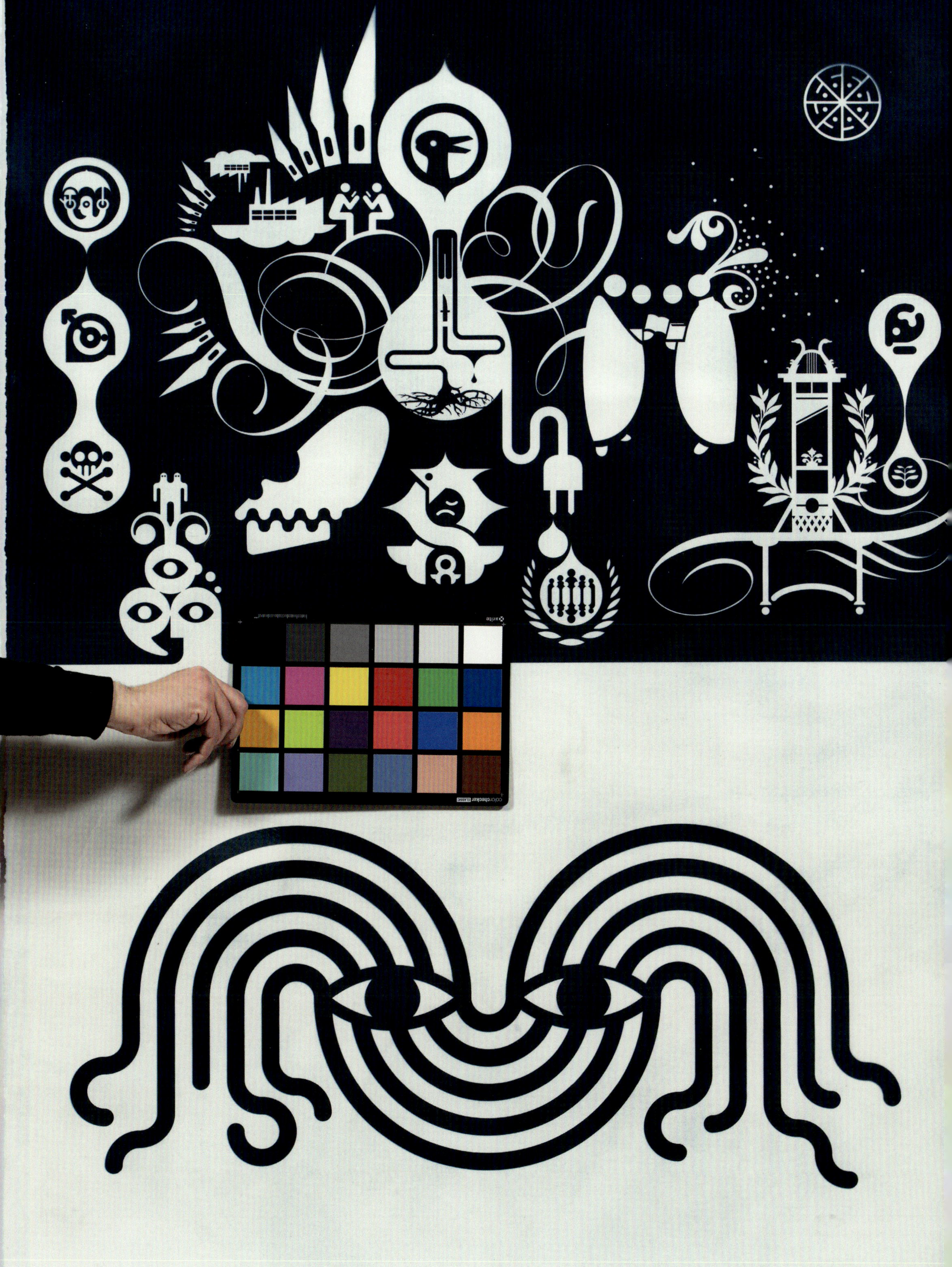

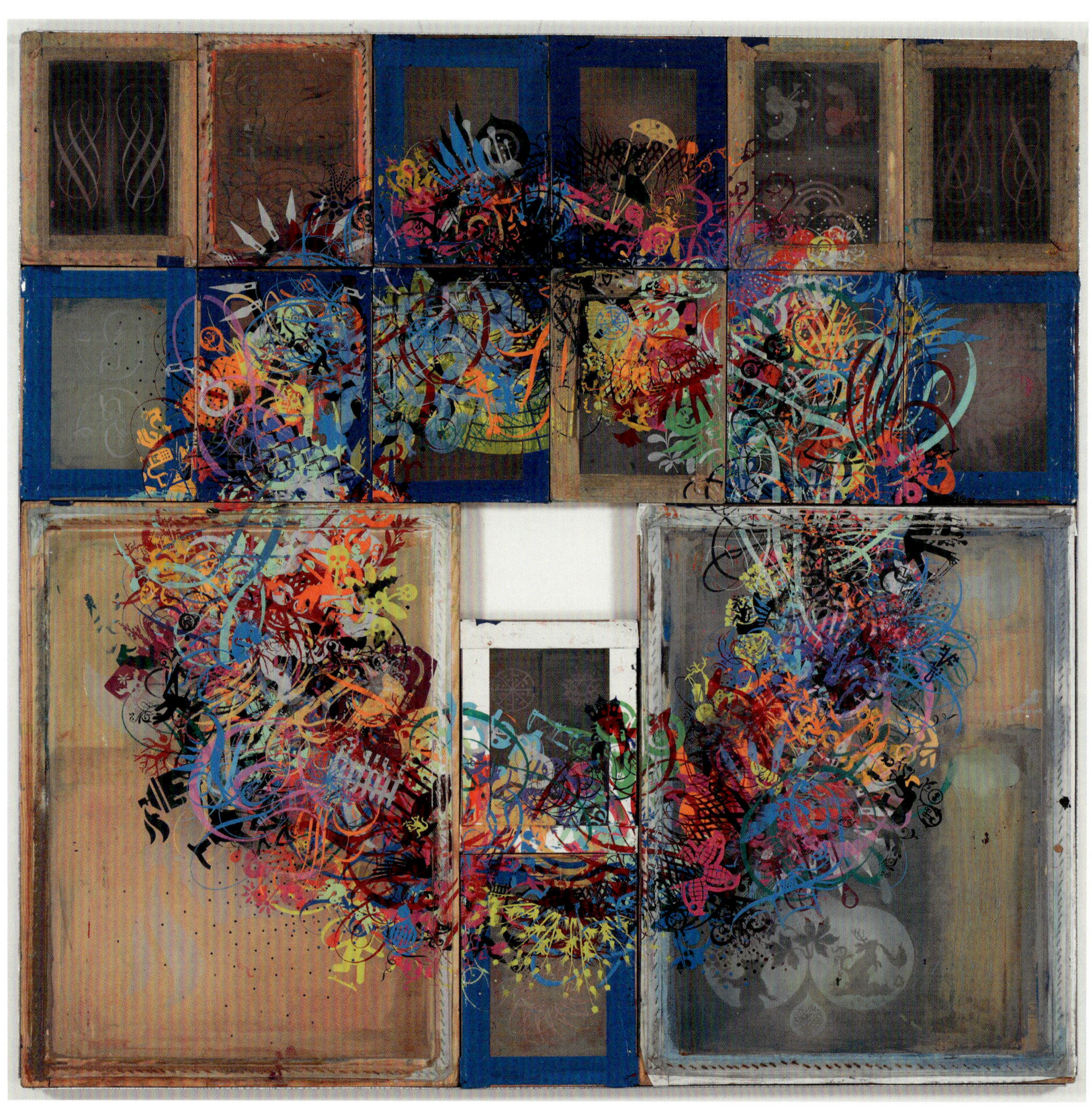

Above: *Screen Combine #47*, 2016, acrylic and photo emulsion on polyester monofilament screens with polyurethane adhesive and polyethylene tape attached to wood frames with aluminum hardware, 72 x 72.25 in. (182.9 x 183.5 cm)
Opposite Page: Untitled (Sketch Process), 2016, ink on custom graph paper, 30 x 22 in. (76.2 x 55.9 cm) and digital vector drawing

Lost in Graphic Translation

Andrew Blauvelt

Although it is known that Ryan McGinness studied graphic design, less has been said about what that might mean in relationship to his artistic practice. For me, as a graphic designer, it is impossible not to see in McGinness's work the process and methods of graphic design. In preparation for his exhibitions, *Studio Views* and *Collection Views* at the Cranbrook Art Museum, McGinness revealed his interest in and the influence of a period of graphic design experimentation at Cranbrook Academy of Art in the 1980s. It was a period with which I was intimately familiar as a graduate student in the department from 1986 to 1988. Led by the husband and wife team of Katherine and Michael McCoy between 1971 and 1995, the duo had built a hothouse of experimental design work in the unlikeliest of locales, in the Midwestern rustbelt of Detroit. Although the program evolved through various phases during these two-plus decades, the late 1980s represented the zenith of the department's most radical guise. Influenced by the literary theory of deconstruction at perhaps the height of postmodernism, its graduate students rejected most of the fundamentals of modern graphic design. For instance, they challenged assumptions about legibility and readability that had been codified in modern typography, they created an anti-aesthetics of bad rather than good form, and they also argued against the linear encoding of messages by designers and for the inherent multiplicity of meanings in the decoding of such communications by readers and viewers. It was a direct assault on the refined sensibilities of the mainstream design profession. The ideas and work of the program were widely circulated in the influential publication, *Cranbrook Design: The New Discourse*, released in 1991—the same time that Ryan McGinness was studying graphic design at Carnegie Mellon University.

There are two important takeaways from the work of Cranbrook's graphic design program as it relates to Ryan's practice that inform both its theory and praxis. First, the program radically undermined the conventional notion of a simplistic, linear, sender-receiver model of communications that had been preached to graphic designers since the postwar period. Such a model privileges the designer as a creator of messages, its de facto encoder. But what happens when this model privileges instead the acts of decoding and the role of readers? Much interest arose in aspects of word play and multiple meanings, the fallibility and instability of language, and the use of ambiguity rather than clarity as a fundamental principle of design, for instance. Second, the program developed a method of graphical layering in compositional design as the visual expression of these new theories. If modernism had been structured around the ethos of less is more and the reduction of (graphic) noise in the channel, then its postmodern equivalent would celebrate a strategy of more is more, whereby visual excess and graphic maximalism would represent the complexities of communication. A multiplicity of images and texts—or in the parlance of postmodernism, the pa-

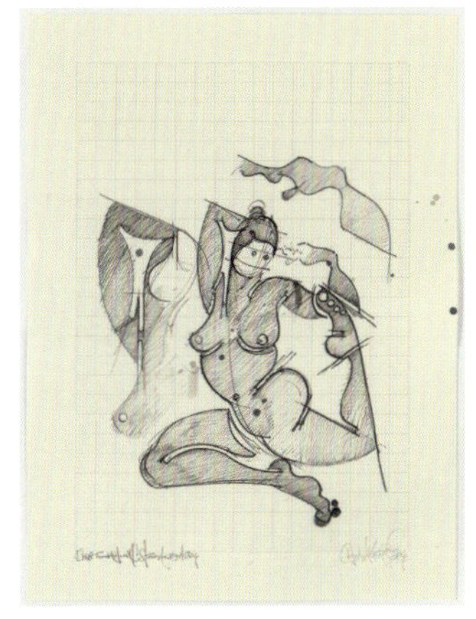

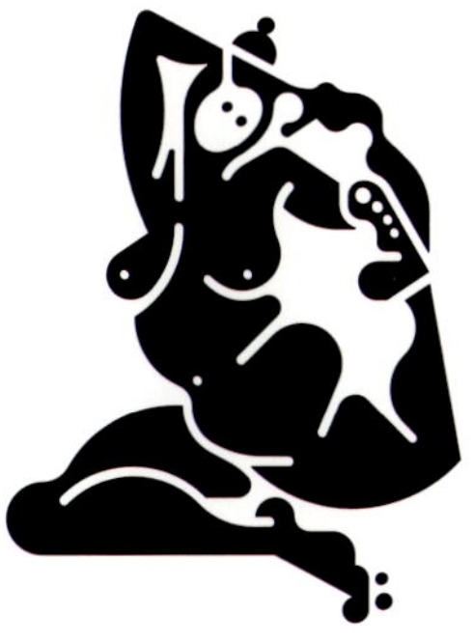

limpsest—could be used, but controlled by designers through the layering process. While Cranbrook's philosophy was squarely aimed at transforming the practice of graphic design, its influence was more widespread.

Perhaps not surprisingly, the postmodernist and poststructuralist inflected work at Cranbrook was decidedly self-reflexive. Essentially, it was design about design. This does not diminish its importance or dismiss its relevance. On the contrary, it represents a kind of maturation of the discipline in so far as the field had attained enough self-awareness and had sufficiently codified its practices to enable its eventual self-critique. During the same period, graphic design had begun to become more socially legible as a cultural artifact—something increasingly distinct and recognizable by non-designers. For instance, in its mainstream guise, graphic design developed the modern company logotype and with it the notion of corporate identities that would beget contemporary branding. Its visual output was always ubiquitous, but now its visual language was quotable. Thus, it would only be a matter of time before graphic design would become the subject, process, and product of art—reversing decades of art's influence on graphic design. If the Pop artist drew inspiration from the world of postwar popular culture, such as its consumer products, ads, and comics, then contemporary artists in the 1980s began mining graphic design's visual language, for instance, in Barbara Kruger's text and image collages, Matt Mullican's cultural symbols, or Ashley Bickerton's appropriation of corporate logos. Later in the 1990s, design began to be expropriated wholesale, treated as kind of a medium itself in the work of artists such as Pae White, Liam Gillick, and Jorge Pardo. With the advent of so-called graphic culture during the same period, street artists who had ascended from the graffiti writers and muralists of the 1970s and 1980s and the skateboarding and rave scenes of the 1990s, the full integration of design into art and art into design seemed complete.

Ryan McGinness represents a distinct position in this kind of graphic art history by using his design skills not to replicate works of mass production, but rather to produce singular and unique works of art. This is true even though McGinness is primarily

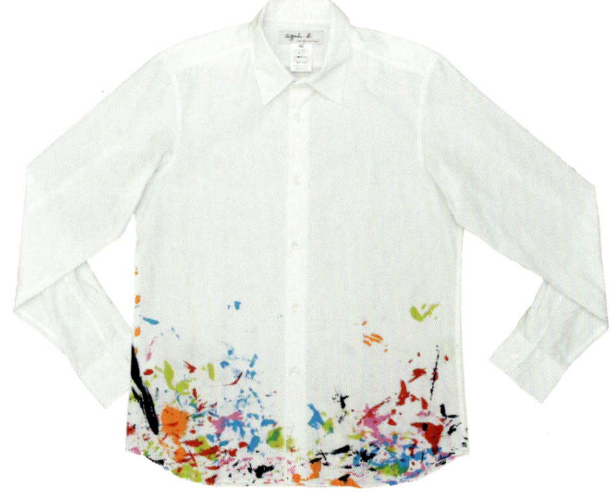

Studio Shirt, 2012, six-color silkscreen ink on 100% cotton agnès b. shirt, two-sided, dimensions vary, published by agnès b., Paris

associated with the printmaking process in general and the method of screen printing in particular. Used to print things like textiles, posters, and t-shirts, silk-screening is a commercial printing technique largely associated with industrial mass production. It was famously used by Andy Warhol, who began his career as a commercial illustrator and art director, at his Factory as a method of fine art production for print editions as well as paintings. Of course, for the Pop artist, the use of screen printing reinforced the movement's infatuation with consumer culture, allowing for bold graphics with bright, flat colors like those found on commercial packages, but also for the reproduction of the photographic image through the enlargement of the finer halftone screen dots used in commercial offset lithography and photogravure, the primary methods used to print illustrated books, magazines, and newspapers. Given its relative ease of use and low cost of operation, screen printing fell into vogue again amongst graphic designers particularly in the 1990s DIY scene as a method to produce self-authored works and, by extension, in the resurgence of gig, or concert promotional, posters. These slapdash productions, however, seem a far cry from the meticulousness of a McGinness print—for instance, the custom formulation of colors or the sharpness of the image in its pull. McGinness frequently uses fluorescent, pearlescent, and metallic paints that are particularly well-suited to the screen printing process. The screen print applies a thicker layer of paint, which allows for a greater optical effect. The use of these same special pigments by graphic designers, although rare because of the added expense, is often in reaction to the ubiquitous nature of process color (CMYK) printing, which became the new normal once cheap desktop color printers landed in everyone's homes, studios, and offices. For McGinness, the use of optically reactive pigments means that reproductions of his work in catalogues printed in CMYK or circulated online through JPGs in RGB deny a true chromatic experience. Thus, the richest and most accurate visual experience of the work can only happen when it is viewed in person. Screen printing also lends itself well to the use of layering, whereby one color is added at a time. Physically overlaying or overprinting paints allows for either great opacity or variable translucency of color. In his most complex and layered designs, McGin-

ness evokes the aesthetic of printer's "make ready." A byproduct of the commercial printing process, make ready are test sheets of paper reused by printers to prepare new jobs for printing. One print job is printed upon another, the result produces striking but unintended collages of new patterns of interconnecting shapes, overlapping fields of type, and various color interactions. Unlike the job printer's make ready, the layering of images and colors in a McGinness canvas is compositionally purposeful. McGinness exploits these optical and physical qualities of printing to great artistic effect.

At the heart of McGinness's process is a special type of drawing technique used by graphic designers to create symbols and icons for a variety of commercial uses. Found in everyday life as corporate logos, on traffic and transit signs, or used as symbols on maps, diagrams, and instructions, these graphic icons comprise a contemporary lexicon of visual communication. As old as the pictograms found in ancient caves and as new as the latest emoji on the smartphone, such symbols rely on a distillation of form and meaning to effectively communicate. Not surprisingly, the drawing skills necessary to create such icons were perfected in graphic design education and training. Known as the graphic or object translation, these drawings are often conducted as student exercises in more process-oriented design programs, such as the one at Carnegie Mellon University where McGinness studied. Designers such as Kurt Hauert popularized the technique through his teaching of courses at the Basel School of Design in Switzerland and through workshops attended by many American designers and educators, who brought the method home to their students. Hauert famously had students draw leaves and lake water using black and white gouache or Plaka, a casein paint with great opacity that produces a velvety matte finish. Today, such drawings are made using computer drawing programs like Adobe Illustrator. Essentially a silhouette, graphic translations are especially attuned to the contours of an object and are rendered from an optimal point-of-view, one that best captures its distinguishing characteristics. A graphic translation is judged on a nexus of qualities, such as its legibility of meaning, economy of form, gestalt as a unified mark, scalability, and the aesthetics of flow—the interaction of positive and

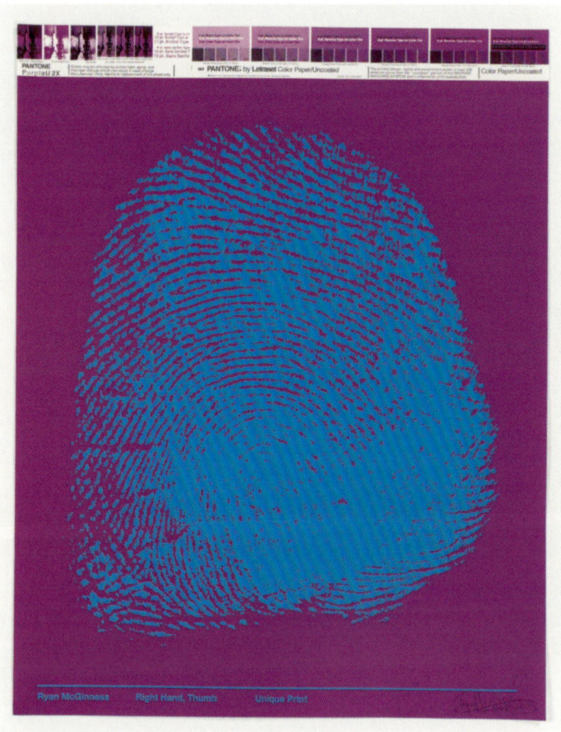
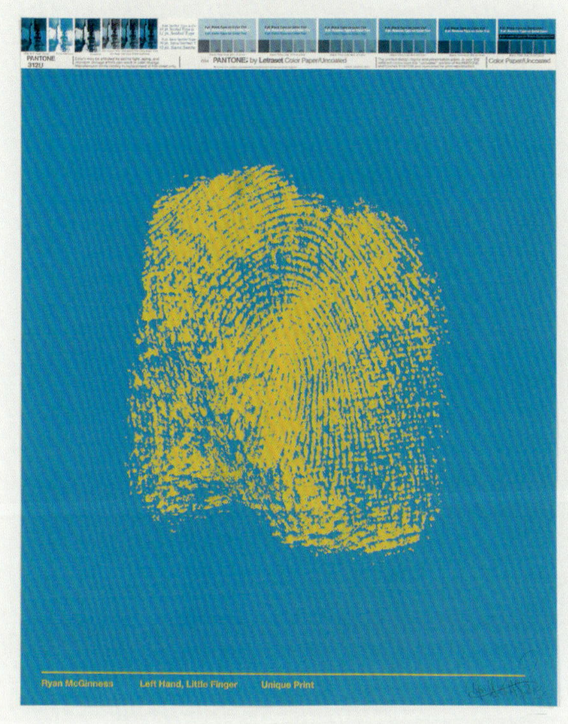
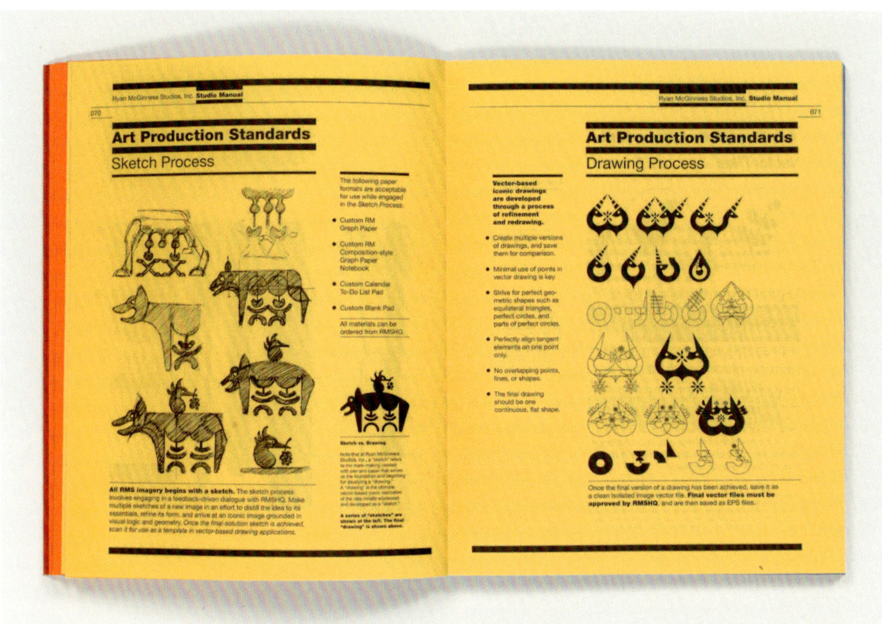
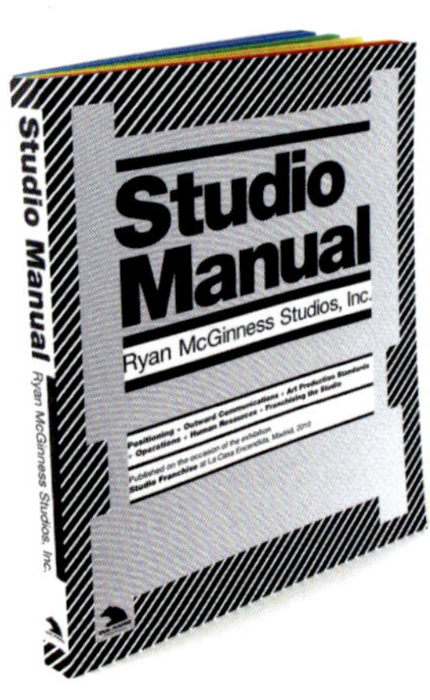

Above: *Fingerprint Prints (Pantone Purple 2X & 312U)*, 2013, ea. unique, acrylic on Pantone by Letraset Color Paper, 26 x 20 in. (66 x 50.8 cm)
Below: *Studio Manual*, 2010, 1C on colored paper, 192 pp., softcover, published by La Casa Encendida, Madrid
Opposite Page: *Supreme Color Formula Guide*, 2000, silkscreen on skateboards, 32 x 8 in. (81.3 x 20.3 cm) ea., published by Supreme, New York

negative space. Such iconography produced using this method privileges the fast read and the universality of the visual to communicate across linguistic borders. Not surprisingly, the form has been embraced by multinational companies to avoid expensive multilingual iterations in their global operations (think of IKEA's pictographic assembly instructions or the symbols used on the dashboards of cars sold globally). McGinness both trades on and disrupts the communicative expectations of such iconography in his art. Shapes become polymorphous and meanings polyglot, as figures open themselves to interpretation. In these symbols, humor delights, sexuality shocks, and ambiguity confounds.

In a related project to his Cranbrook exhibitions, *Wayfinding*, a skate park installation in downtown Detroit, McGinness deploys more than 70 metal signs to frame the space. Produced like conventional traffic signs, using the same graphic films and aluminum substrates, the marks cover the gamut of the McGinness pictorial library: two fingers guide a skateboard, evoking the Yellow Pages logo; two middle fingers are joined in double indignation; the maneki-neko, or beckoning cat, appears but with scissors in its belly; a spray-paint can shoots flames while dissolving into paint drips; a metronome sits atop buckets; a body lies in bondage; and so on. These signs demand to be decoded not simply recognized and obeyed. Like the Tower of Babel, they speak in many different tongues, some meanings are familiar, while others are not. Many signs mix and fuse symbols in hybrid combinations that leave us in a communicative limbo. Not so much the artist. If shared communication of content is the assumed obligation of the designer, then for McGinness, the artist, the signs do not point to external content as much as they do to his own practice as their ultimate source of meaning. Since language generates its meaning through its systematic deployment and context, the meaning of any piece of graphic ornamentation or symbolic iconography when viewed in isolation or even as a grouping is merely fragmentary. In other words, trying to read these symbols as if they were design fails to understand that they perform as art.

In *Studio Views*, McGinness reaches a new stage of self-reflexivity. Thirty-five canvases wrap the four walls of the gallery and depict the artist's studio. Sharing a common horizon line, they form a panorama for the viewer. All is flattened and compressed into this unified picture plane: the saw horse printing tables, desks and other studio furniture, merchandise like skate decks and t-shirts, the wigs, the silkscreens, and, of course, other paintings. This is a metanarrative about art and its making as well as its reification. The process is the art that becomes the product. Just like the experimental work from Cranbrook that inspired McGinness, it contains the seeds of a self-critique, pointing as it does to the artist's own studio, but it also suggests a larger commentary about the field of art using the tools and techniques of design. Once autonomous works of art are now rendered as just another symbol among many other symbols in this painting of all paintings. The five-gallon buckets used to lift a drying canvas are on the same plane, literally, as the painting itself. Therein lies the power of graphic design to assimilate into its two-dimensional world, the world itself. The meanings, however, escape this thin plane of representation and may remain forever beautifully lost in graphic translation.

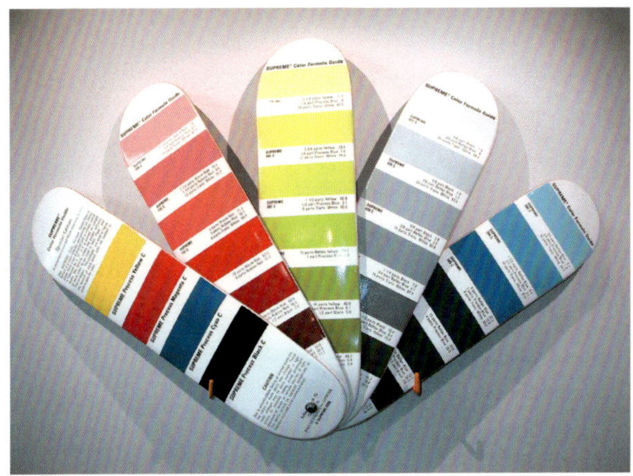

Parallel Studio Views (Detail with color calibration chart held by photographer), 2017, acrylic on linen, 84 x 60 in. (213.4 x 152.4 cm)

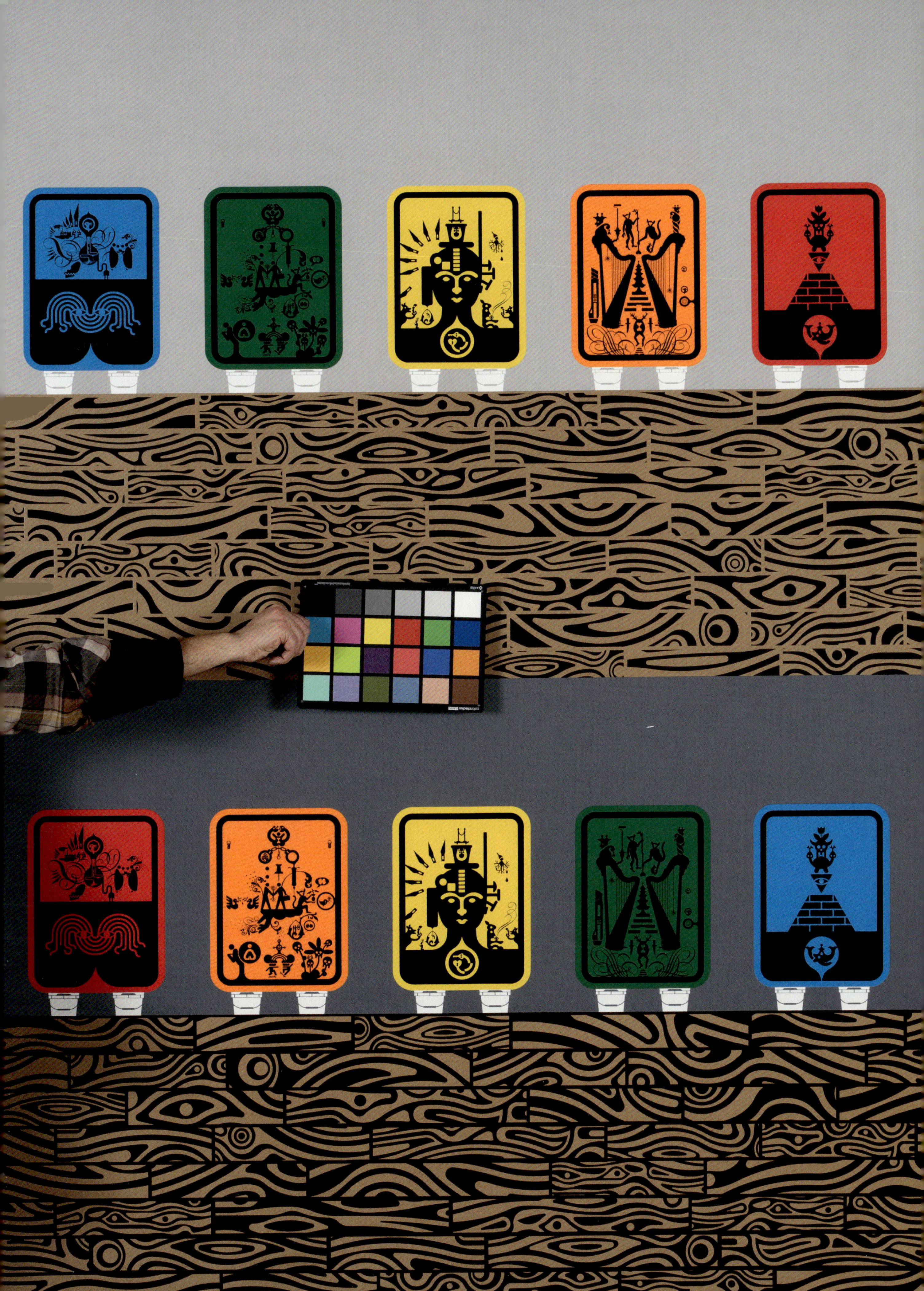

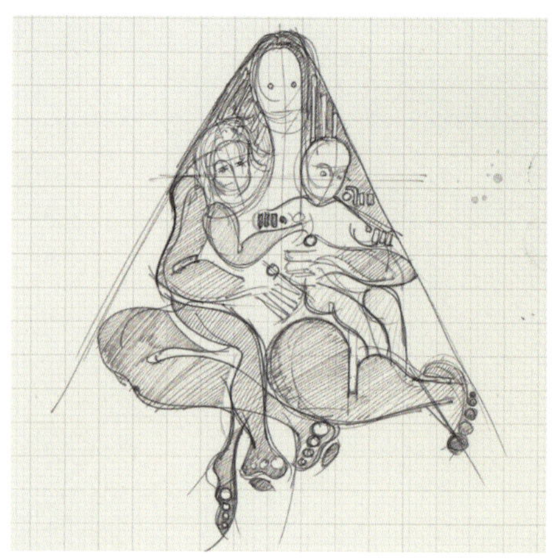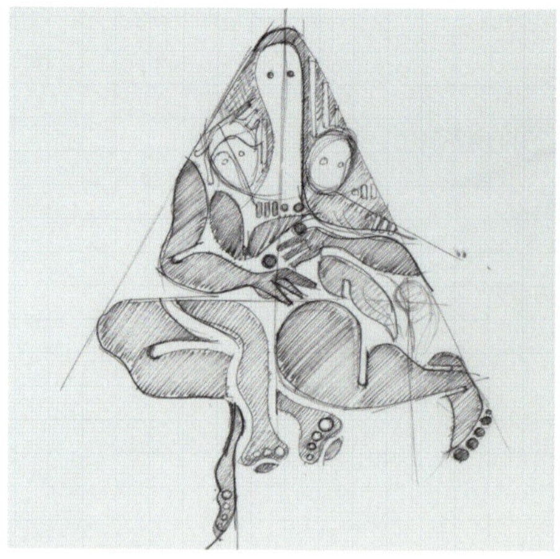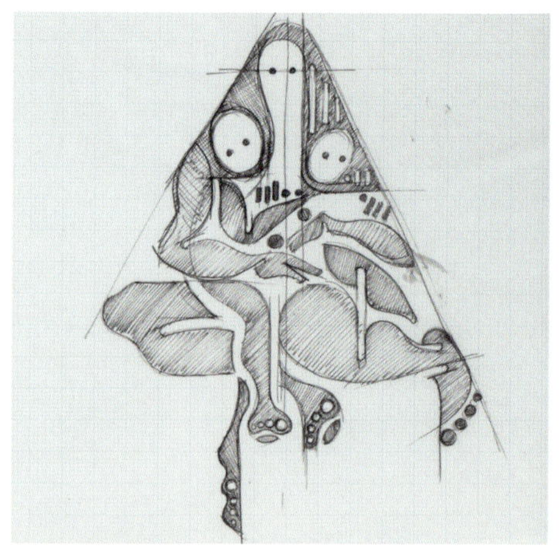

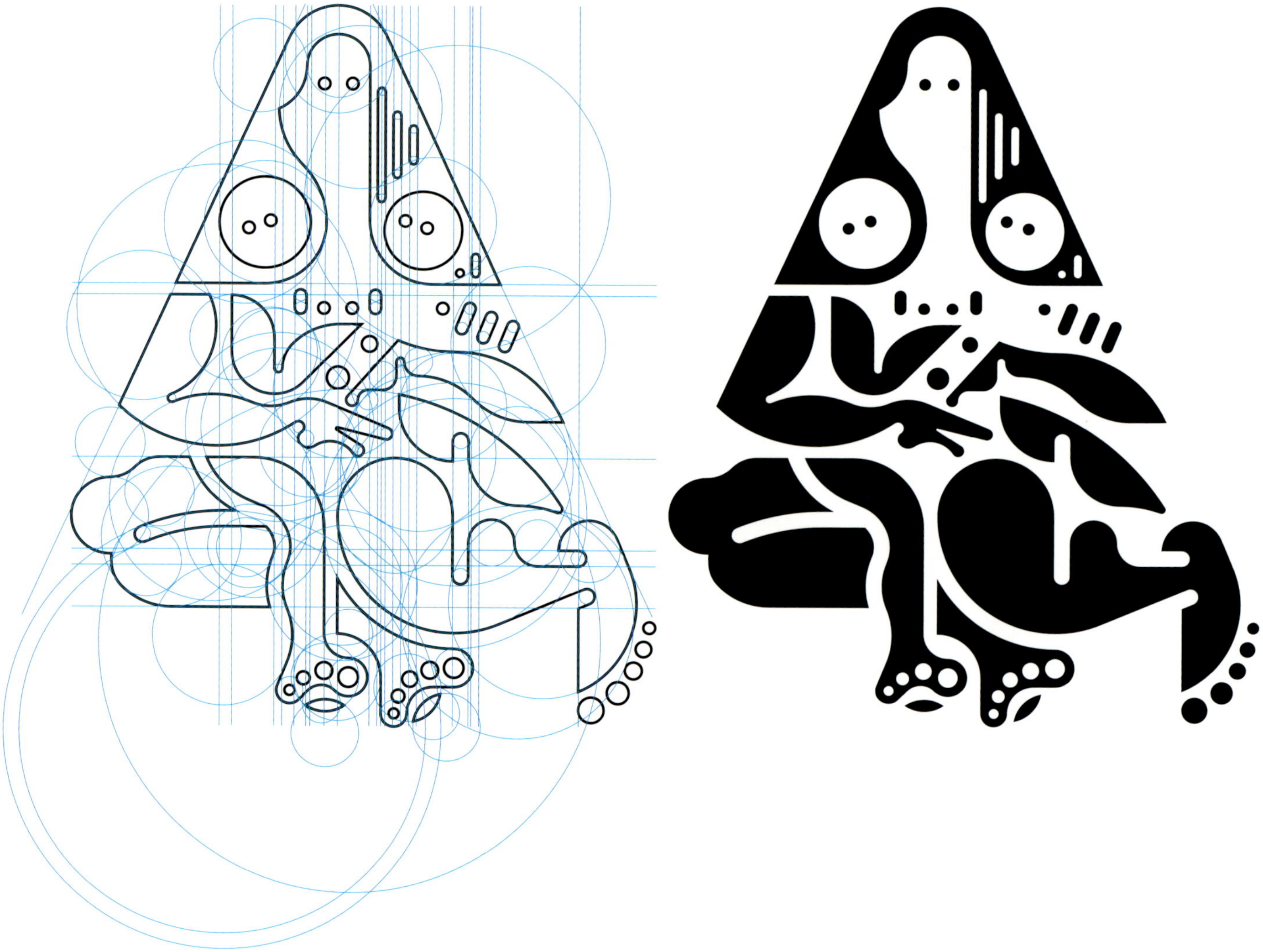

Above: *Mother & Child Sketch Process Sheets* (Details), 2015, ink on custom graph paper and ink on quad-ruled vellum, 30 x 22 in. (76.2 x 55.9 cm) ea.; Below: digital drawing process and final vector drawing

Mother & Child

Ben Sutton

"I'm interested in the push and pull between the figurative and the abstract," Ryan McGinness says.[1] This new series of 50 screenprint monoprints, *Mother & Child*, pushes toward abstraction through the layering of McGinness' stylized pictograms, personal in origin yet imbued with a playful universality using one of Western art history's most ubiquitous motifs.

Starting from photographs he shot of his wife and daughters, McGinness created sequences of drawings, each time stripping away details to reveal essential geometric lines and forms, a process that eventually resulted in twelve monochrome images depicting a mother holding her children. The prints consist of at least three (but often many more) of these hieroglyphlike images printed one atop the other in his trademark saturated and neon inks, as well as shimmering gold and silver. The layering makes the original pictograms harder to decipher, while drawing the viewer's attention to isolated details revealed in the process: a sequence of shrinking dots forming the toes of an outstretched foot; the wild strands of hair in an otherwise poised image; the elegant symmetry of a mother's legs under a precariously sprawled child. In many of the prints, additional images emerge the longer one looks, with ghostly traces of concealed ink registering as shifts in texture beneath subsequent layers. The superimposition of images draws out their shared features, offering glimpses of a kind of underlying DNA of mother-and-child iconography dating back centuries. "In my figure drawing stage, I am gathering data," McGinness says of his process. "As I develop those sketches by tracing and re-drawing, I am analyzing the data. With my final drawings, I draw conclusions."[2]

The graphic composition of the *Mother & Child* series echo art historical antecedents, from the earliest surviving "Virgin and Child" painting at Saint Catherine's Monastery in Egypt of the 6th century, to Medieval and Renaissance versions from golden Byzantine icons, to Botticelli's tender rendering in 1480, right up to more contemporary touchstones like, say, Annie Leibovitz's 2014 photograph of Kim Kardashian, Kanye West, and their first child. McGinness' prints not only add to the mix of this sprawling visual genealogy, but also rely on it for legibility. The image of a mother holding her offspring is thoroughly enshrined in the canon of art history, while also speaking to the universal human experience of holding and being held as a child. This is crucial for McGinness, who always strives to achieve the "anonymous authoritative visual vocabulary" of the clip art that first piqued his interest in visual culture when he was in high school.[3] In *Mother & Child*, he seems to have found one of the essential building blocks of our shared visual vocabulary, one that integrates personal experience with a wealth of earlier artworks. McGinness' manipulations of that iconic composition dazzle not only through their color palettes, but also through the economy and elegance of their pared-down forms, which strive for global legibility while remaining distinctly his own.

1 Jessica Womack, "A Visit with Ryan McGinness at Lower East Side Printshop," INSIDE/OUT online content, October 7, 2015, https://www.moma.org/explore/in-side_out/2015/10/07/a-visit-with-ryan-mcginness-at-lower-east-side-printshop/ [accessed May 8, 2017].
2 Alessandra Codinha, "The Male Gaze Under a Blacklight," Maker Magazine, Winter 2013, 52.
3 Gerhard Stochl, "Talking Skateboarding, Instagram, and Glow-in-the-Dark Art with Ryan McGinness," Creators online content, July 17, 2015, https://creators.vice.com/en_us/article/talking-skateboarding-instagram-and-glow-in-the-dark-art-with-ryan-mc-ginness [accessed May 8, 2017].

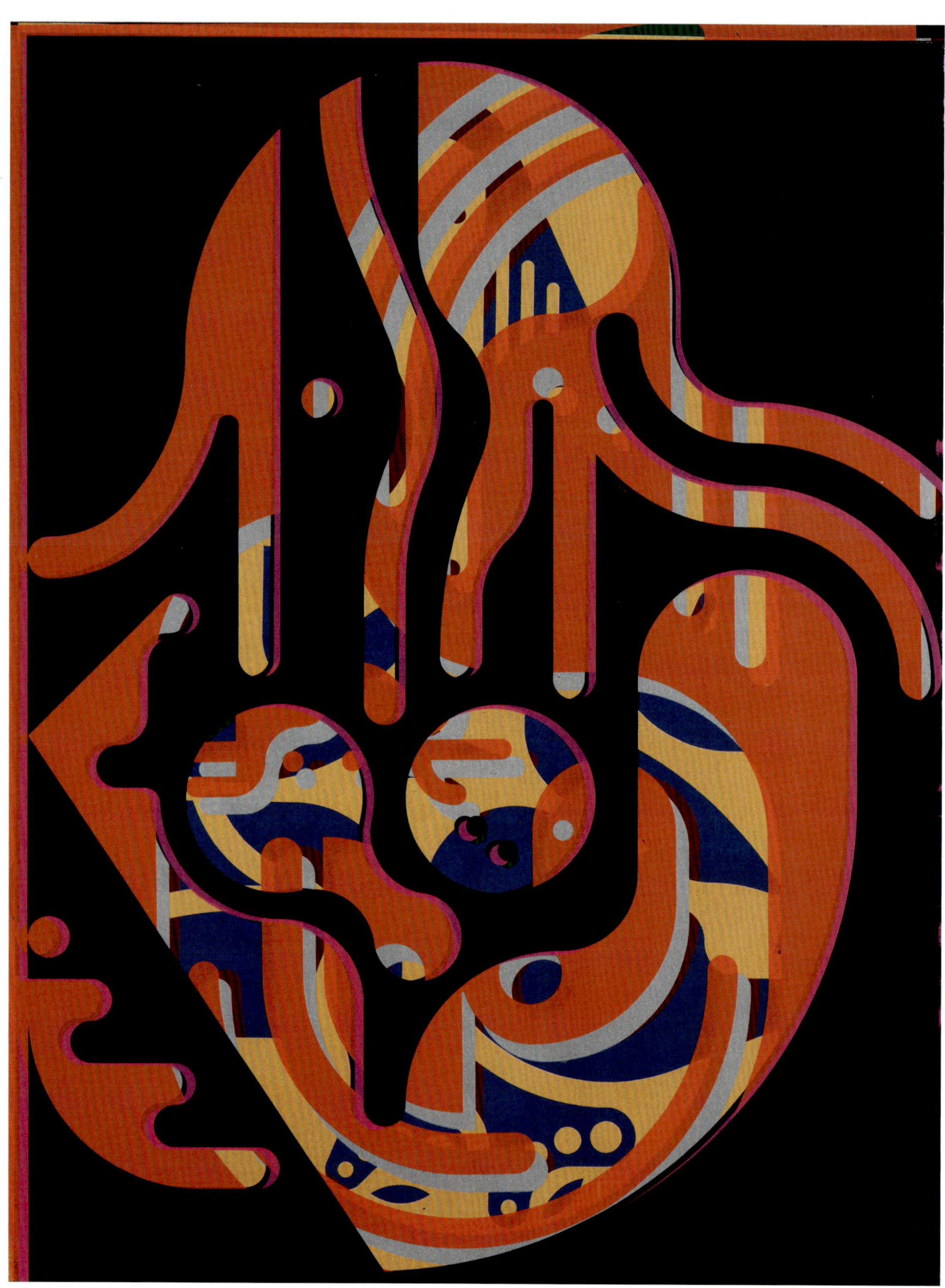

Mother & Child, 2017, acrylic on linen, 30 x 22 in. (76.2 x 55.9 cm)

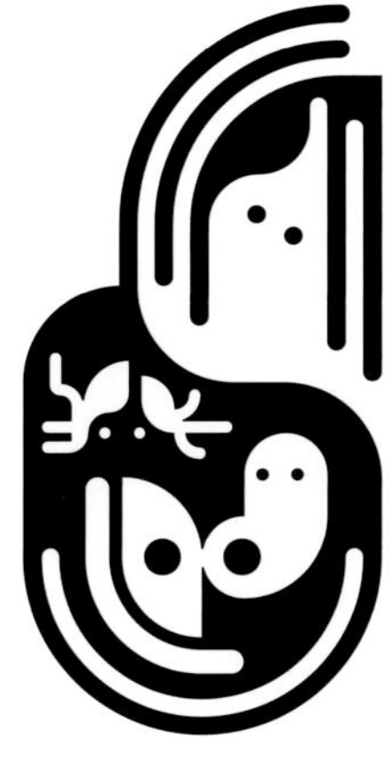
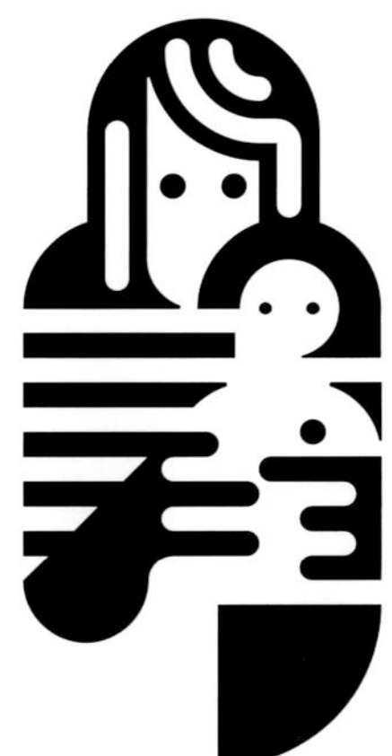
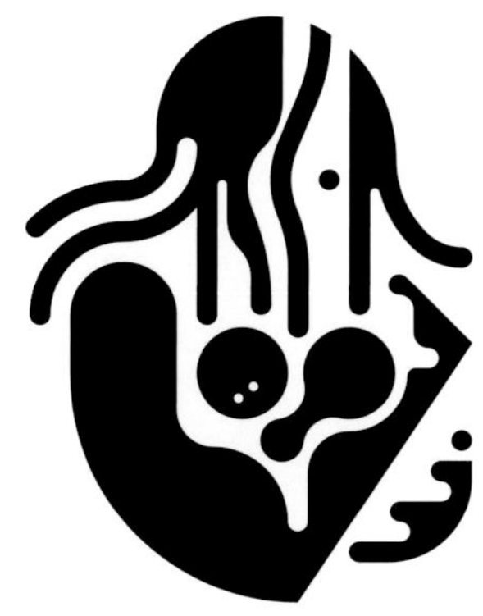
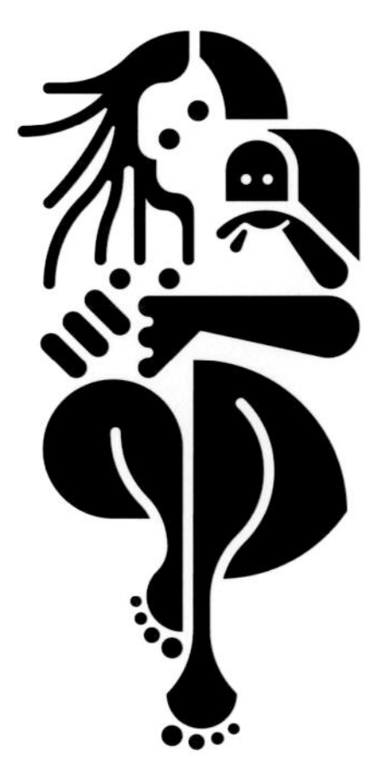
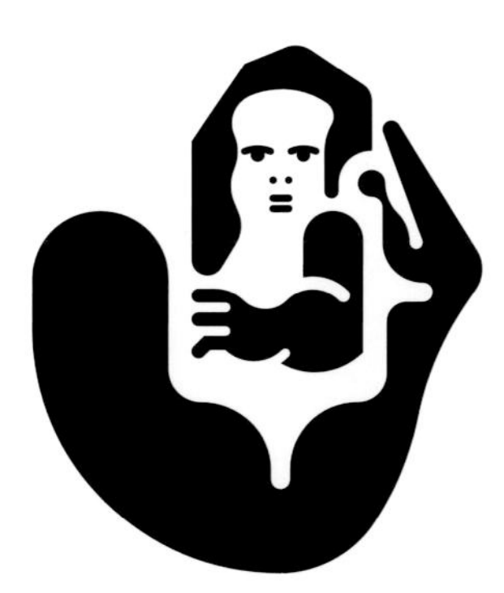
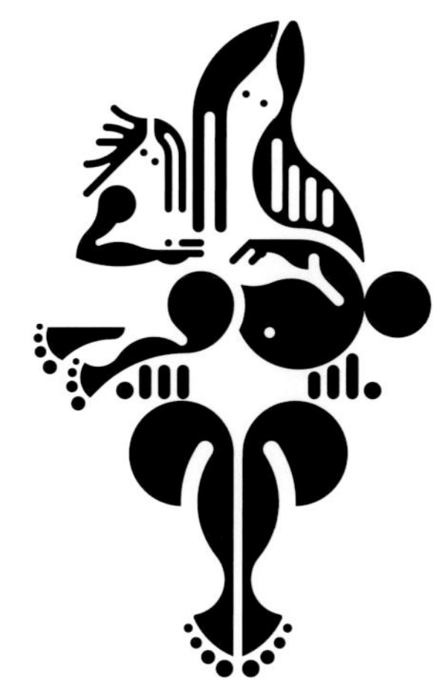
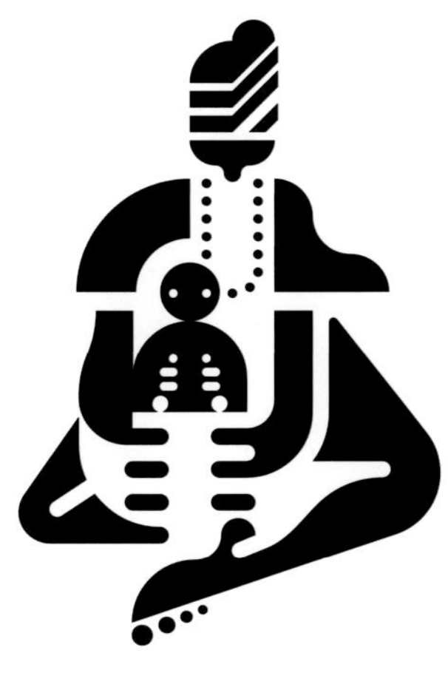
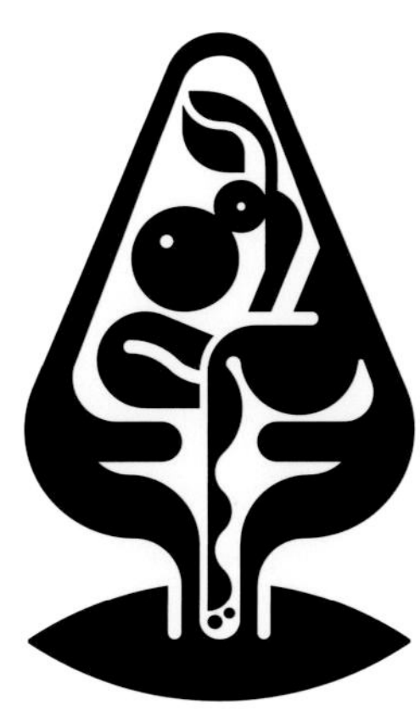
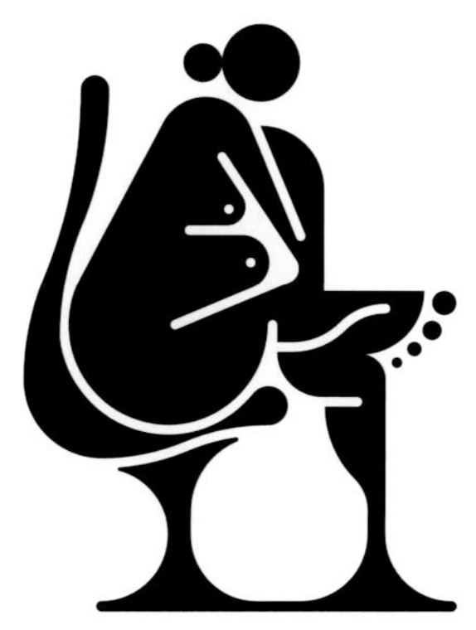

Mother & Child, 2014-2016, digital vector drawings

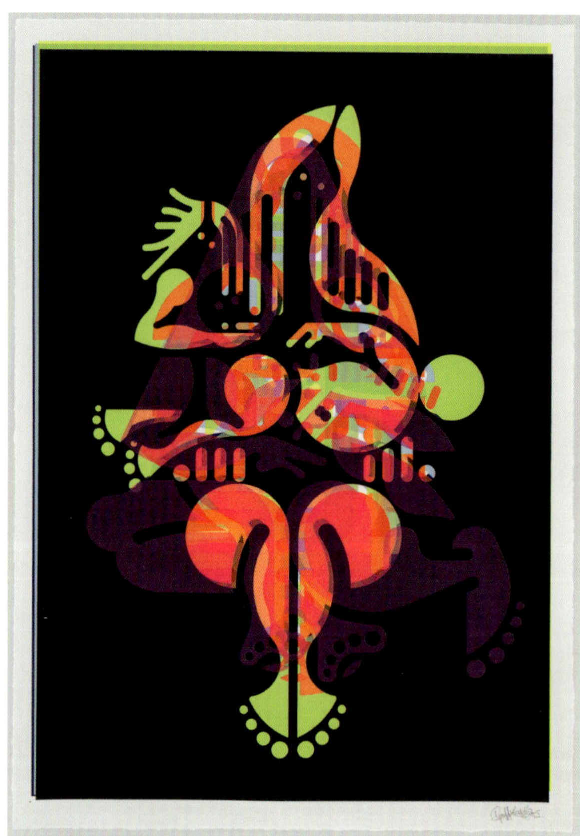 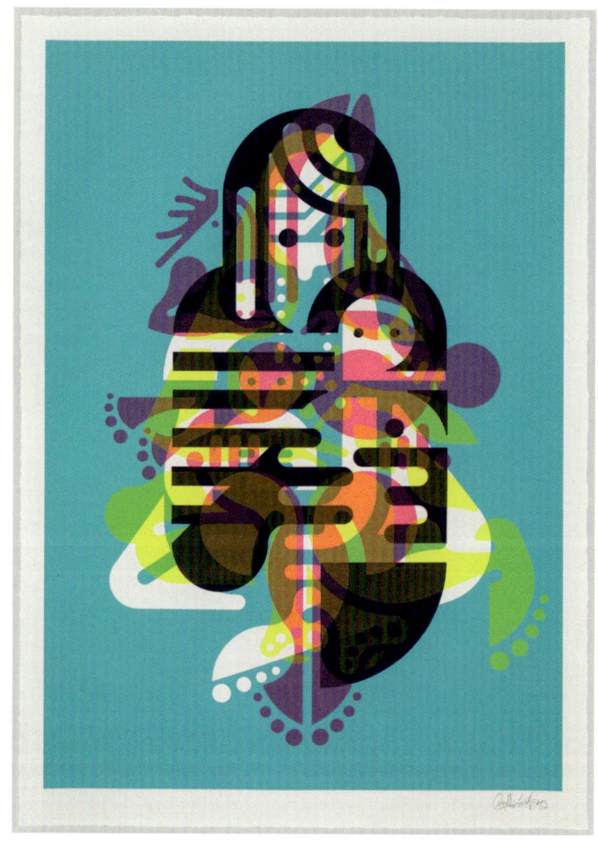

Mother & Child (Monoprints #33, #49, #34, & #42), 2015, unique screenprints on Lana paper, 43.5 x 30 in. (110.5 x 76.2 cm) ea., published by Lower East Side Printshop, New York

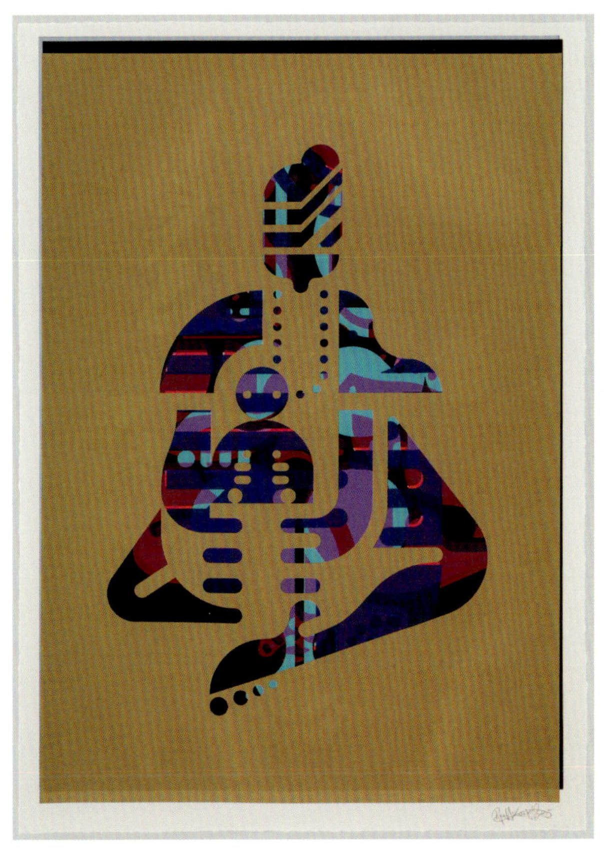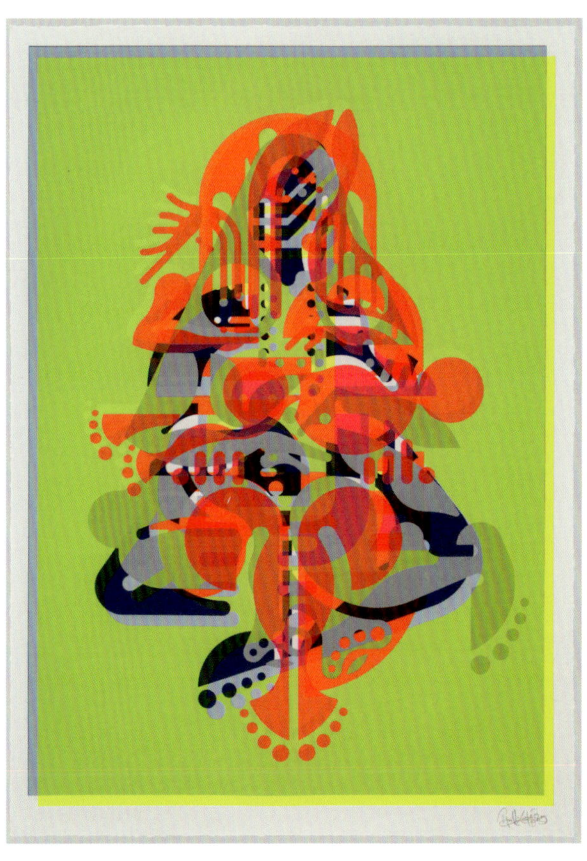

Sipping Soup with a Knife (Detail with color calibration chart held by photographer), 2017, acrylic on linen, 84 x 60 in. (213.4 x 152.4 cm)

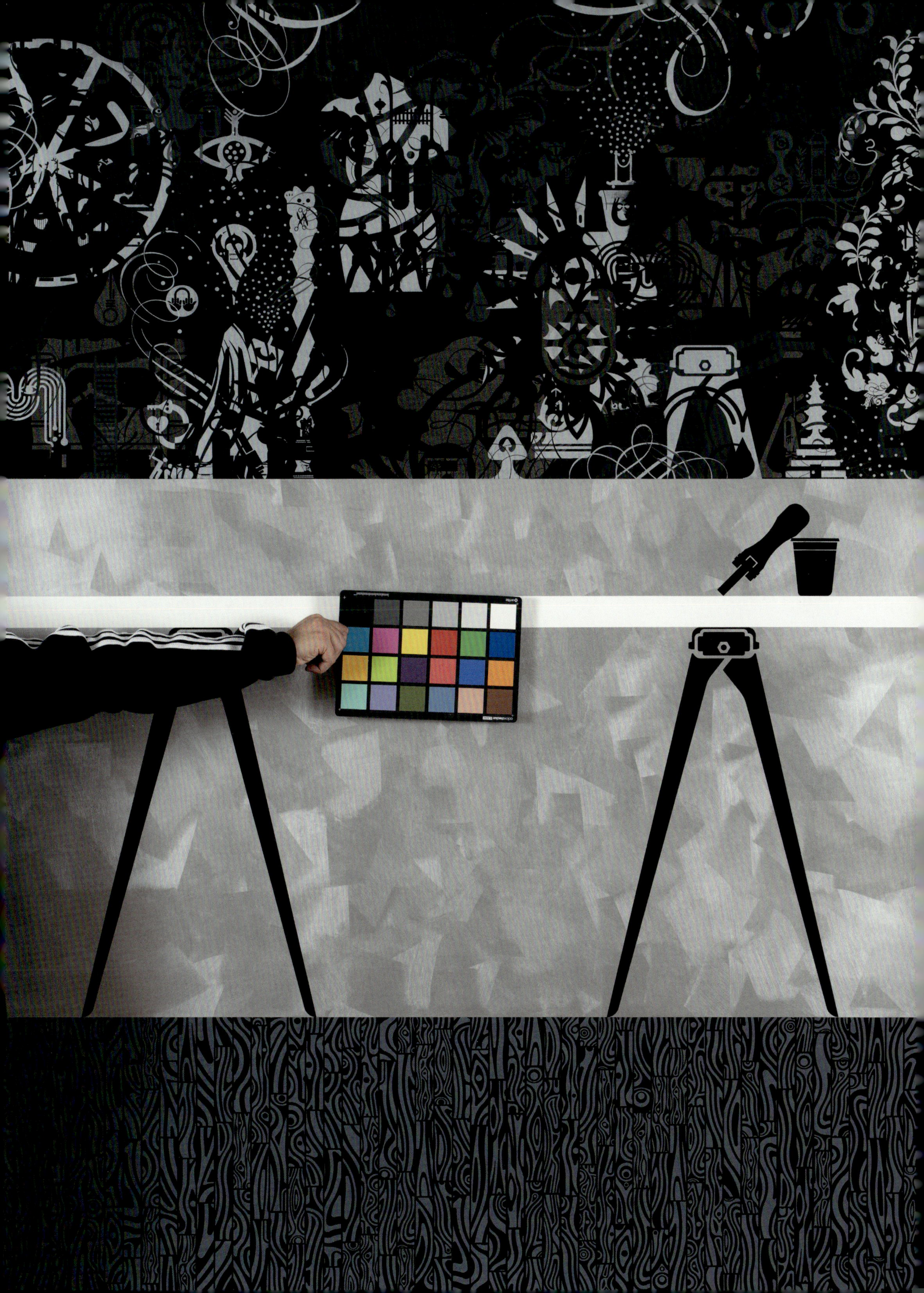

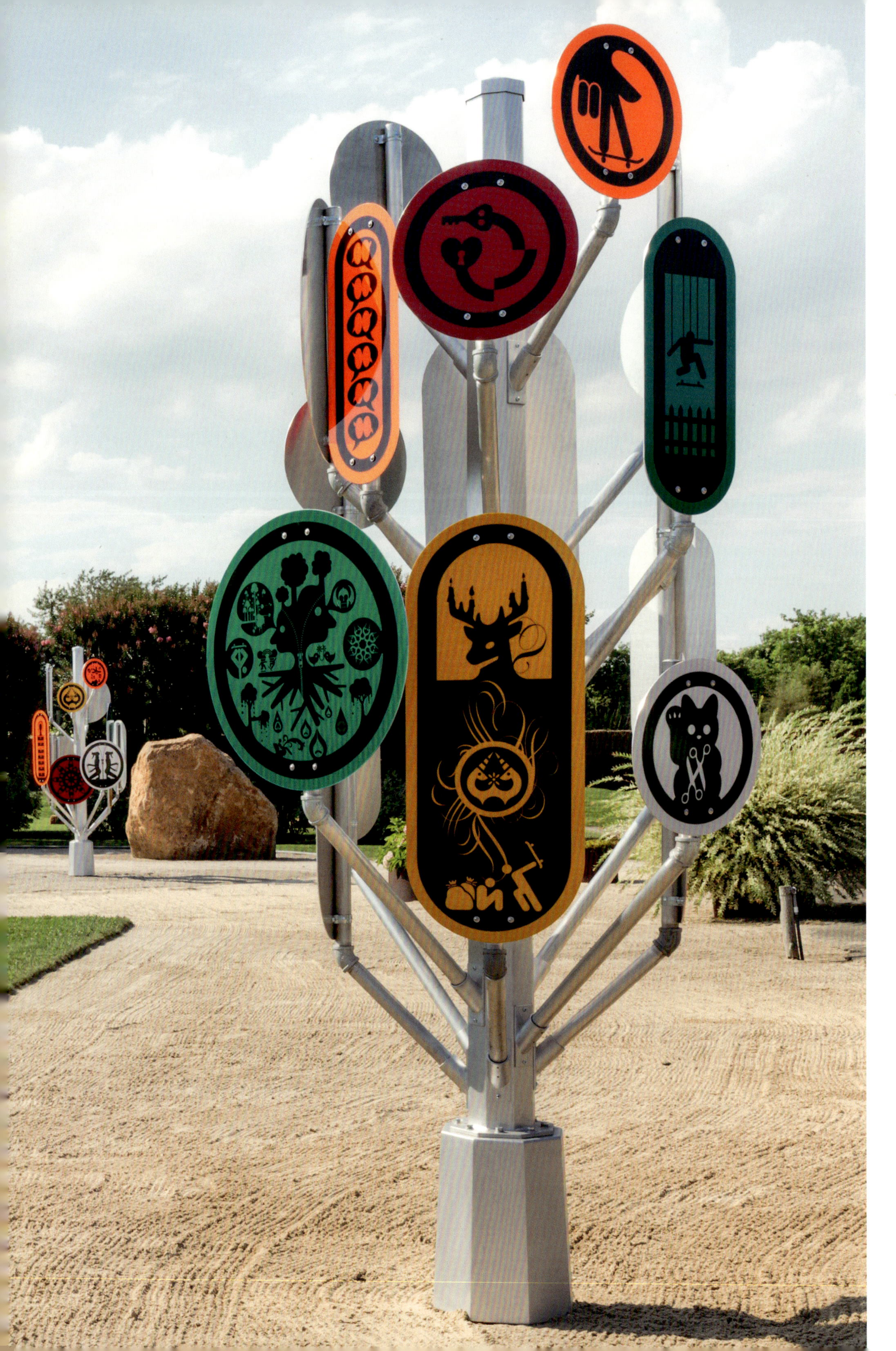

In the Forest of Signs

Carlo McCormick

Whatever twists and turns art may make in the relative favor or disfavor awarded any paradigm of style or content at a given moment, there is always a perennial divide between those who feel that less is more and those who feel, rather, that more is, well, never enough. These opposing attitudes, or competing aesthetics, have borne different names over the years, but let us simply call the former a kind of Minimalism and the latter a matter of Maximalism. Try it on your own art or on any art you look at, and you'll note the inherent difference between, say, a manner of brevity and reduction, versus expansiveness and detail.

Though this distinction is perhaps not as polemic as some of the debates fine art likes to get into, as a functioning polarity, it is fundamental to the kind of art we like and relate to. I mention all of this because Ryan McGinness, more so than just about any artist I have ever encountered, is somehow both. This contradiction in terms is central to his art, or rather it is more like the simultaneity of these terms within the same creative practice that makes his art so challenging and provocative in our visual landscape.

When McGinness first started showing his work in New York in the late '90s, sometimes in proper galleries but just as often in less pristine downtown conditions with the pop-up feel of a kind of DIY intervention, I recall with some embarrassment now that it all seemed a bit thin. Too much of a distillation into some precious essence, it was easy to mistake his rather arch mode of pictorial abbreviation as something far closer to very clever design work than actual fine art. Still in his twenties back then, Ryan was very much drawing from his background and prior tenure in commercial graphic design. Perhaps it was just too easy to read—for legibility was

its premise and mandate—that it could be misread just as easily. What appeared then as a wittily updated form of post-modern clip art was rather more complex and subversive than it seemed. As a culture we were getting used to redundancies, slipping away from the necessity of invention towards the inevitability of novelty, so McGinness' revival of arcane pictographic terms as a selfless (almost corporate) argot of non-self expression looked to be yet another, admittedly peculiar, invocation of Pop. It was, and it was not.

Ryan McGinness' early explorations in the terse language of symbols and icons are remarkably just as articulate, spot on, funny and fresh today as they were at the time. Let alone the faddishness that afflicts contemporary art, by the measure of industrial and commercial graphics, the ability to still look good and relevant a decade and a half later is an epic achievement. That's not accidental or incidental, but deliberate and essential to the way he worked. Pop Art's examination of consumer culture, of course, borrowed heavily from commercial forms in terms of production, content and style—and probably more so than most realized if you compare, for instance, Warhol's most famous canvases of the early '60s with Roger Coleman's *Ark* magazine in England from the late '50s. But Ryan wasn't so much following the path of Pop into the garden of products, as he was boldly stepping off towards an entirely different direction. Pop's all about looking at the field of comics, magazines, movies and supermarket shelves. McGinness was storming the back rooms of capitalist coercion where the merchants of desire were divining the lexicon of identifiers by which everyone would come to read the corporate landscape. He didn't want to emulate their products or mimic their sales spiel, he was after the esoteric language by which

Sign Trees, 2015, digitally printed high reflective vinyl on aluminum signs with painted aluminum and steel structure and hardware, 142 x 58 x 58 in. (360.7 x 147.3 x 147.3 cm) ea.

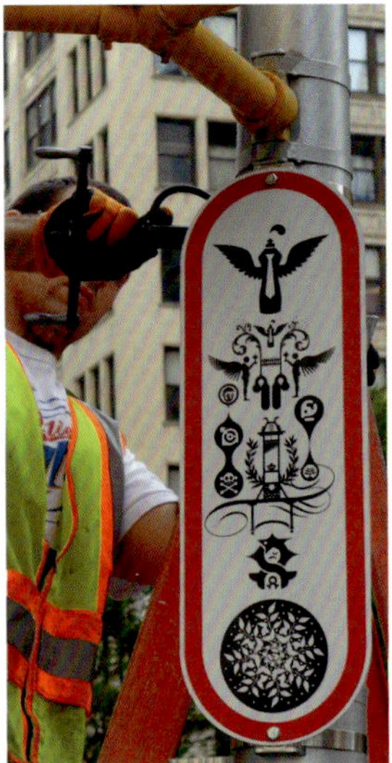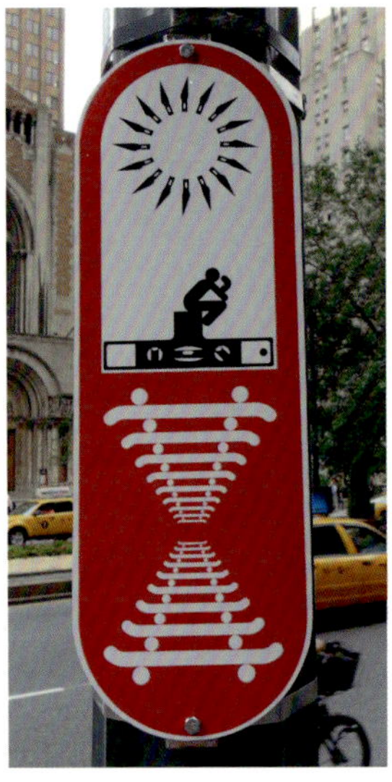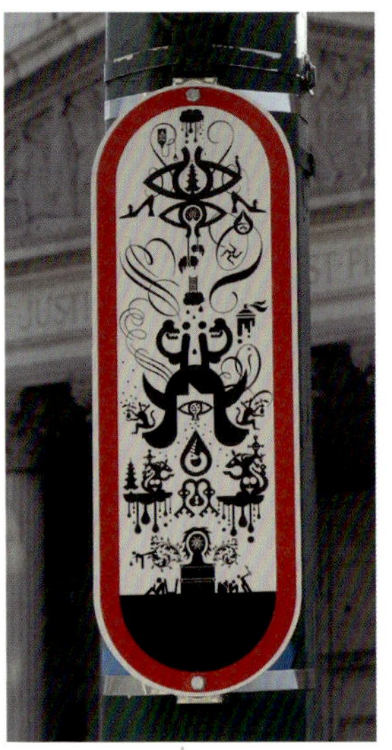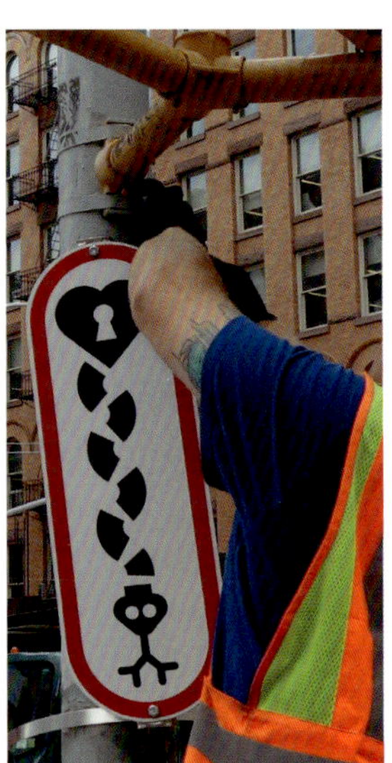

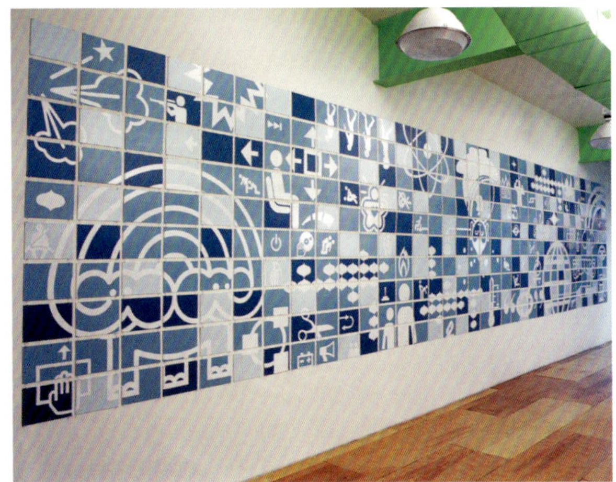

brand identity is made manifest.

By the time McGinness brought together the sum of his singular icons into his first conceptually acute body of work, *Flatness Is God*, in 1999, the achievement took on a gravitas that couldn't simply be dismissed as some whim or elaborate joke. The totality was compendious and cohesive. He had, in just a period of a few short years, created an entire visual language all of his own, something monumental and unmistakable, the kind of thing many of the world's greatest artists take lifetimes to develop. It was certainly significant enough that he could have stopped right then and there. He had more than enough to make a successful career in design and exercise an ample impact on the arts for years to come. What many of us have come to appreciate most about this artist, however, is that for all the exactness and precision of his thinking, he is cursed with a restless mind. If he had stopped there he might just be the most important lexicographer of the past century, but this was just the beginning.

To realize how the most reductive of signs could convey an immense amount of information, or how those very signs could so easily infect our way of seeing and become so much a part of us that we stop, yield or watch our step on command and even draw deeply personal and internalized associations with a wide variety of rapidly recognizable trade-

Above: *Signs* (Details), 2014, fifty vinyl on aluminum signs fabricated and installed by the New York City Department of Transportation, 24 x 8 in. (60.96 x 20.32 cm) ea., New York

Below: *Part of Everything*, 2000, enamel on 360 canvas boards, 96 x 480 in. (91.4 x 1219.2 cm) installation view, Alife, New York

marks and logos, is like a new science of perception for our mass mediated age. Knowing this expansive alphabet, all the messages they can convey and even how their common usage can insidiously tap into deep emotional resonances within the individual, is one thing, but really having something to actually say with that language is quite another. Where he has taken that pictographic language in the years following, up to the very present, proves that McGinness is not merely a master communicator; he's a provocateur and a poet of the highest order. What began as a definitive study on how we read this public language of social authority and, in the marketplace, the highly trademarked emblems of near equal command, led the artist to an ontological examination of how these systems have altered the very nature of our daily experience.

Prolific to a point that is nearly pathological, it would be impossible here to iterate the innumerable ways Ryan McGinness has developed and expanded upon his inventory of ideograms in recent years. Along the way, he has produced a deftly chic and irresistibly desirable assortment of artist multiples as a kind of examination through mimesis of our design-driven product culture. He undermined those very same processes of co-branding artists with commerce that had made him such a celebrated and in-demand figure in youth culture with a radical undertaking at fellow commercial/fine artist Shepard Fairey's first Los Angeles gallery with a show called *Sponsorship*, in which all the participating companies were represented simply by their logo on the wall in various sizes according to how much they offered the artist in terms of sponsorship. There was the marathon endeavor of staging fifty consecutive parties in 52 weeks to delve into the social dynamics of communal conviviality as aesthetic and conceptual theatrics, and more recently, the disassembled pin-up figure of the mud-flap nude into a formalist language of primary geometric forms available for high modernist interpretation. He even did the converse of that this past year with his *Studio Visit* where he reduced the wonderful complexity of masterworks within the Virginia Museum of Fine Arts into a set of highly simplified icons. Most frequently, however, Ryan has chosen to amass his bare-bones semiotics into miasmic onslaughts of visual over-

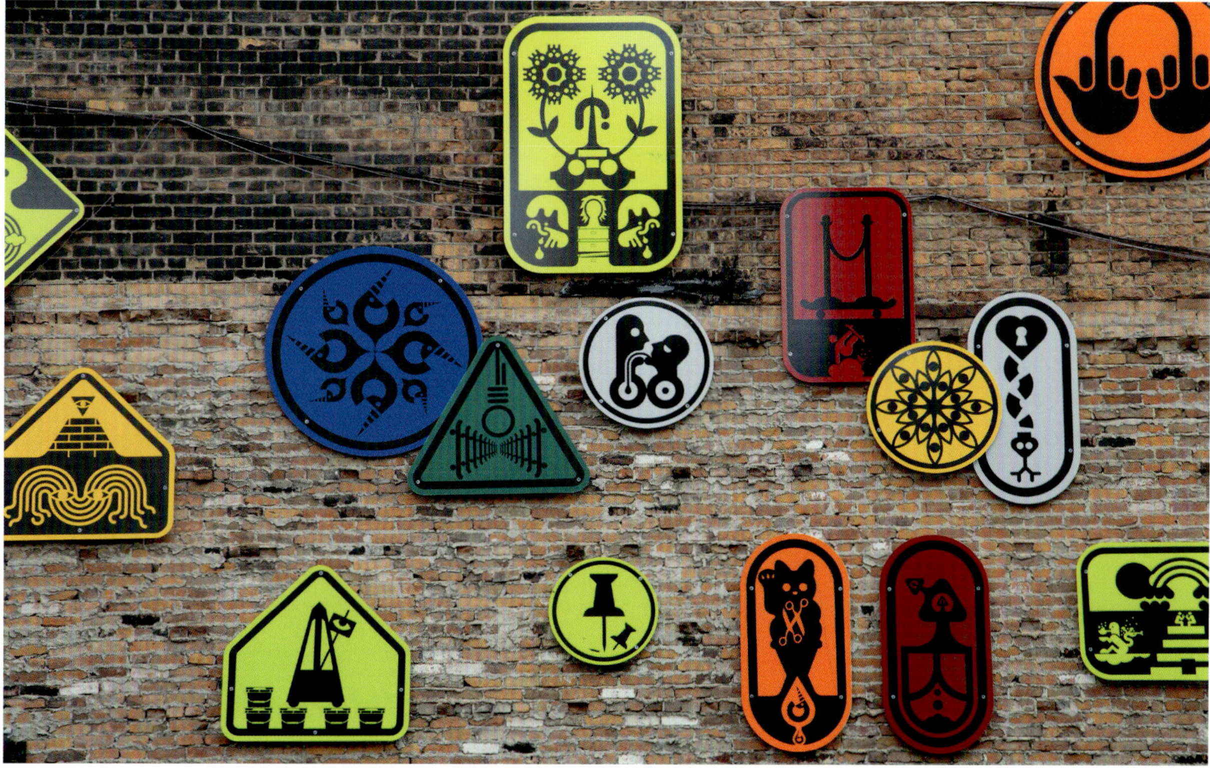

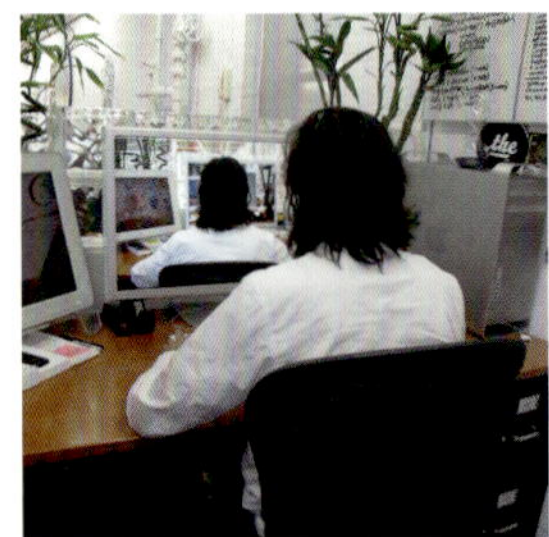
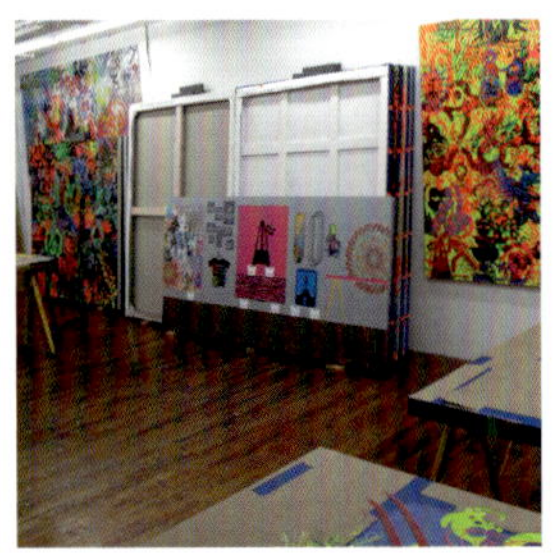
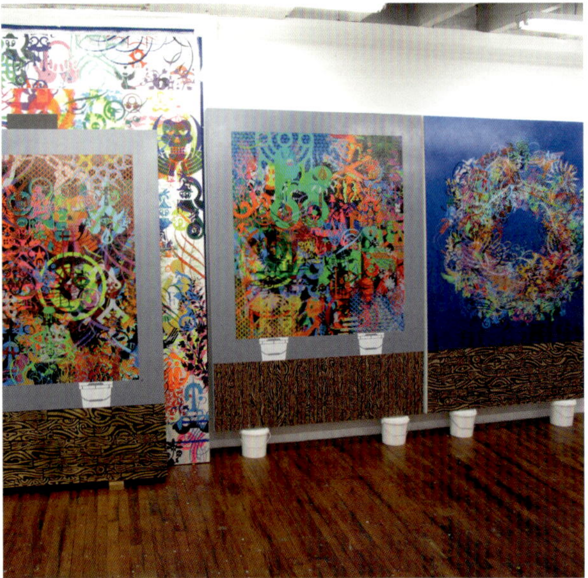
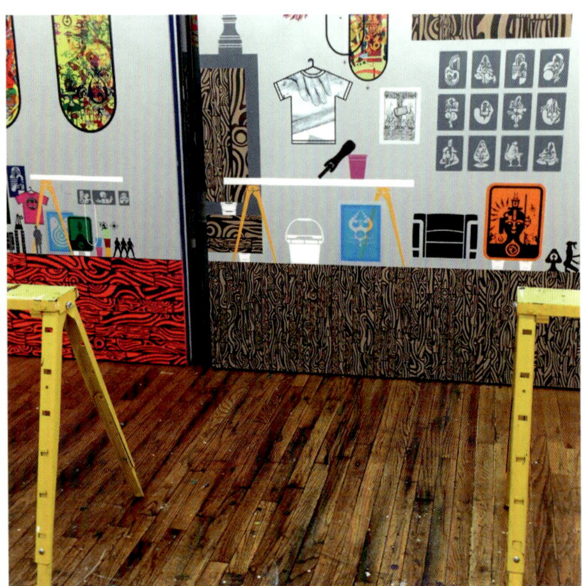
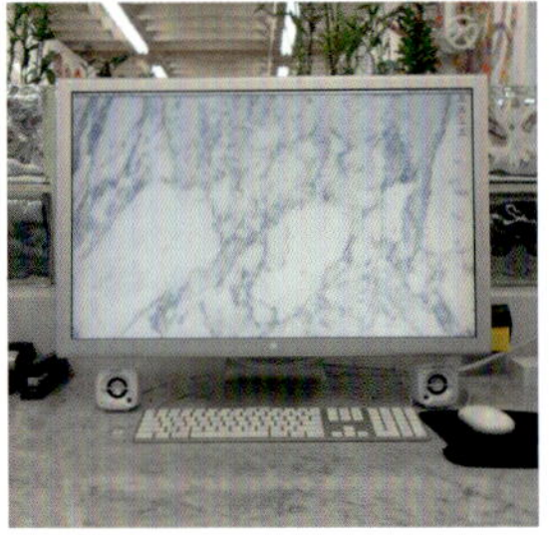
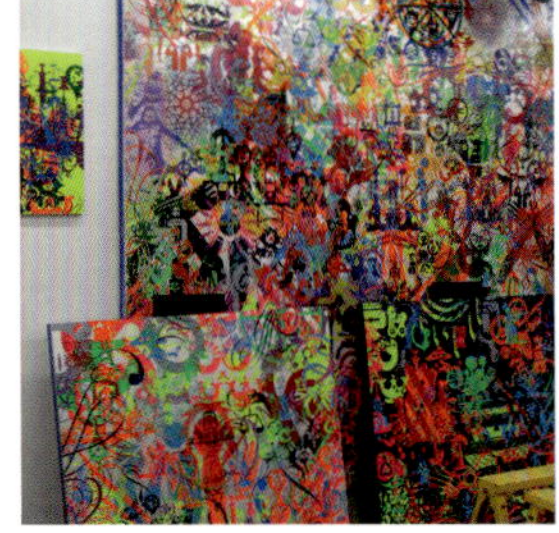

Studio views, New York, 2014-2017

load that defy the facile clarity of their terms—notably so in two major bodies of work, the *Mindscapes* begining in 2000 and the *Black Holes* beginning in 2005.

It is to this latter impulse, so much at odds with the minimalist tendencies inherent in his starkly deciphered sign-language as to create a befuddling frisson, that we were drawn back to McGinness' studio once again for what has become like some bi-yearly check on the zeitgeist. There, as always, it is to confront that impossible gap between language and understanding, to see something strangely familiar yet disquietly foreign and, in registering the entirety, feel that dissociative lag by which cognition must drag the verity of content kicking and screaming from the multiplicities of context. "What do you think?" he asks, "These are my paintings in paintings, like my work is all folding in on itself." Well, think is not exactly the right word for how you're likely to react when Ryan pulls out all the stops. It's all so much more primal than that. When art yanks on you that hard, the pull is overwhelming, not something you can rationalize with logic but wholly vertiginous, closer to the awe one registers before the sublime, a kind of fear you can't just talk away. Structurally, his art can make perfect sense, but as a sensory experience, it's dangerously close to the exquisite psychic panic of utter confusion. Much like his *Mindscapes* and *Black Hole* paintings, excess trumps comprehension, the surfeit subsumes certainty.

As a strict matter of perspective, there is some grounding. McGinness' Pictures in Pictures offer a kind of studio view with the maelstrom at its center, carefully framed by the quotidian elements of wood flooring or the buckets upon which a painting might rest as post-modern trompe l'oeil situational landscape—but these effects are about as comforting as being able to see the narrow ledge you're standing on after you've climbed out the window of a very tall building. Knowing there is something solid under your feet does little to ameliorate the unfathomable spectacle of what lies beyond. Nietzsche parsed the human condition as preferring "the void as a purpose than the void of purpose," and even if McGinness has an abiding optimism that is far from the nihilism of Nietzsche, his art has an uncanny way

of playing right along that thin line of intentionality where meaning and oblivion clutch close to one another in a mortal dance. He allows us the judicious cogency of less is more, but he also raises that storm of superfluity that wracks and ruins the architecture of signification into the traumatic rubble of desperate loss. It's as if he uses the building blocks of visual language to build a Tower of Babel befitting the contemporary polyglot of culture's wanton referencing, assembling it all to an unfeasible height for the glorious purpose of watching it implode.

Semiotics, in the hands of Ryan McGinness, is not just the tool by which we interpret our very modes of communication; it is the topography of a human affliction in which too many signs distress comprehension to the ends of confusion. He described it to us as "metadata work," explaining the subject matter as "information about information." In part, he asserts this is his reaction to the disembodiment of fine art into the trivialized medium of .jpegs in our digital age. Better versed in the abilities afforded by computers than most artists, save those who work solely in digital art, Ryan maintains he uses computers only as tools of necessity along the way rather than any end to themselves, insisting that it is "really important to make things and embed information in those objects." That's why he wouldn't even talk to us about what he was doing now until we came to look at the work directly in the studio, where he's painting the pictorial equivalent of big data, the big picture of all the pictures put together, the fearful symmetry that can only be gleaned by too much at once. Much like the use of fluorescent paint in his black light paintings, the artist is concerned with the experiential aspects of art that cannot be reduced to a reproduction, and as he puts it, "creates something you have to see in person and forces a specific time/space experience of the work."

Signals Painting (Detail with color calibration chart held by photographer), 2016, acrylic on linen, 84 x 60 in. (213.4 x 152.4 cm)

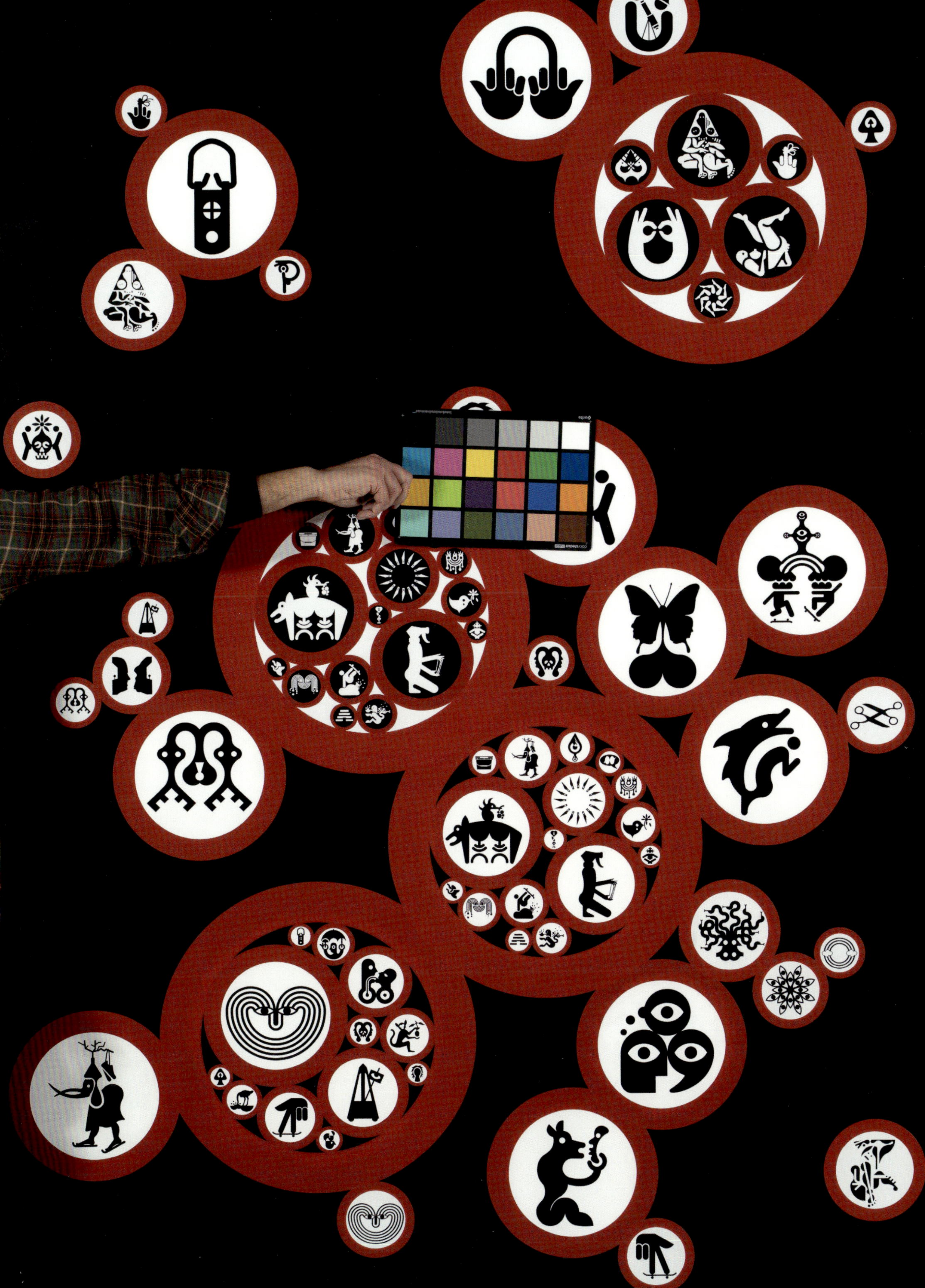

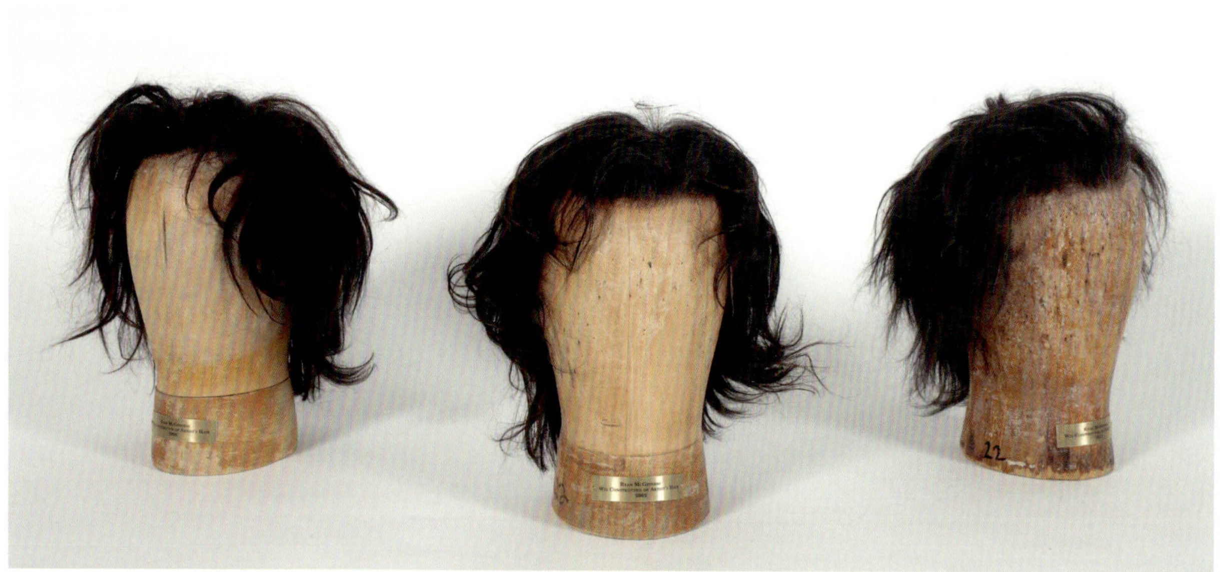

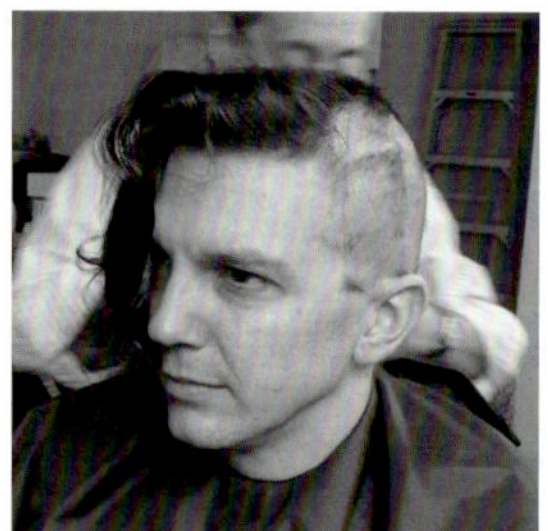

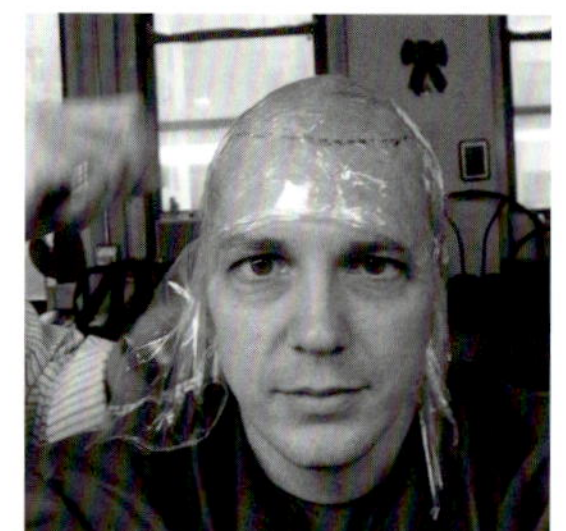

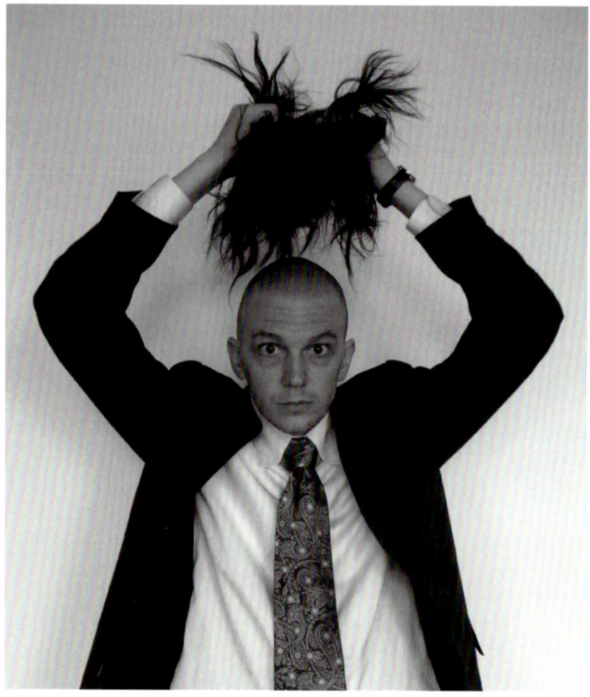

Above: *Wigs*, 2008, 2009, & 2011, artist's hair with stretch lace cap (hand tied construction) on wood head forms, 13.5 x 8.5 in. (34.3 x 21.6 cm) ea. Below: Photos of wig-making process, 2008

Shock & Aww

Bill Powers

It's hard to imagine that anyone could outdo the shock value of Andy Warhol's famous fright wigs, but painter Ryan McGinness has achieved just that with a set of wigs he's created using clippings of his own hair. Fixed somewhere between *Silence of the Lambs* and Locks of Love, perhaps the most disturbing aspect of this project is that he wears them around in public, unbeknownst to the uninitiated. Sure, you can tell something's off about him—primally we know such things—but it's the pinpointing that proves elusive. You can have a look for yourself the next time he has a public opening. Ryan will be the guy in the white dress shirt—for over the past twenty years he's only worn white shirts—and the strange upside-down beard on his head. I think it was Henri Matisse who liked to dress up before heading to his studio, because he considered the act of creation an aesthetic experience therefore demanding that an artist present himself to the canvas in the best possible light. McGinness has absconded with this concept and morphed it to meet his own twisted split ends.

What was your idea behind this project?
During a lecture I gave sixteen years ago, someone in the audience asked if I was wearing a wig. I wasn't, but it started me thinking about wigs, and then really liking the idea of wearing a wig as a way of standardizing my appearance in an effort to achieve total efficiency. Although I had adopted a limited set of clothing variables by that time, I hadn't addressed the hair situation. So for a few years, I outlined the idea in my sketchbook and developed a plan and schedule for growing the wigs. I revisited those plans six years later when I was working on the *Varied Editions* exhibition at Pace Prints in 2007. With the pieces in that show, I wanted to push the idea of making unique objects within a set of variables. This wig project would have been a good fit for that concept, but I didn't have the time required to grow hair the three wigs I needed to make my point. Anyways, I eventually completed the triptych by the end of 2011, and they became part of the *Metadata* series of works.

Were you influenced by Andy Warhol's wigs?
Of course! Andy's fright wigs are an obvious precursor to my wigs. However, it's always been important to me that the hair in my wigs is real. It's my genuine hair. This difference underscores my critique of Warhol's dehumanizing approach to art-making.

So the wigs are definitely your own hair?
Yes. I had to grow my hair an inch longer than I wanted the wigs to be so they had the length needed to tie each hair to the lace cap. In using my own hair, these wigs have become simultaneously the symbols and the referents. These objects have folded in on themselves!

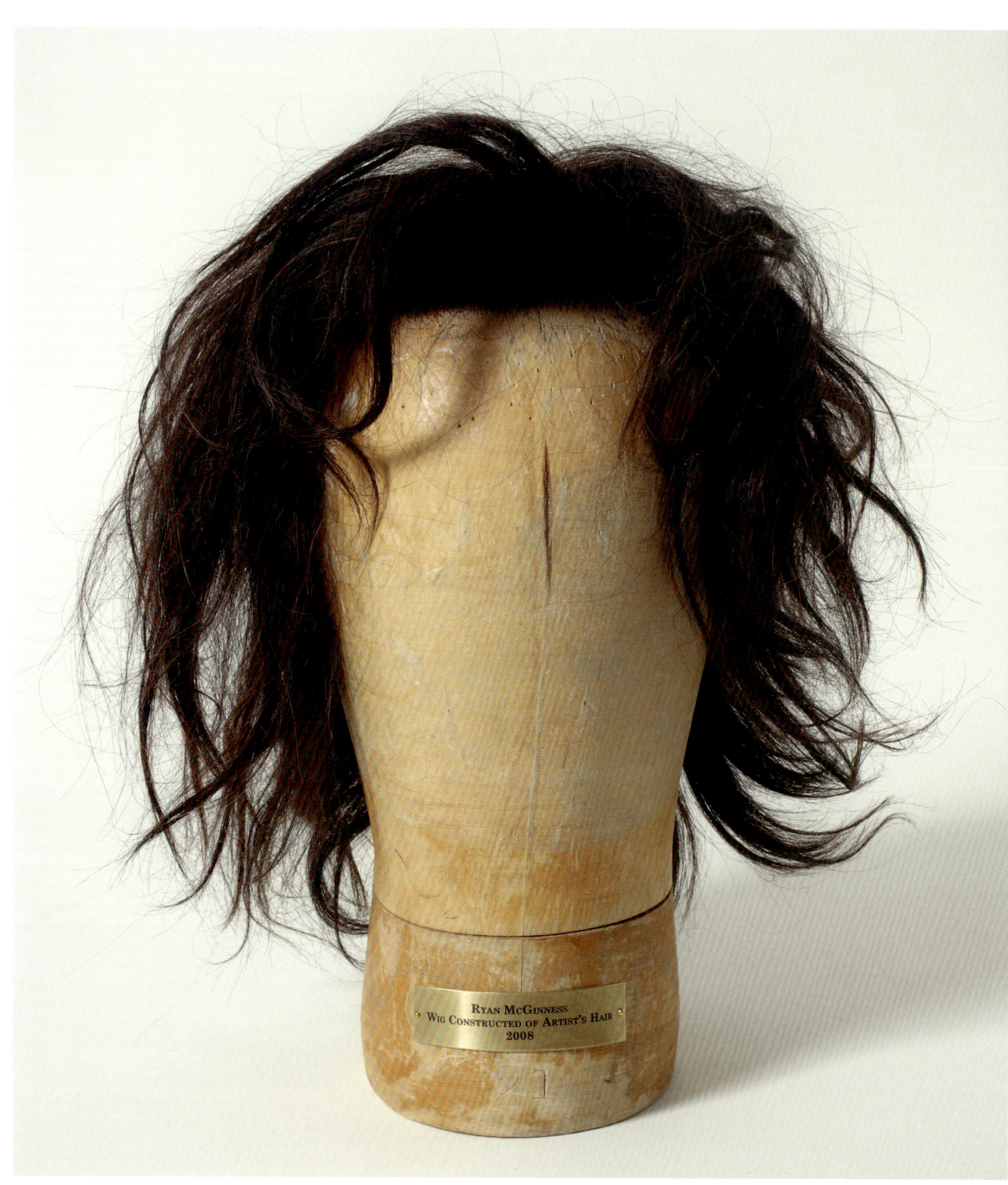

44   *Wig*, 2008, artist's hair with stretch lace cap (hand tied construction) on wood head forms, 13.5 x 8.5 in. (34.3 x 21.6 cm)

Opposite Page: Michael Halsband contact sheet of outtakes from photoshoot, 2011, 12 x 9.5 in.

How did you find wigmakers?
Jeffrey Deitch recommended Bob Kelly Wig Creations in midtown Manhattan. Apparently Vanessa Beecroft used them for her models' wigs. But what was more exciting for me was that they were the wigmakers for *Saturday Night Live*. Bob Kelly was a legend in his field. He created wigs for the Met Opera, numerous Broadway productions, and even did makeup and hair for the Beatles' first live American TV performance, on *The Ed Sullivan Show*. Sadly, he passed away before my last wig was made, which I had to have woven by one of Bob's apprentices.

Have all three wigs ever been shown together?
Only recently in the *Studio Views* exhibition at the Cranbrook Art Museum. The first two were shown in the *Studio Franchise* exhibition in 2010 at La Casa Encendida in Madrid.

Is there any variation among the three wigs?
Yes. Each is inherently unique, of course. And, much to my chagrin, each has progressively more grey highlights.

Do you consider this work to be a fashion statement?
I didn't, but now that you suggest it, I suppose it is. The wigs, are quite literally, a second skin and premised on costuming.

What's been the reaction to the wigs?
Most people think they're creepy. I have been asked to take my wig off during moments of intimacy.

What have you learned about yourself, art, and grooming from doing this?
About myself: An informal poll suggests that people like me better with long hair. About art: Almost all art is about art. If it isn't, then it is outsider art. About grooming: My hair grows fast.

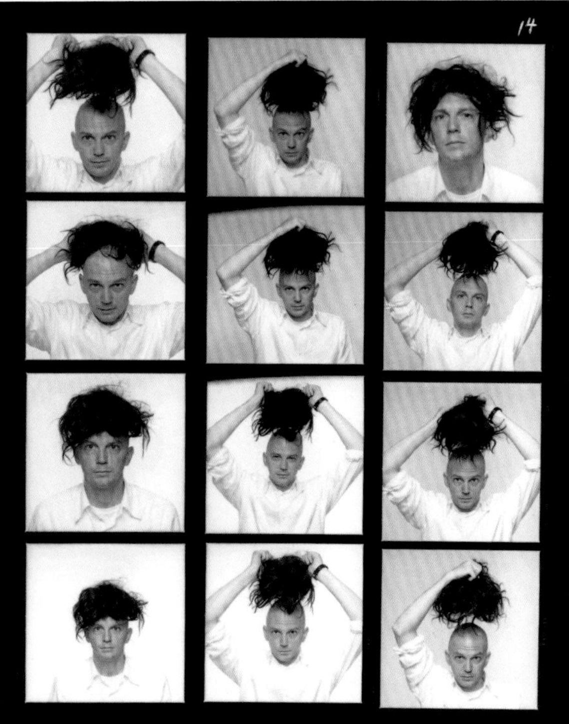

Untitled (with color calibration chart held by photographer),
2016, digital print on canvas, 30 x 22 in. (76.2 x 55.9 cm)

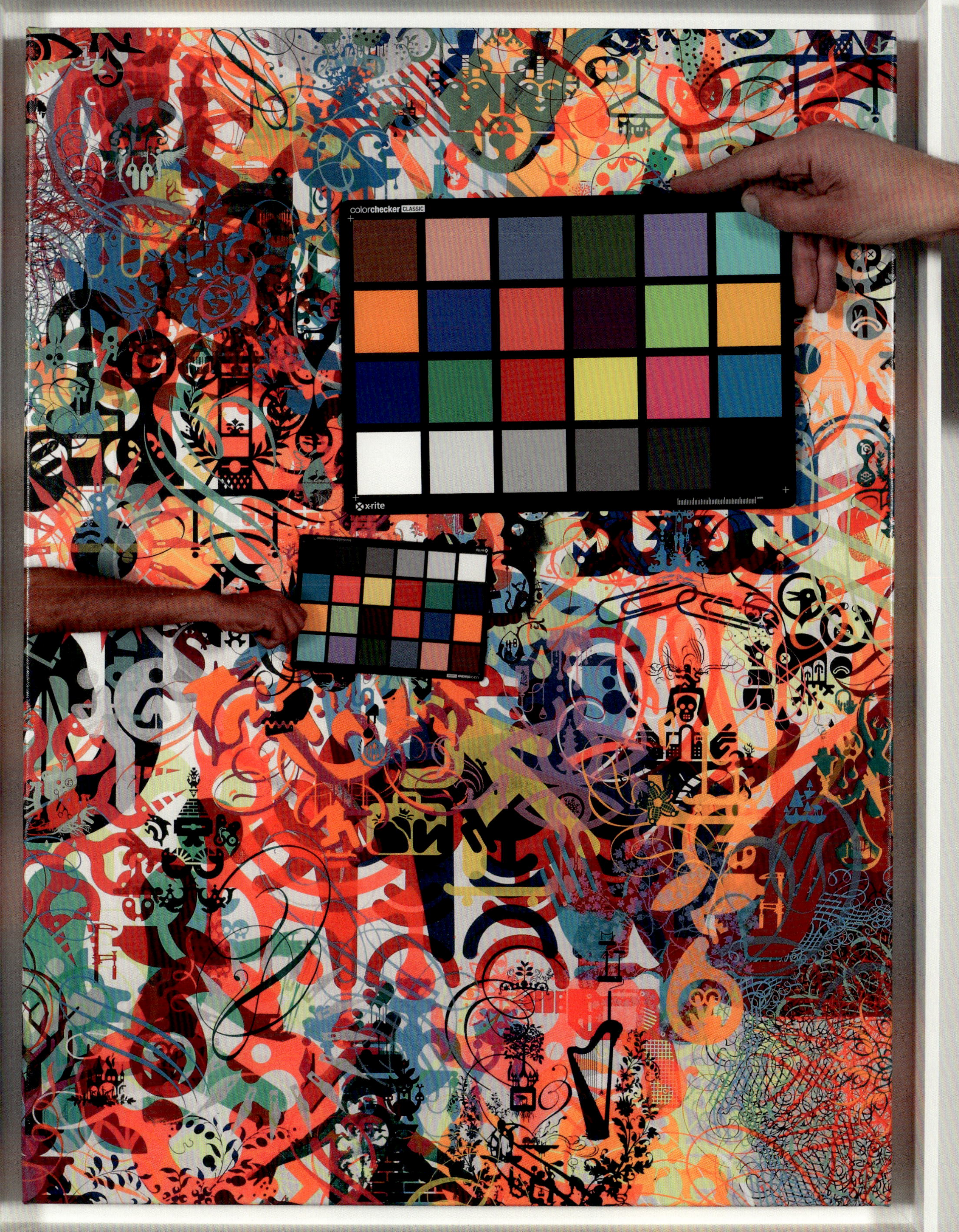

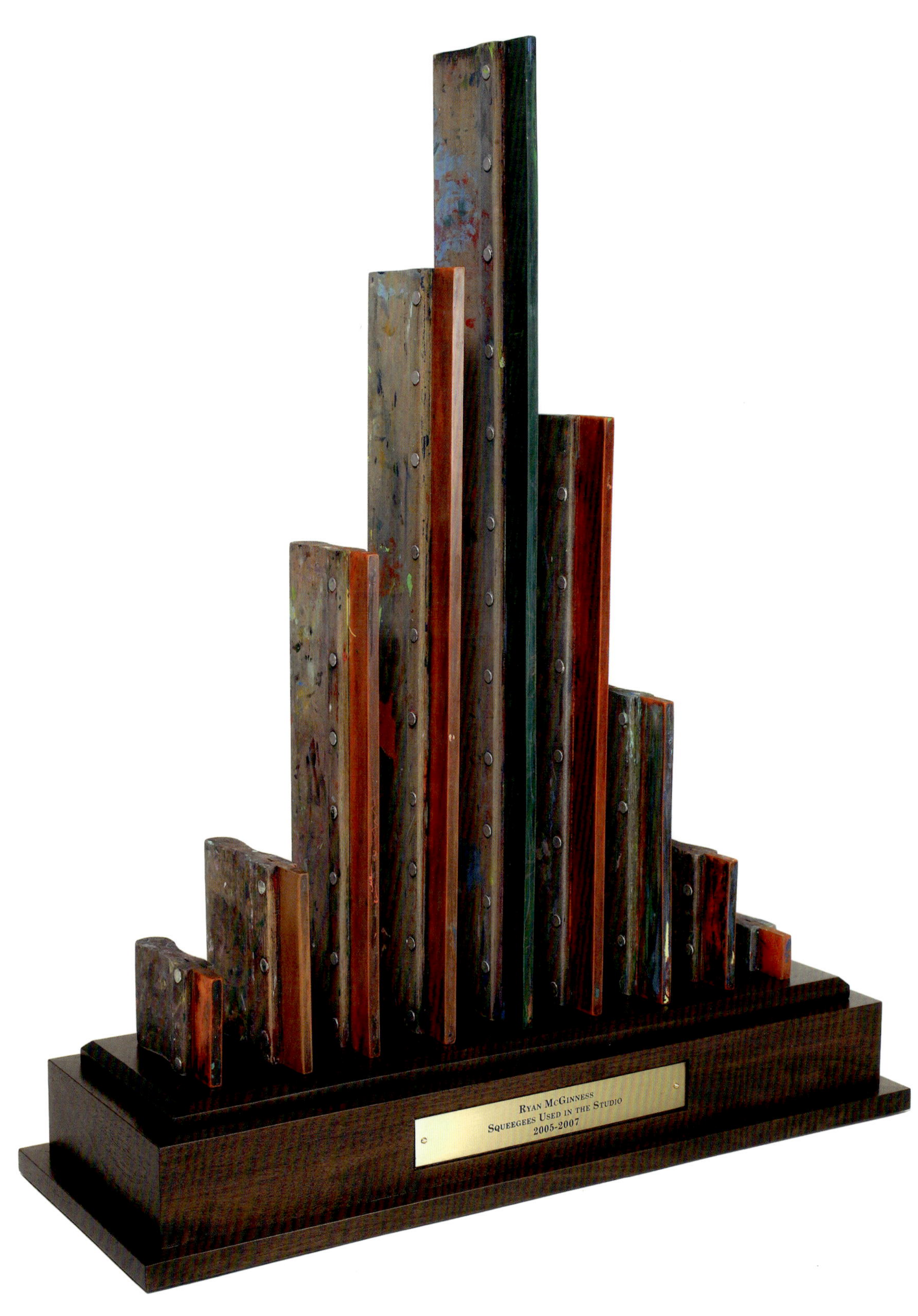

Squeegee Trophy (2005-2007), 2011, used squeegees, wood, and brass
plate, 34.75 x 28 x 10 in. (88.3 x 71.1 x 25.4 cm)

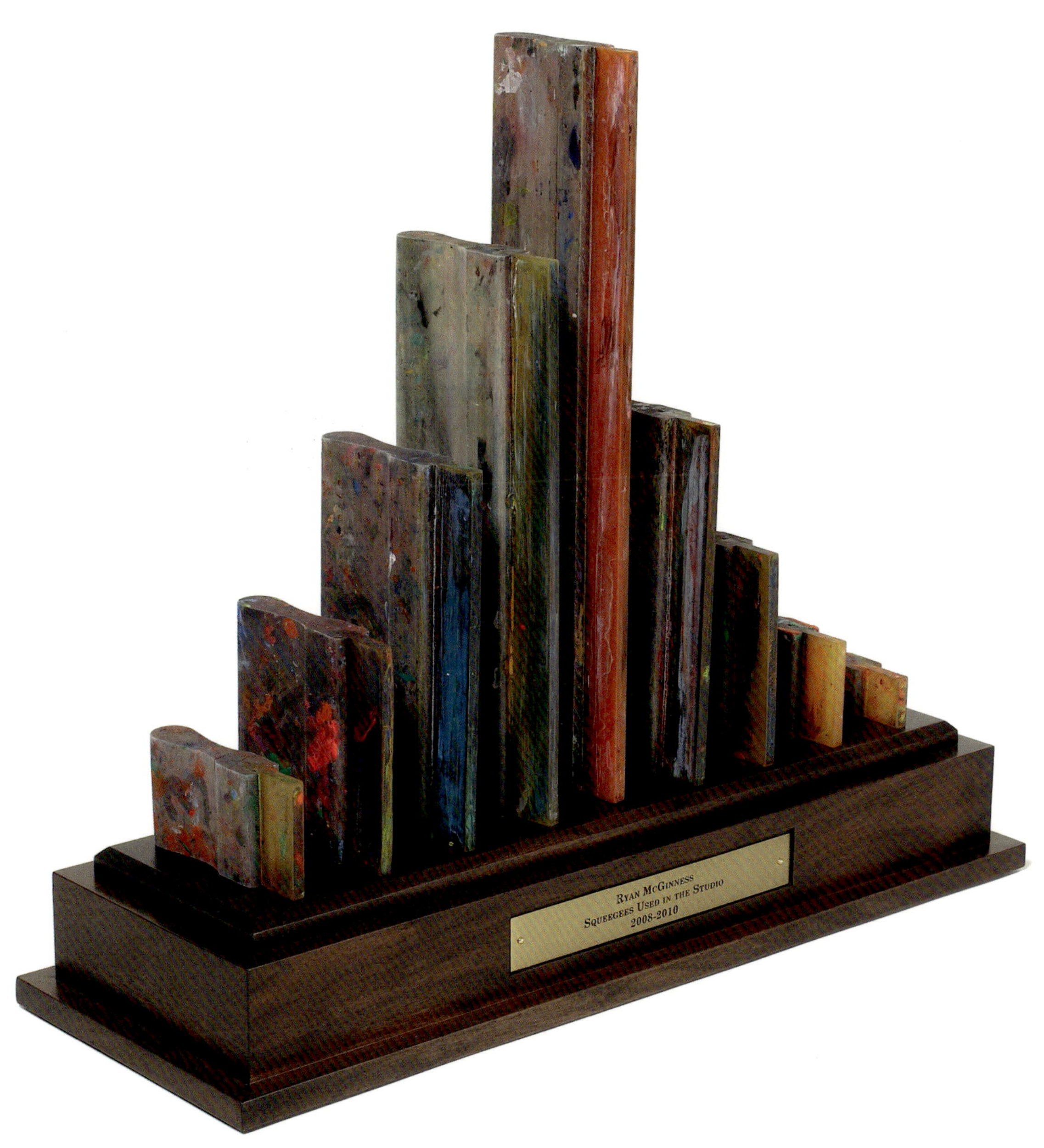

Squeegee Trophy (2008-2010), 2011, used squeegees, wood, and brass
plate, 25.75 x 28 x 10 in. (65.4 x 71.1 x 25.4 cm)

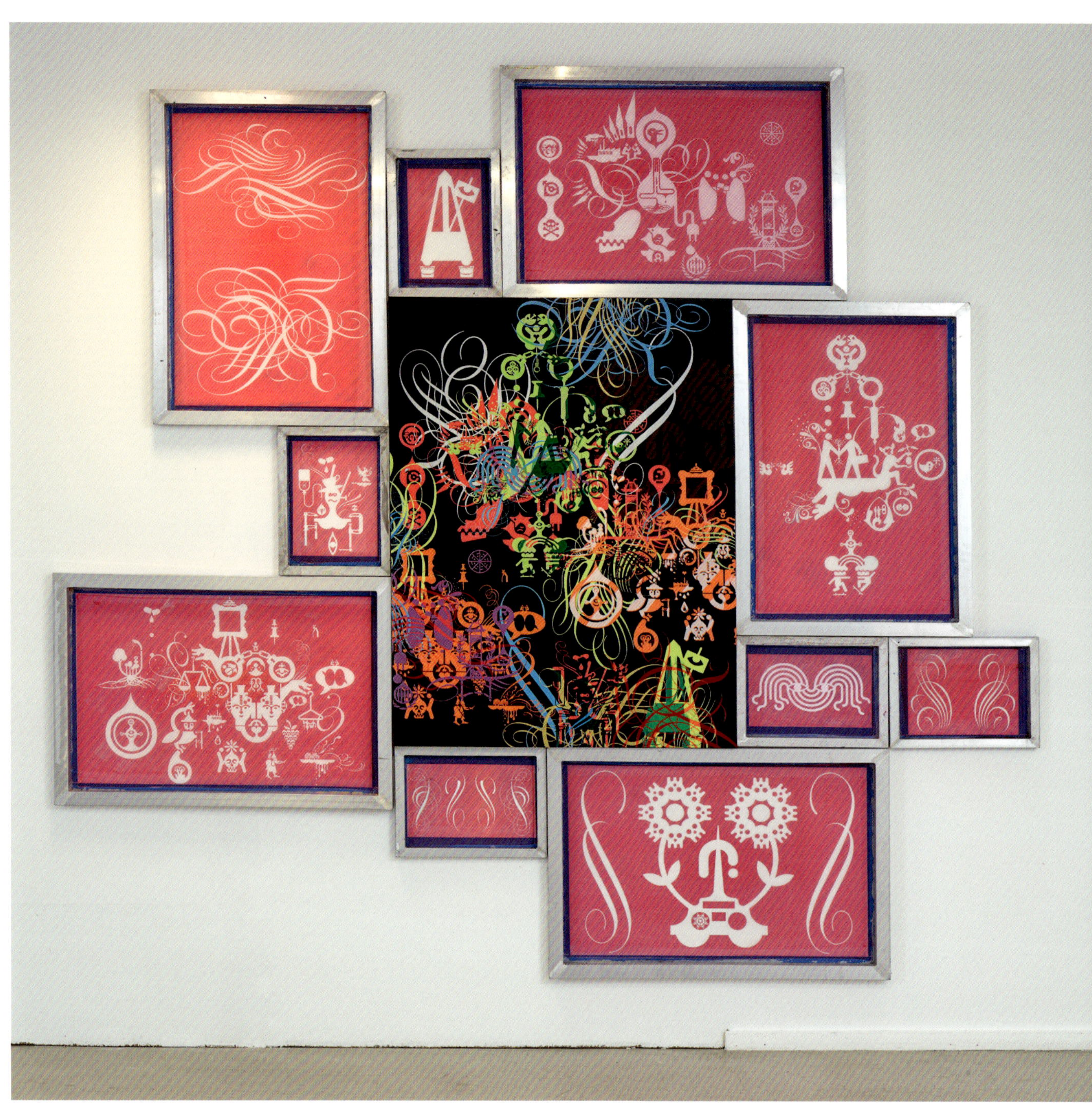

Closed System Painting (Language Slows Thought), 2014, oil and acrylic on wood panel, 48 x 36 in. (121.9 x 91.4 cm) with ten silkscreens, each: acrylic paint residue and photo emulsion on polyester monofilament screen with polyurethane adhesive and polyethylene tape attached to aluminum frame, 36 x 25 in. (91.4 x 63.5 cm) and 16 x 12 in. (40.6 x 30.5 cm), overall dimension: 98 x 104 in. (248.9 x 264.2 cm)

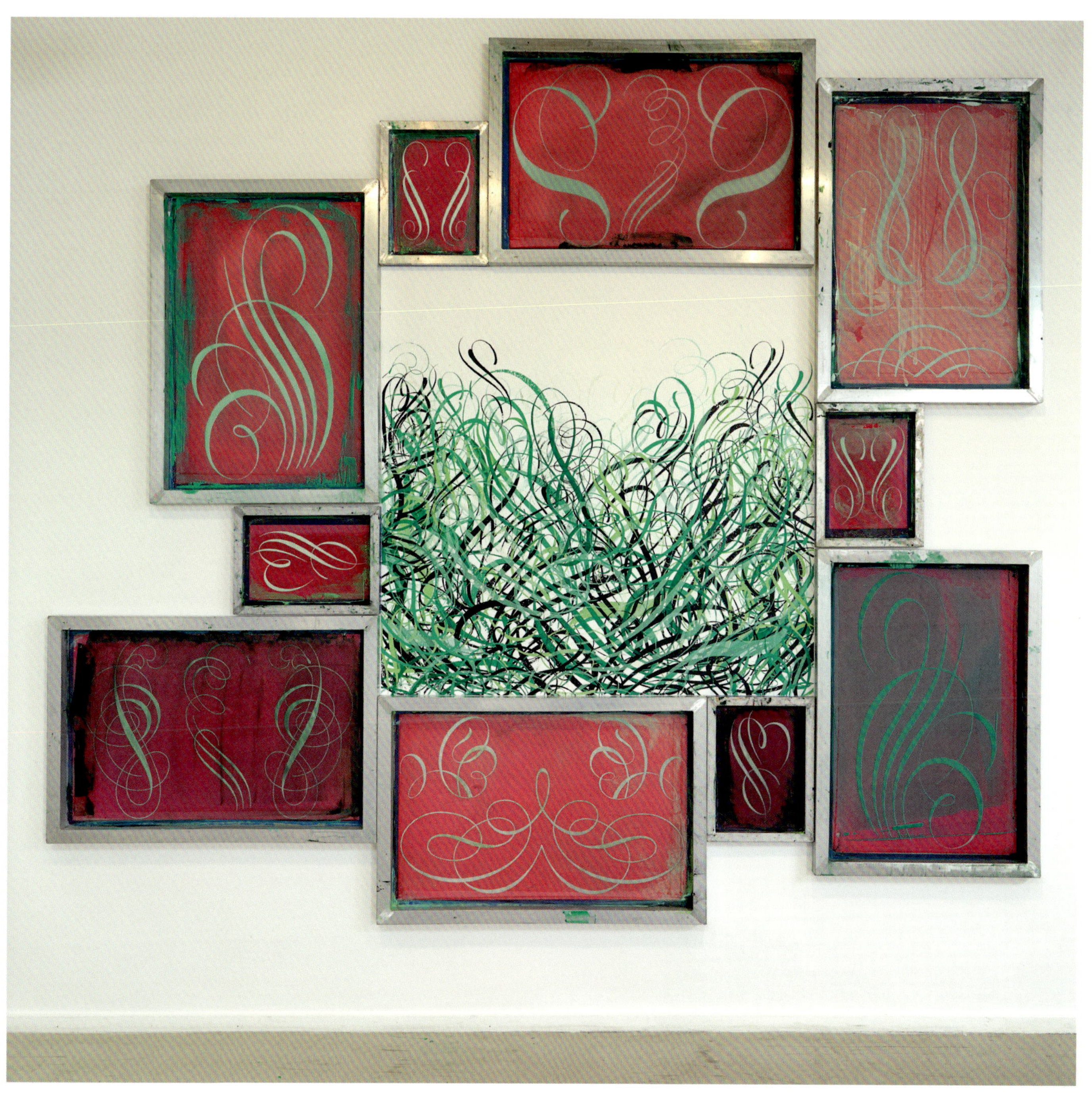

Closed System Wall Painting (Flourishes), 2014, site-specific acrylic on wall, 48 x 48 in. (121.9 x 121.9 cm) with ten silkscreens, each: acrylic paint residue and photo emulsion on polyester monofilament screen with polyurethane adhesive and polyethylene tape attached to aluminum frame, 36 x 25 in. (91.4 x 63.5 cm) and 16 x 12 in. (40.6 x 30.5 cm), overall dimension: 98 x 109 in. (248.9 x 276.9 cm)

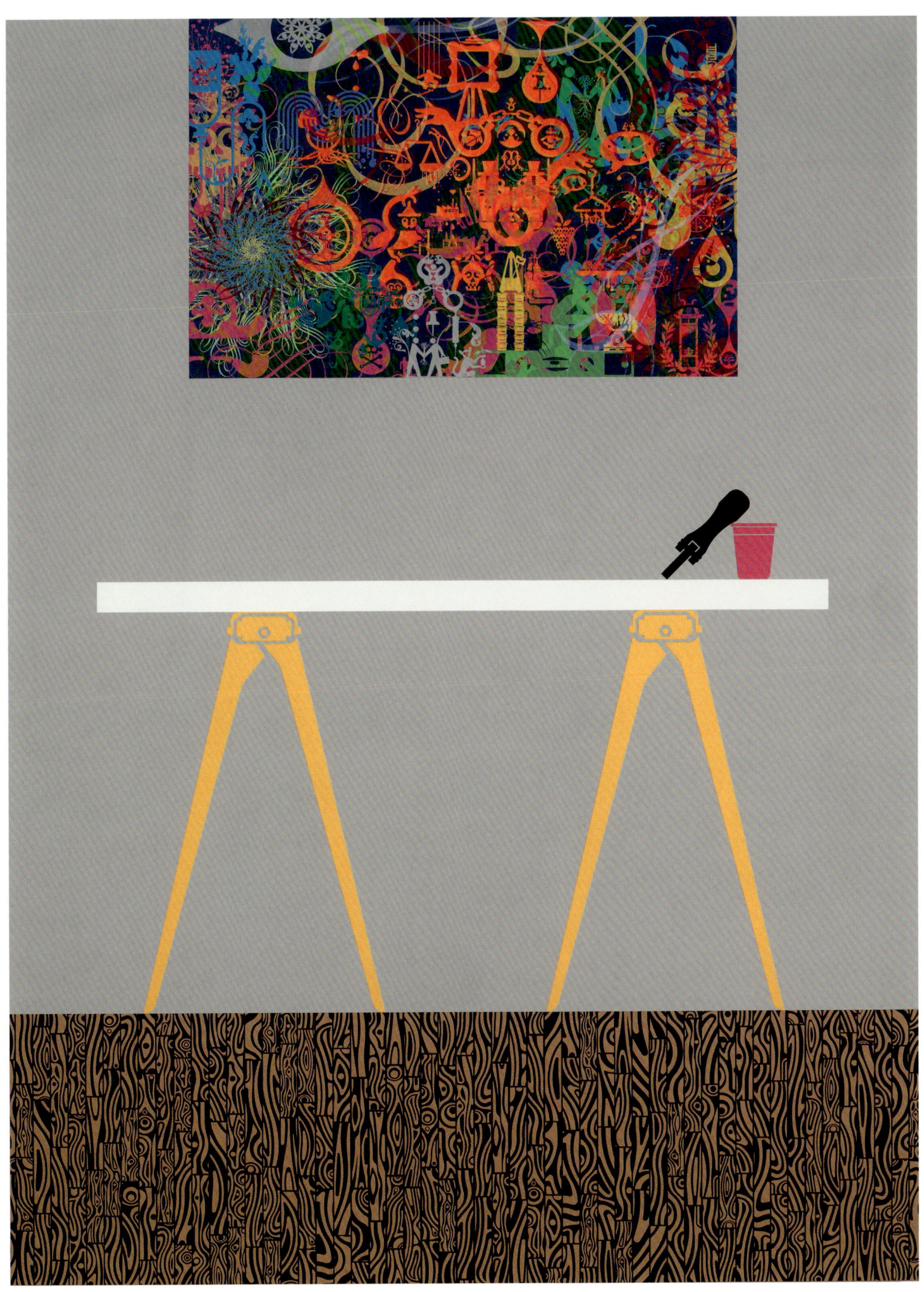

The Maker Doesn't Want It. The Buyer Doesn't Use It. The User Doesn't See It., 2016, acrylic on linen, 84 x 60 in. (213.4 x 152.4 cm)

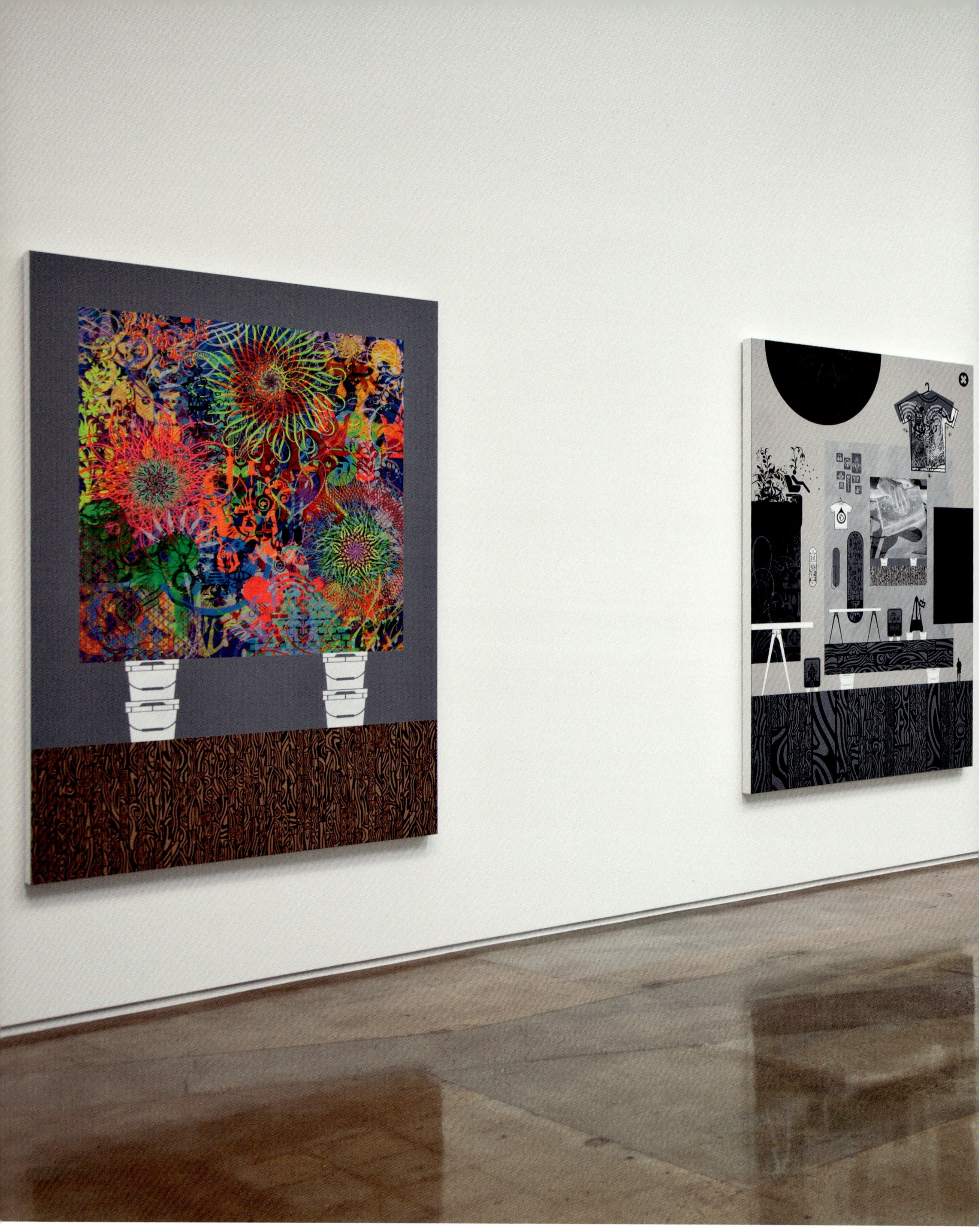

#metadata, 2016, installation view, Kohn Gallery, Los Angeles

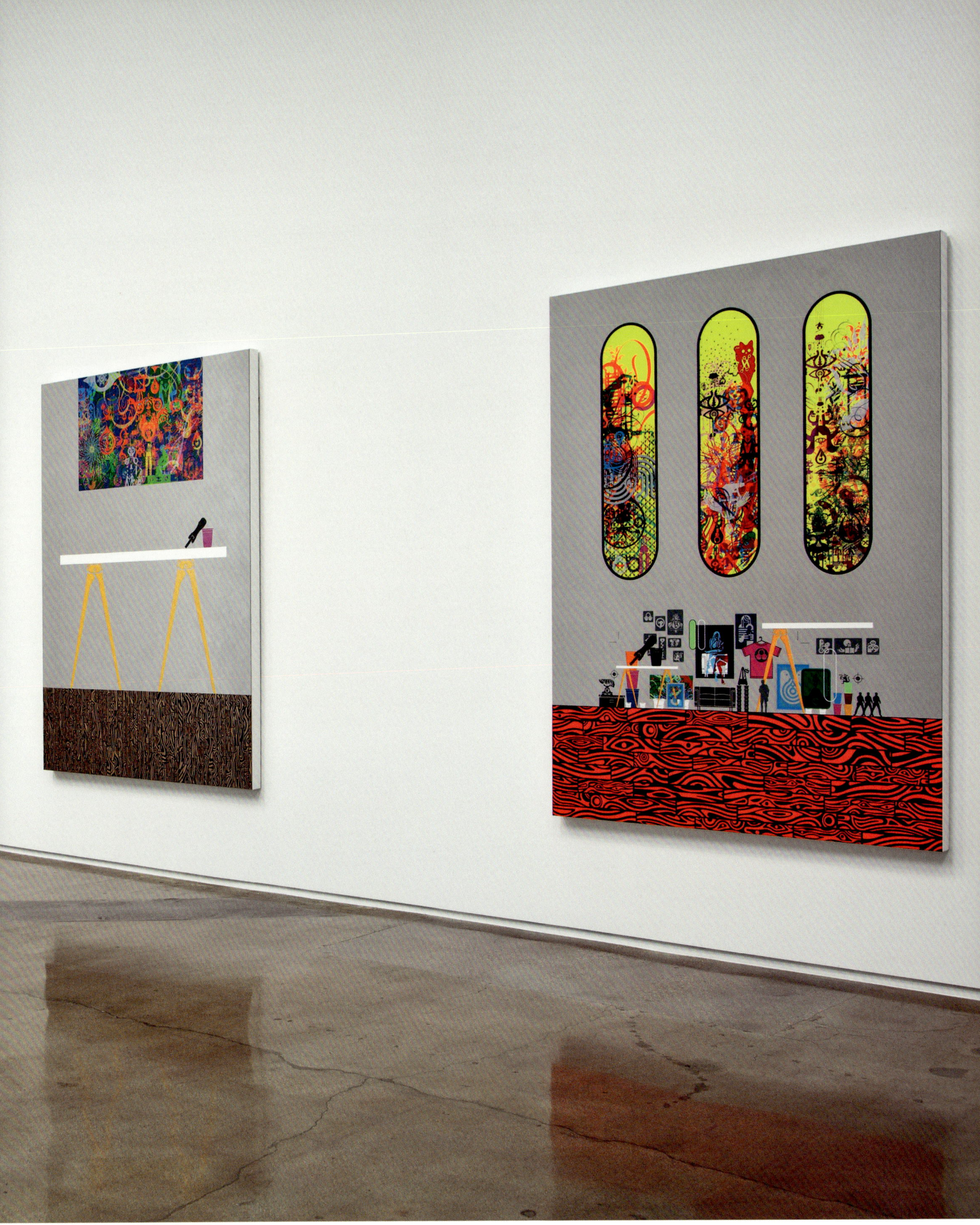

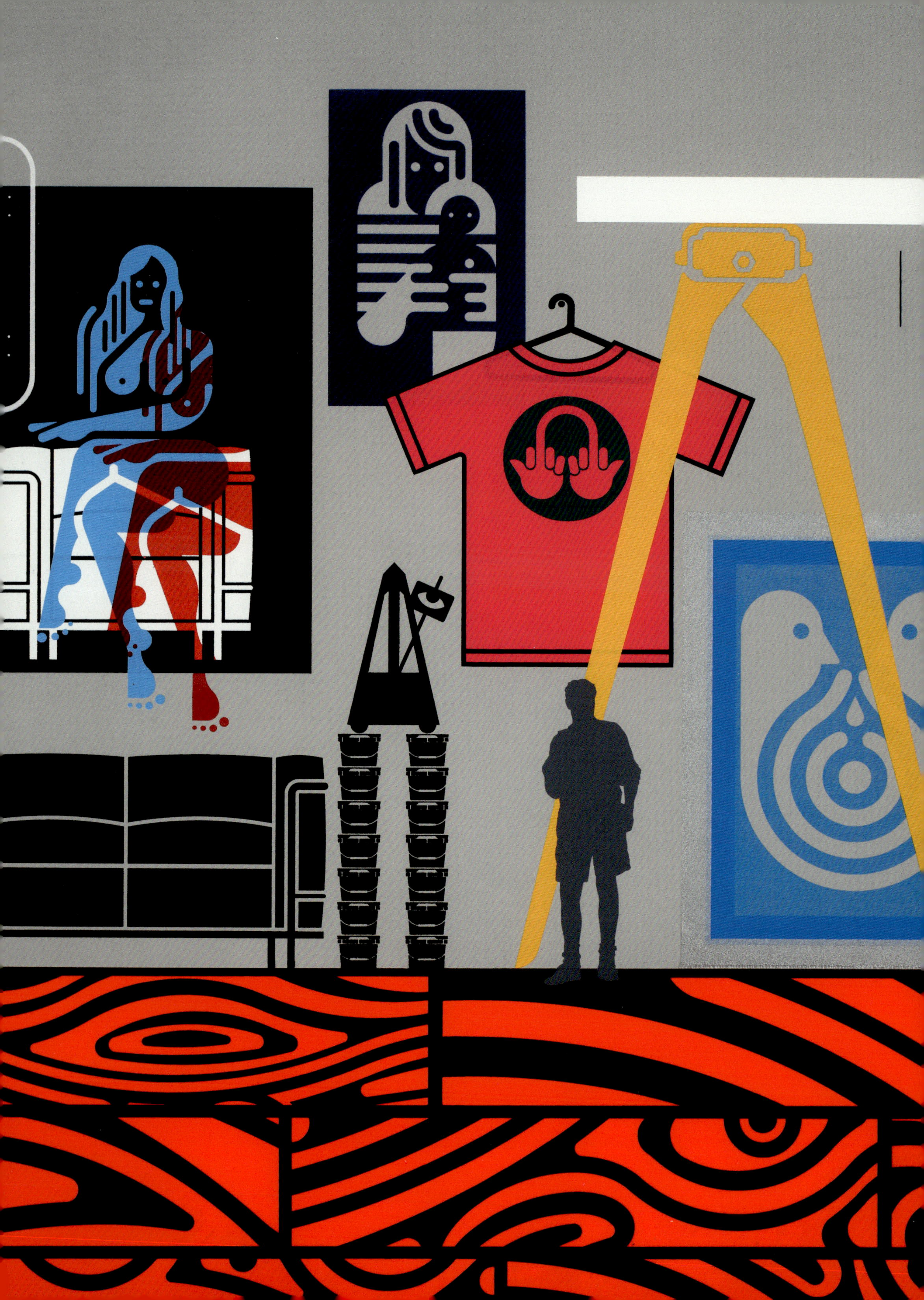

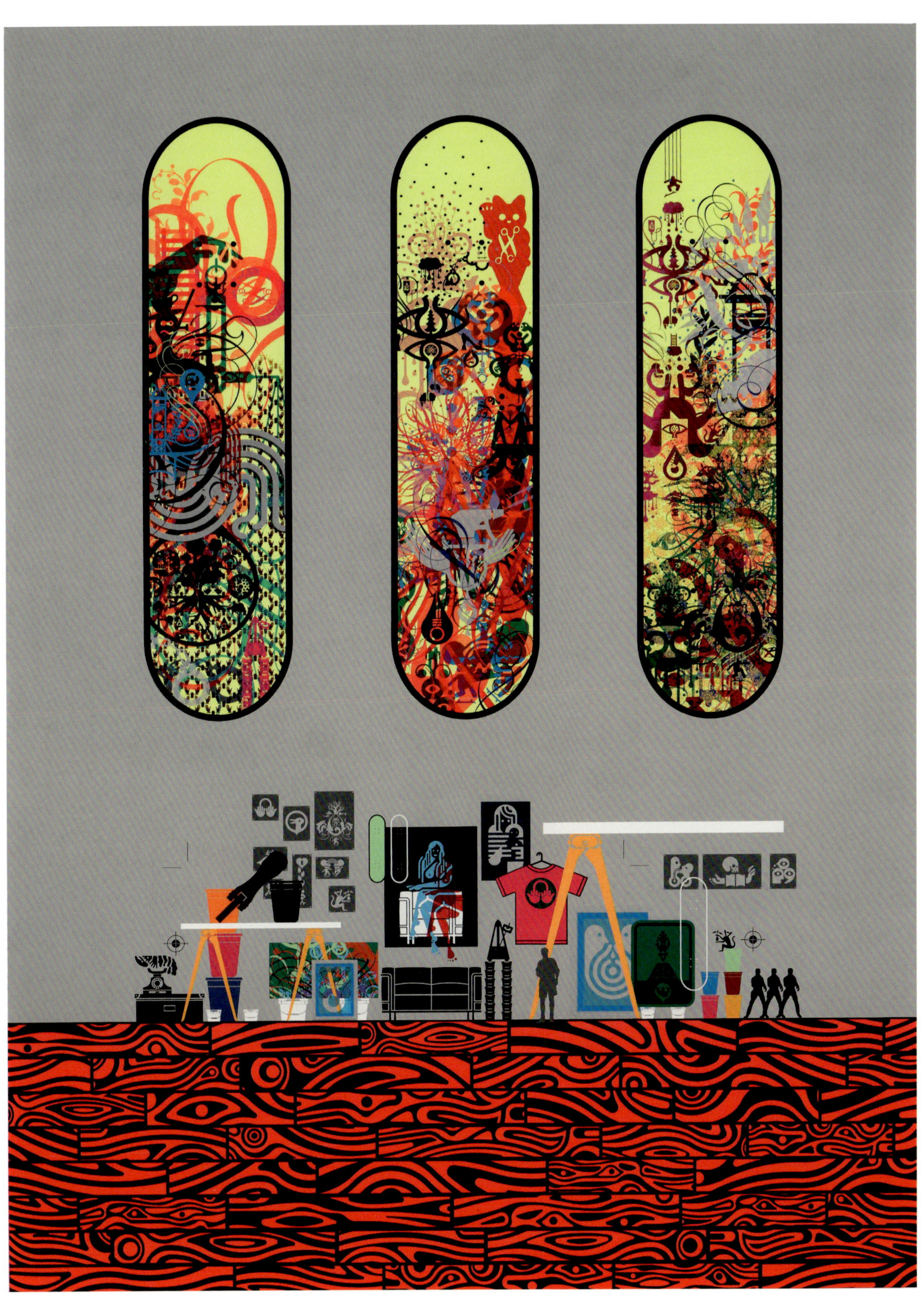

Exit to Exist, 2016, acrylic on linen, 84 x 60 in. (213.4 x 152.4 cm)
Opposite Page: Detail

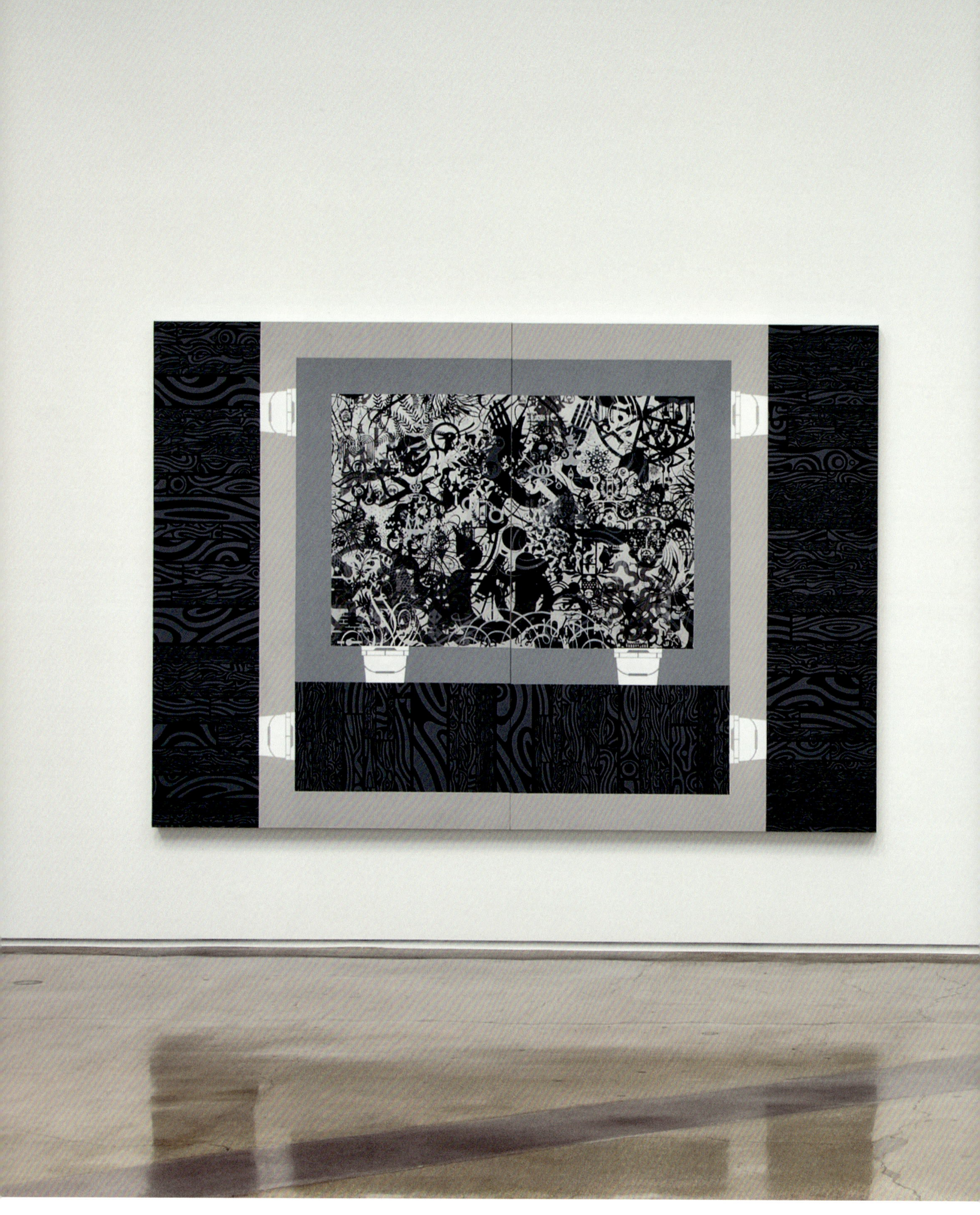

The Meaning of Meaning, 2016, diptych, acrylic on linen, 84 x 60 in.
(213.4 x 152.4 cm) each, 84 x 120 in. (213.4 x 304.8 cm) total

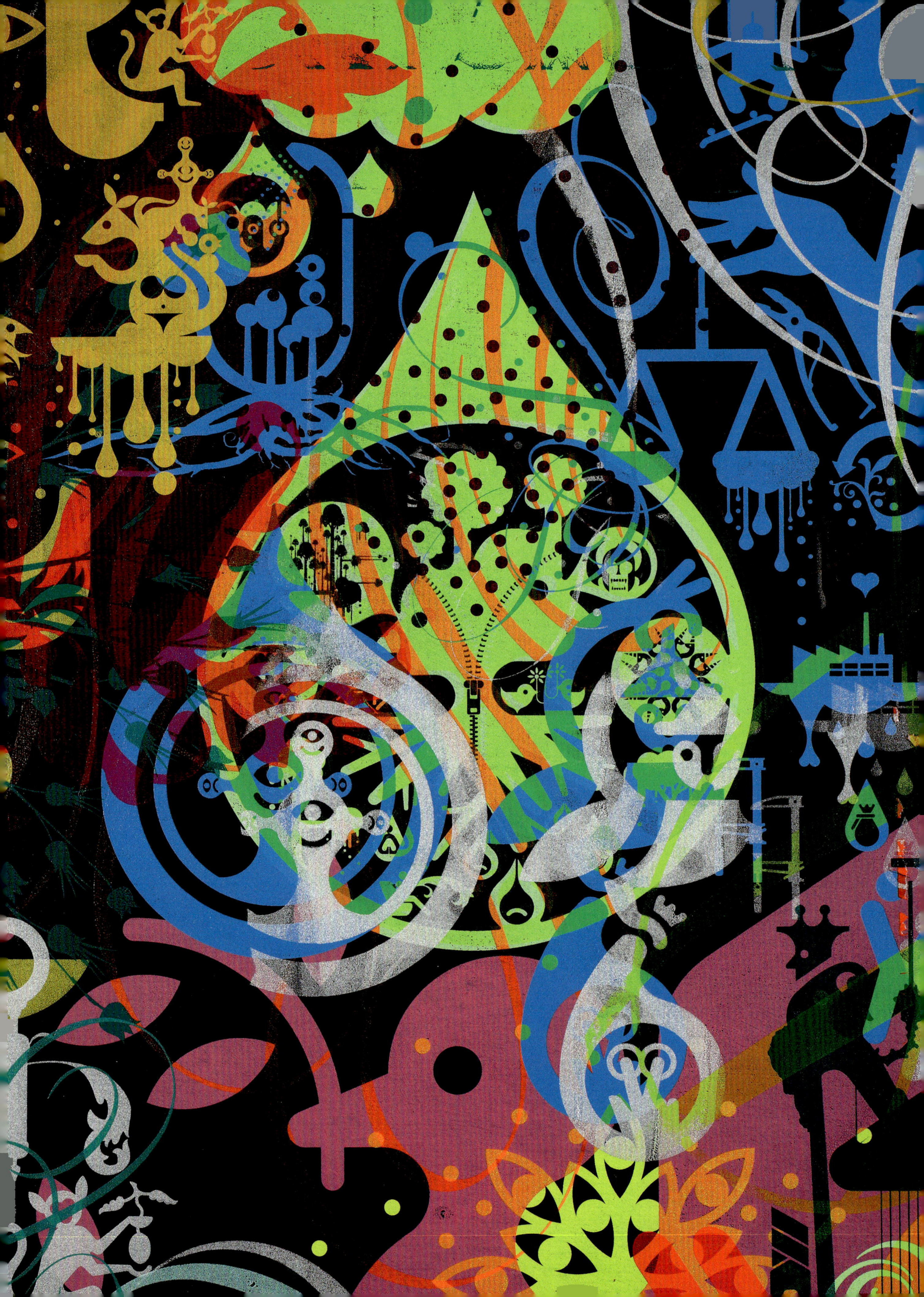

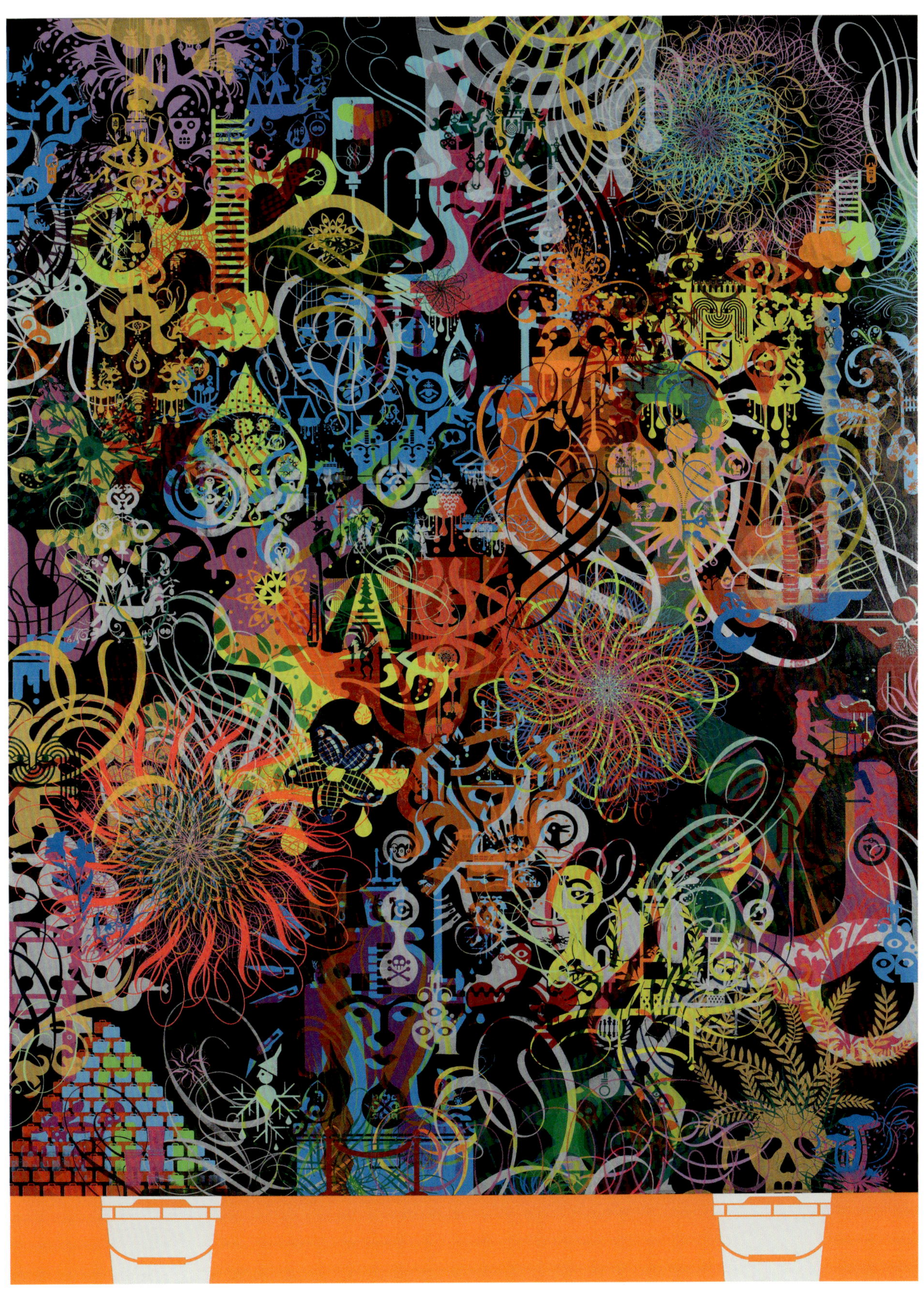

It's a Thing, 2016, acrylic on linen, 84 x 60 in. (213.4 x 152.4 cm)
Opposite Page: Detail

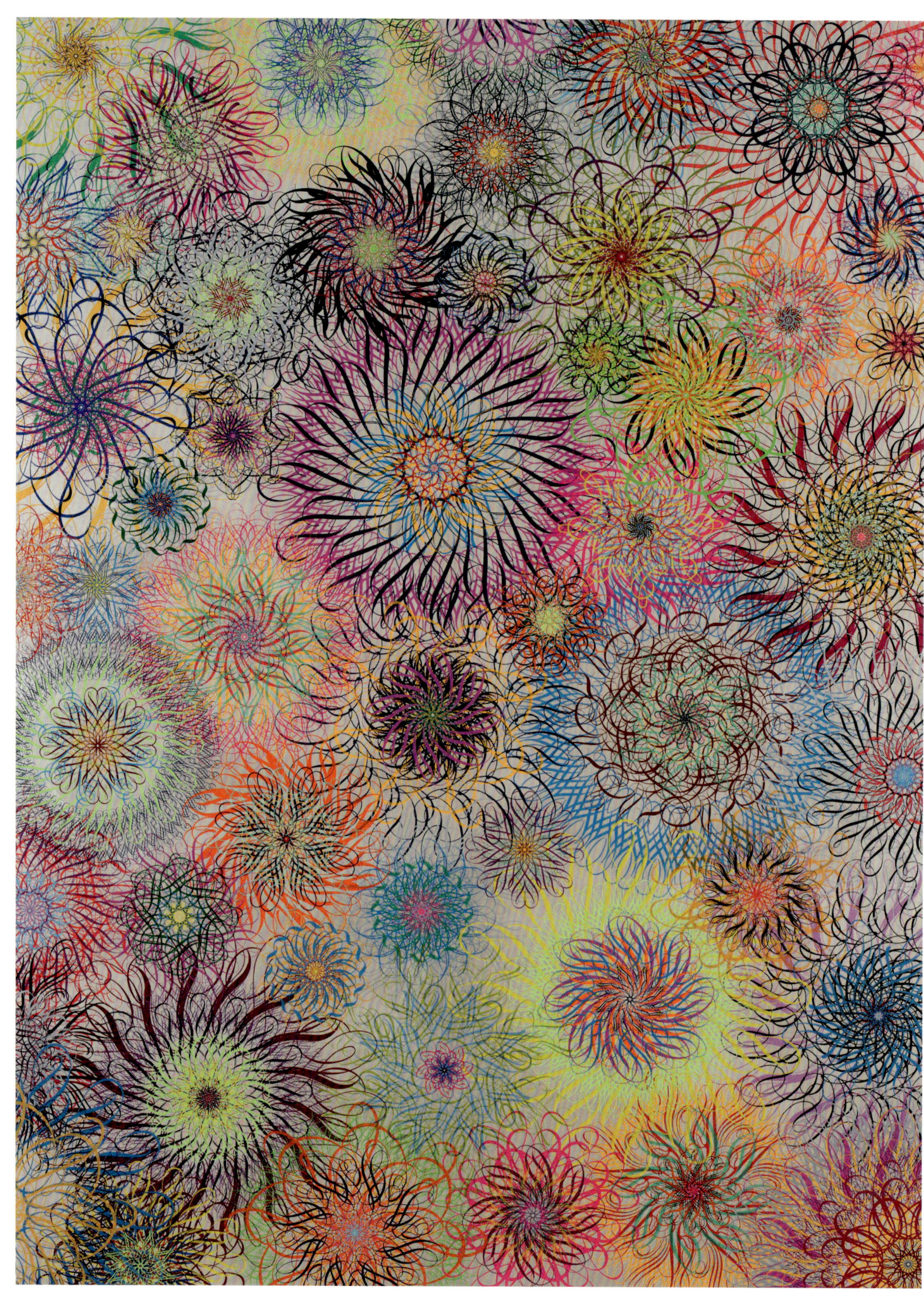

Dark Energy, 2017, acrylic on linen, 84 x 60 in. (213.4 x 152.4 cm)
Opposite Page: Detail

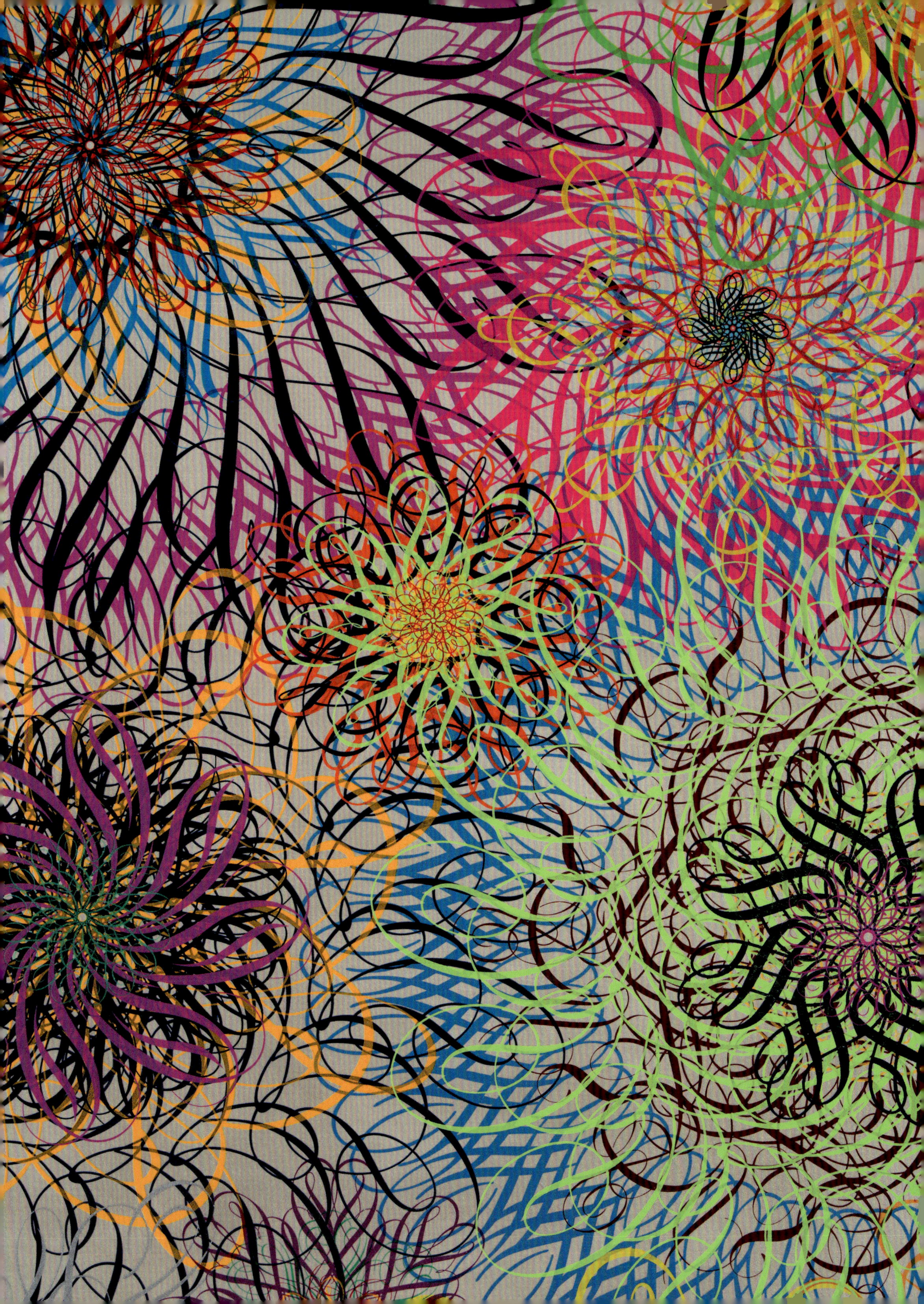

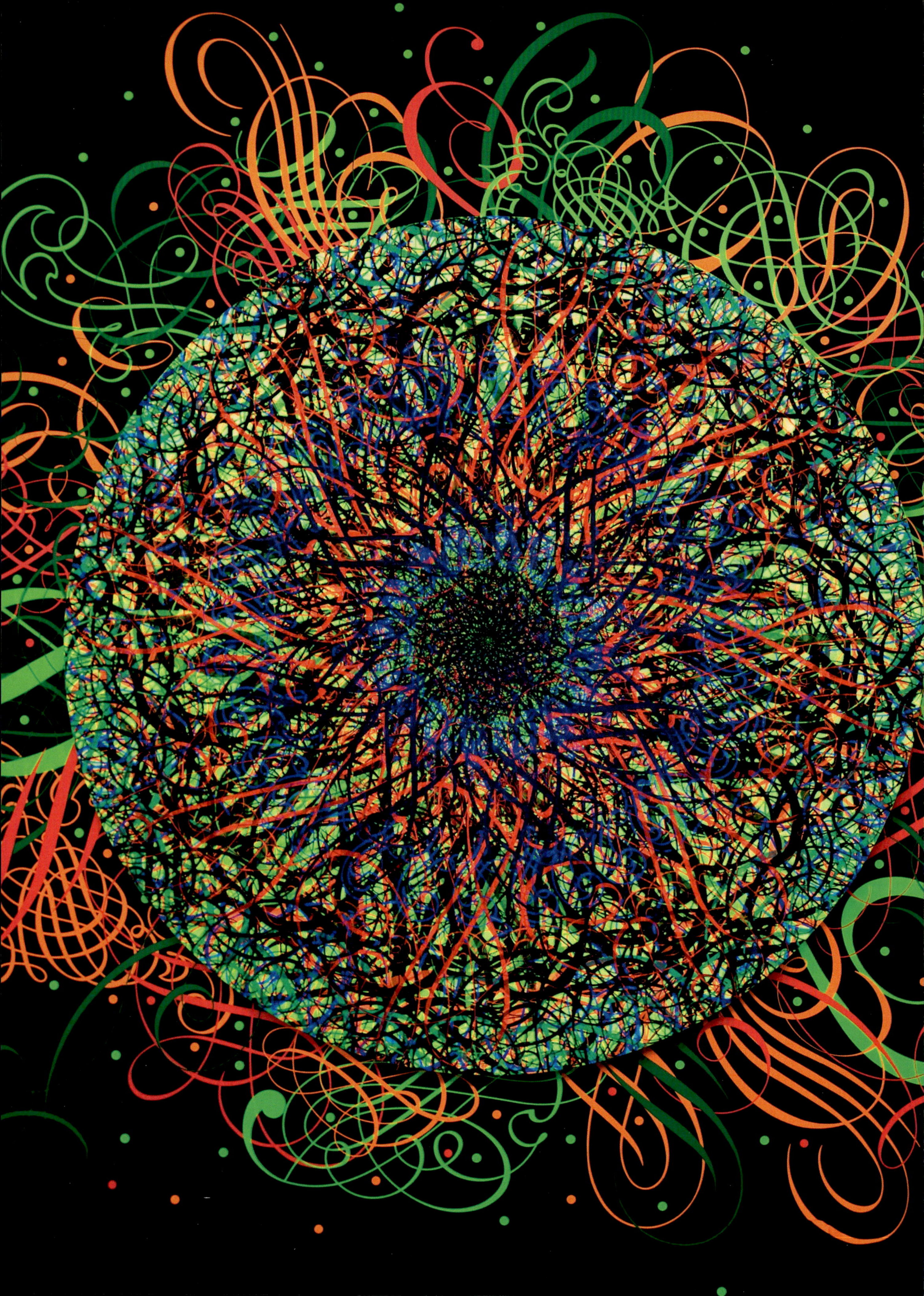

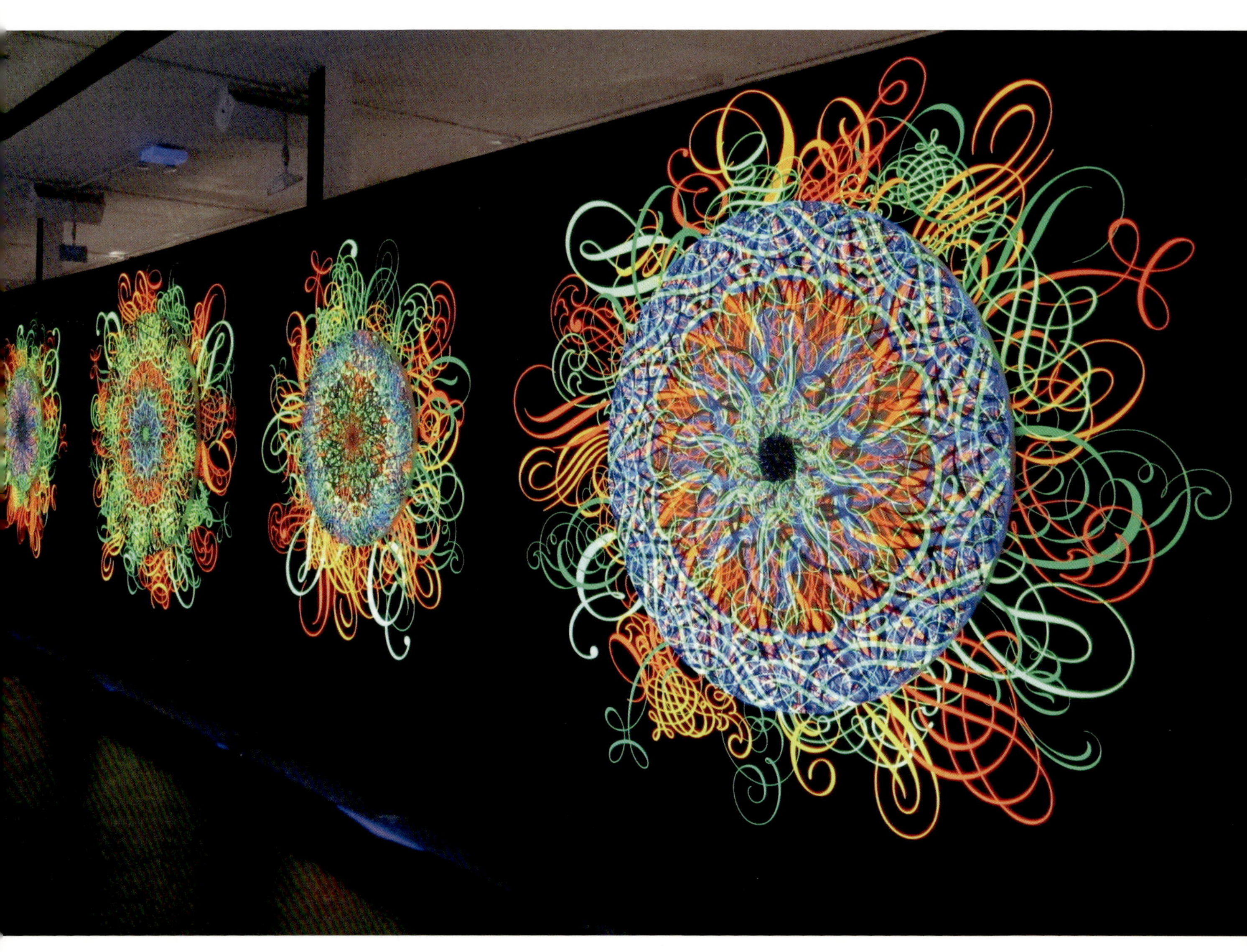

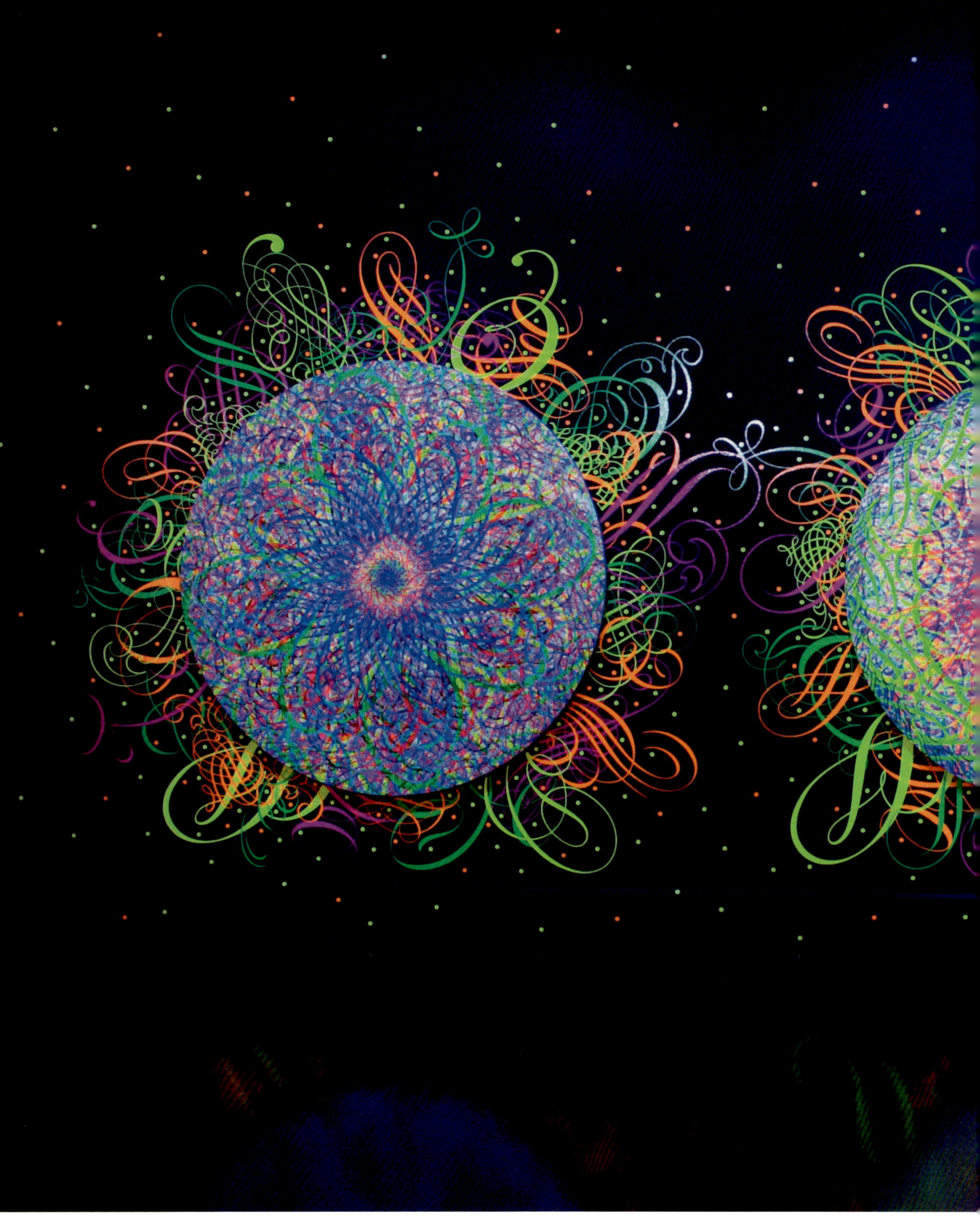

Aesthetic Comfort, 2008, installation view, Cincinnati Art Museum, Cincinnati

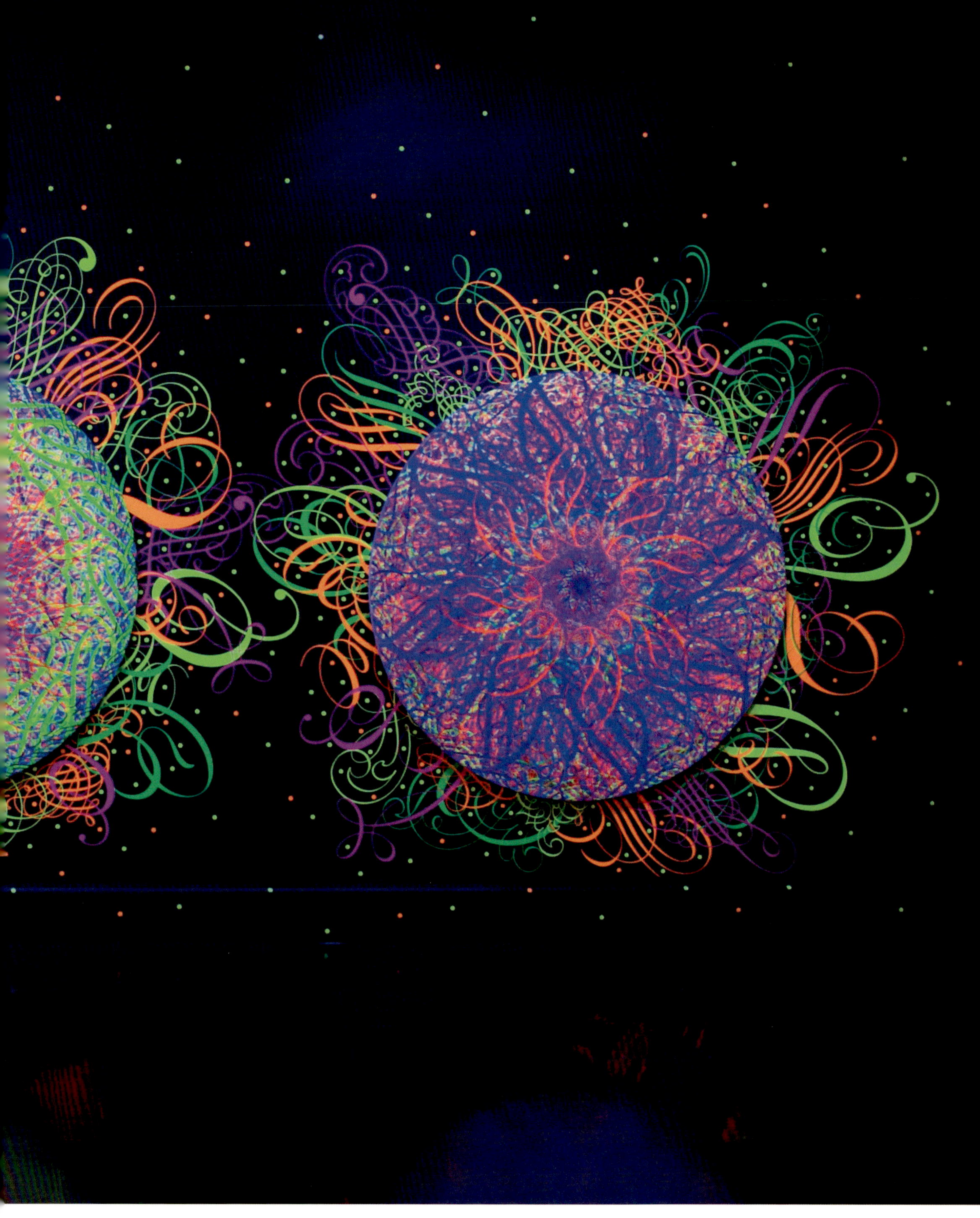

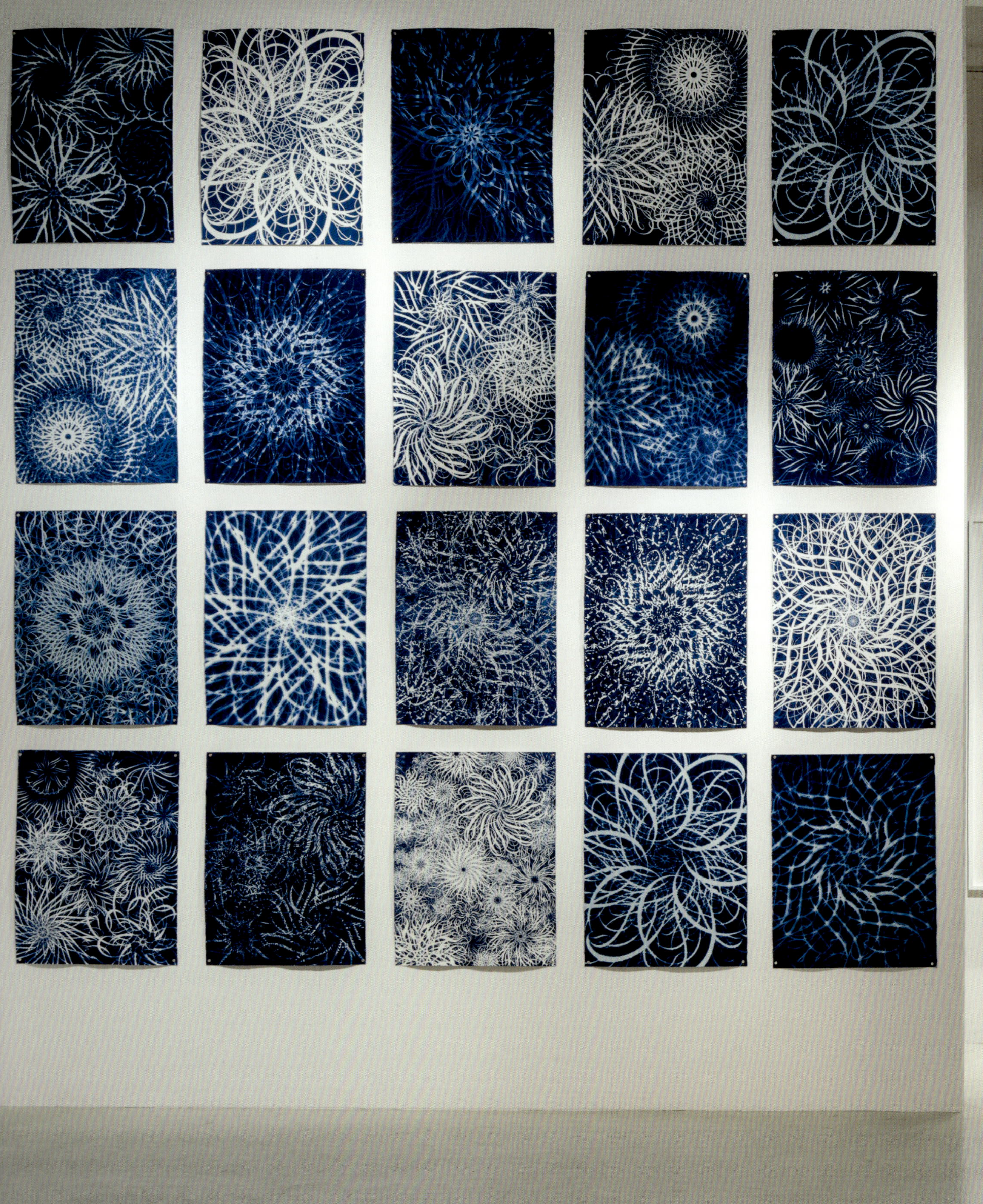

Ocular Evidence, 2017, installation view, Quint Gallery, San Diego

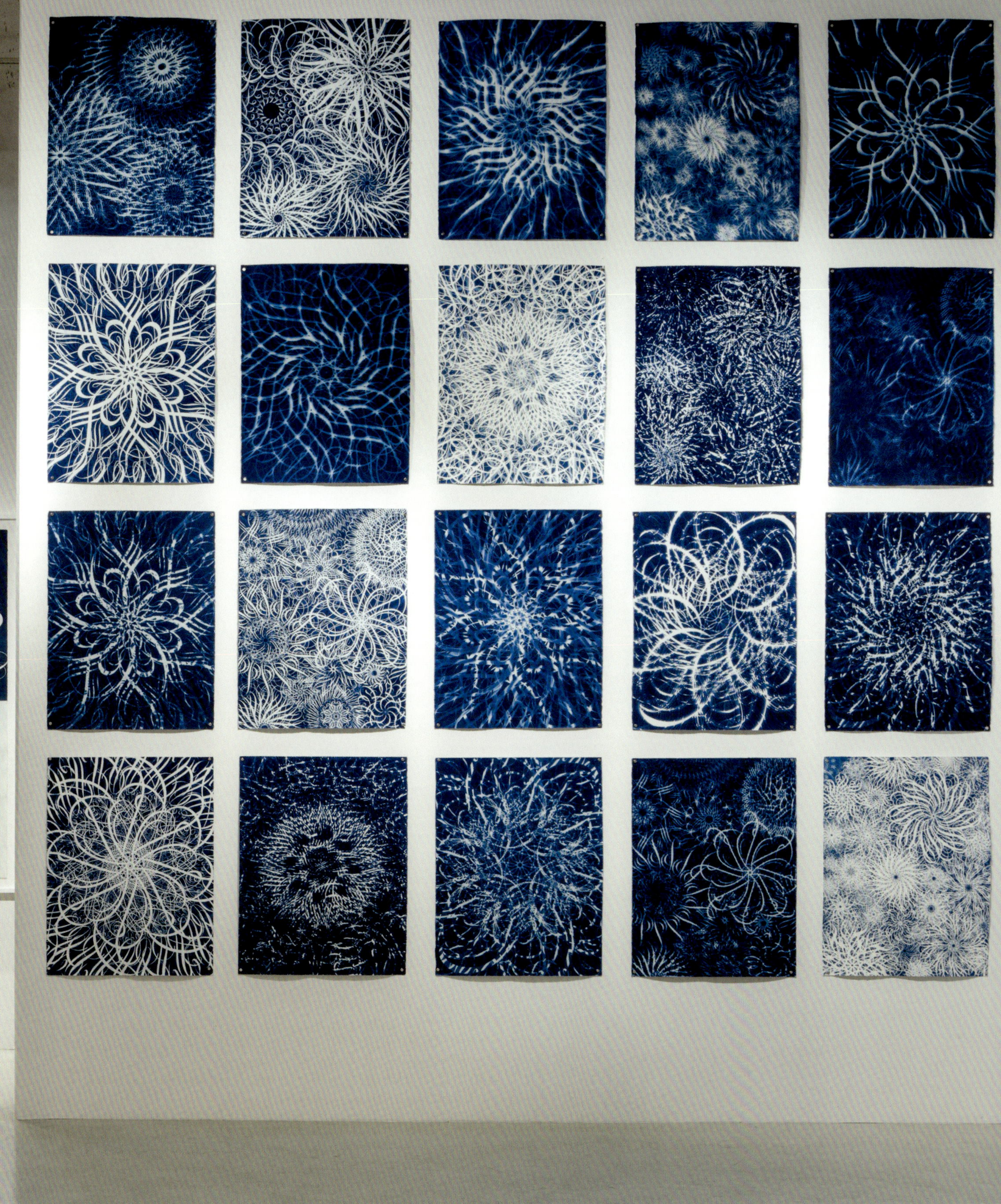

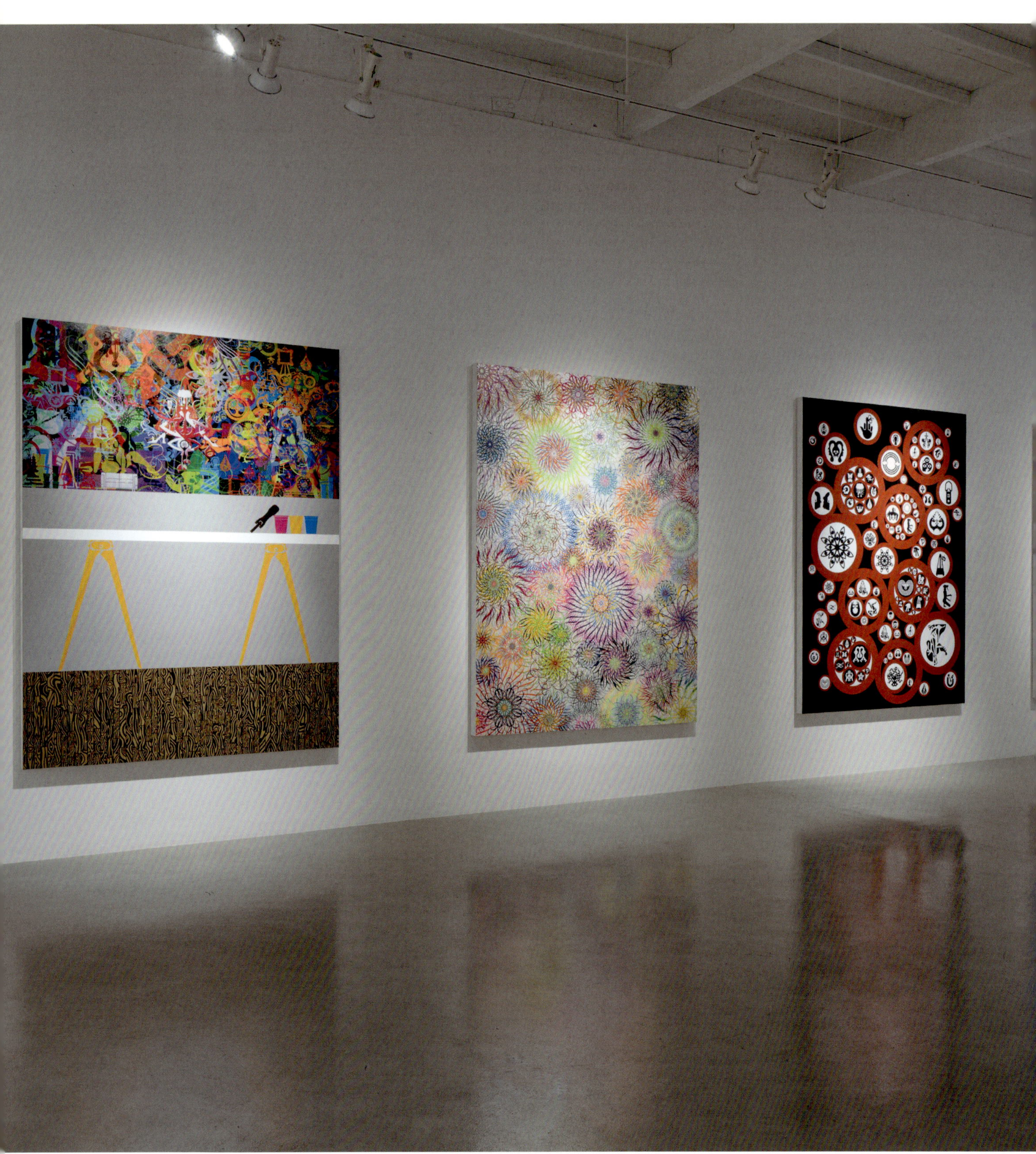

Ocular Evidence, 2017, installation view, Quint Gallery, San Diego

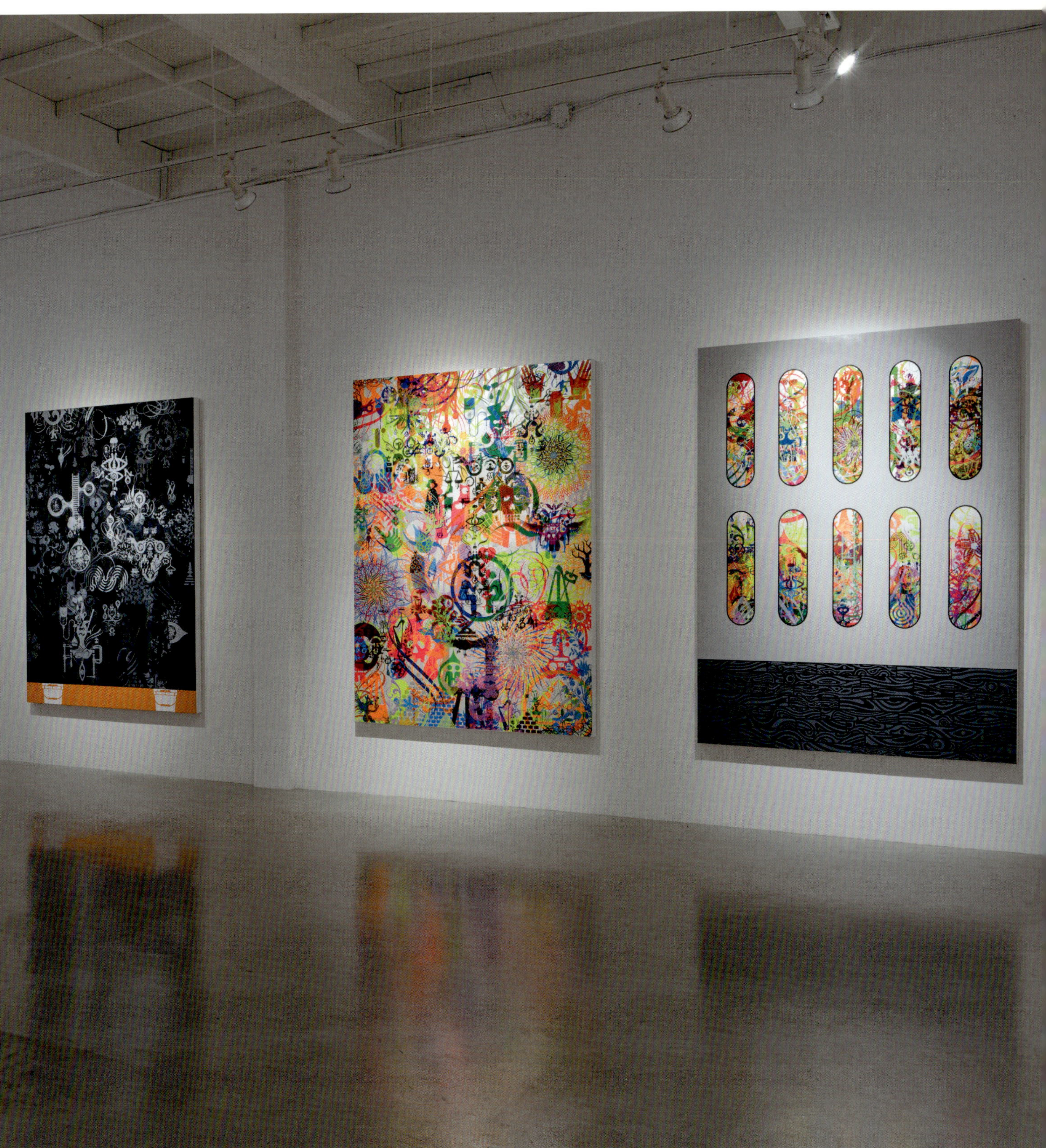

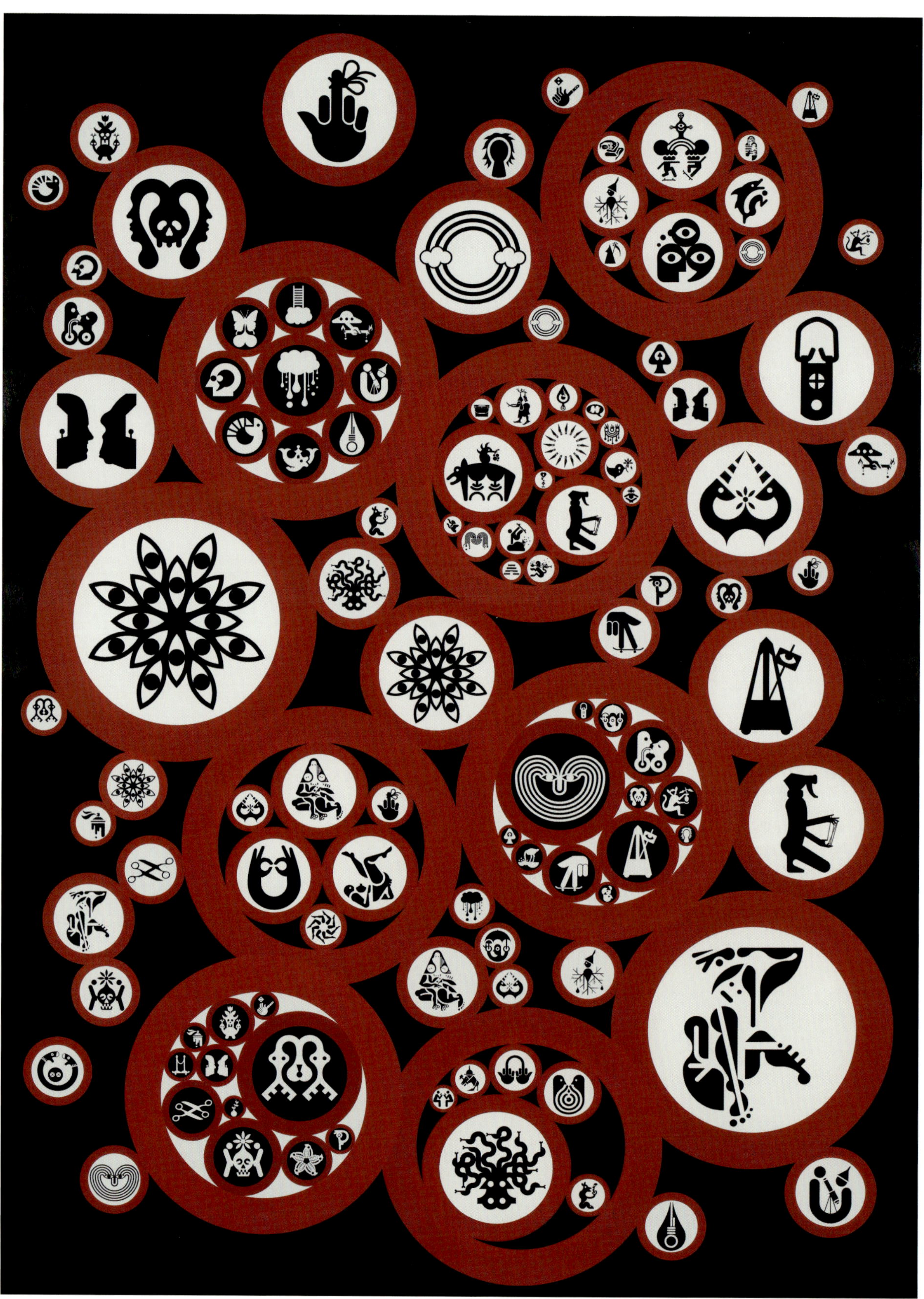

Signals Painting #5, 2016, acrylic on linen, 84 x 60 in.
(213.4 x 152.4 cm)

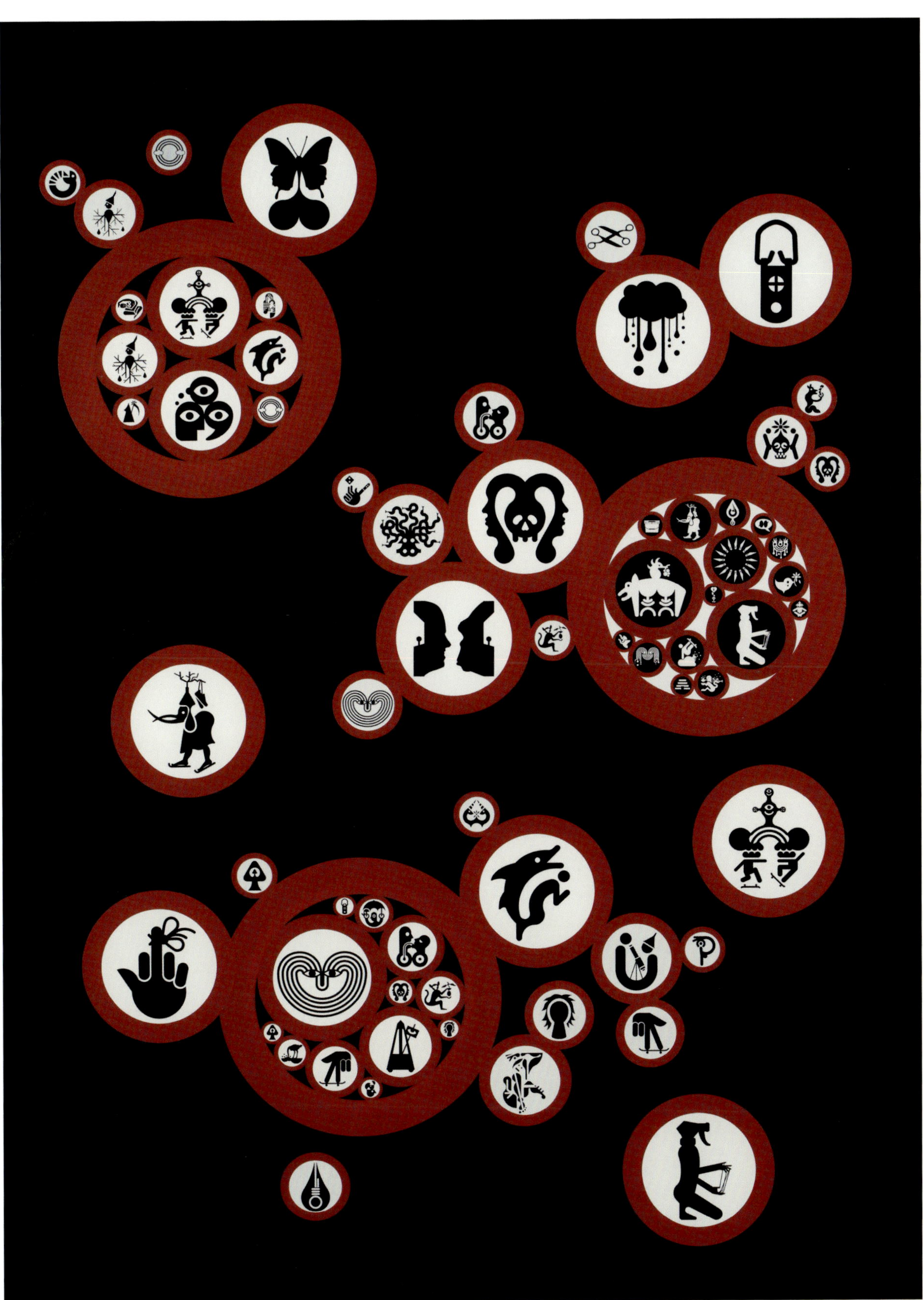

Signals Painting #7, 2016, acrylic on linen, 84 x 60 in.
(213.4 x 152.4 cm)

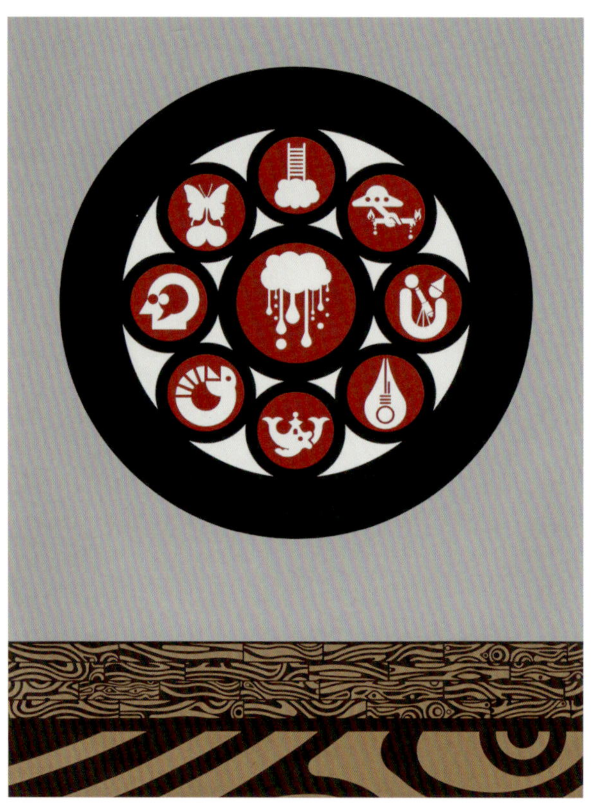
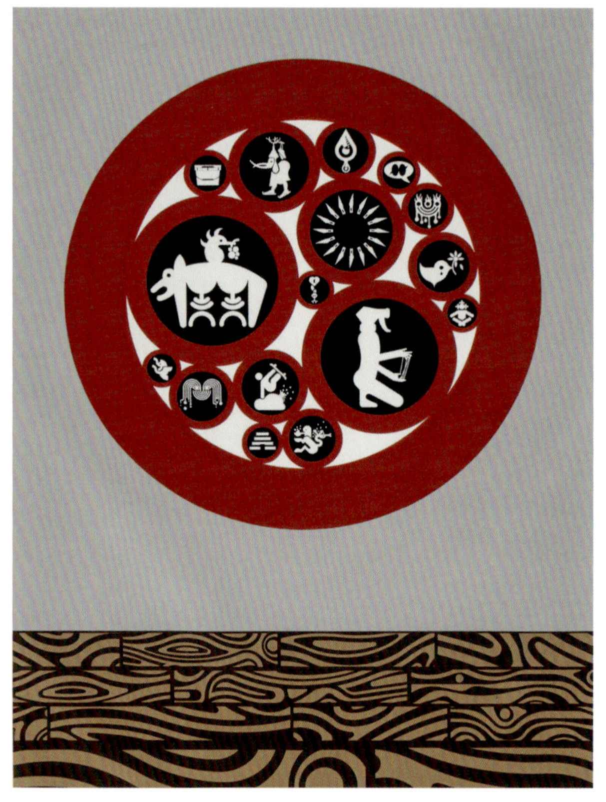
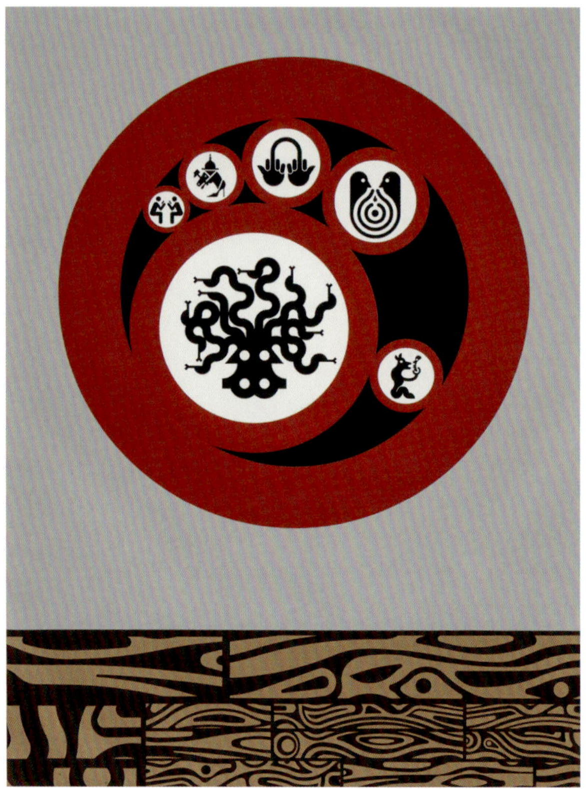
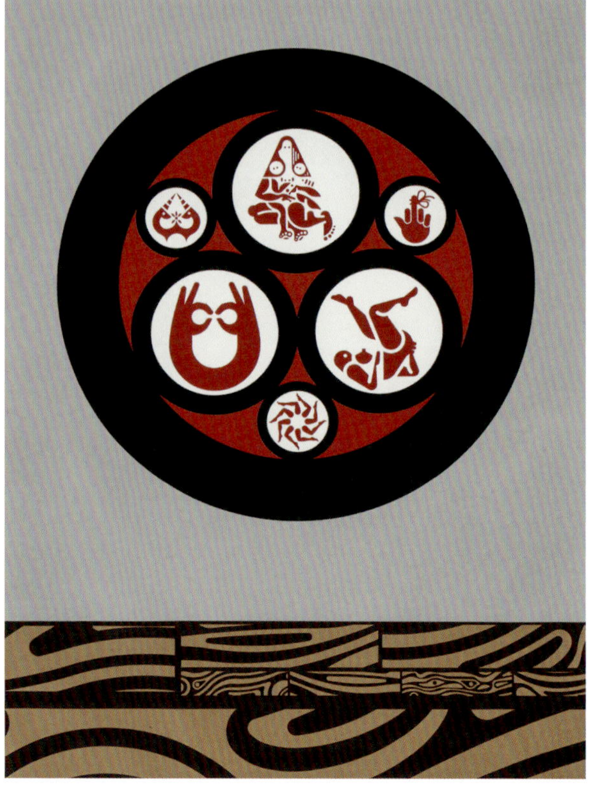

Signals Studio Views (3D, 1B, 6A, 2C), 2016, acrylic on linen,
30 x 22 in. (76.2 x 55.9 cm) ea.

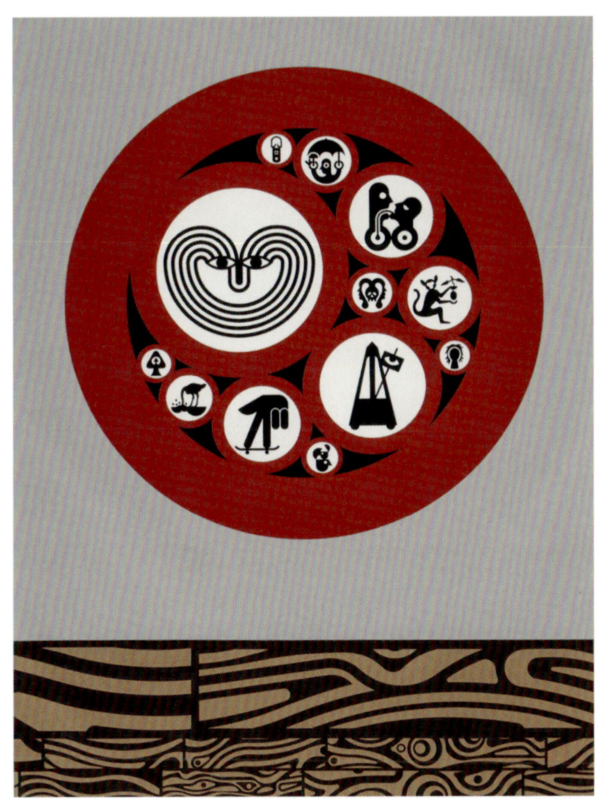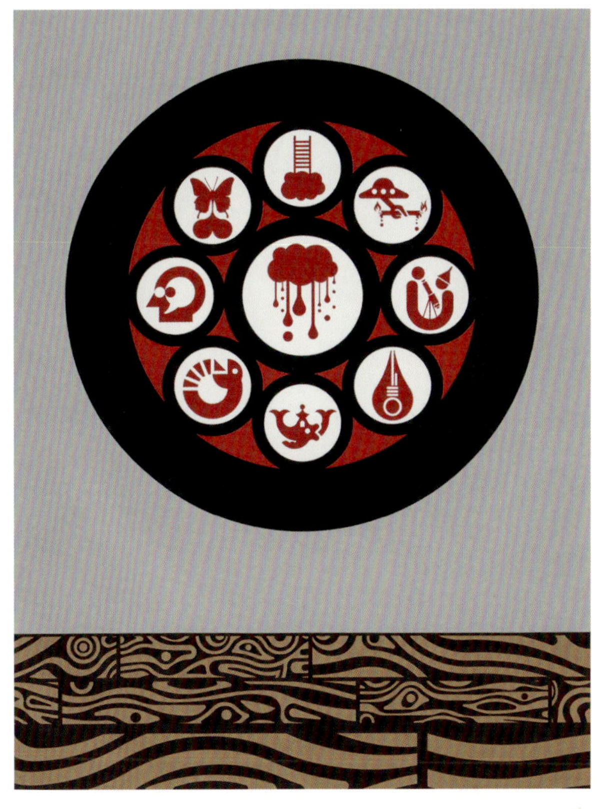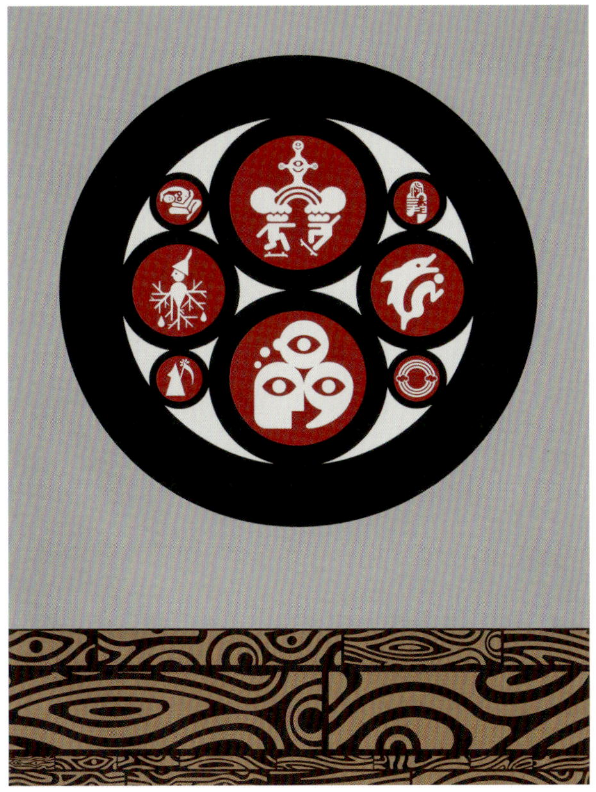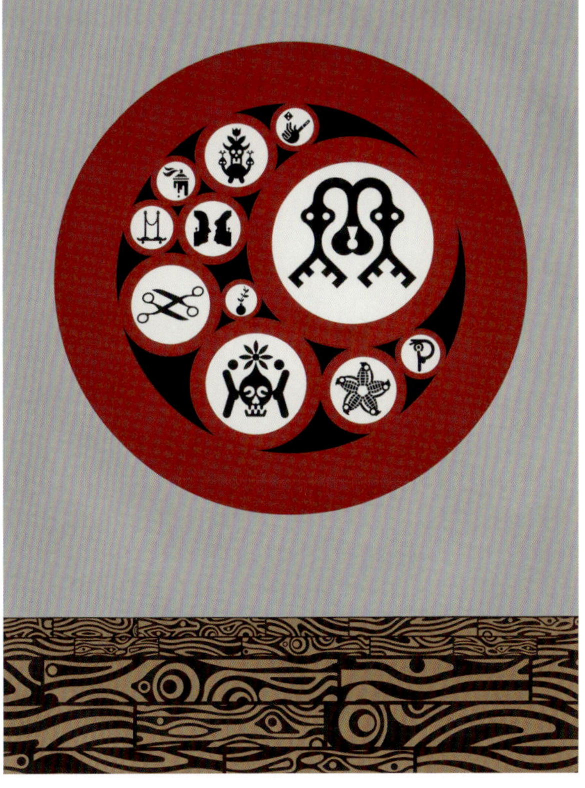

Signals Studio Views (5A, 3C, 4D, 7A), 2016, acrylic on linen,
30 x 22 in. (76.2 x 55.9 cm) ea.

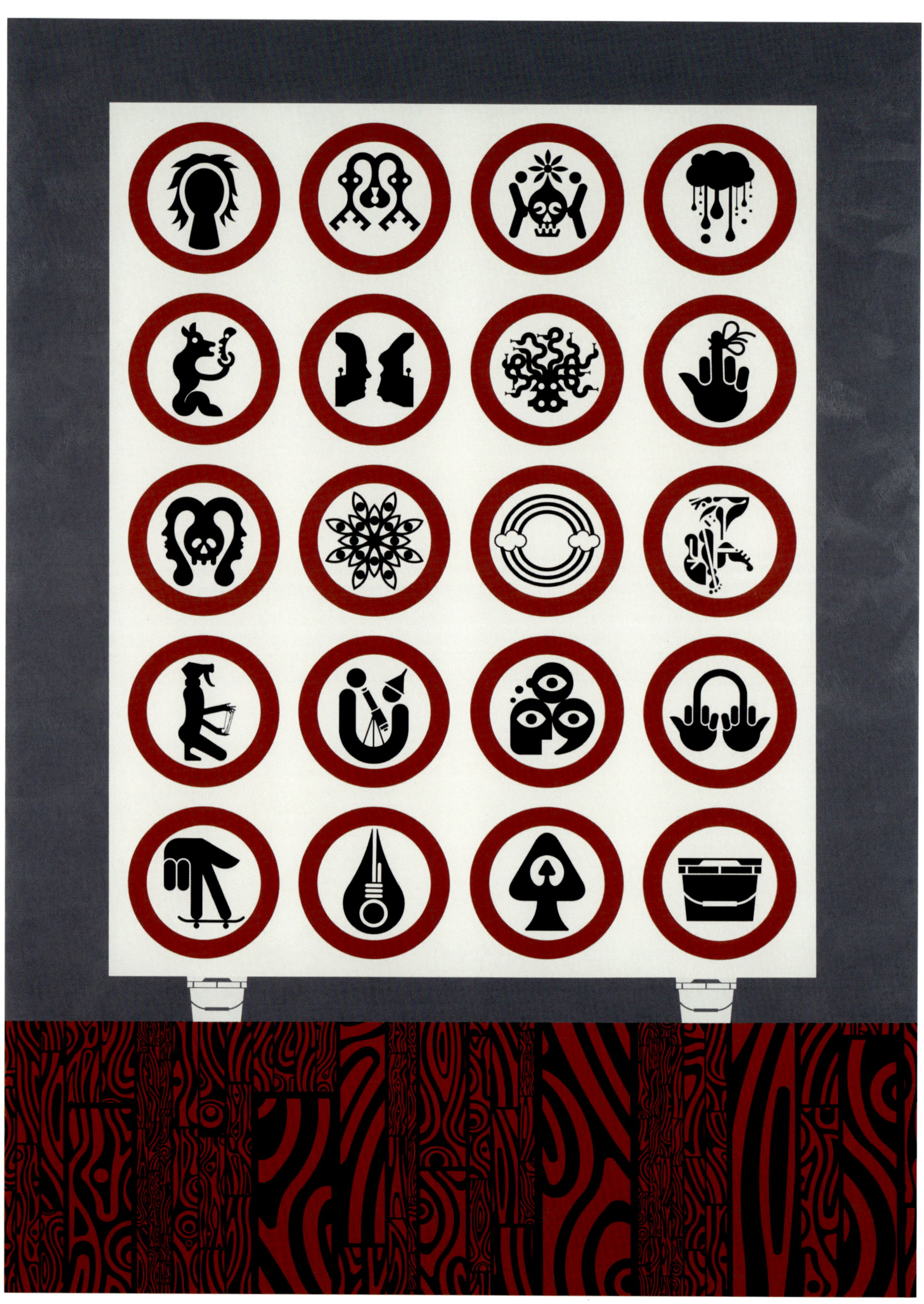

Signals (Wig) Studio View, 2016, acrylic on linen, 84 x 60 in.
(213.4 x 152.4 cm)

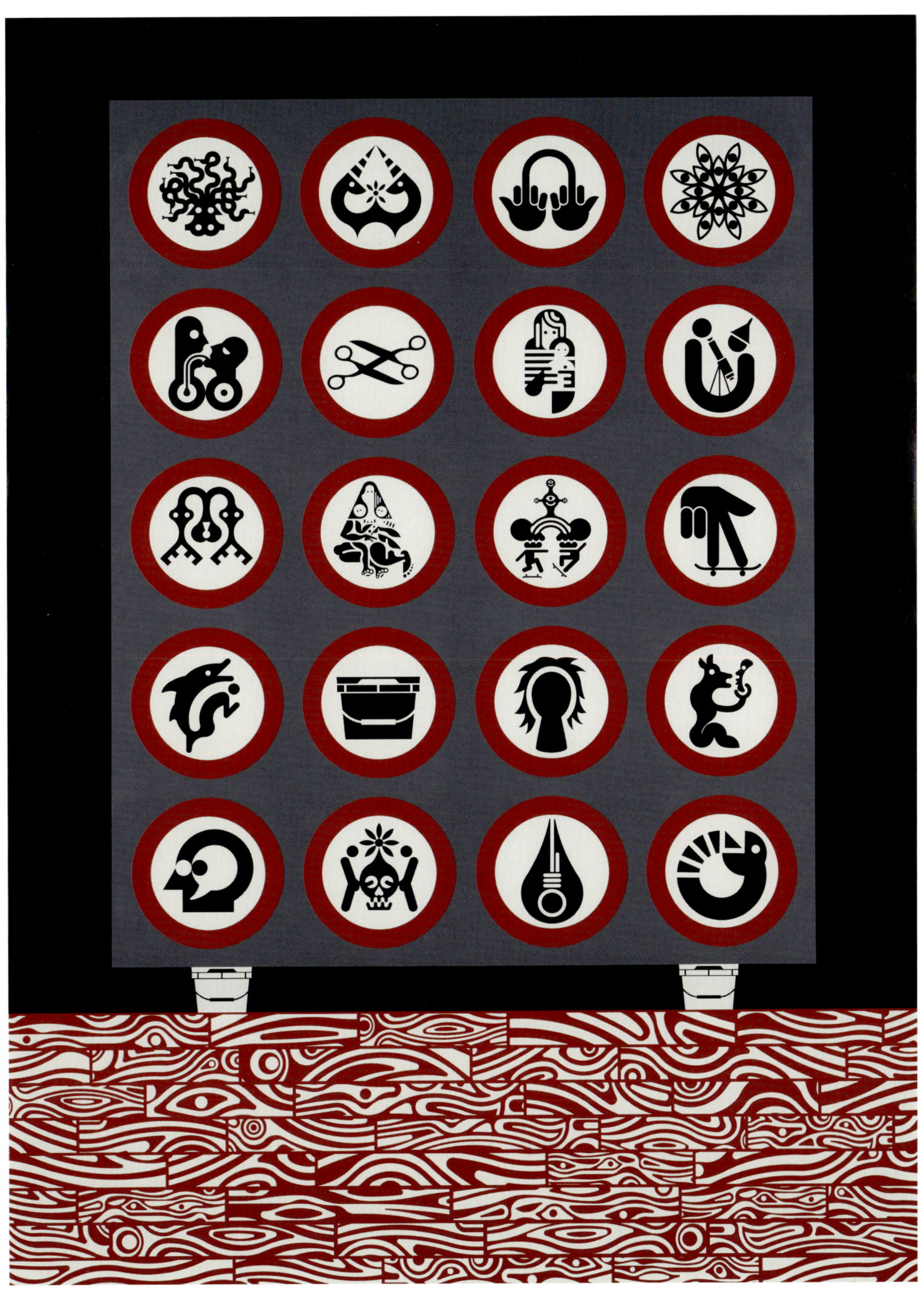

Signals (Medusa) Studio View, 2016, acrylic on linen, 84 x 60 in.
(213.4 x 152.4 cm)

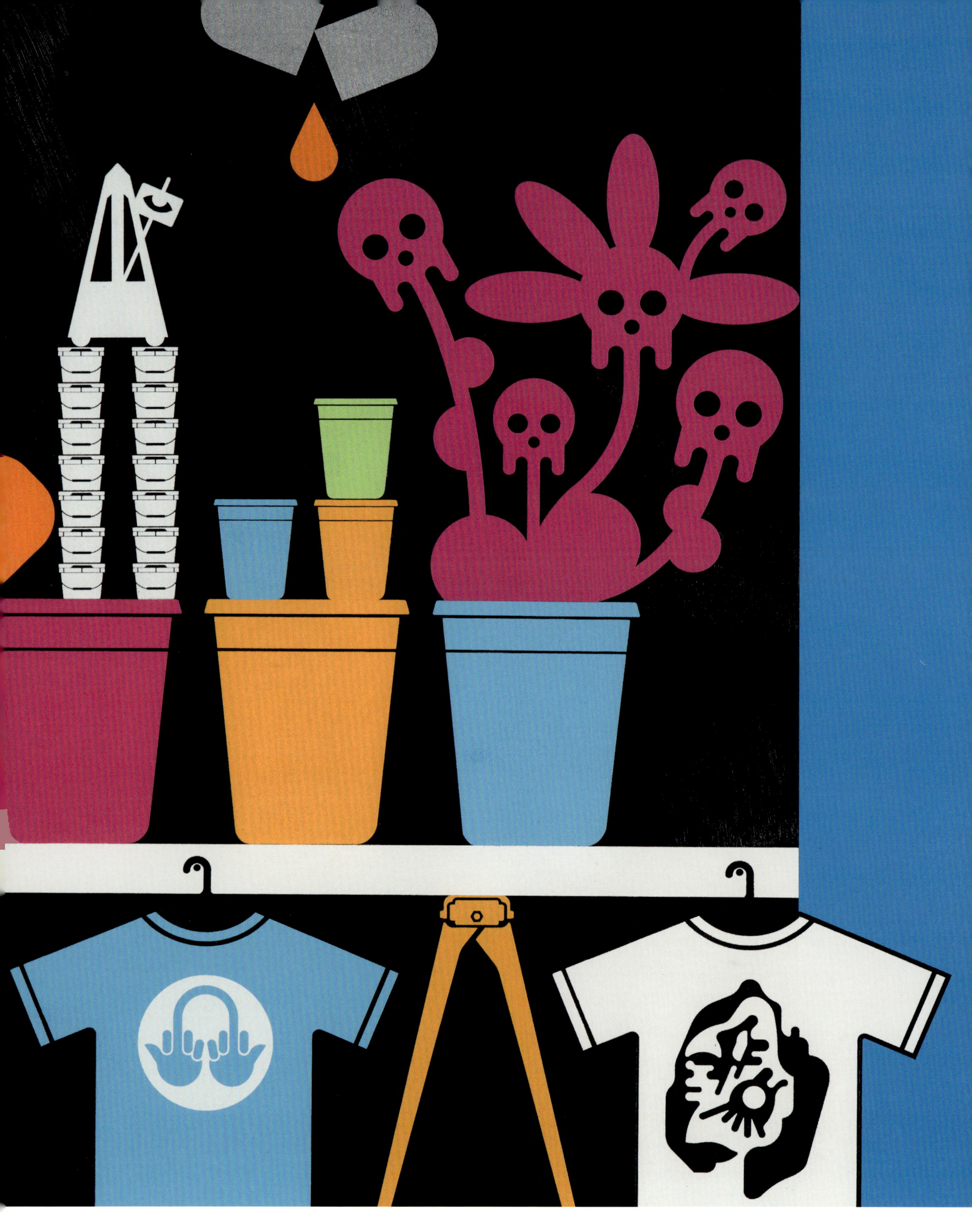

Opposite Page: *Don't Stress the Machine* (in studio), 2017, acrylic on linen, 84 x 60 in. (213.4 x 152.4 cm); Above: Detail

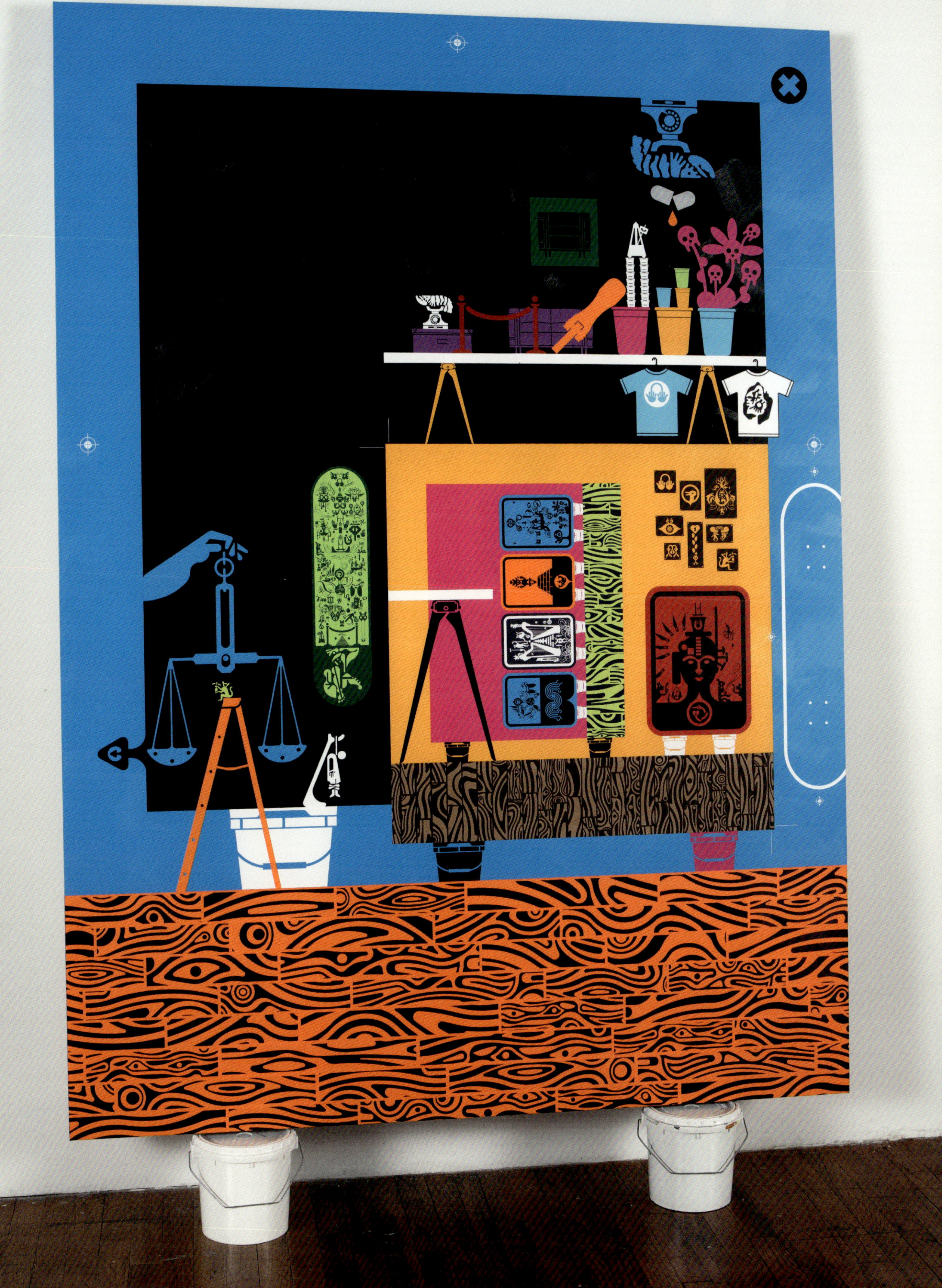

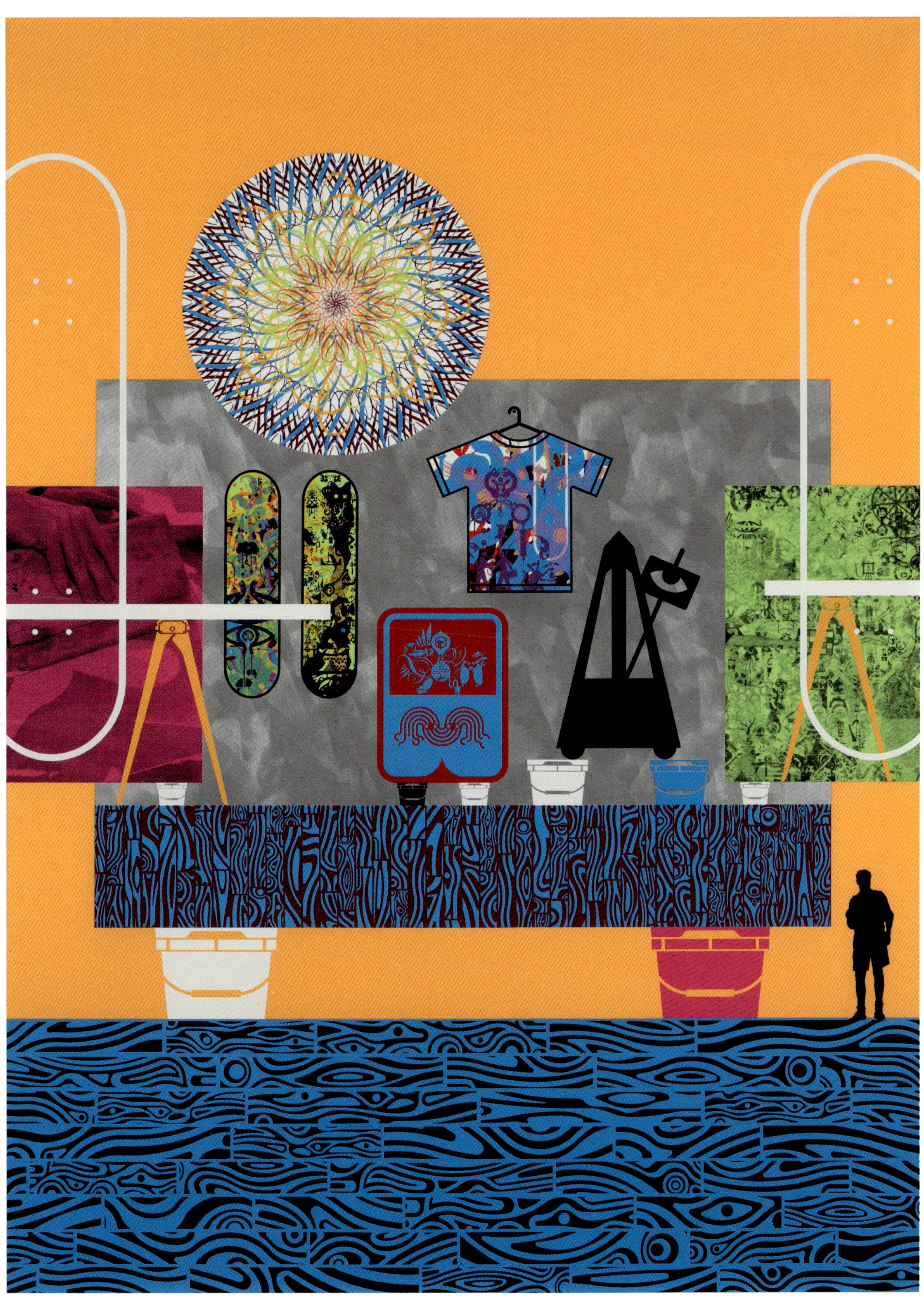

Internal Logic, 2017, acrylic on linen, 84 x 60 in. (213.4 x 152.4 cm)

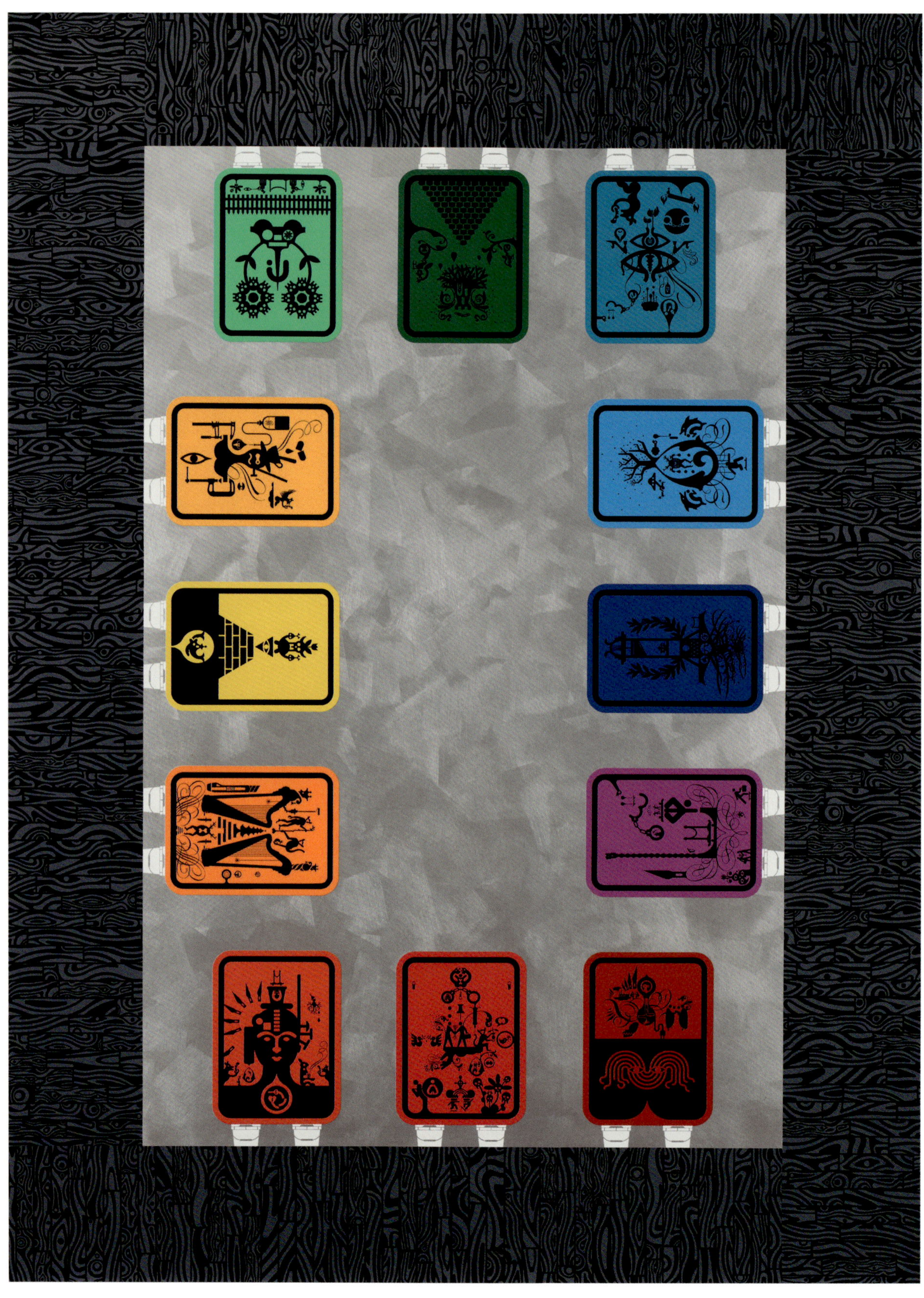

Calendar Color Spectrum, 2017, acrylic on linen, 84 x 60 in. (213.4 x 152.4 cm)

Opposite Page: *Solar Calendar* (in studio), 2017, acrylic on linen, 84 x 60 in. (213.4 x 152.4 cm)

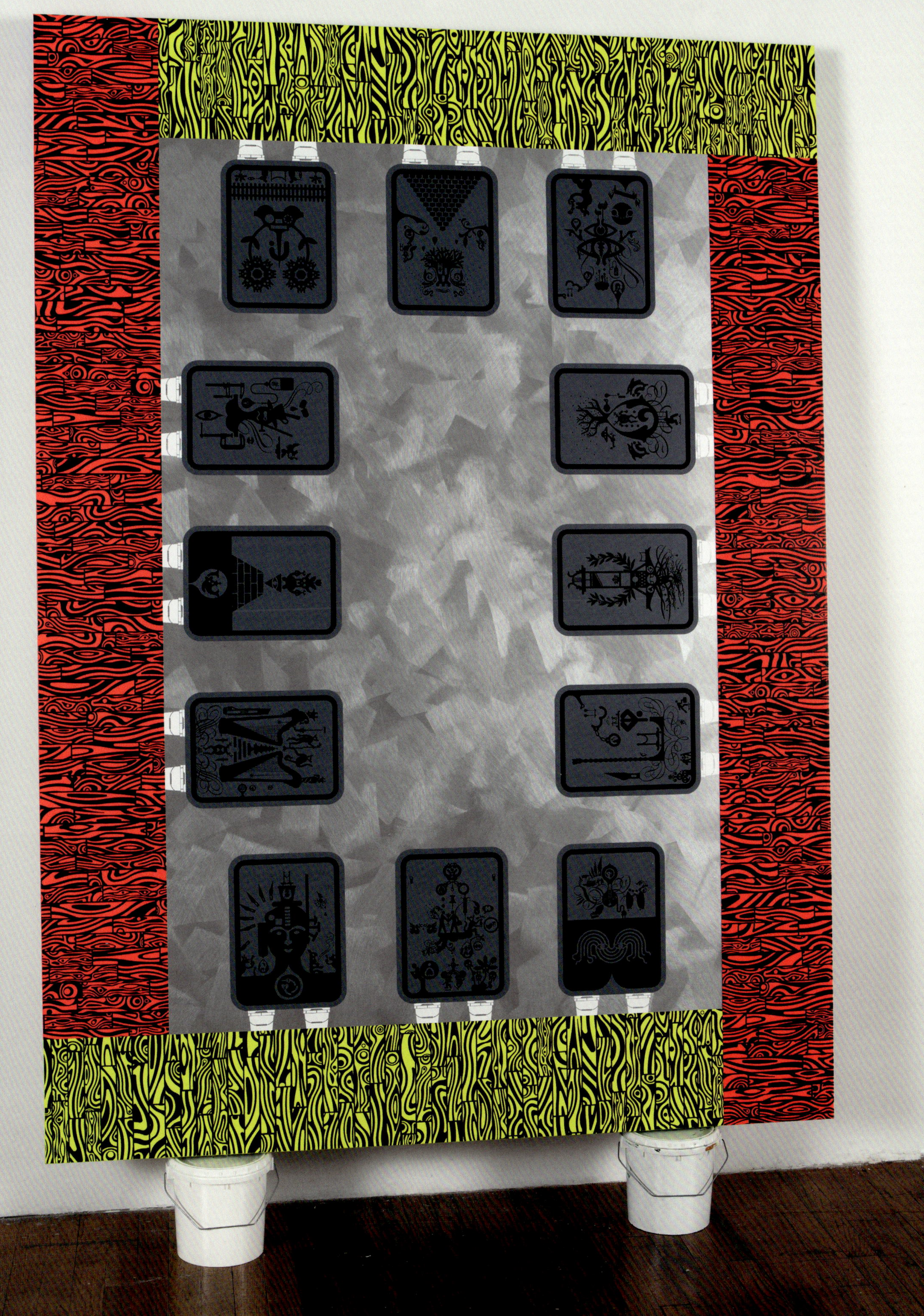

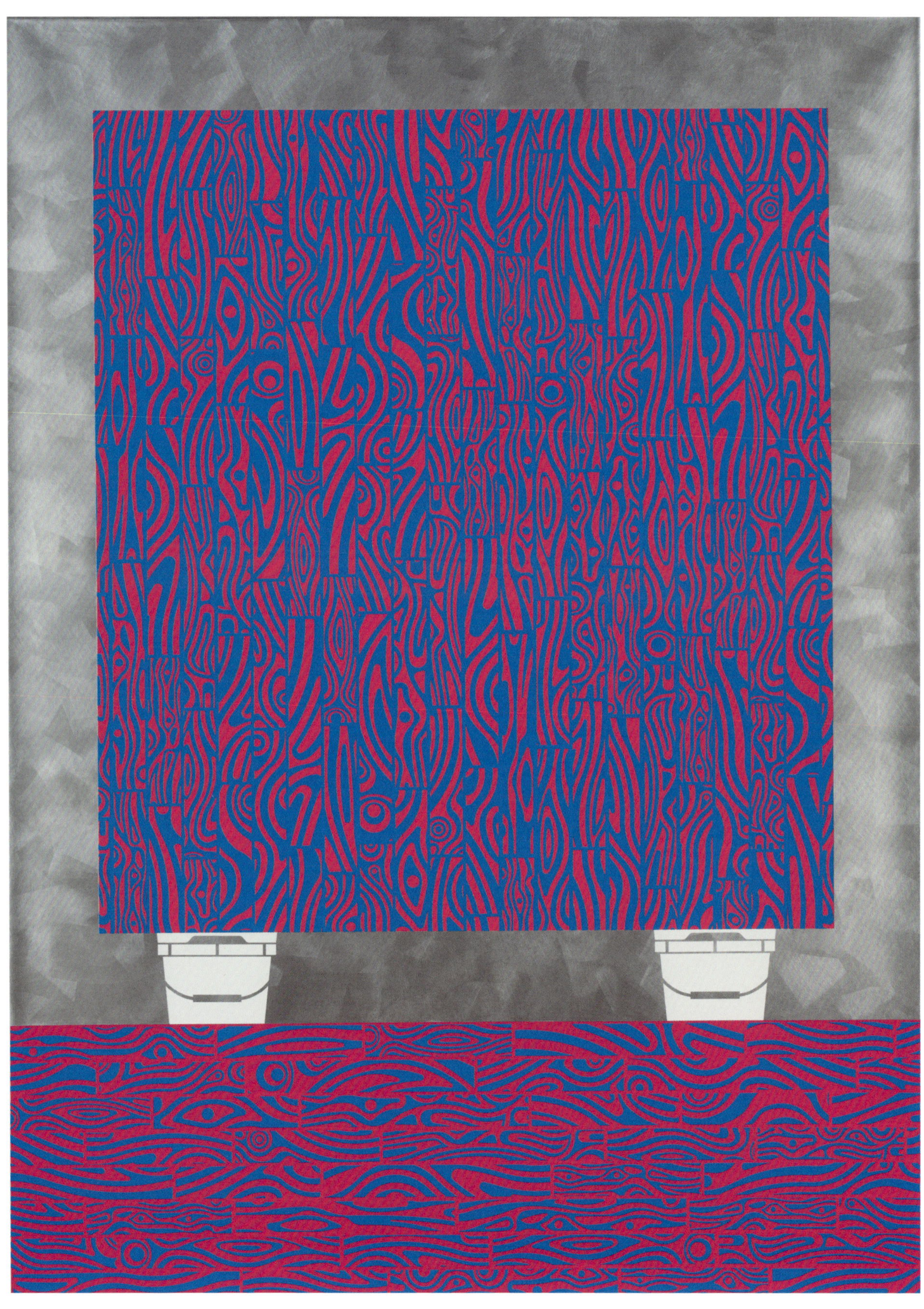

Studio Floor, 2017, acrylic on linen, 84 x 60 in. (213.4 x 152.4 cm)

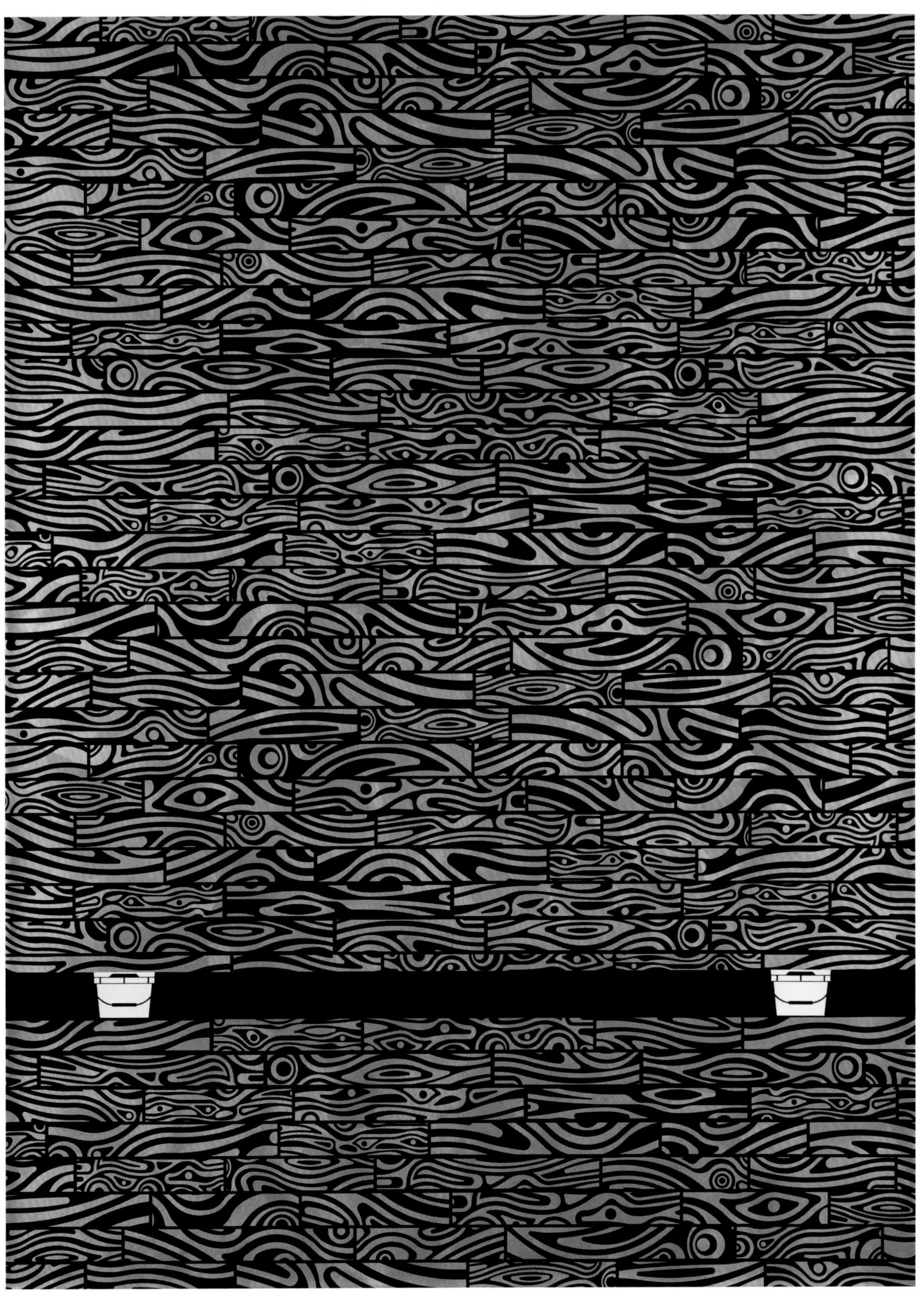

Evidence, 2017, acrylic on linen, 84 x 60 in. (213.4 x 152.4 cm)

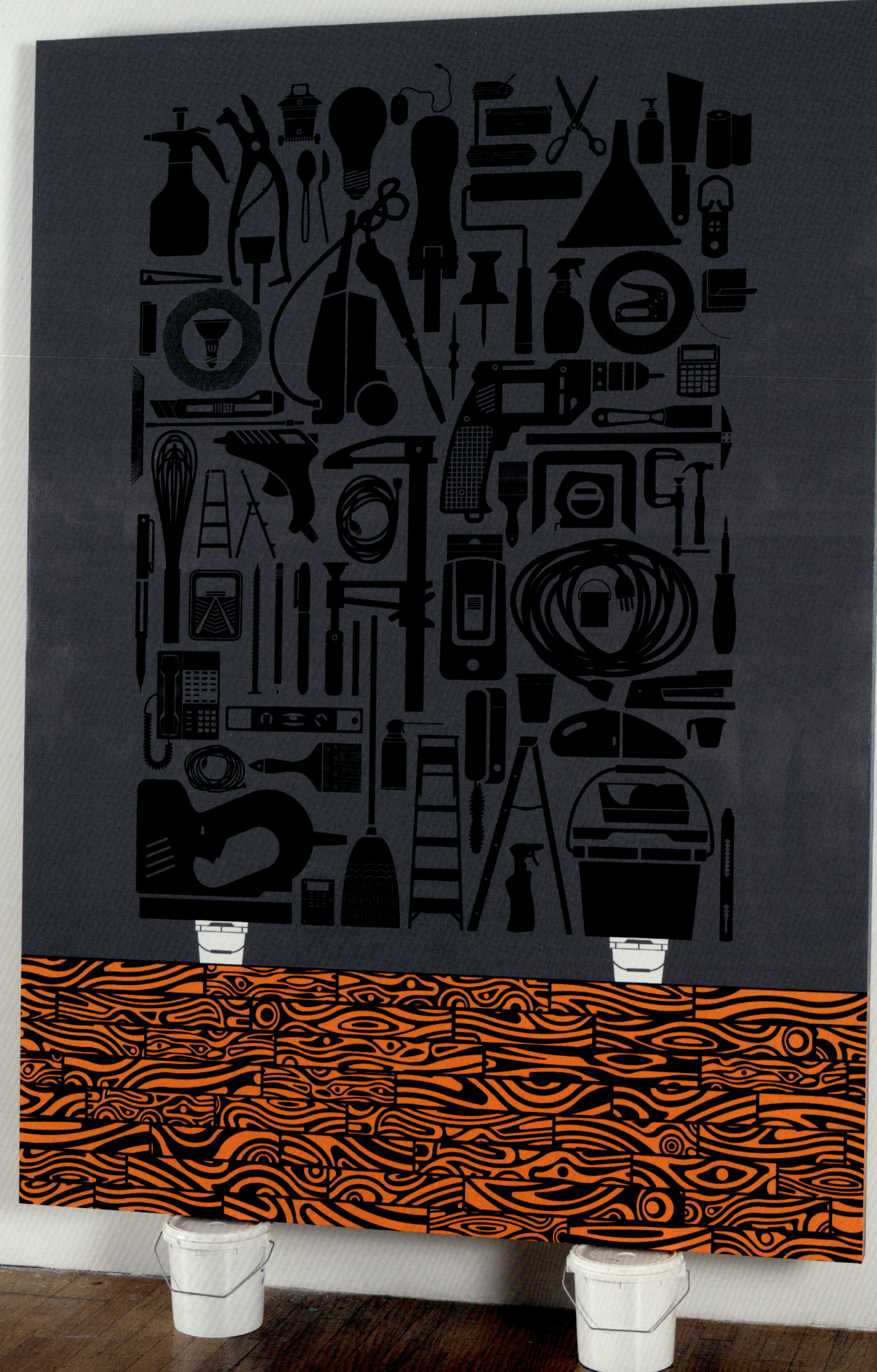

Studio Tools (in studio), 2017, acrylic on linen, 84 x 60 in.
(213.4 x 152.4 cm)

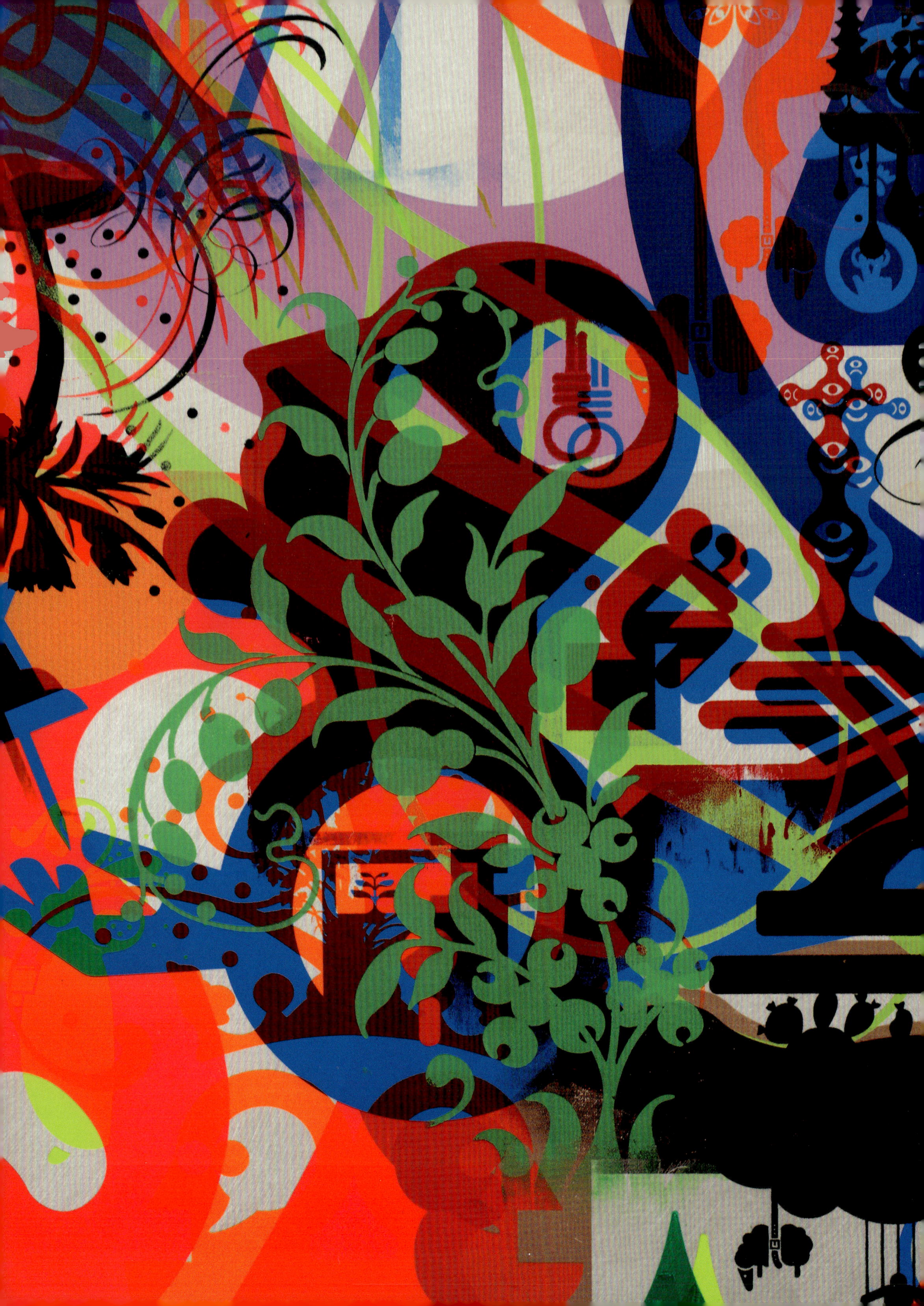

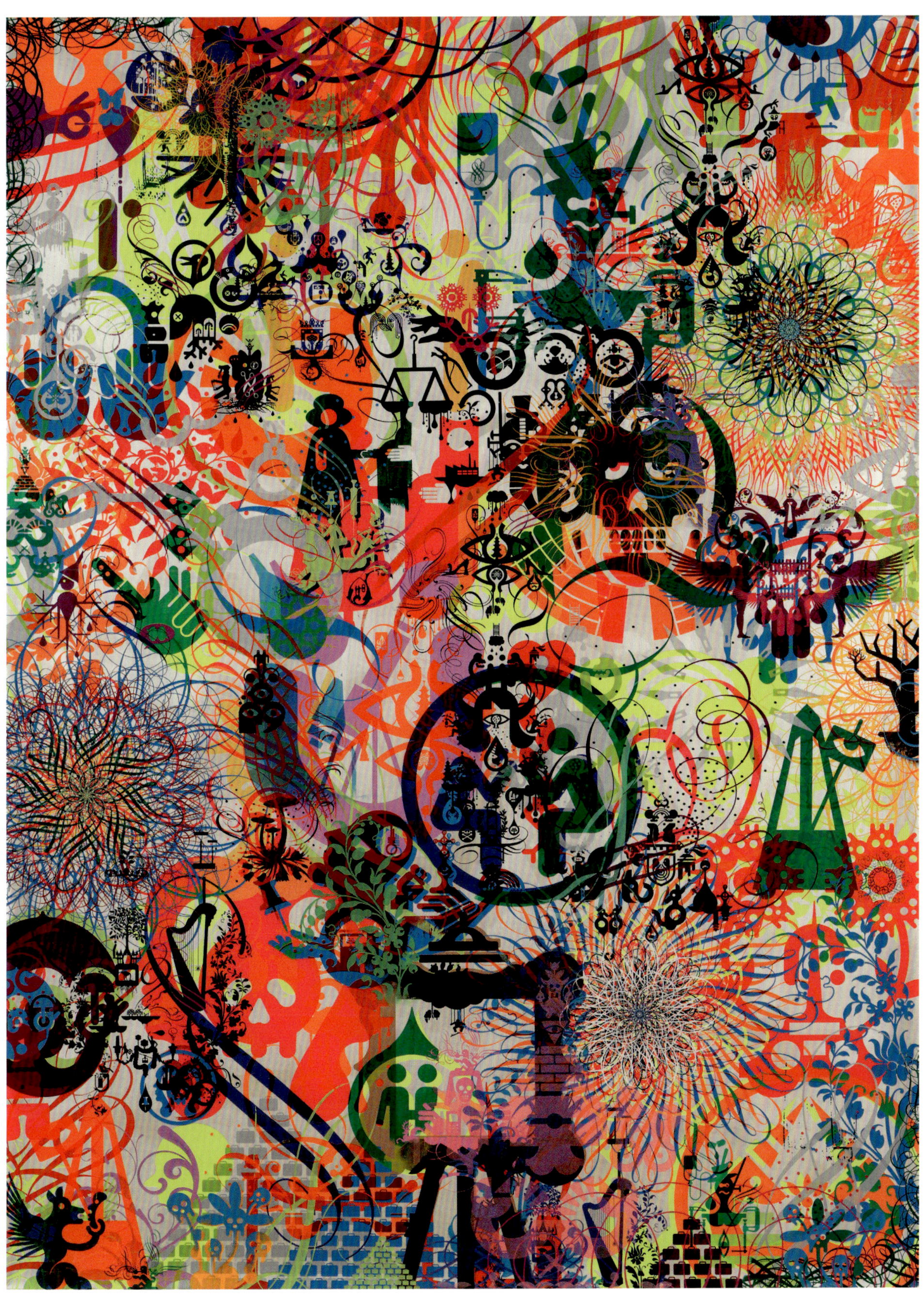

Import Data, 2016, acrylic on linen, 84 x 60 in. (213.4 x 152.4 cm)
Opposite Page: Detail

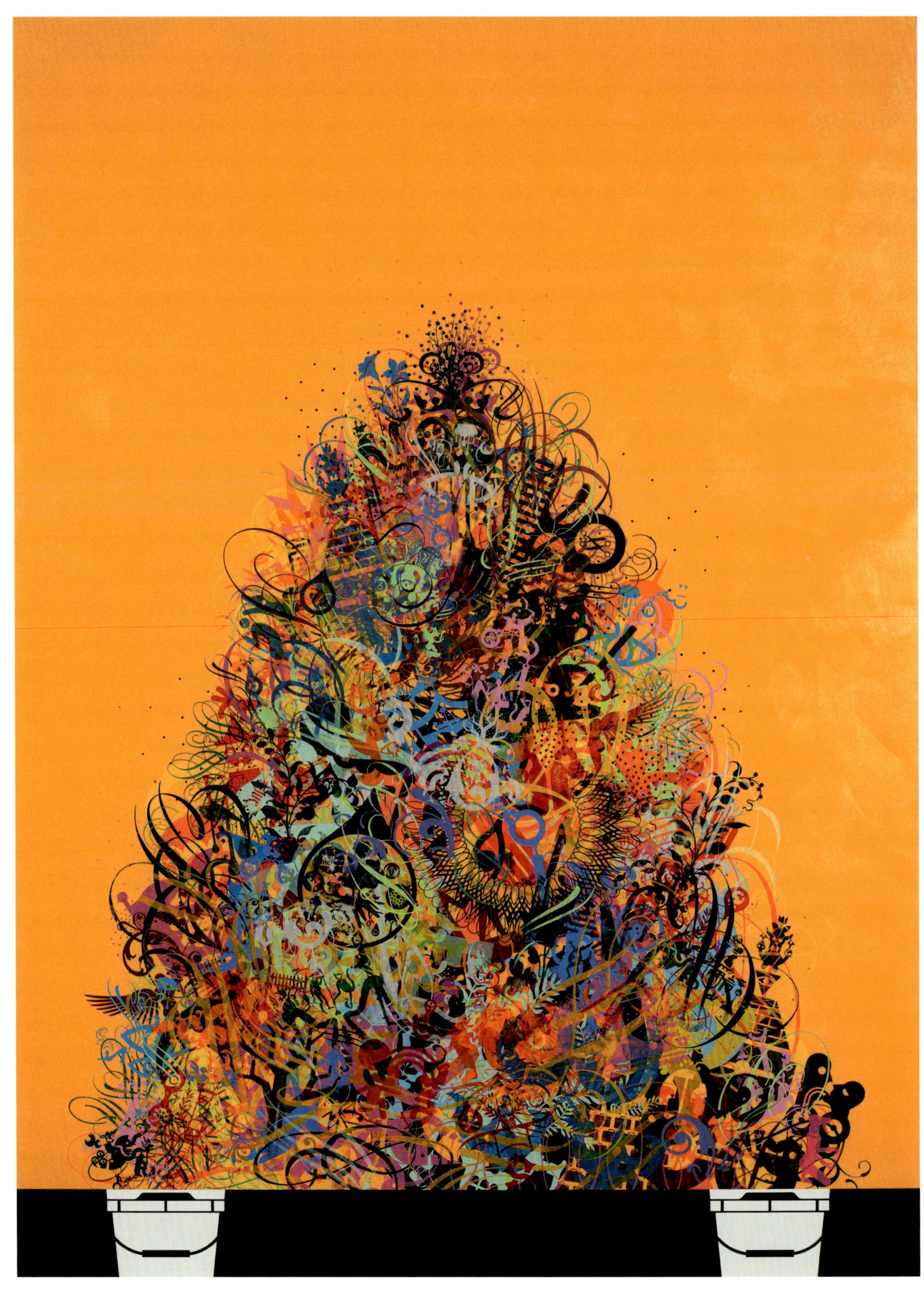

The Local Knowledge Problem, 2016, acrylic on linen, 84 x 60 in.
(213.4 x 152.4 cm); Opposite Page: Detail

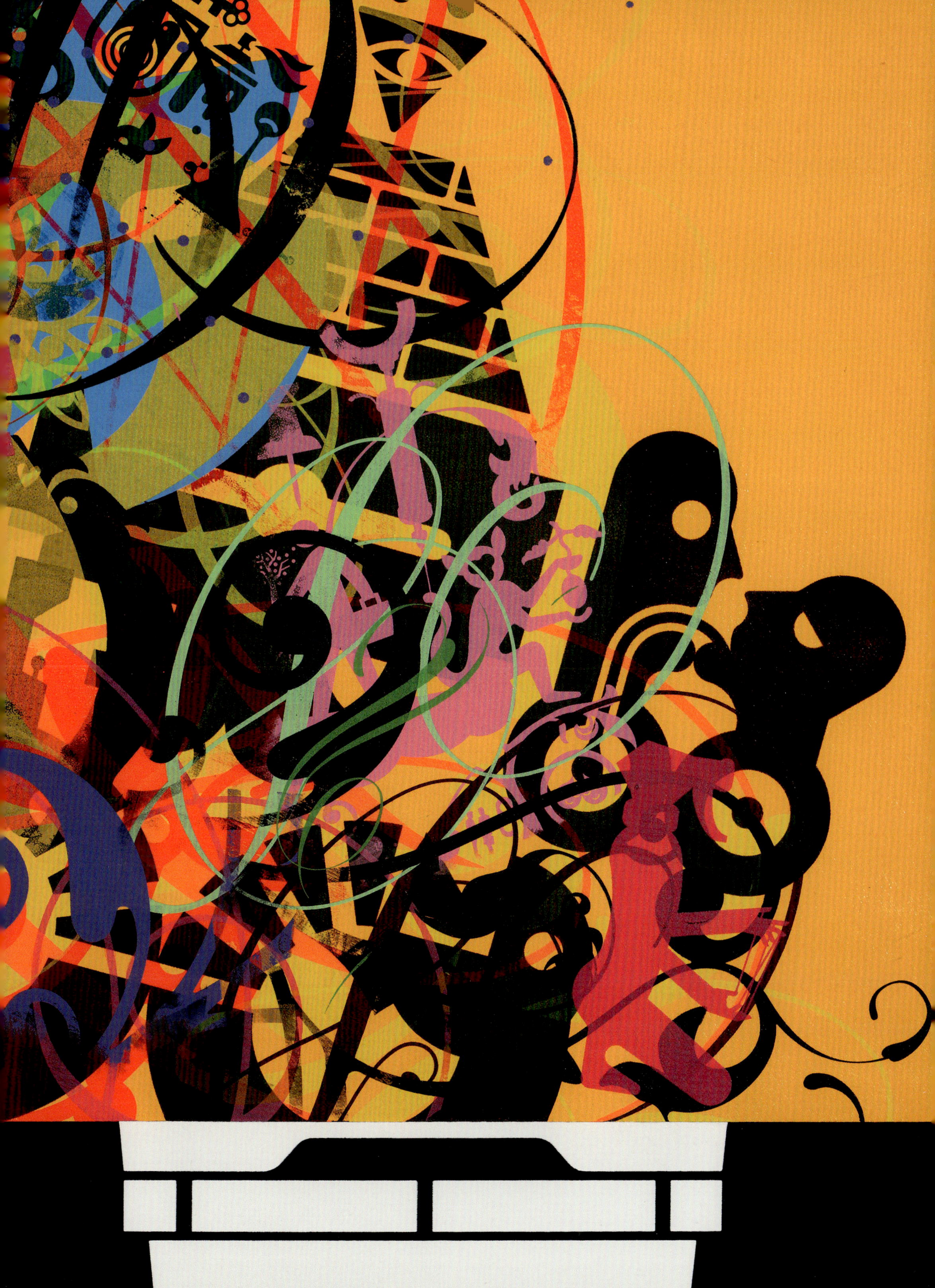

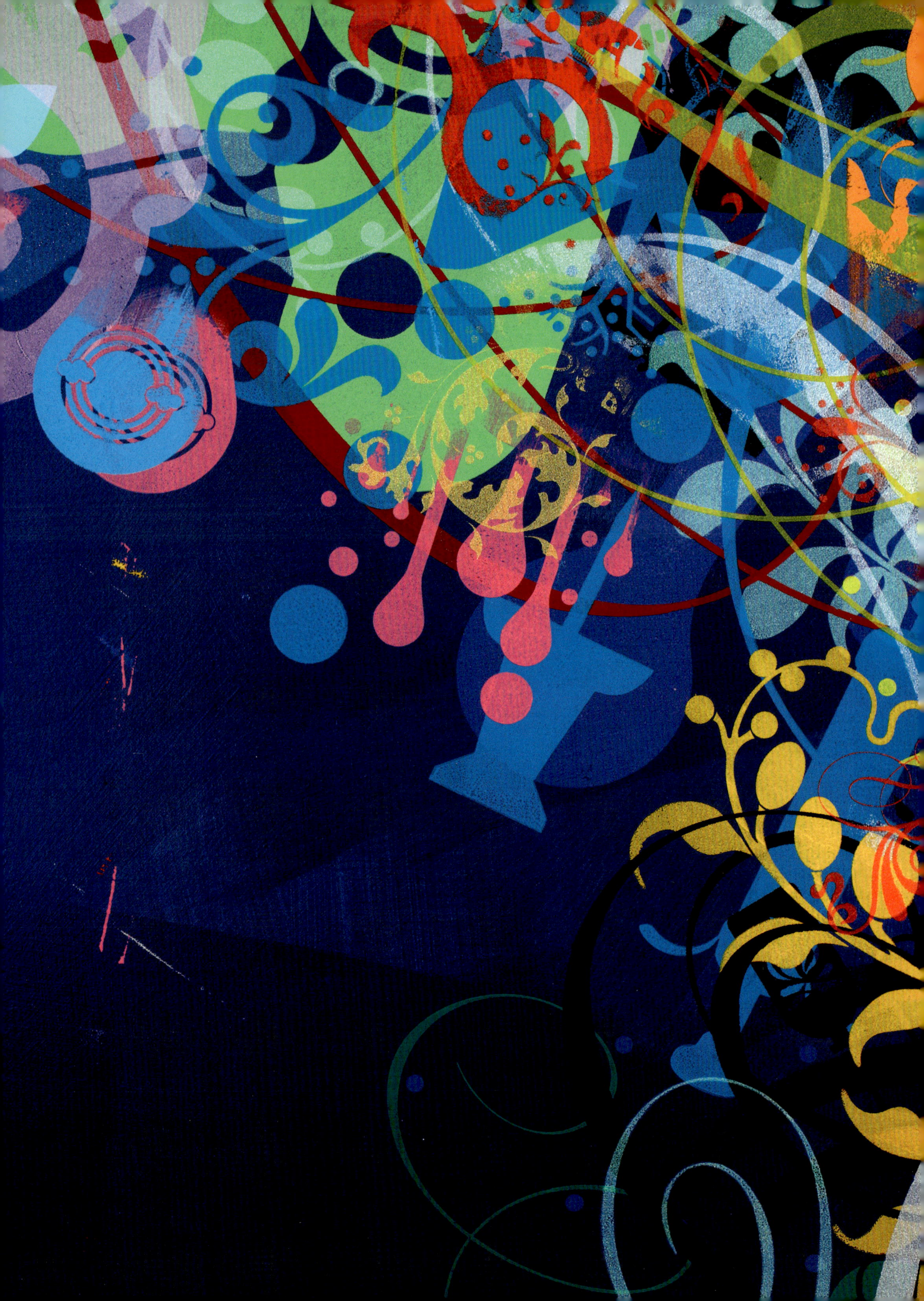

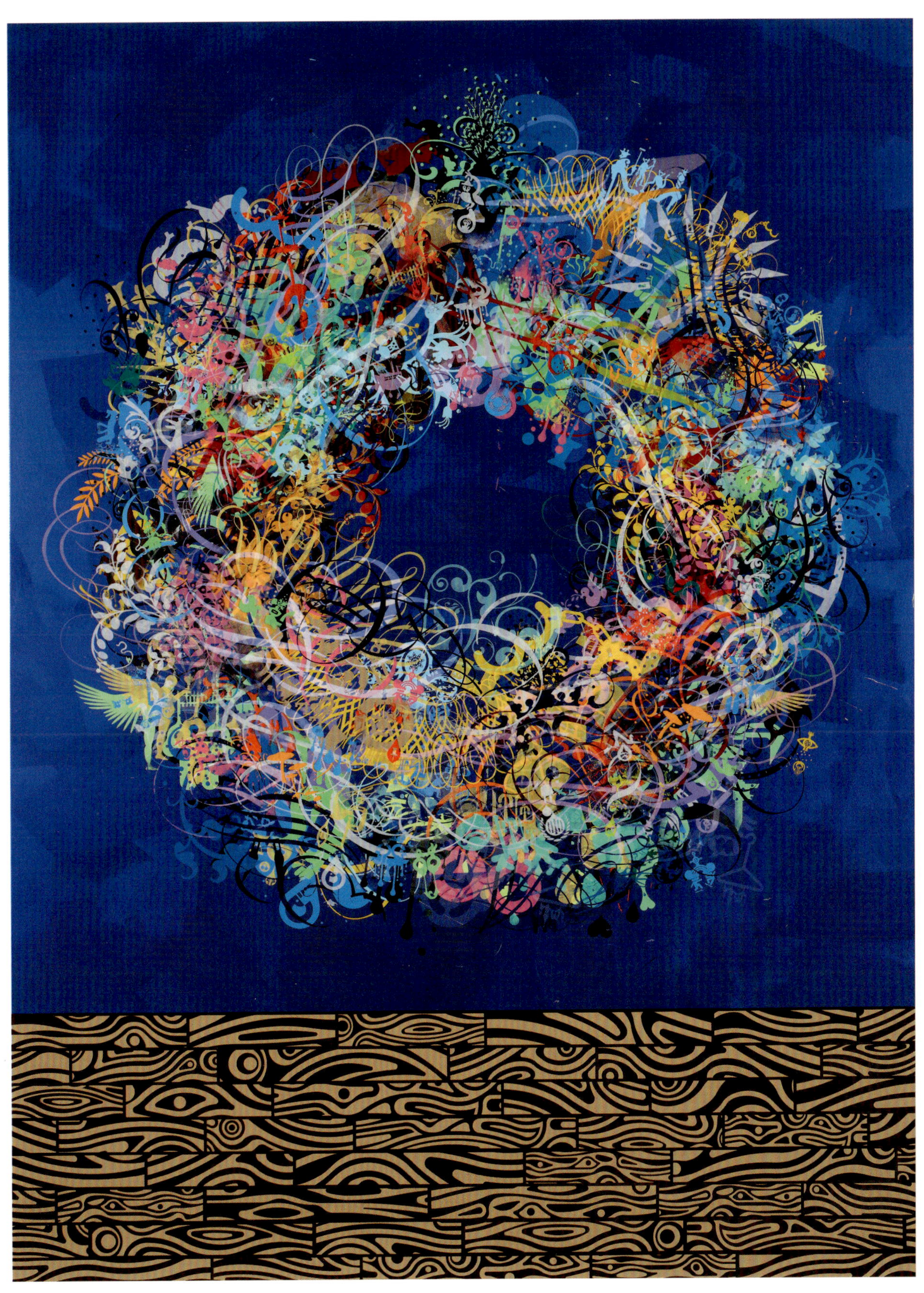

Four Is a Four-letter Word, 2015, acrylic on linen, 84 x 60 in. (213.4 x 152.4 cm); Opposite Page: Detail

Figure Drawings in Neon (Christy, Thea, and Zelina), 2014, argon and mercury in 8mm glass tube with electrical components in artist's frame, 60 x 60 in. (152.4 x 152.4 cm)

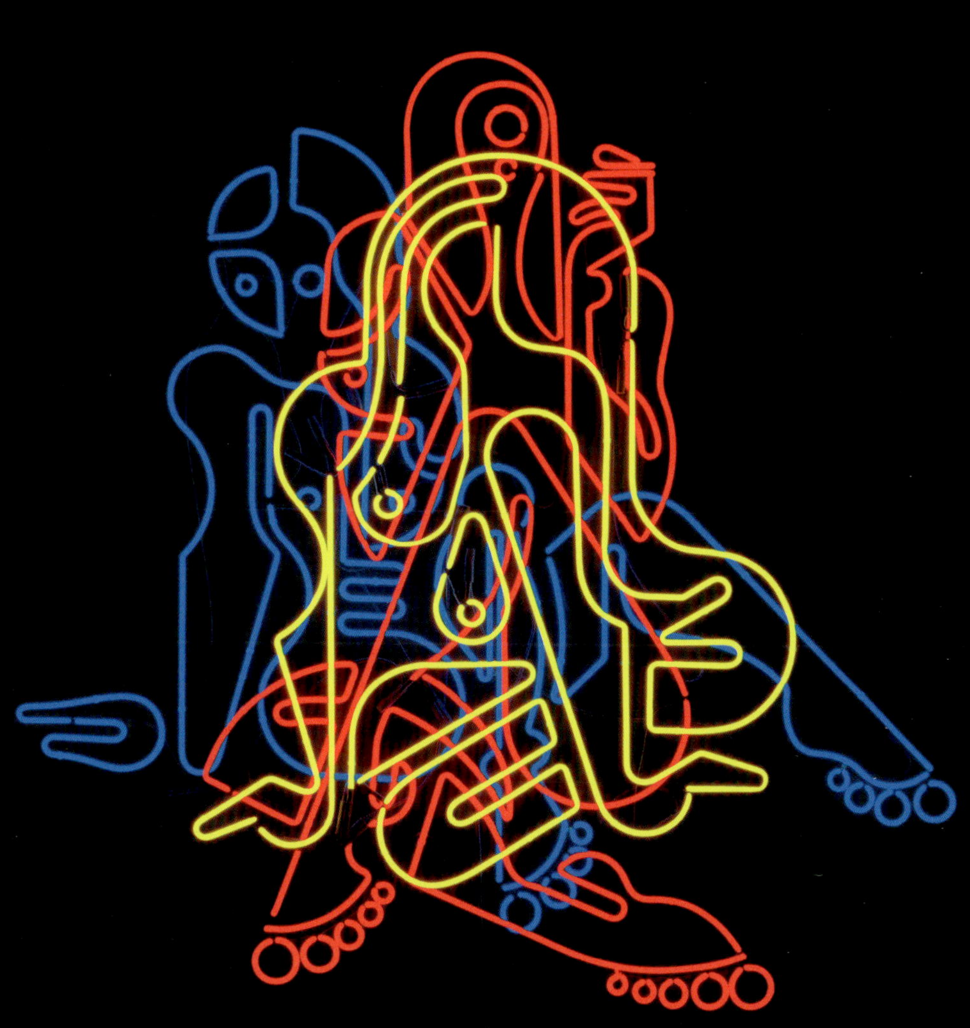

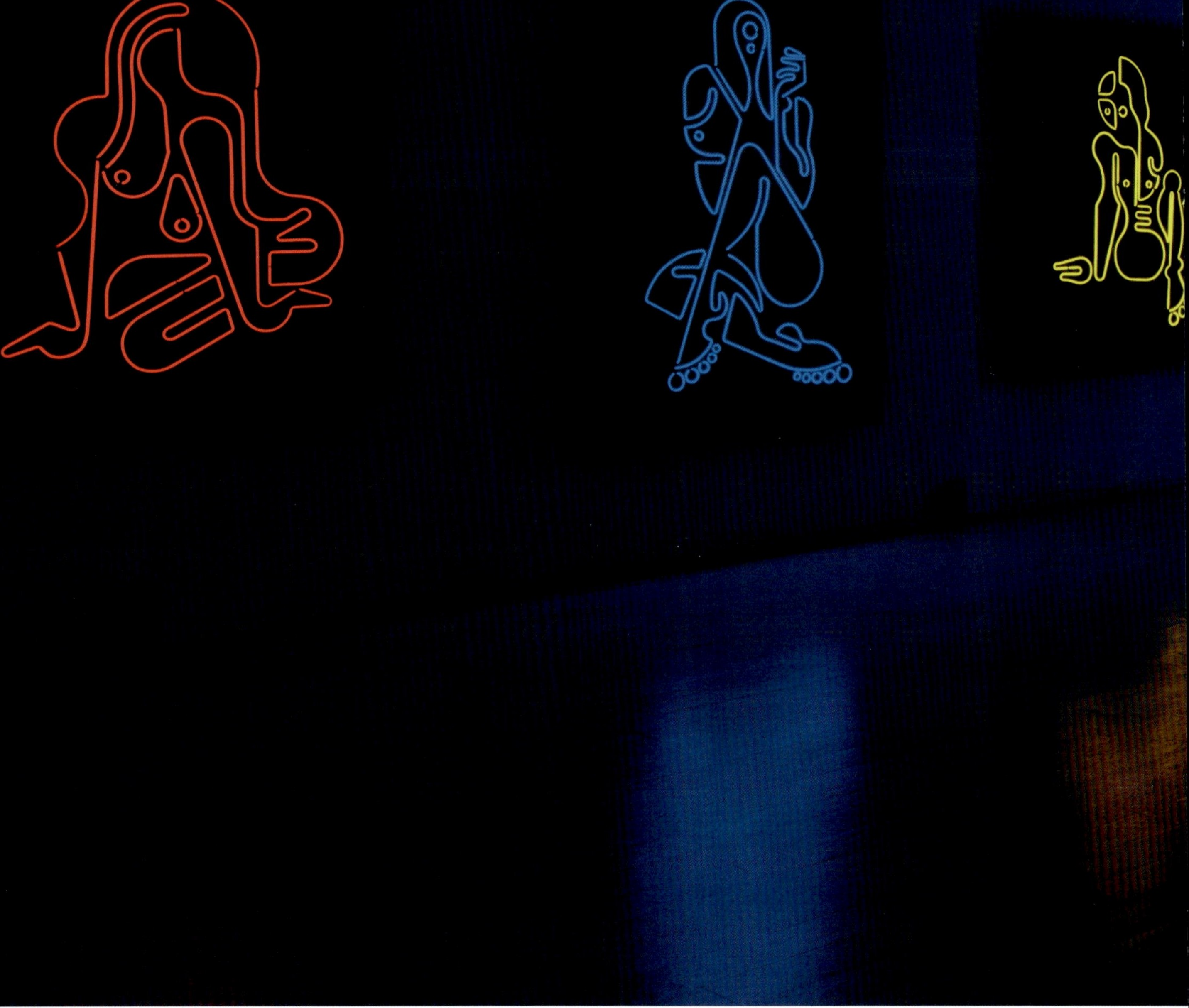

Figure Drawings, 2014, installation view, Pace Prints, New York

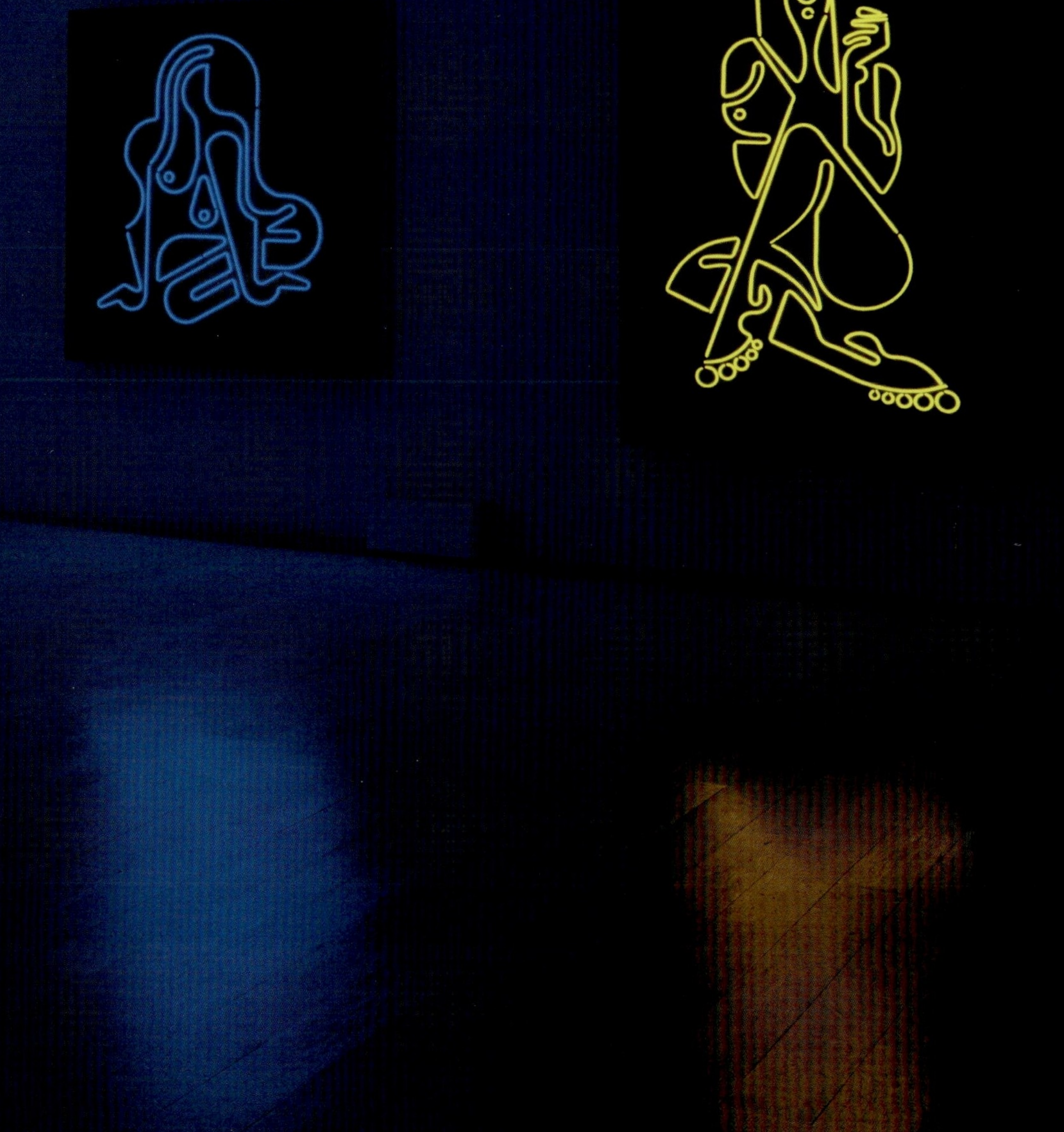

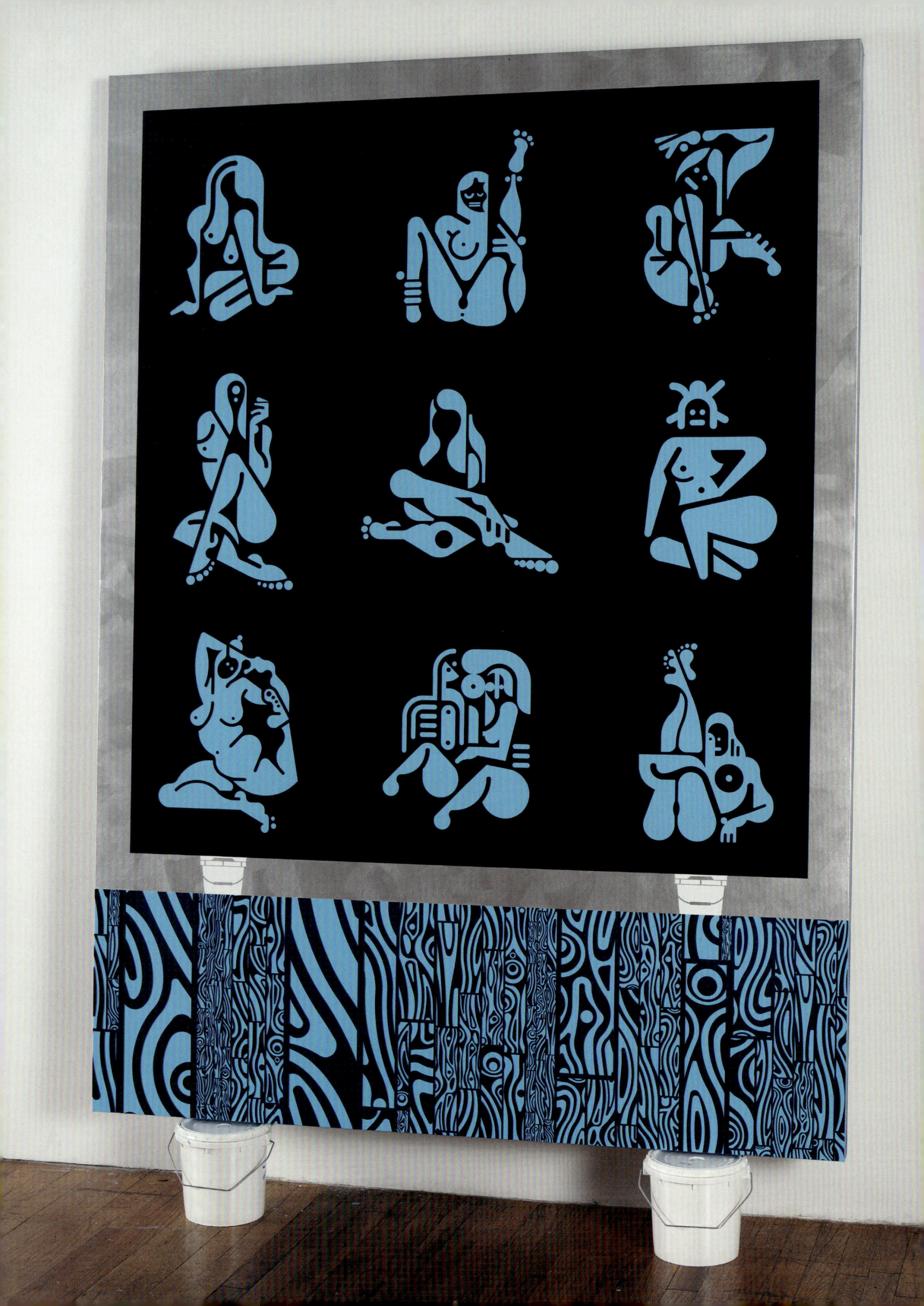

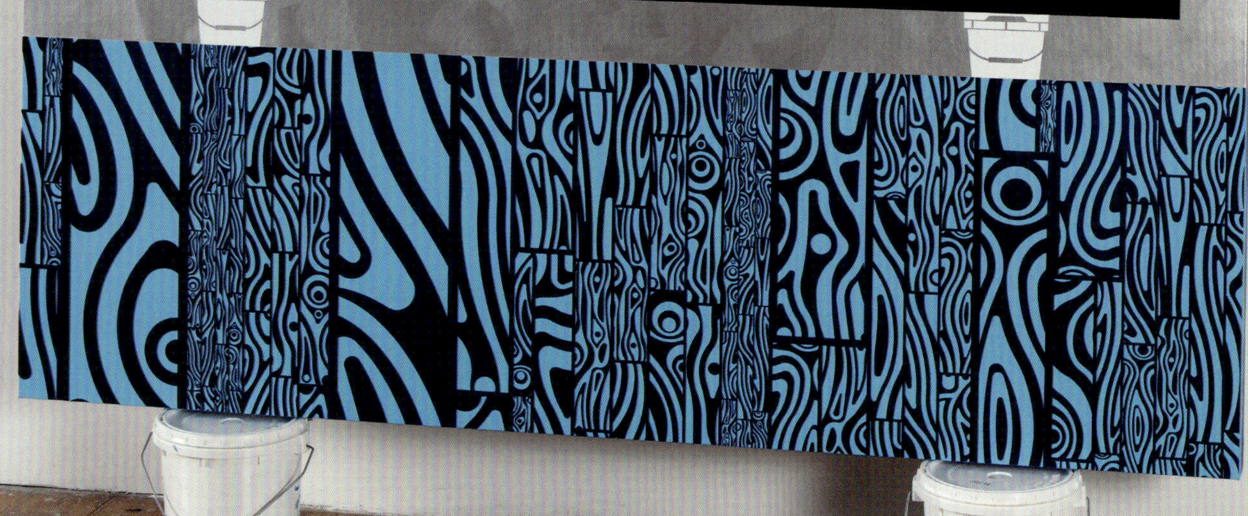

Painting of Nine Figures in Studio, 2017, acrylic on linen, 84 x 60 in.
(213.4 x 152.4 cm)

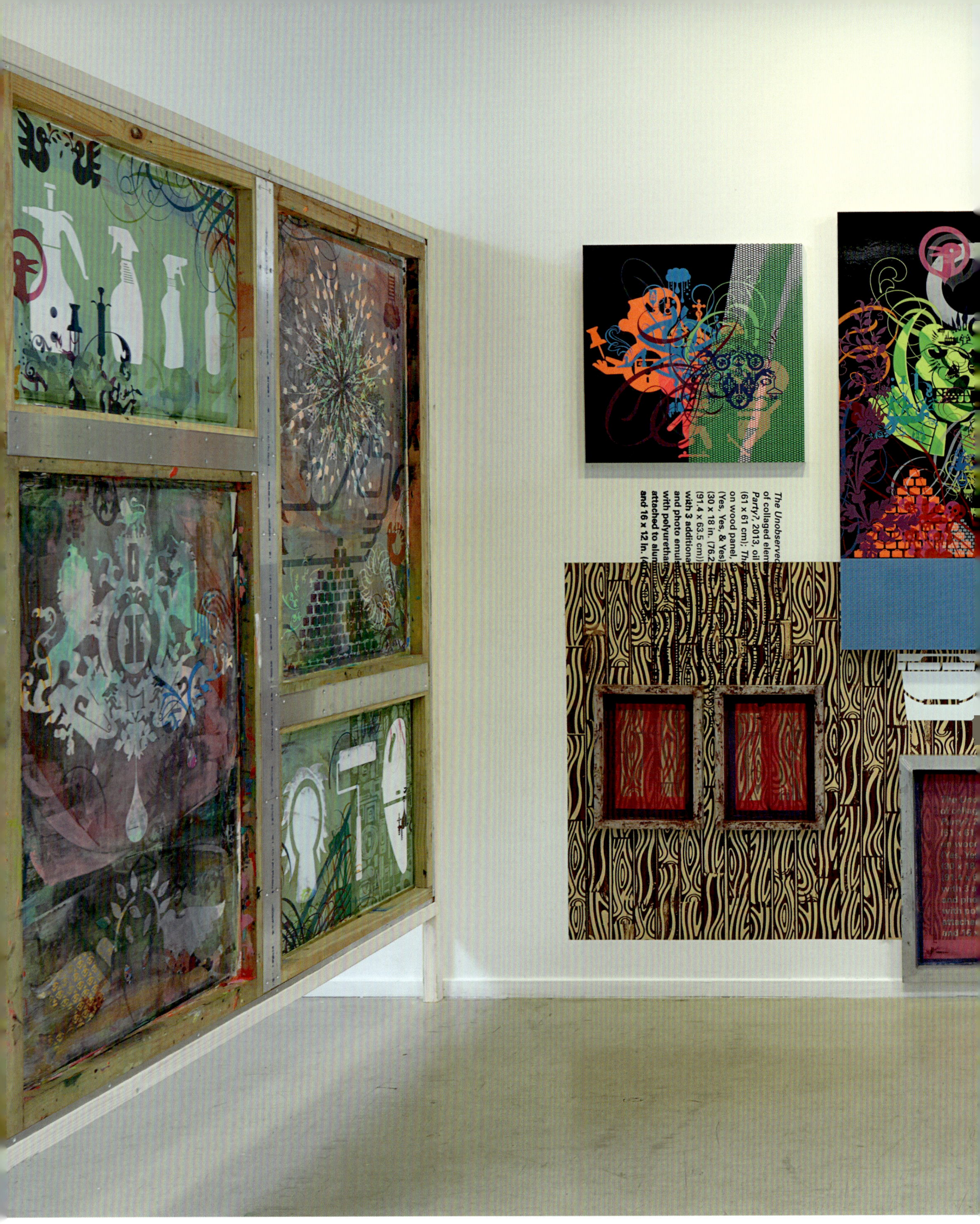

Everything Is Everywhere, 2014, installation view, Galerie Ron Mandos, Amsterdam; Opposite Page: Detail

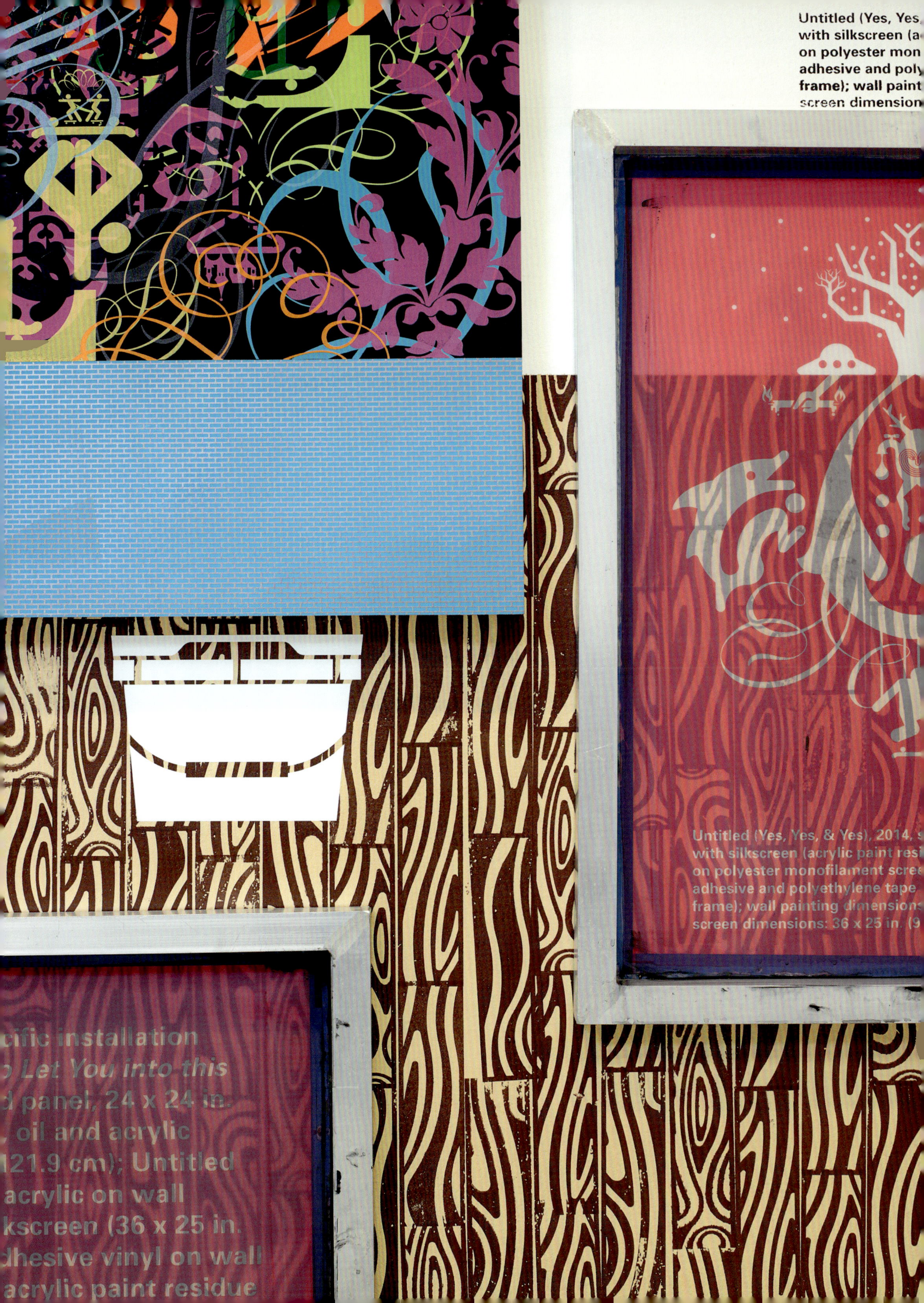
Untitled (Yes, Yes,
with silkscreen (a
on polyester mon
adhesive and poly
frame); wall paint
screen dimension
Untitled (Yes, Yes, & Yes), 2014,
with silkscreen (acrylic paint resi
on polyester monofilament scree
adhesive and polyethylene tape
frame); wall painting dimensions
screen dimensions: 36 x 25 in. (9
ific installation
Let You into this
panel, 24 x 24 in.
oil and acrylic
121.9 cm); Untitled
acrylic on wall
kscreen (36 x 25 in.
dhesive vinyl on wall
acrylic paint residue

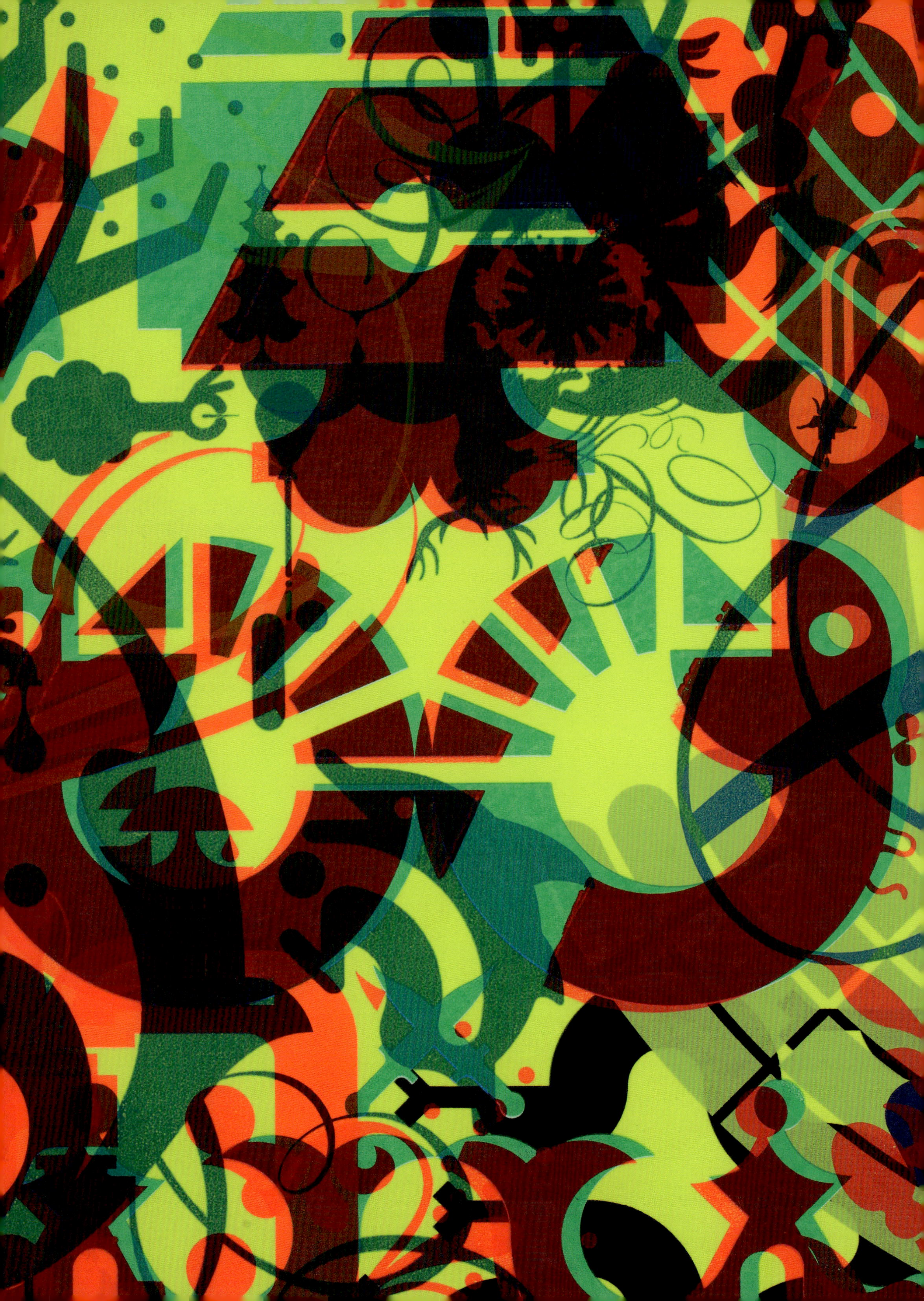

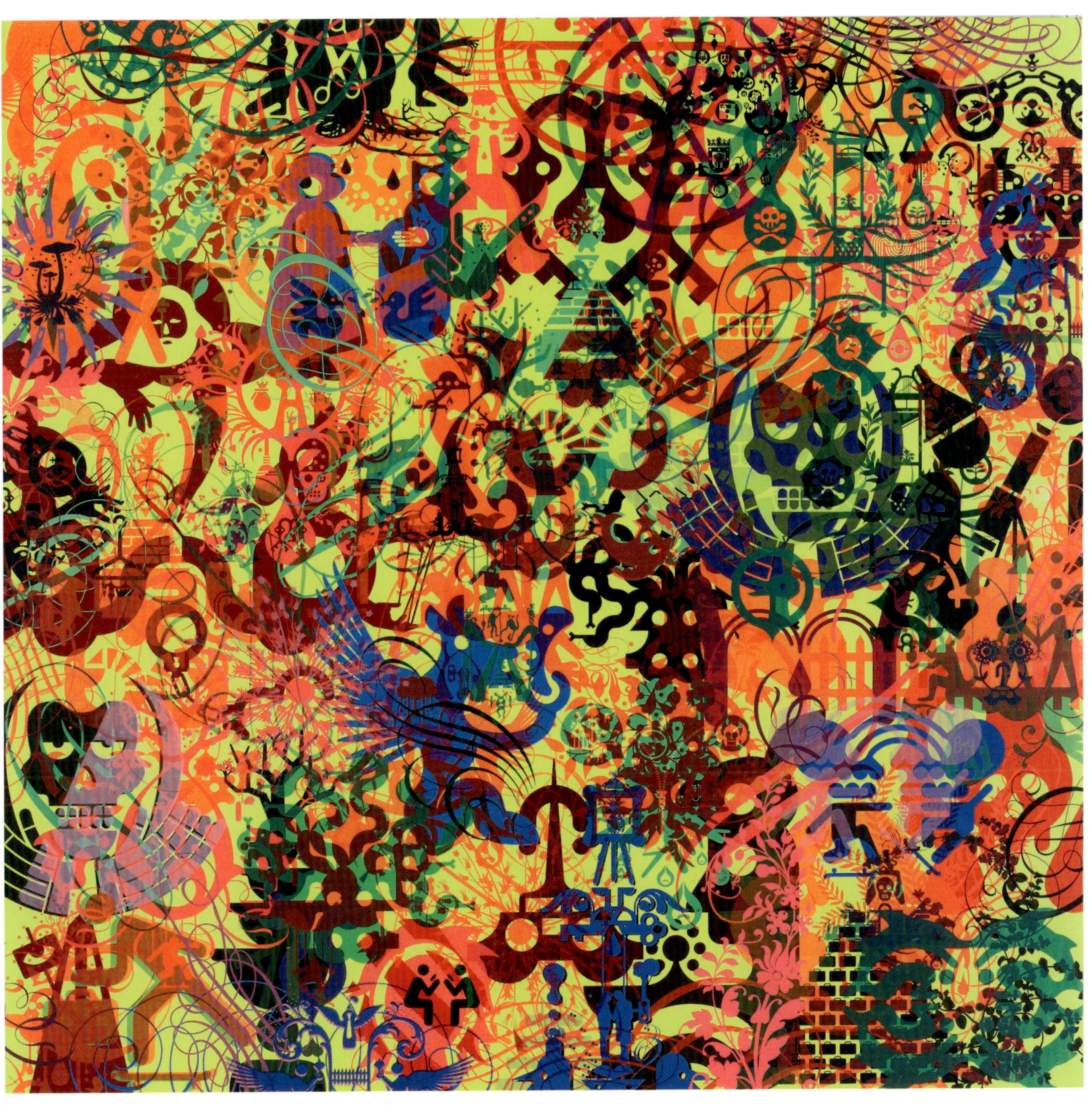

The Cosmic Giggle, 2013, acrylic on canvas, 72 x 72 in.
(182.9 x 182.9 cm); Opposite Page: Detail

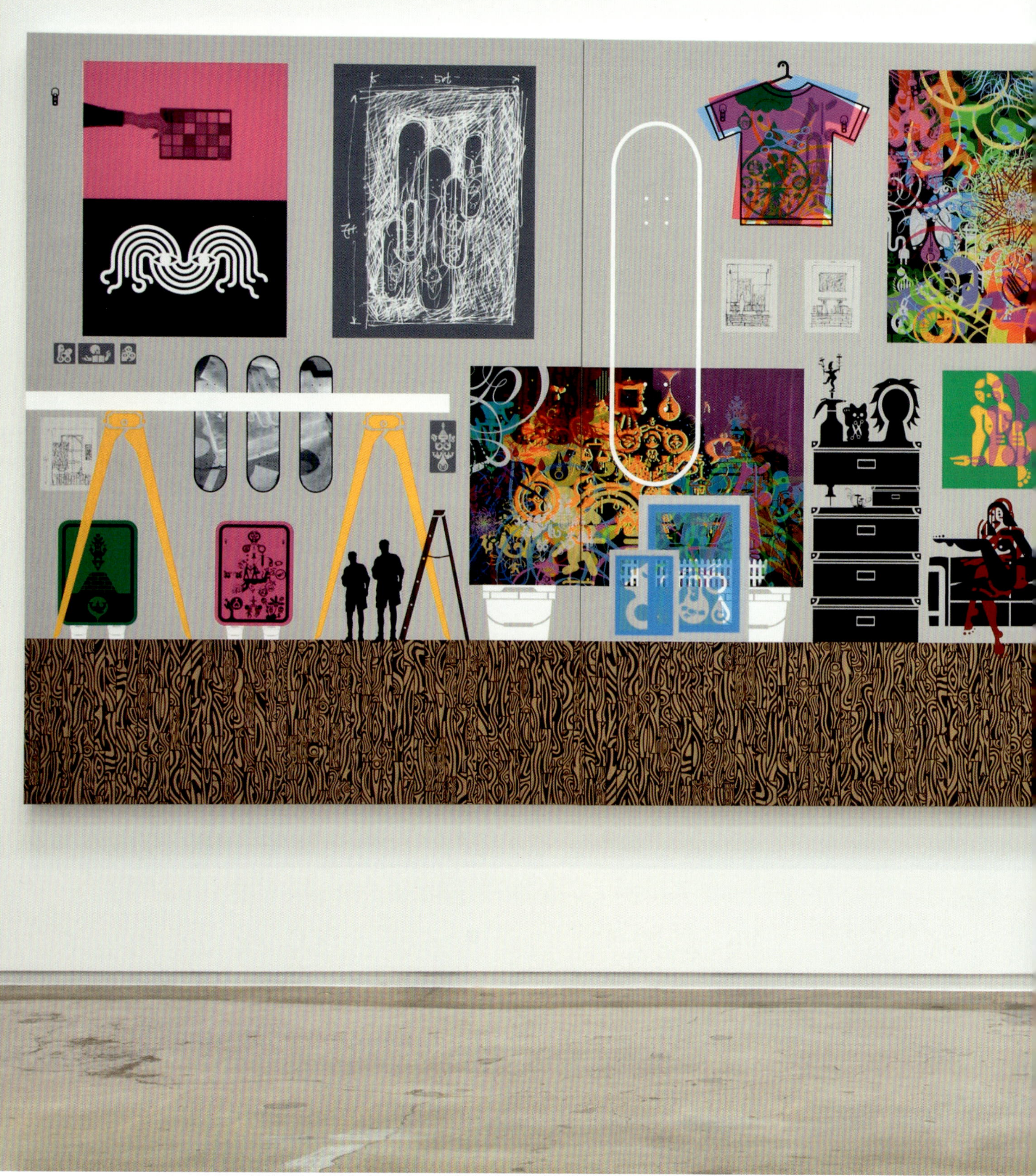

The Logic of this Work Is Stronger than the Logic of the World in which it Exists, 2016, quadriptych, acrylic on linen, 84 x 60 in. (213.4 x 152.4 cm) each, 84 x 240 in. (213.4 x 609.6 cm) total

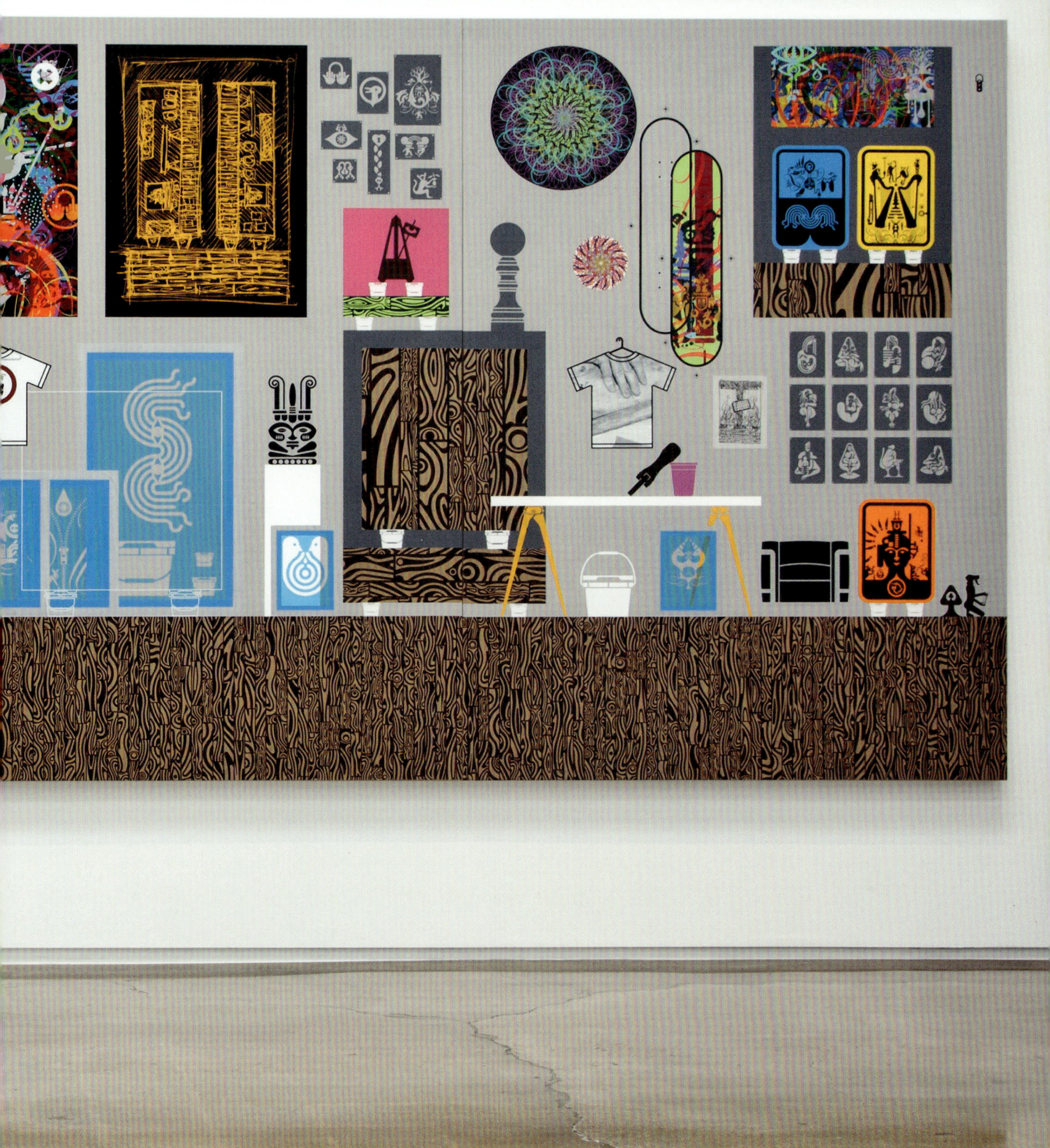

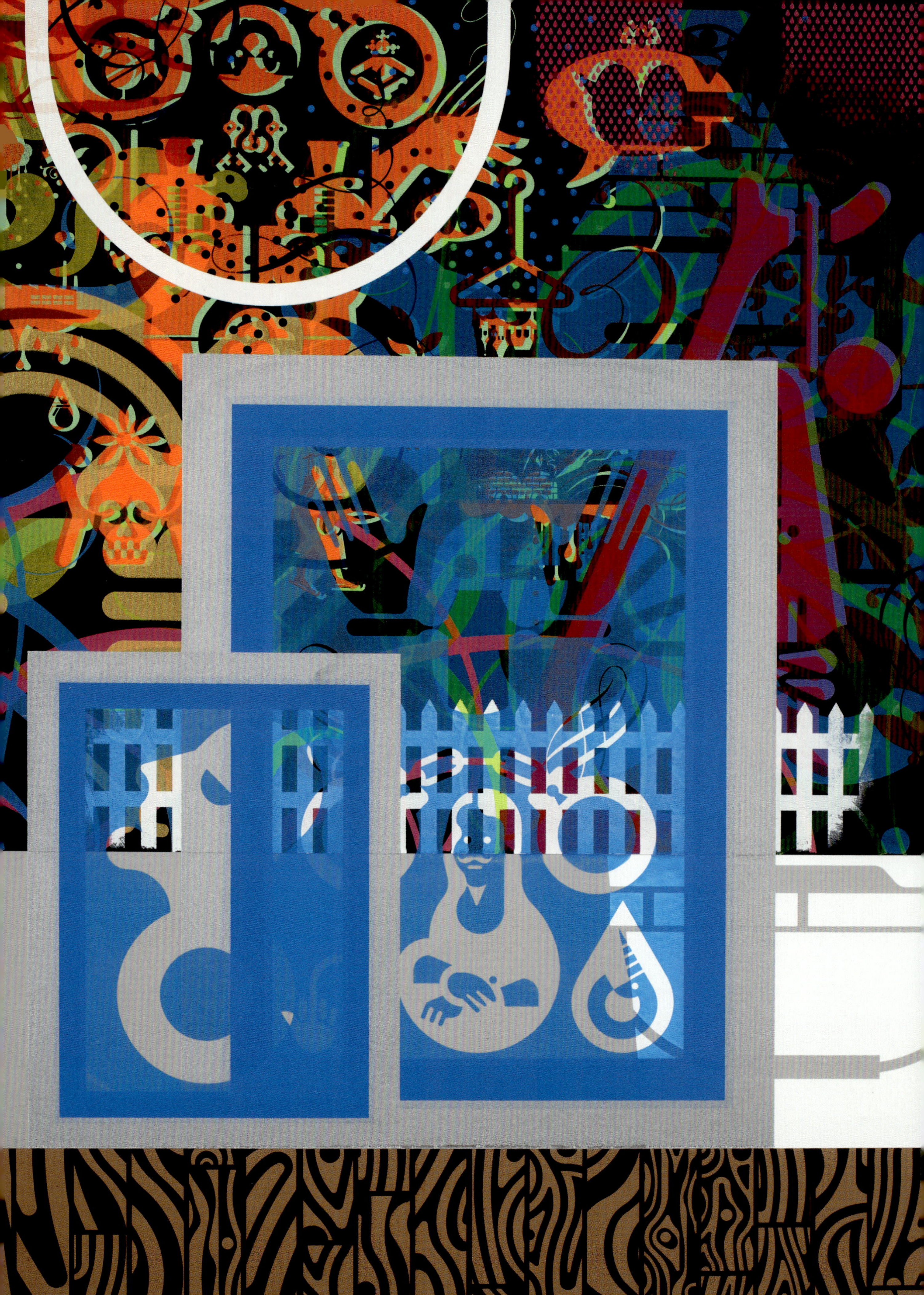

The Logic of this Work Is Stronger than the Logic of the World in which it Exists (Detail), 2016, quadriptych, acrylic on linen, 84 x 60 in. (213.4 x 152.4 cm) each, 84 x 240 in. (213.4 x 609.6 cm) total

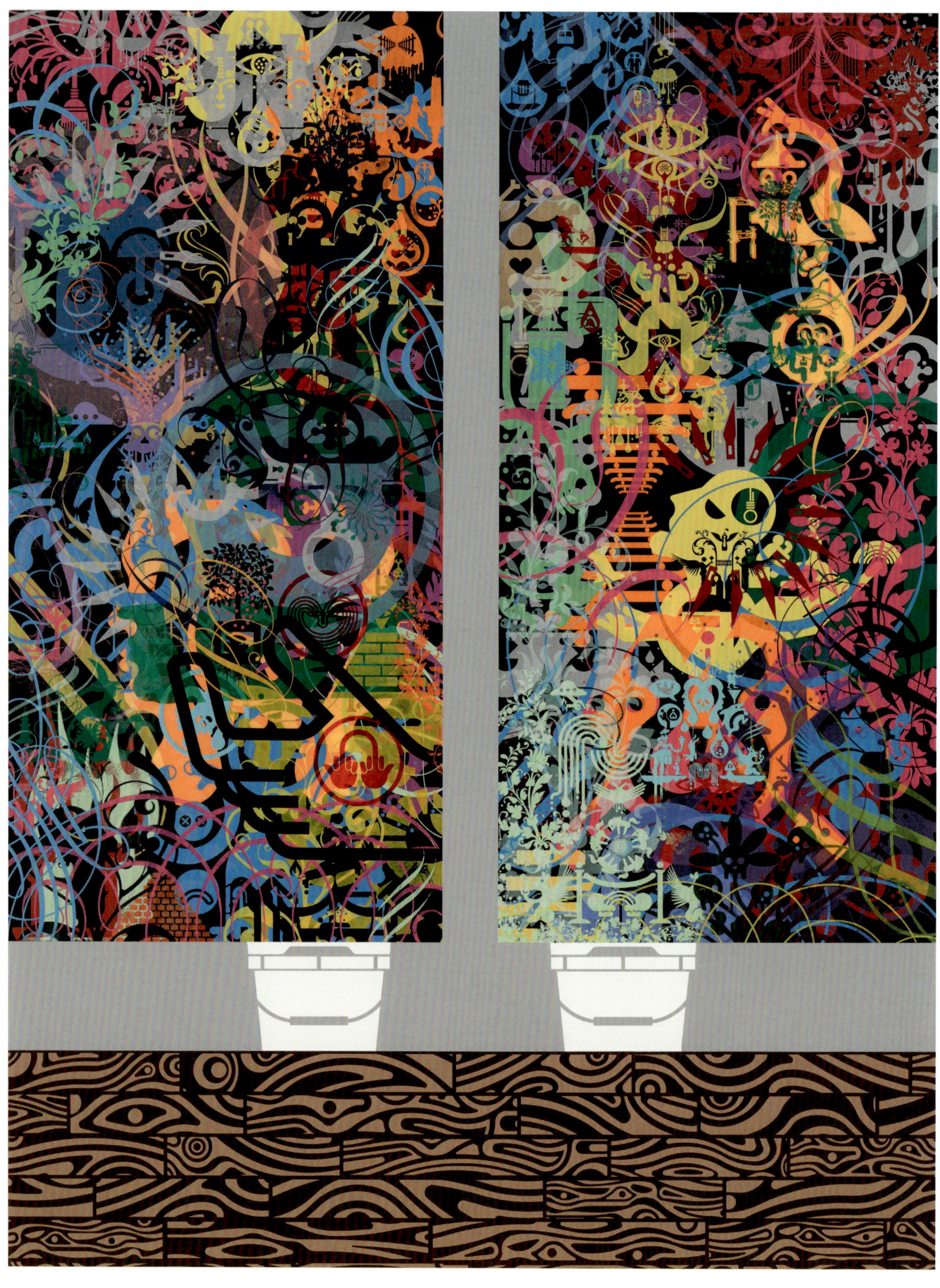

108 *Script Kitties*, 2016, acrylic on wood panel, 69.5 x 51.125 in.
(176.5 x 129.9 cm); Opposite Page: Detail

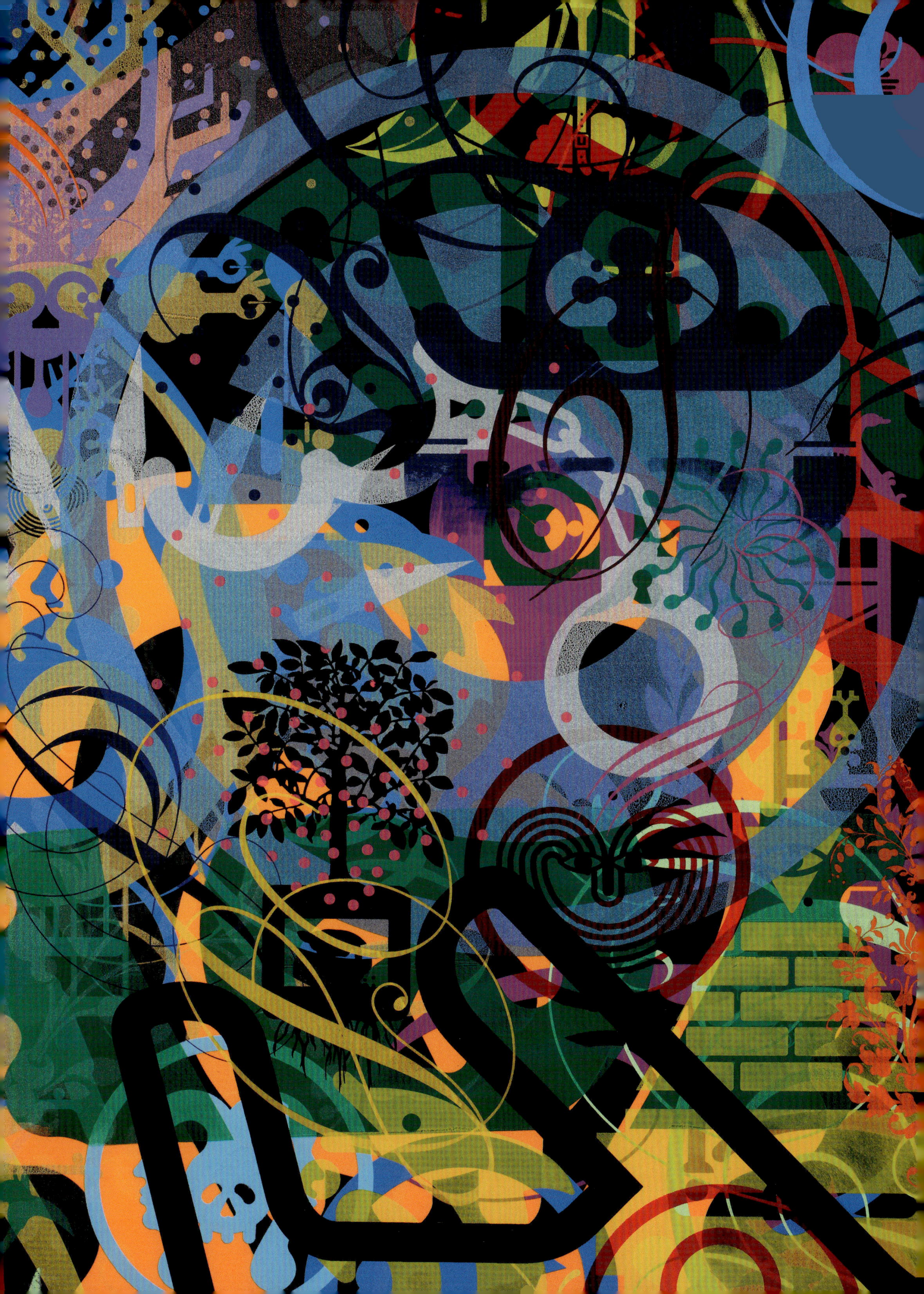

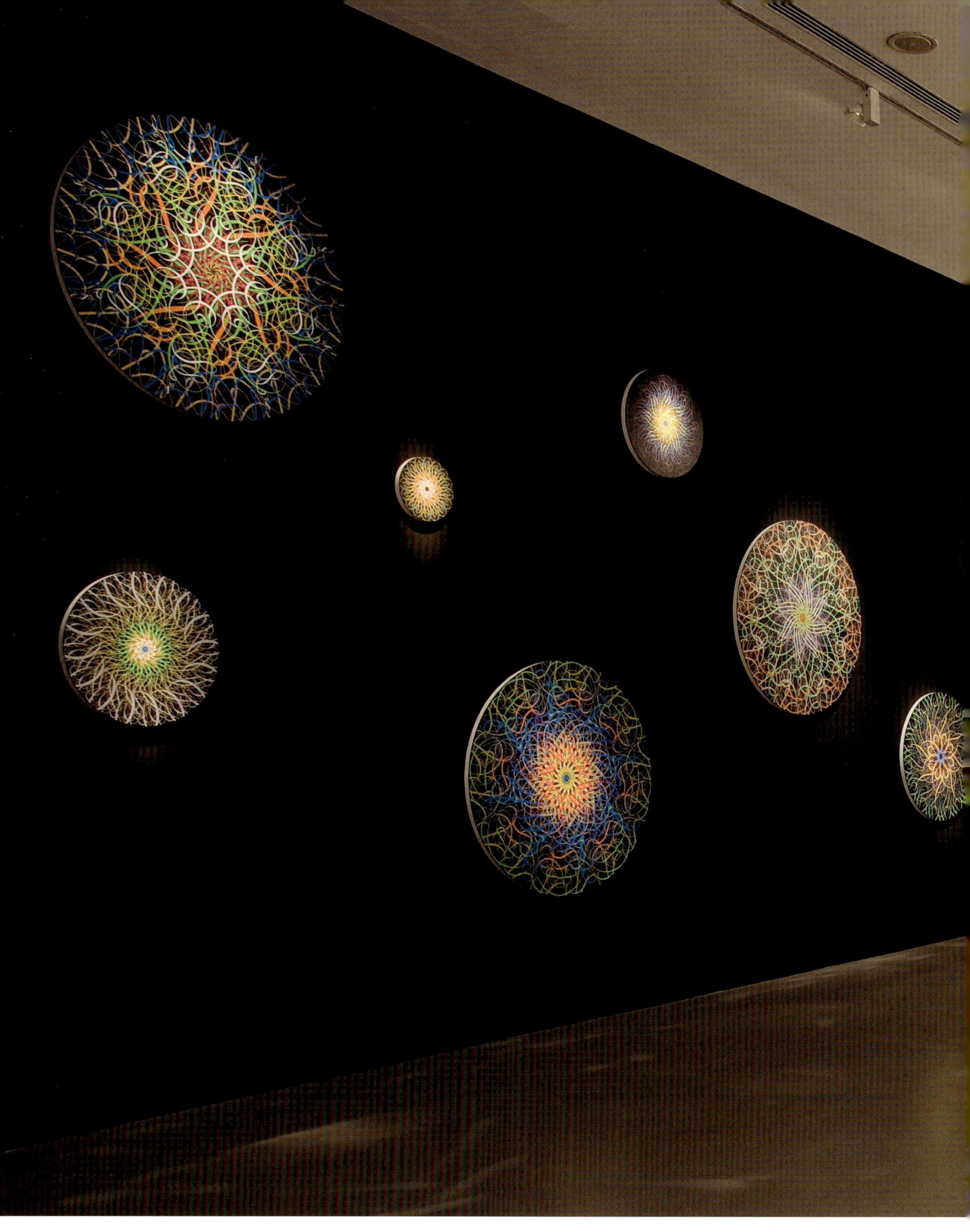

Studio Frànchise, 2010, installation view, La Casa Encendida, Madrid

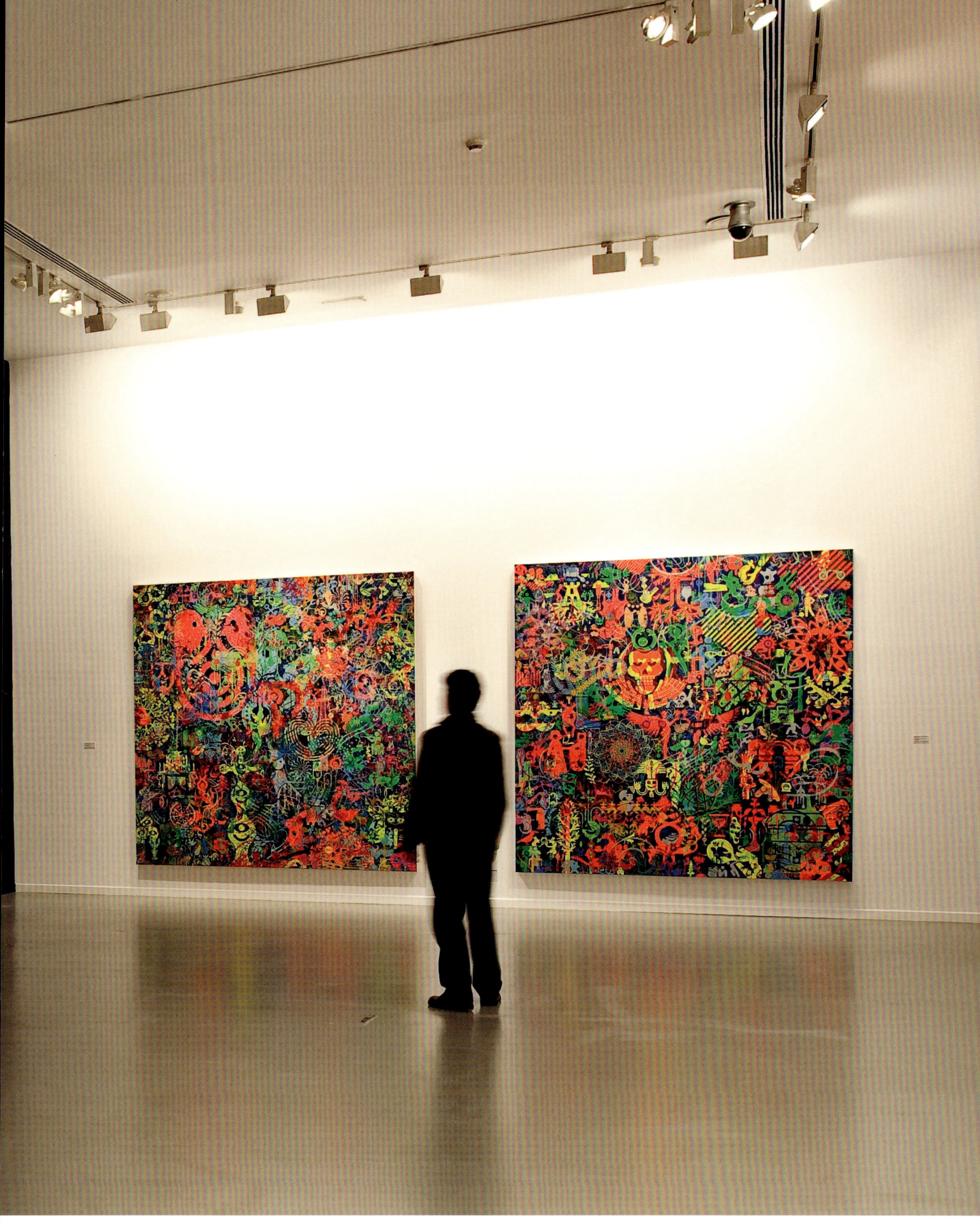

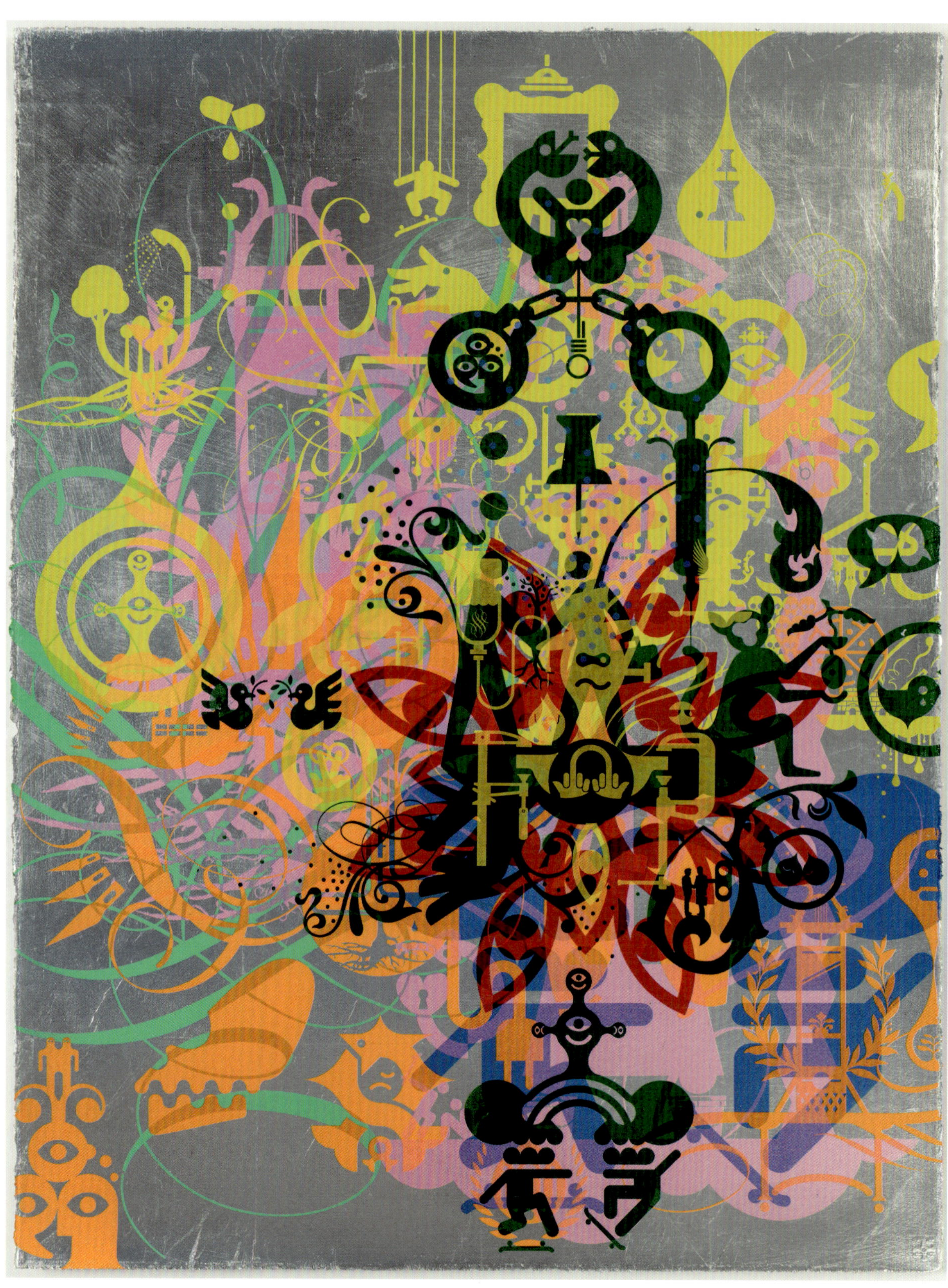

The Creator's Bias (C), 2017, acrylic and metal leaf on paper,
30 x 22 in. (76.2 x 55.9 cm)

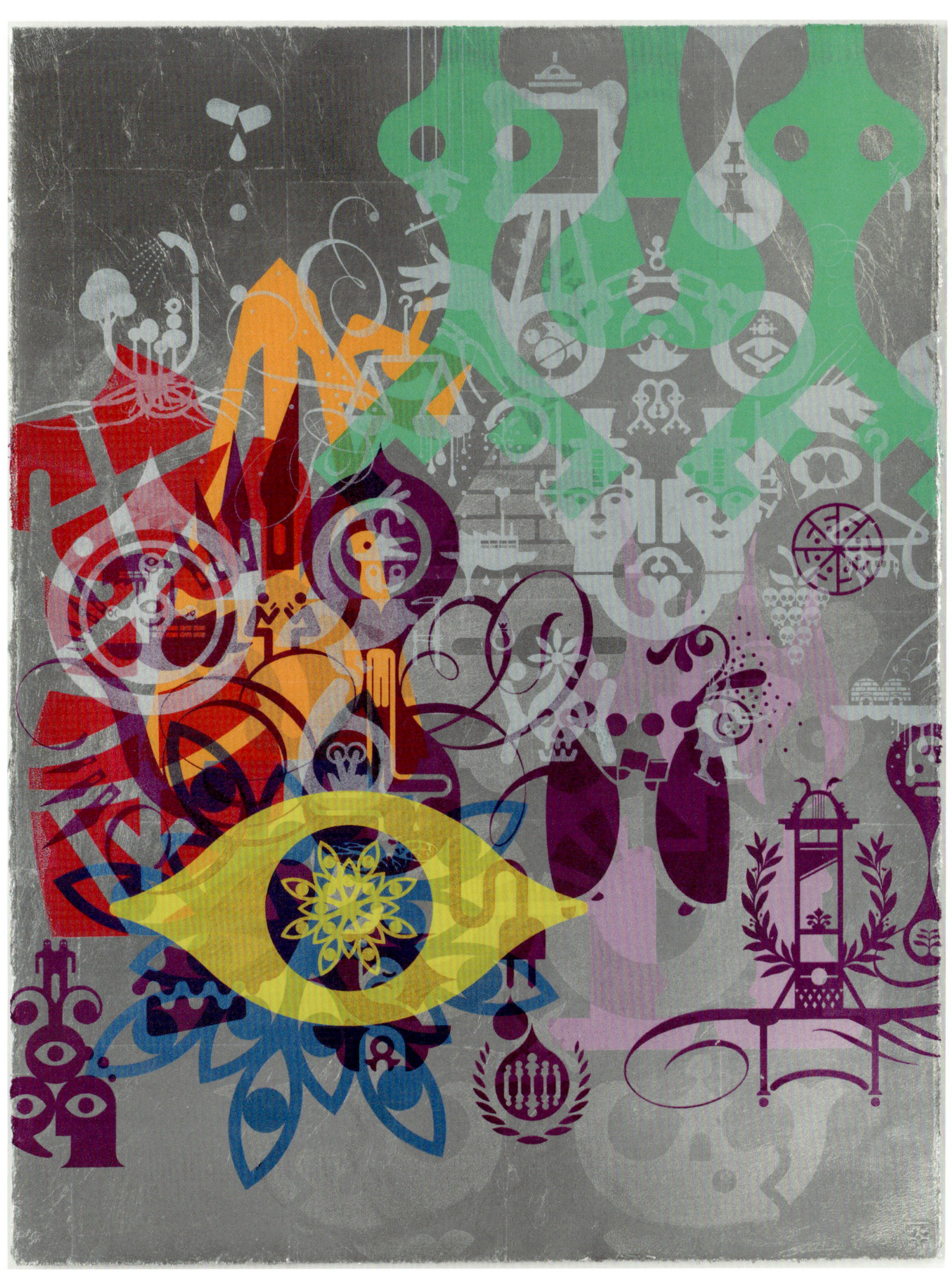

The Creator's Bias (I), 2017, acrylic and metal leaf on paper,
30 x 22 in. (76.2 x 55.9 cm)

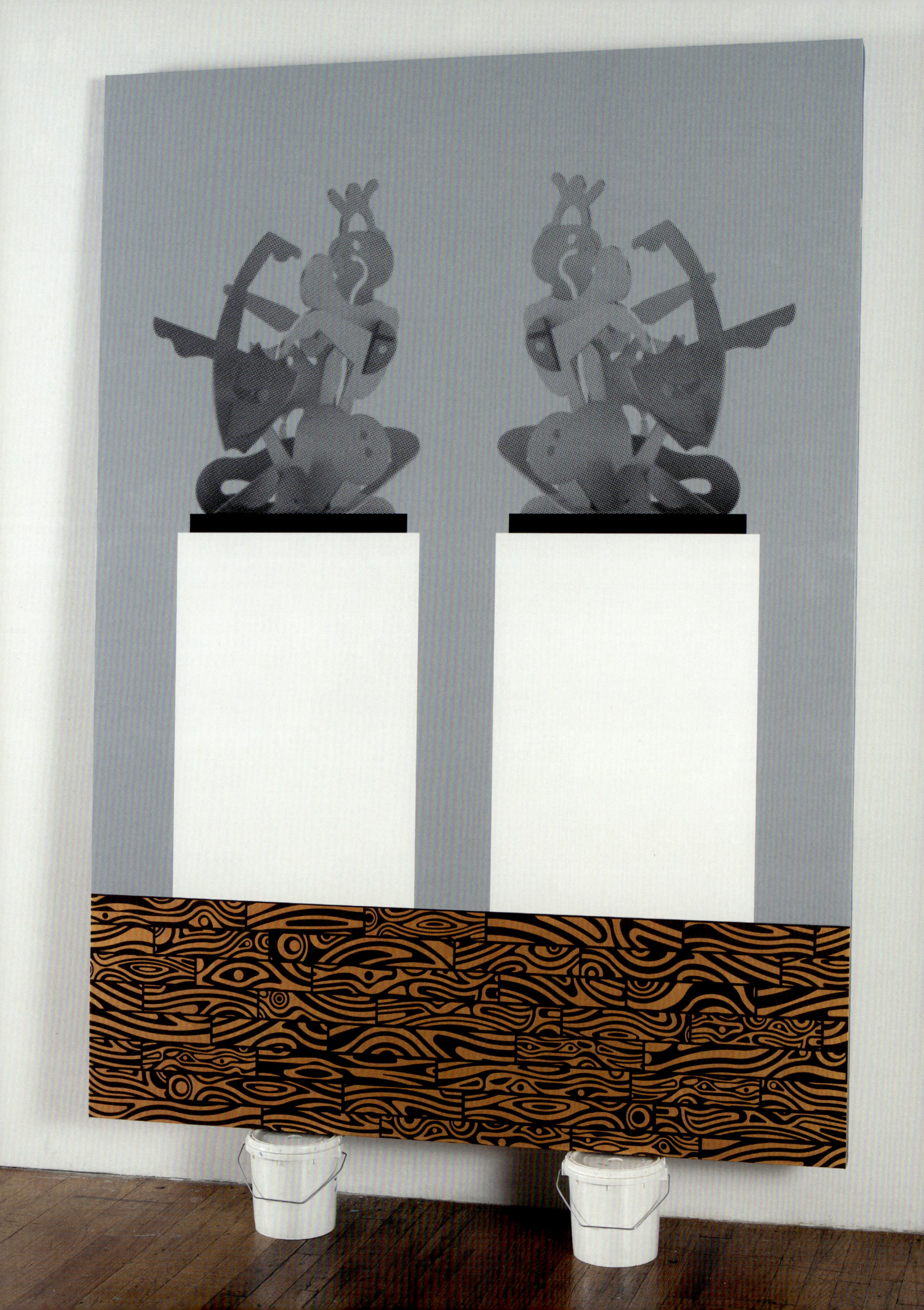

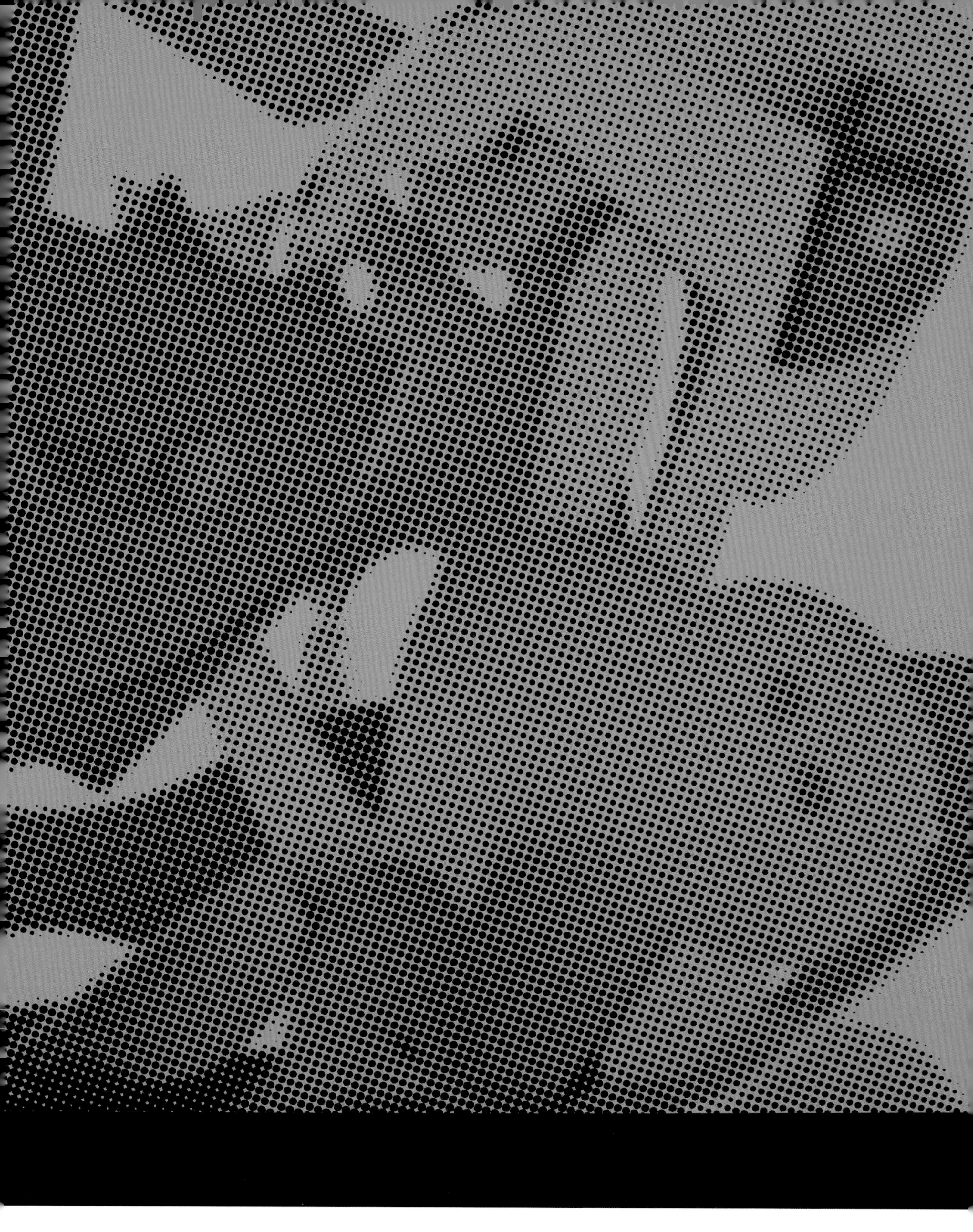

Opposite Page: *Painting of Halftone Photos (Mirrored) of Sculpture on Pedestals in Studio* (in studio), 2017, acrylic on linen, 84 x 60 in. (213.4 x 152.4 cm); Above: Detail

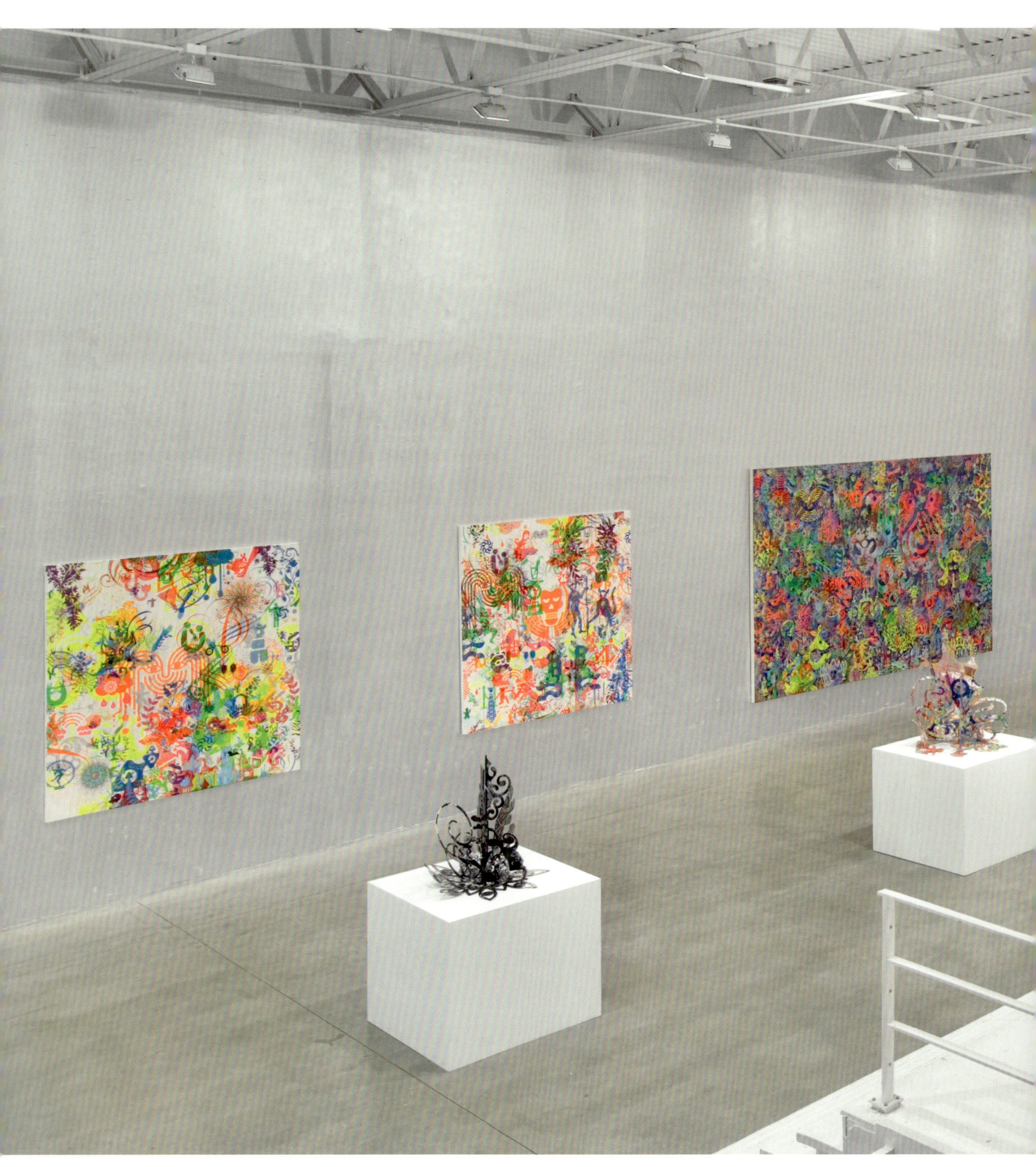

Ryan McGinness Works, 2009, installation view, Deitch Projects, New York
Following Spread: *Roy G. Biv*, 2009, oil and acrylic on 7 wood panels in aluminum frames,
96 x 48 in. (243.8 x 121.9 cm) ea., 96 x 336 in. (243.8 x 853.4 cm) total

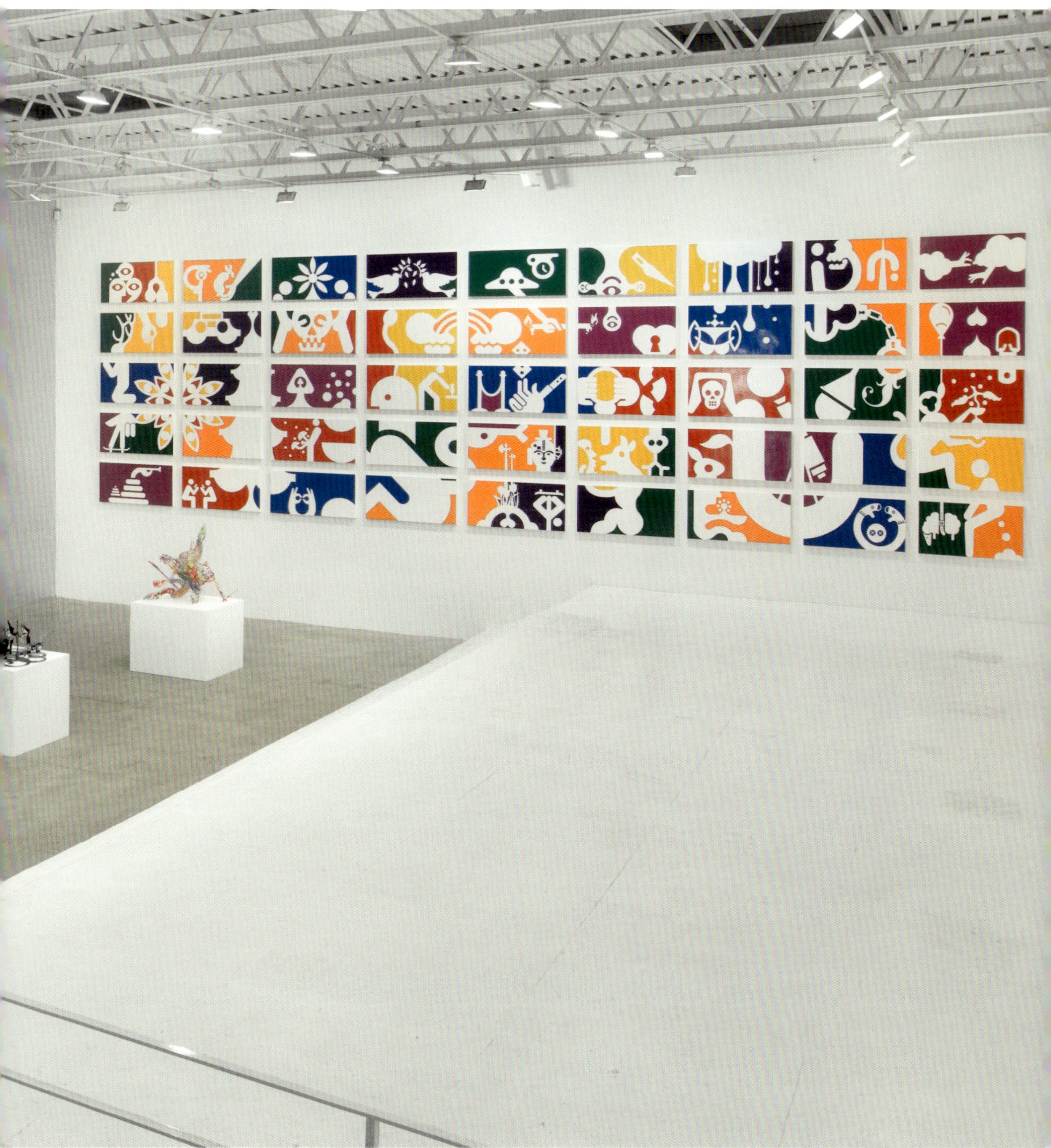

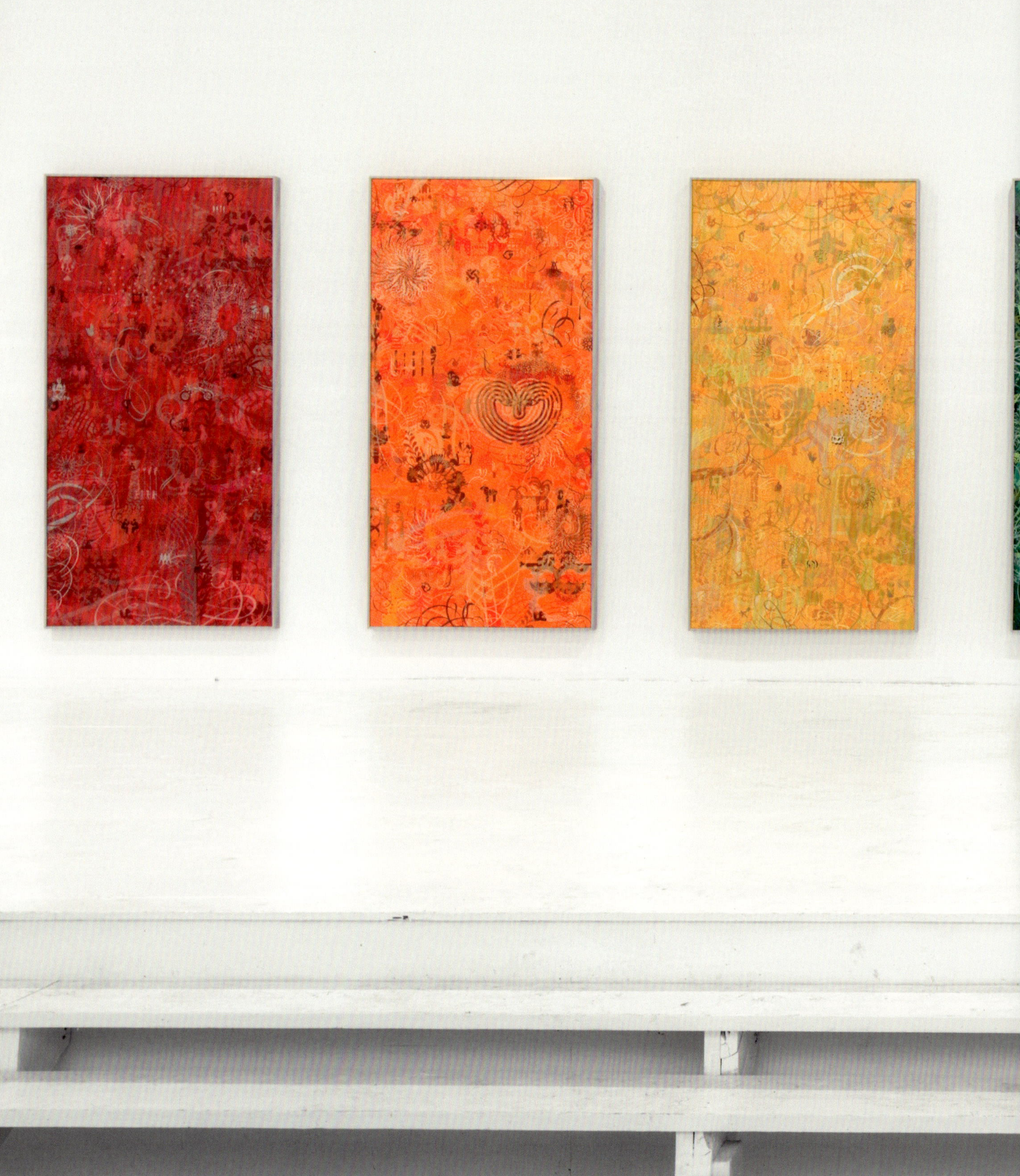

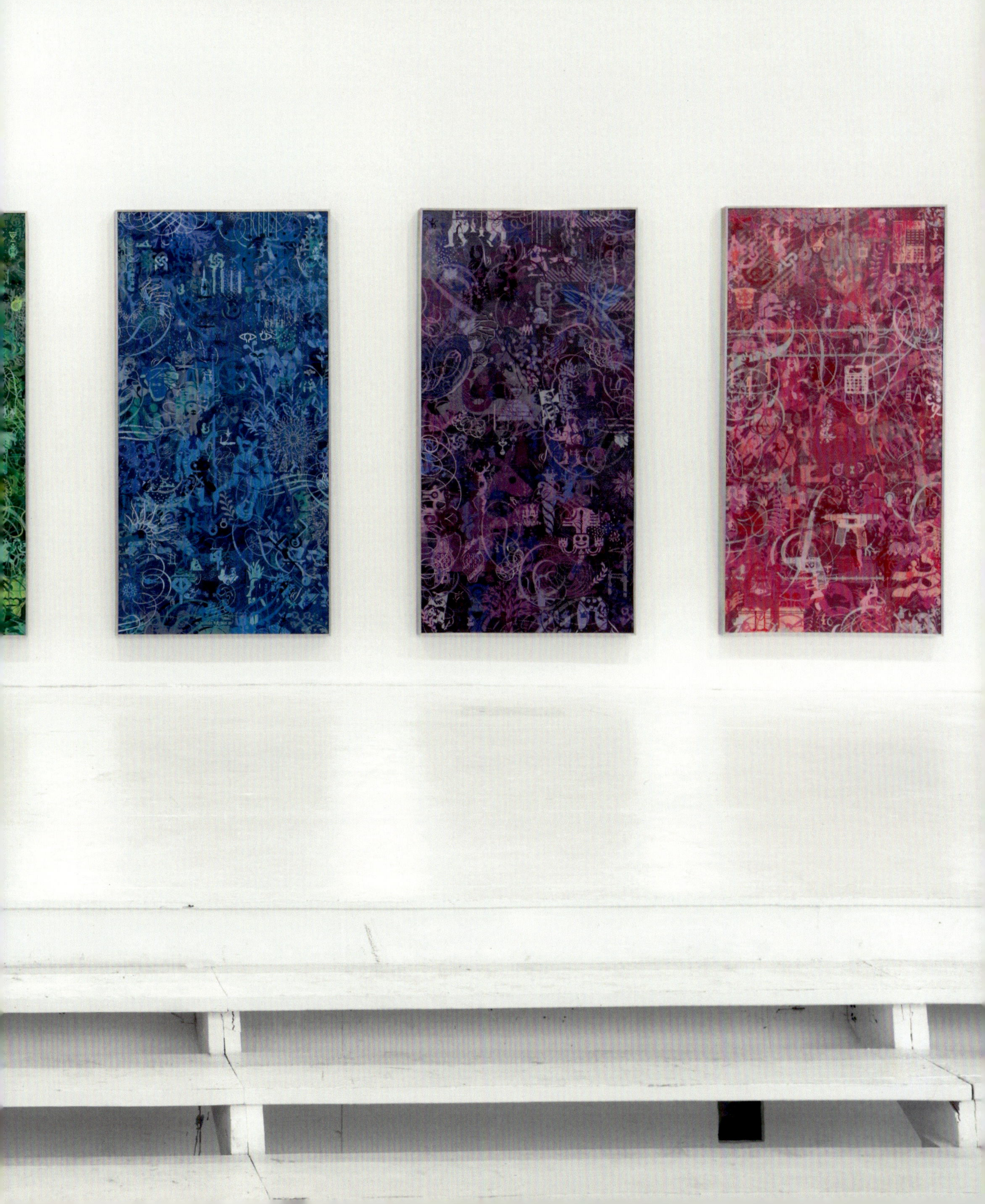

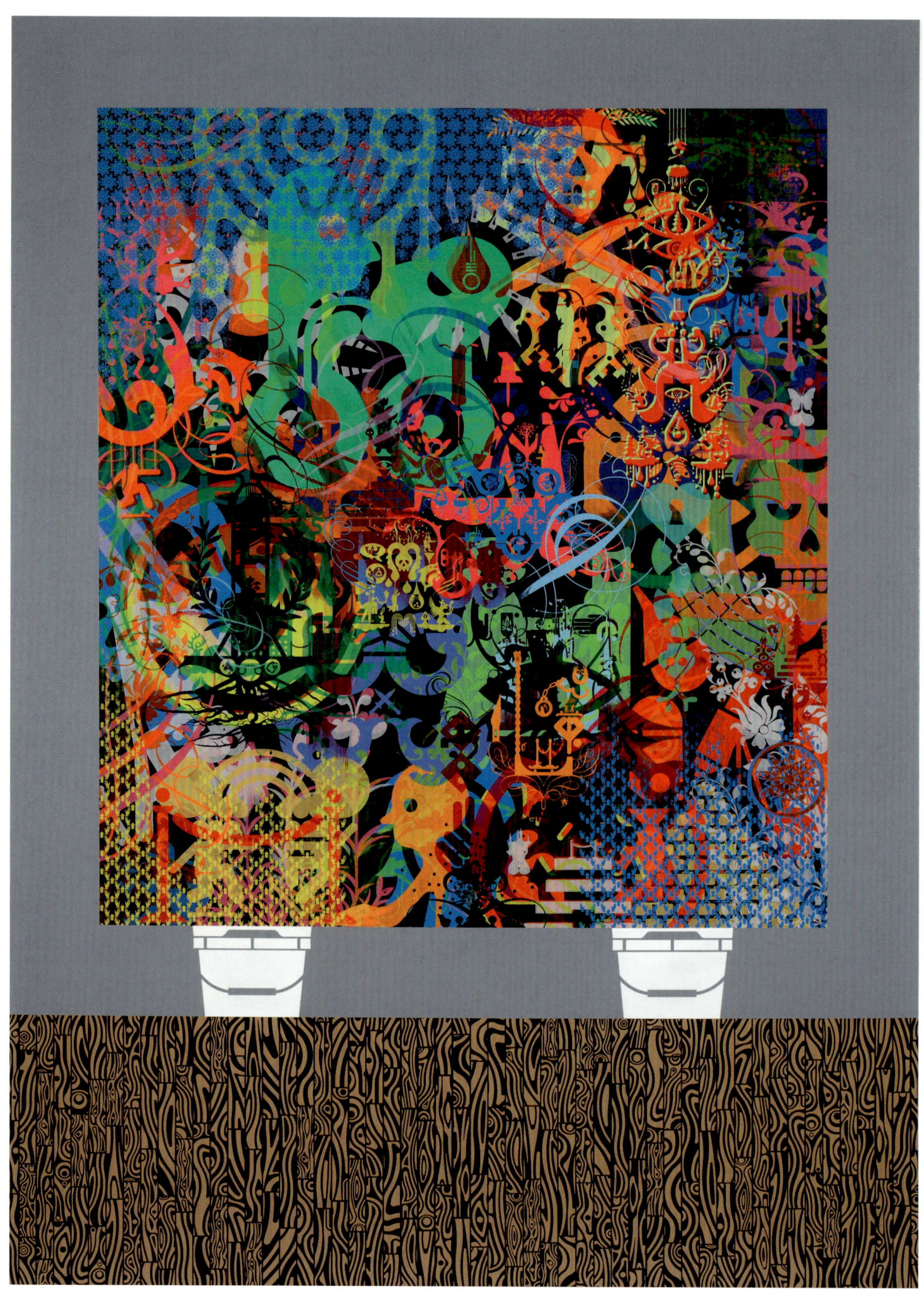

Making Someone Else's Bed, 2015, acrylic on linen, 84 x 60 in.
(213.4 x 152.4 cm); Opposite Page: Detail

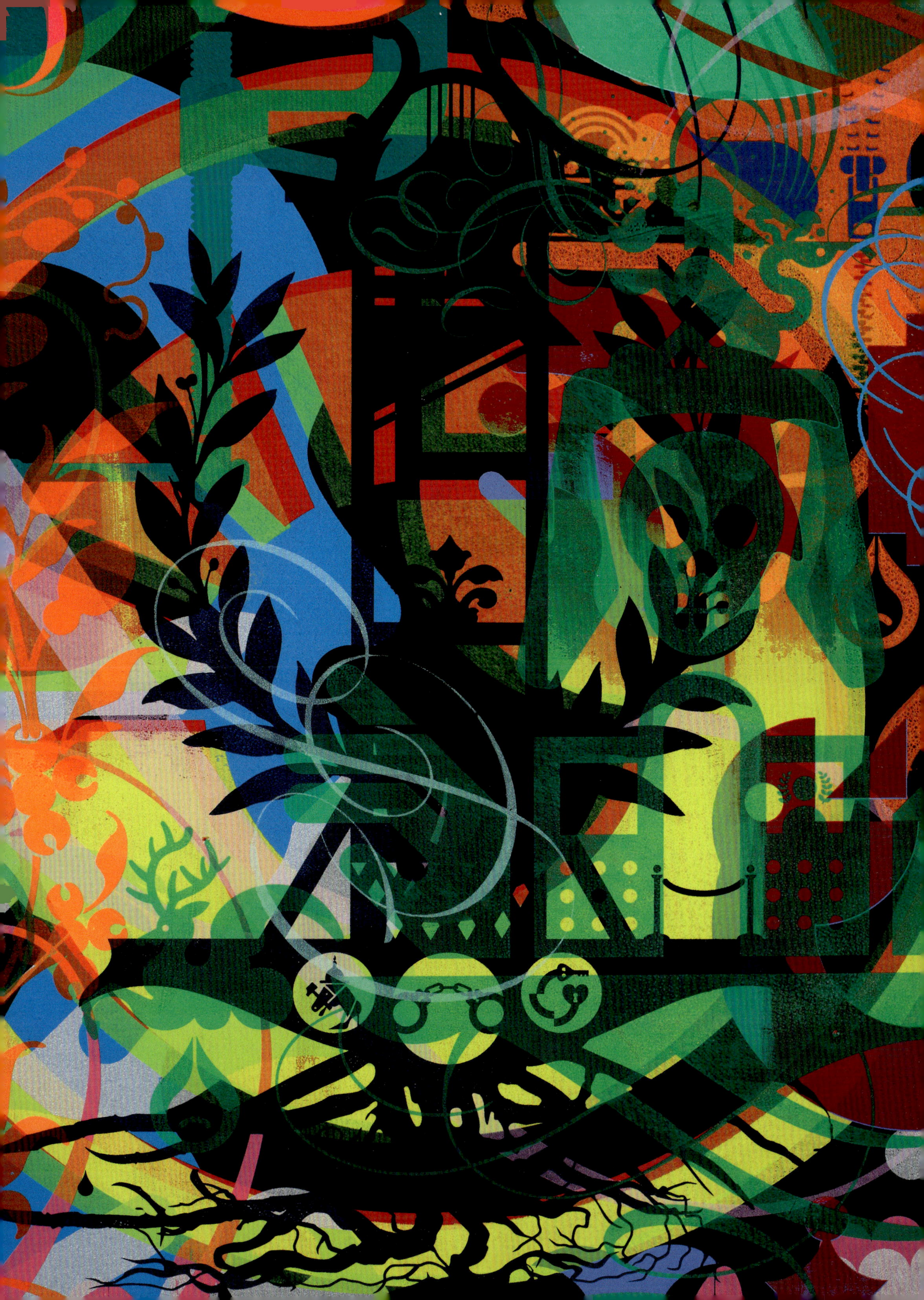

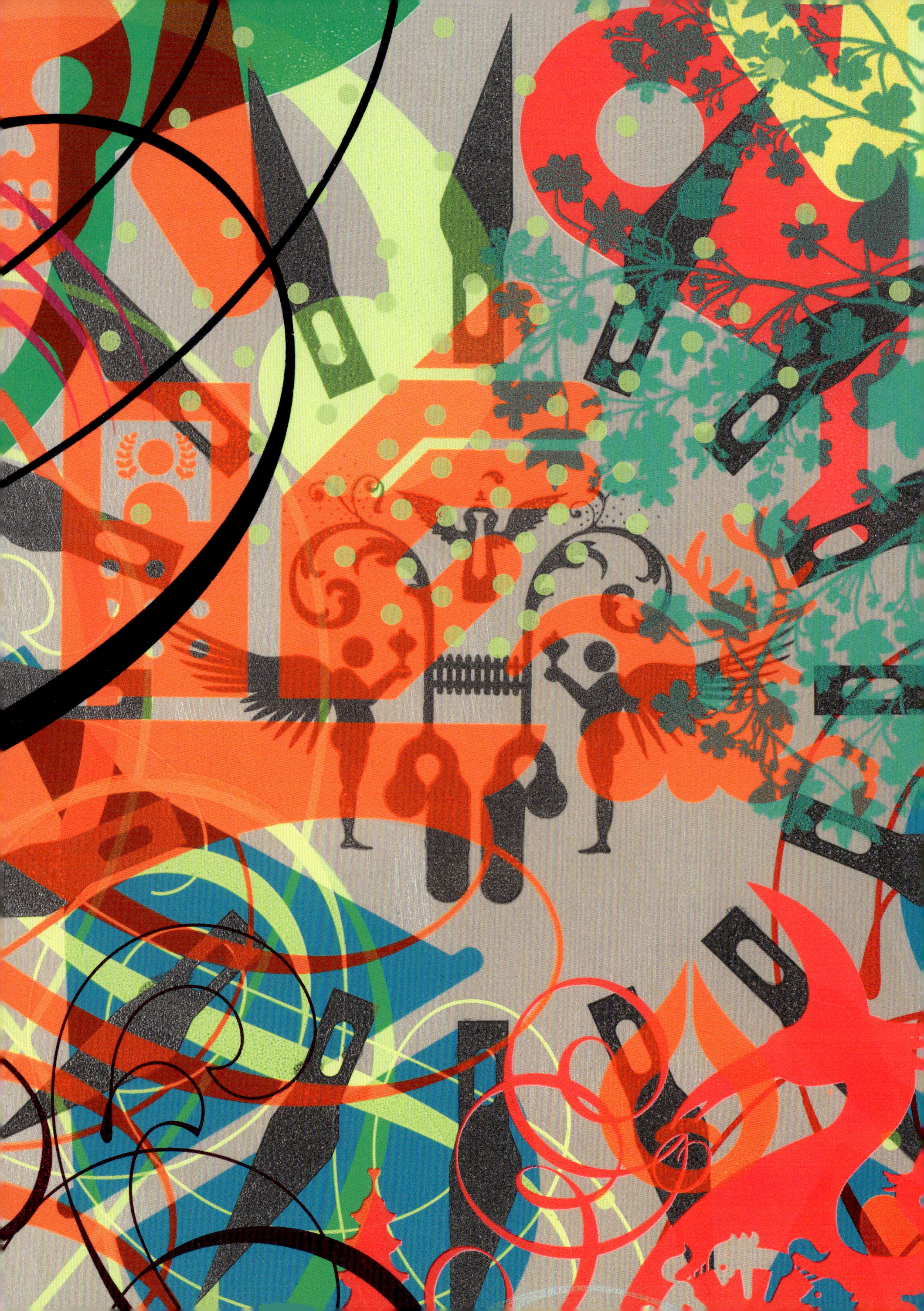

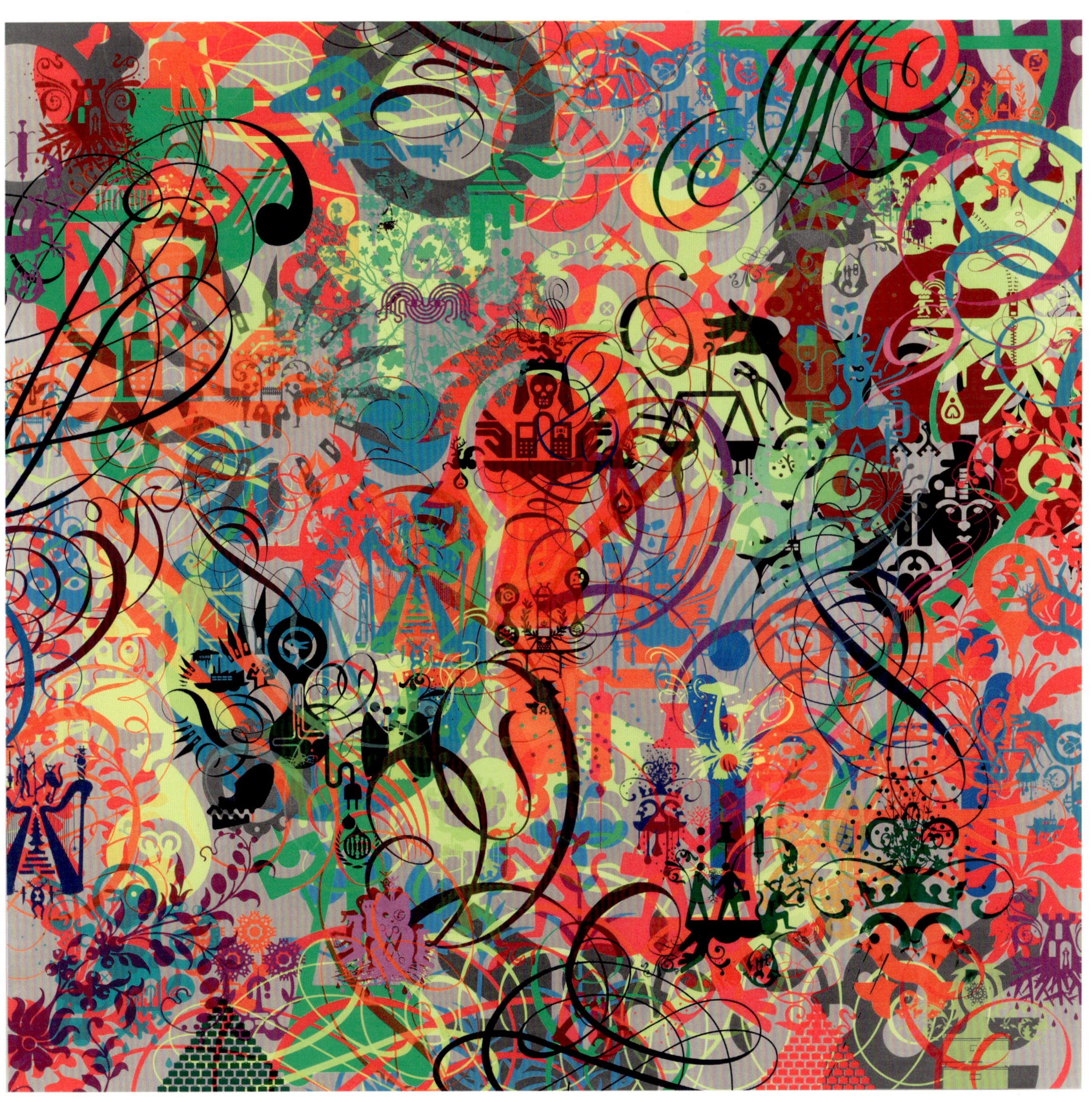

Dreamality, 2013, acrylic on wood panel, 48 x 48 in.
(121.9 x 121.9 cm); Opposite Page: Detail

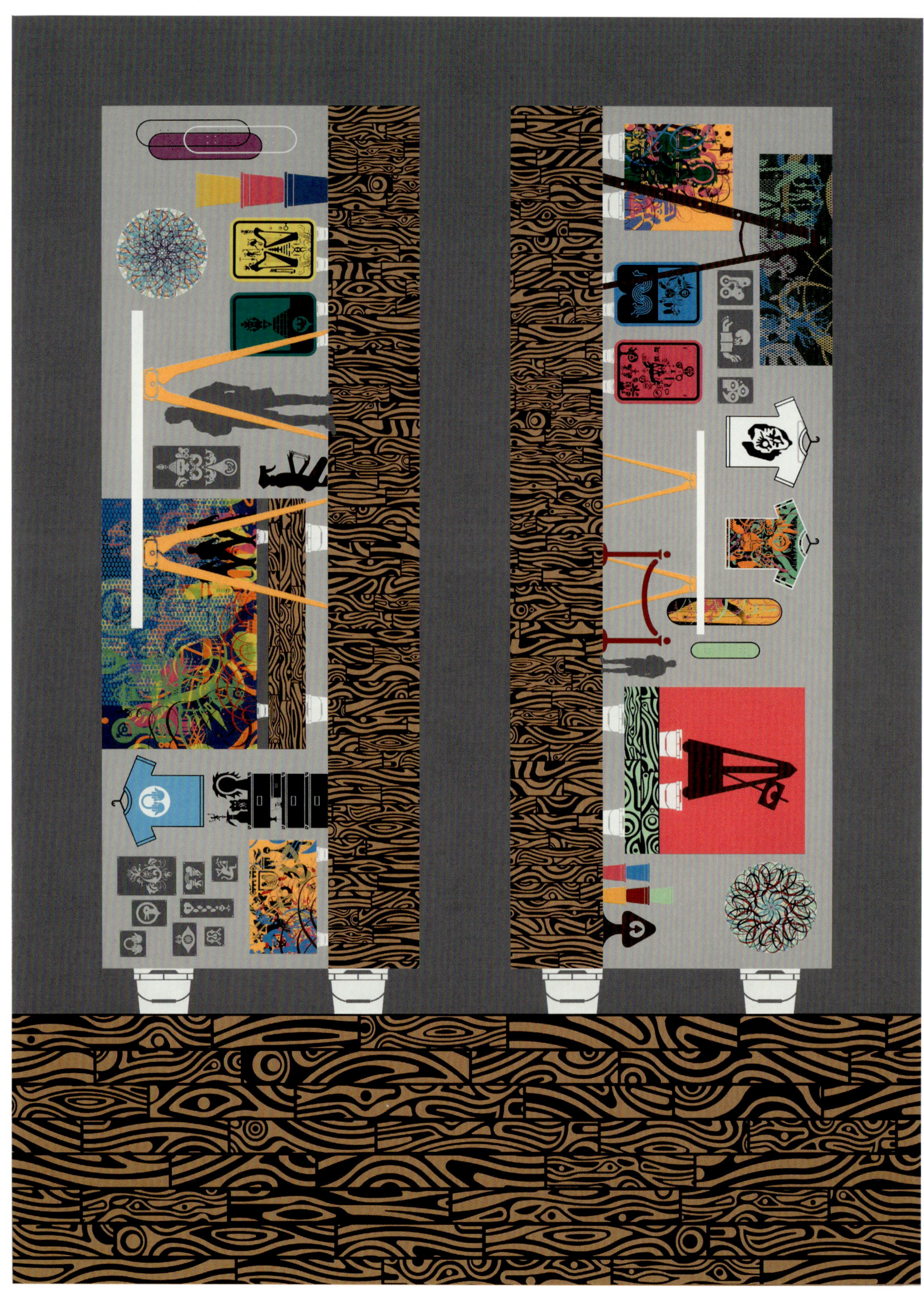

The Universe Is in Us, 2016, acrylic on linen, 84 x 60 in.
(213.4 x 152.4 cm); Opposite Page: Detail

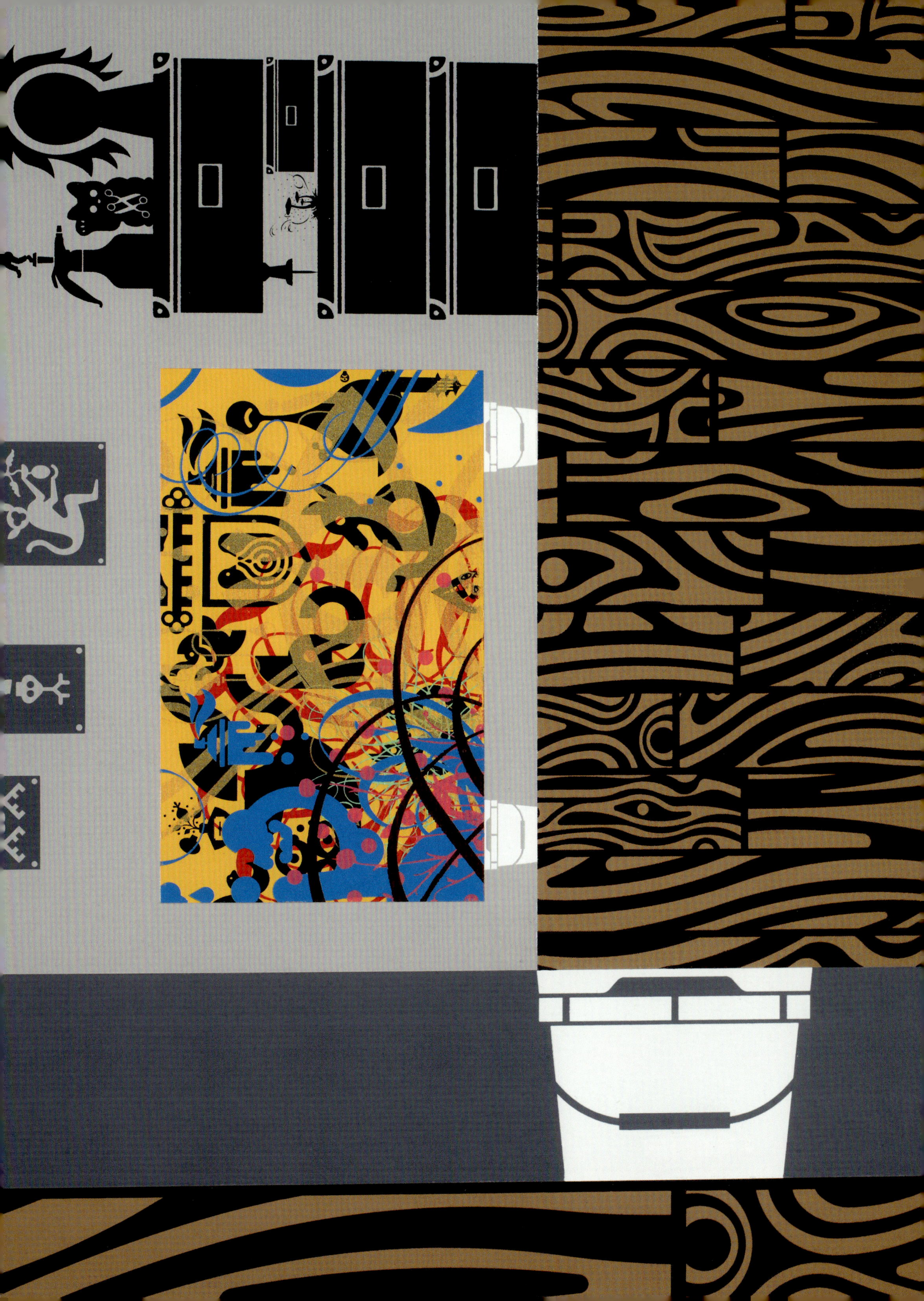

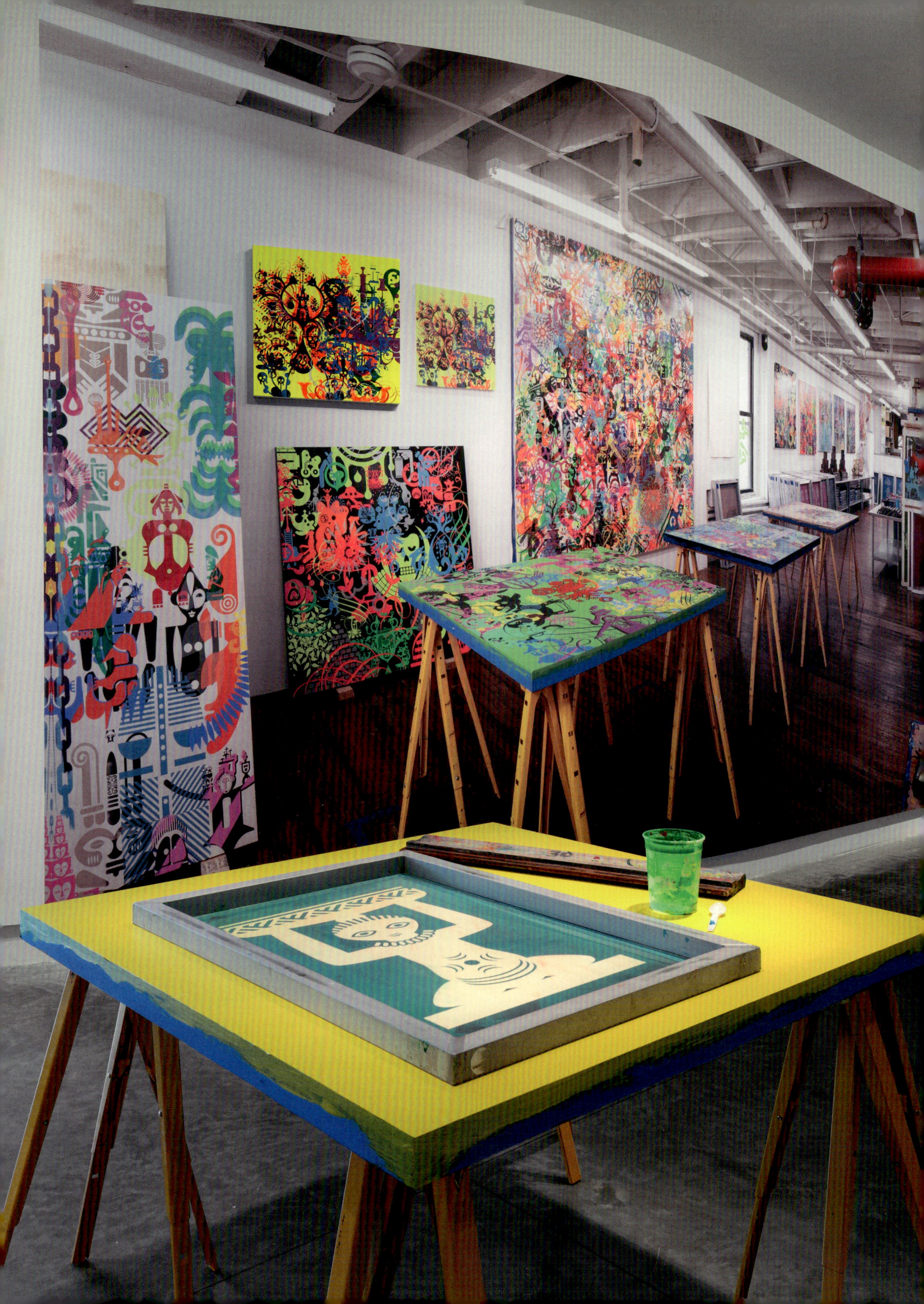

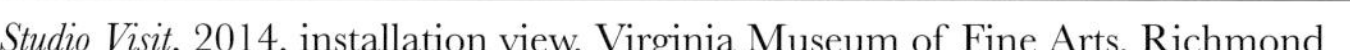

Studio Visit, 2014, installation view, Virginia Museum of Fine Arts, Richmond

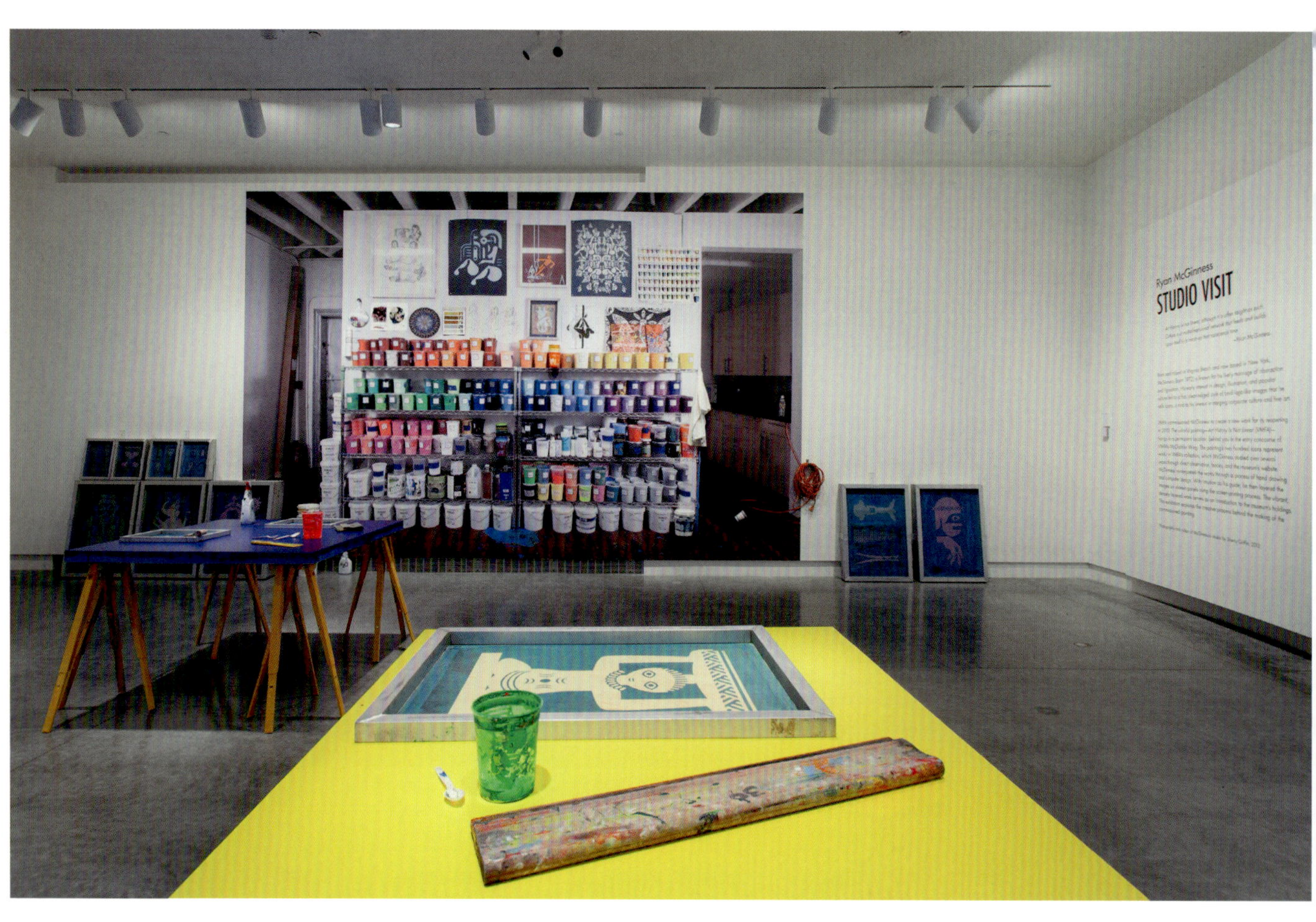

Studio Visit, 2014, installation view, Virginia Museum of Fine Arts, Richmond

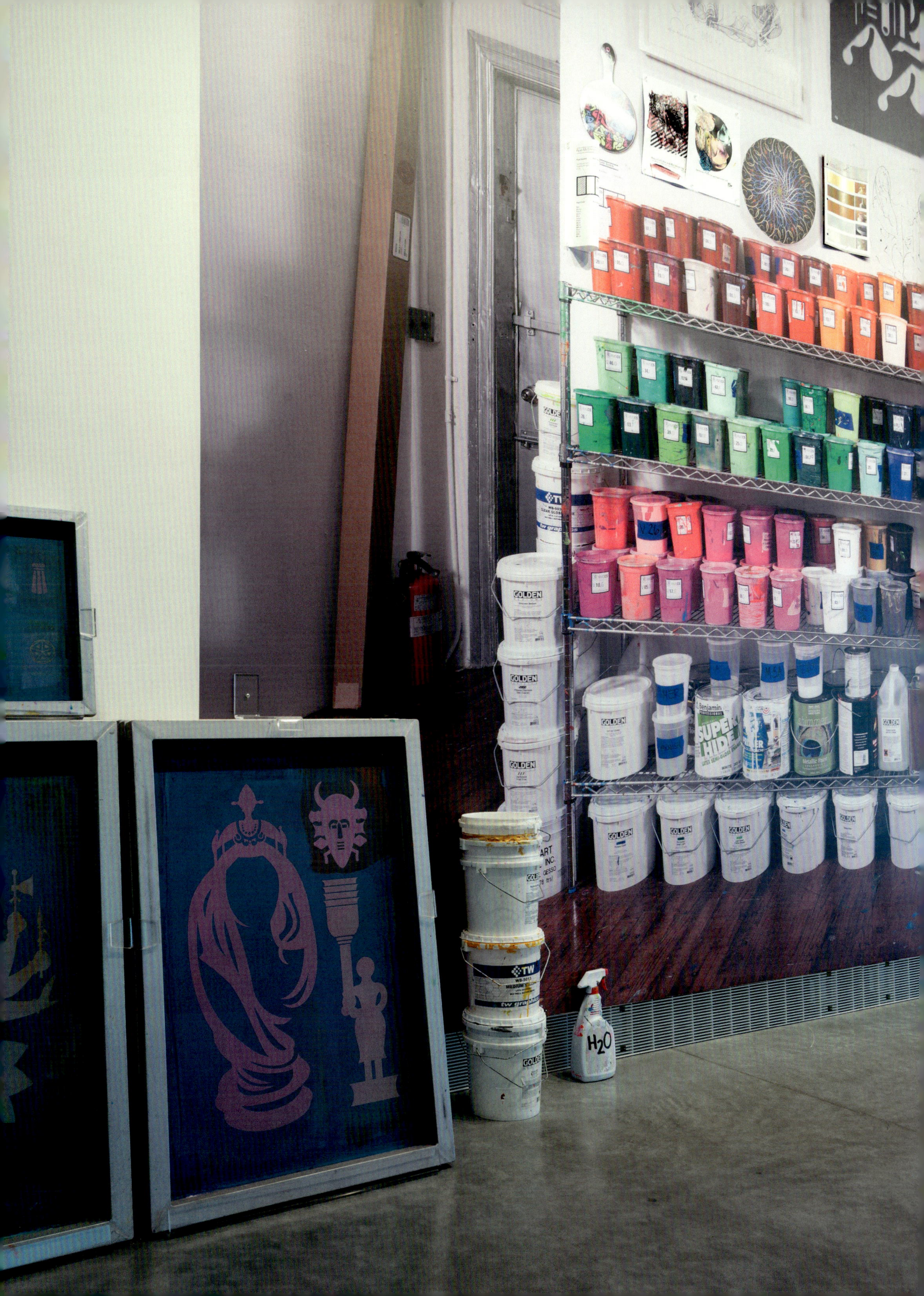

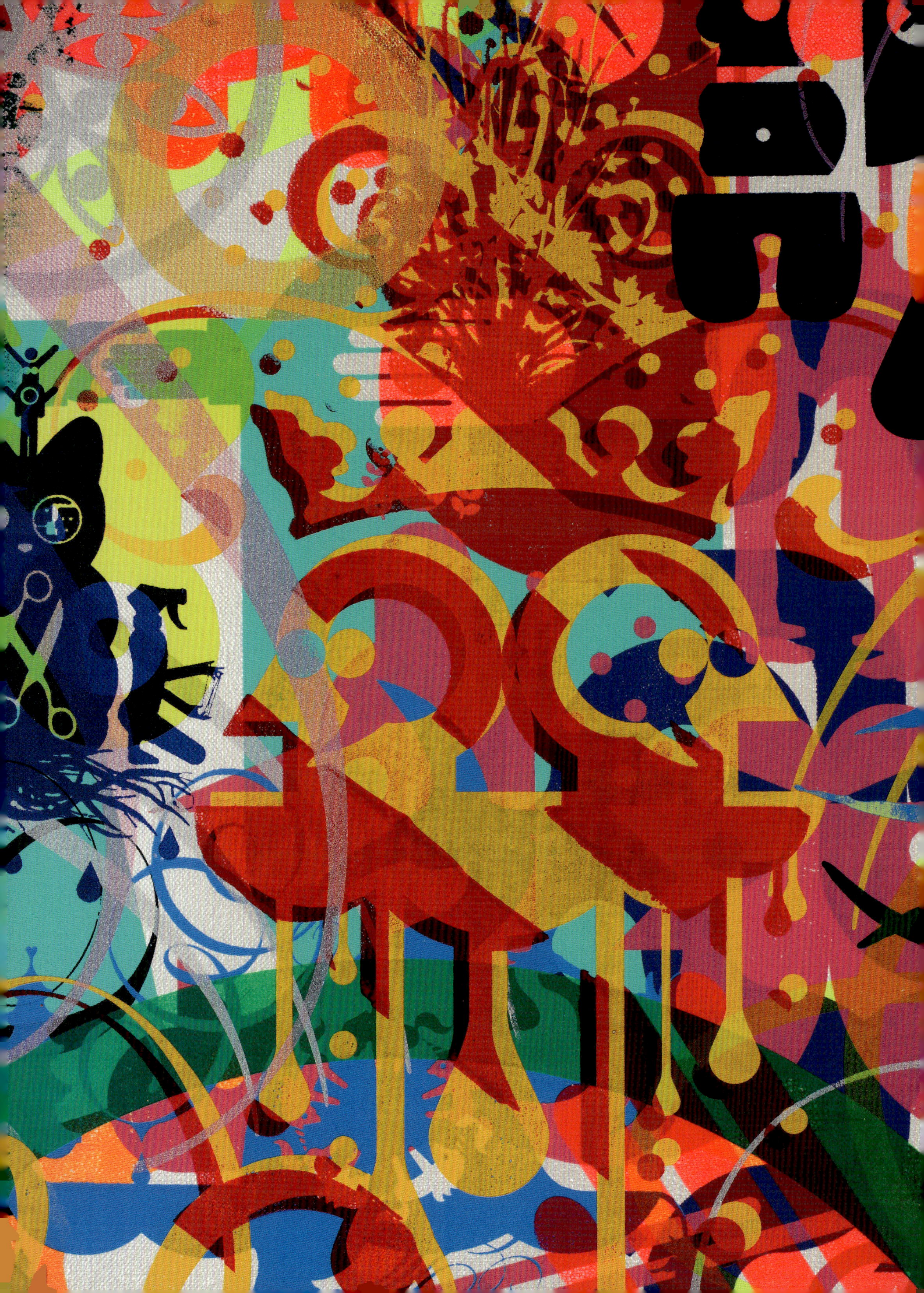

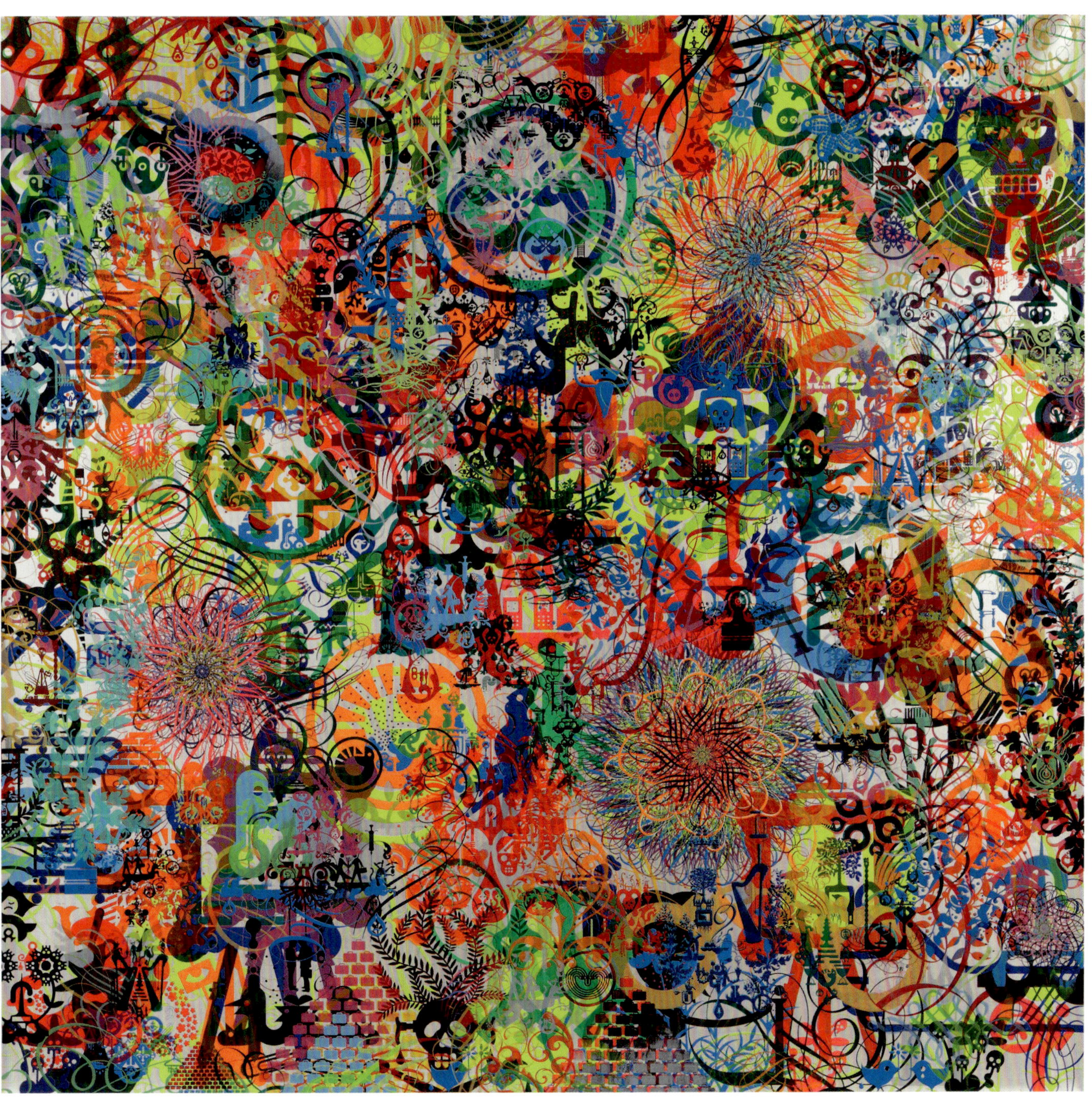

The World of You, 2015, acrylic on linen, 96 x 96 in. (243.8 x 243.8 cm); Opposite Page: Detail

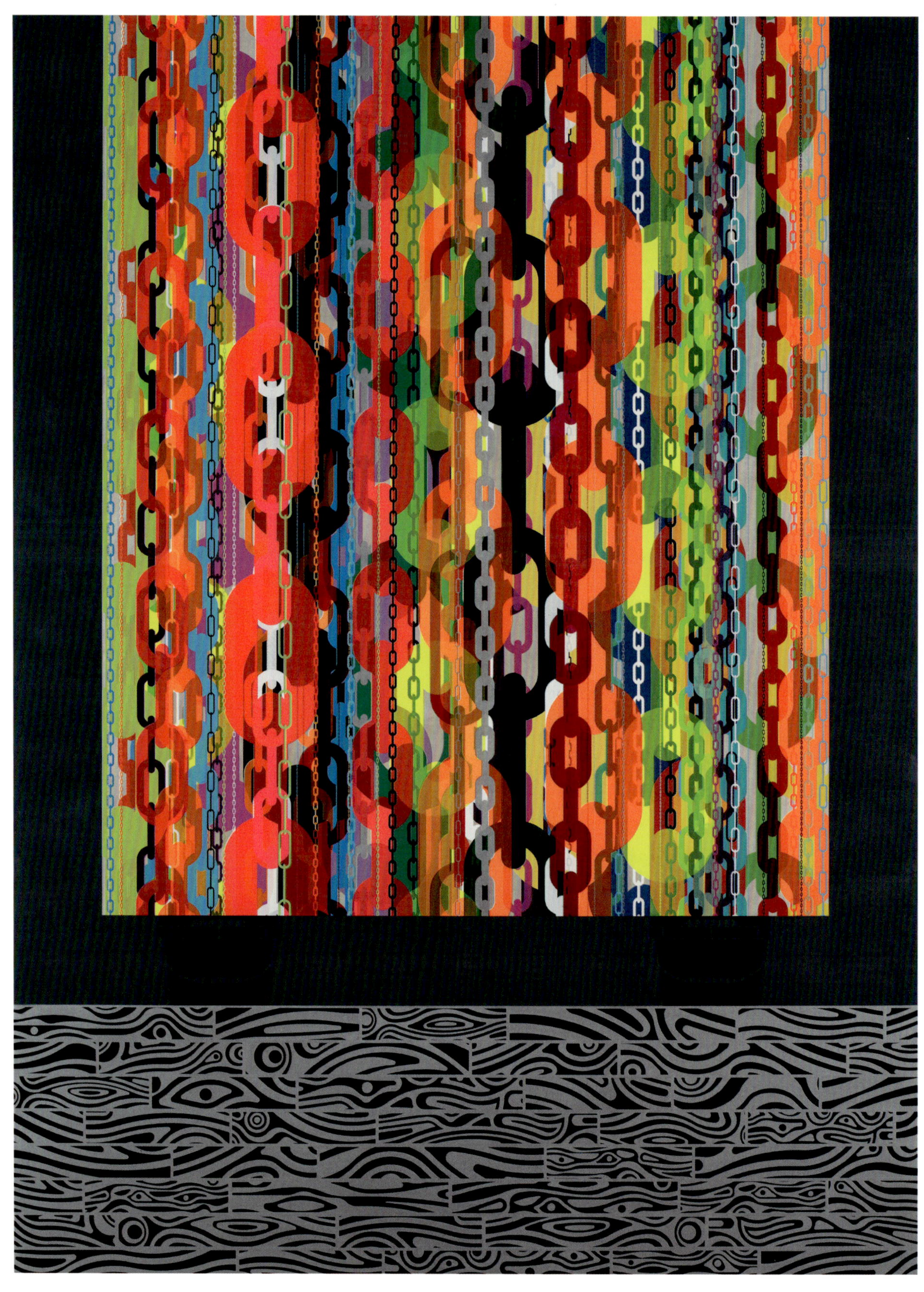

Chains Painting in Studio, 2017, acrylic on linen, 84 x 60 in.
(213.4 x 152.4 cm); Opposite Page: Detail

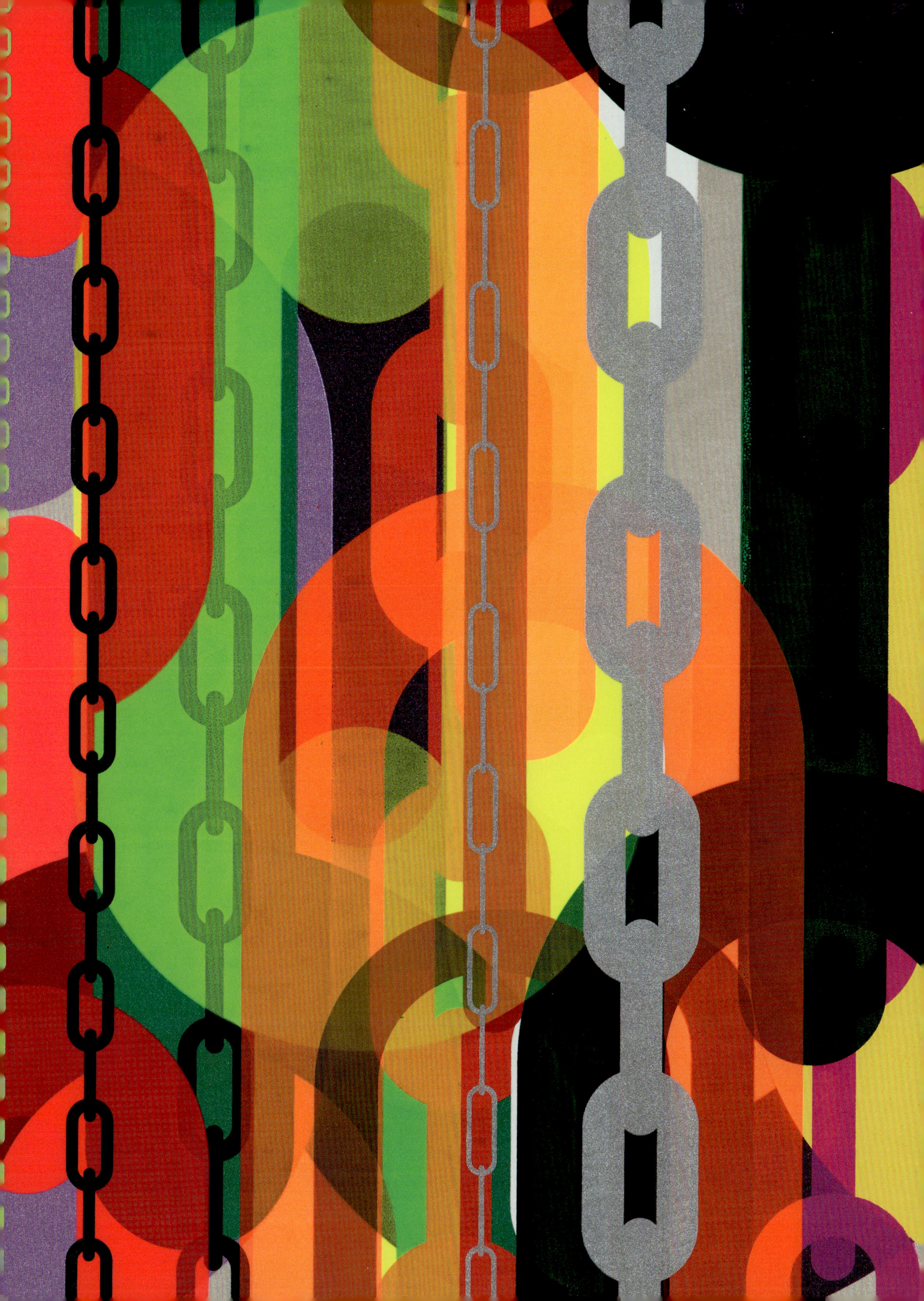

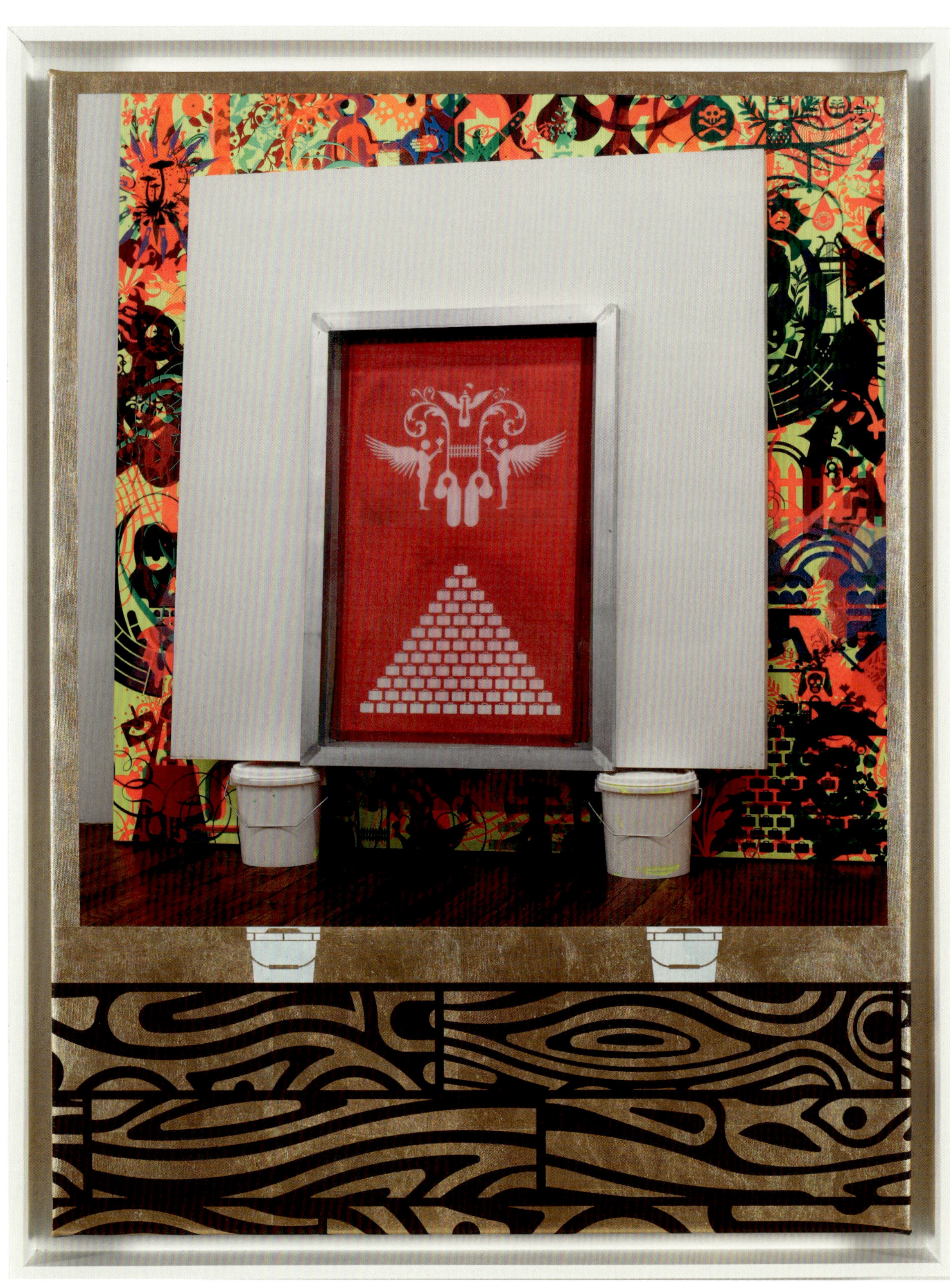

134   Untitled, 2016, acrylic, metal leaf and digital print on canvas,
30 x 22 in. (76.2 x 55.9 cm)

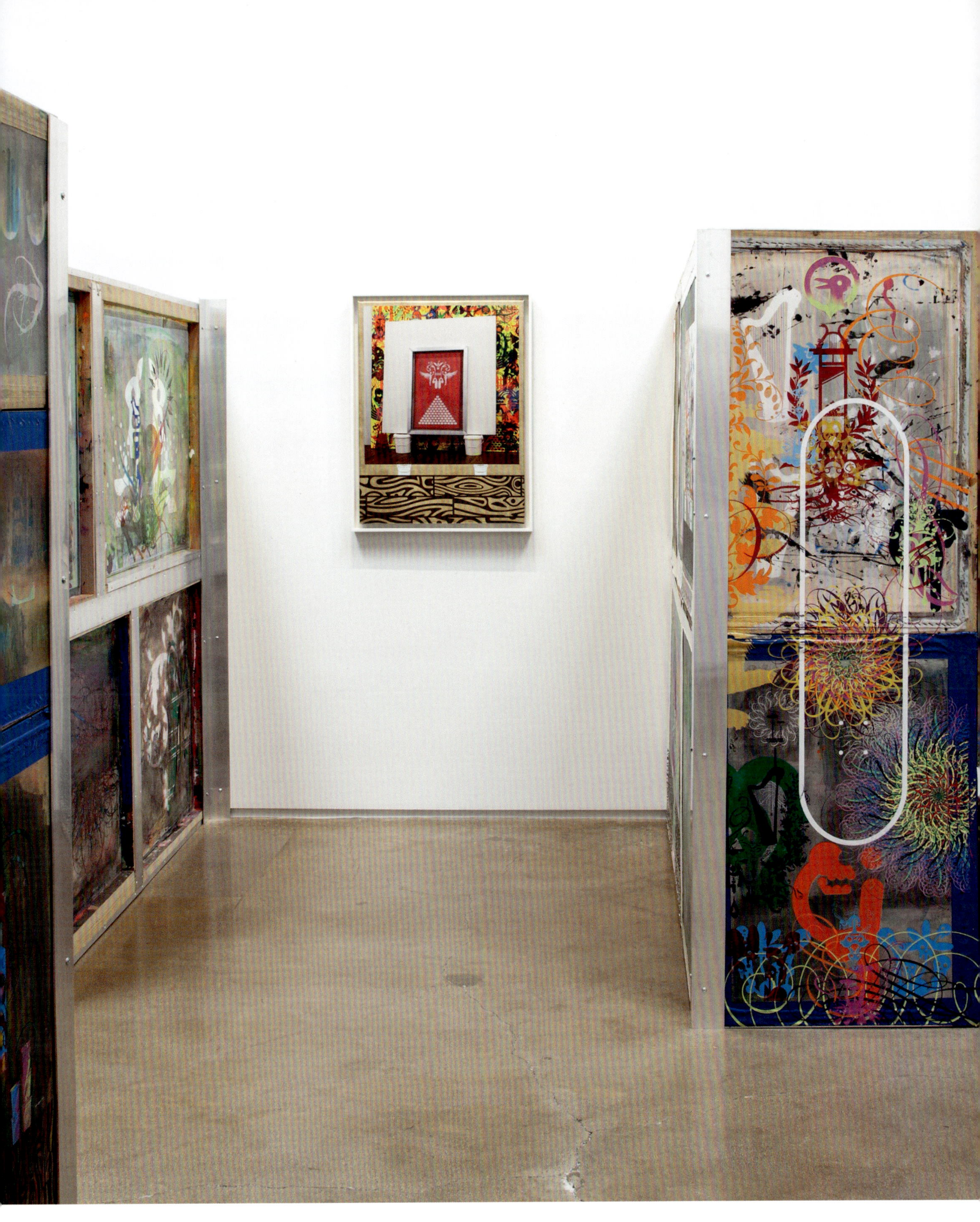

#metadata, 2016, installation view, Kohn Gallery, Los Angeles

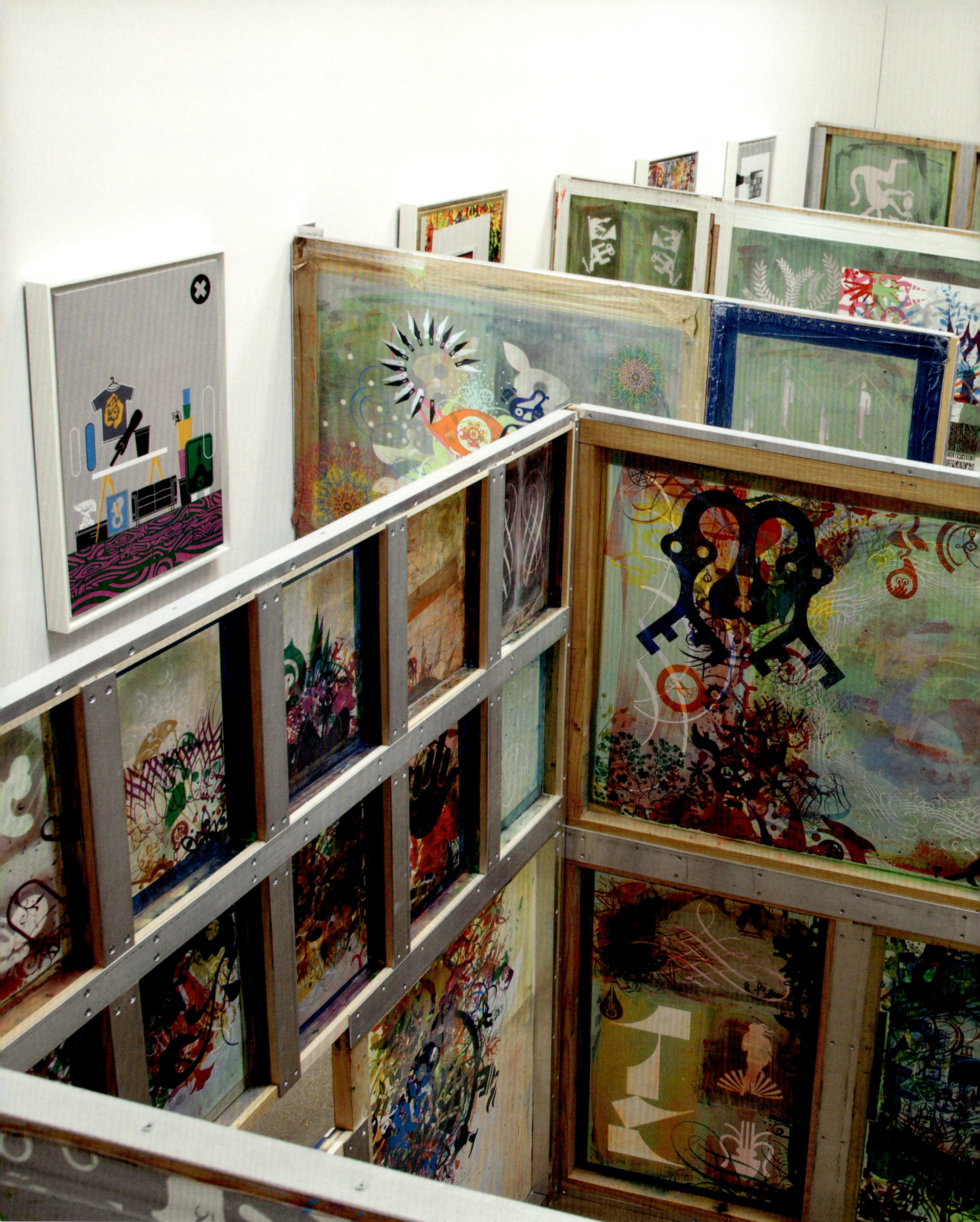

#metadata, 2016, installation view, Kohn Gallery, Los Angeles

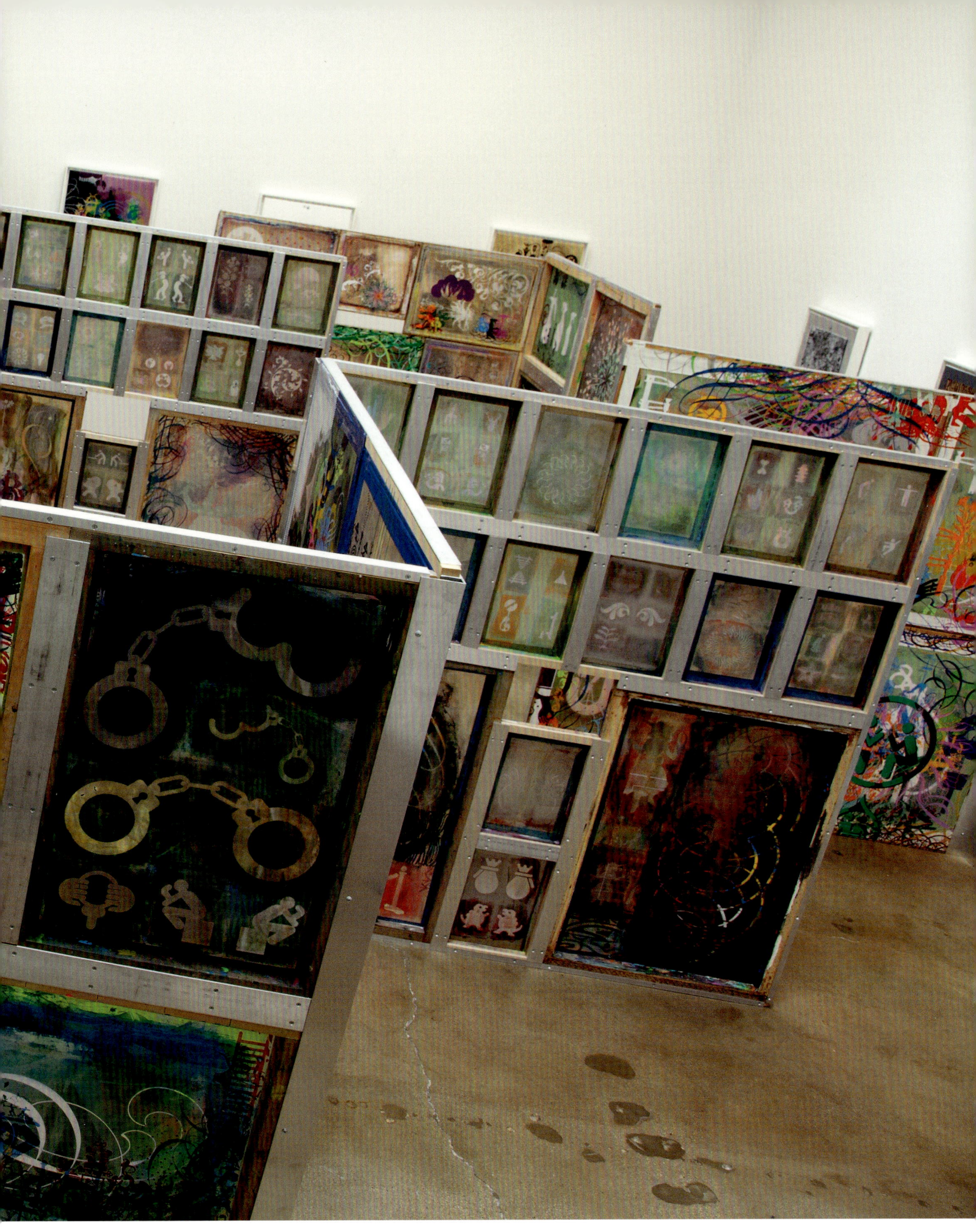

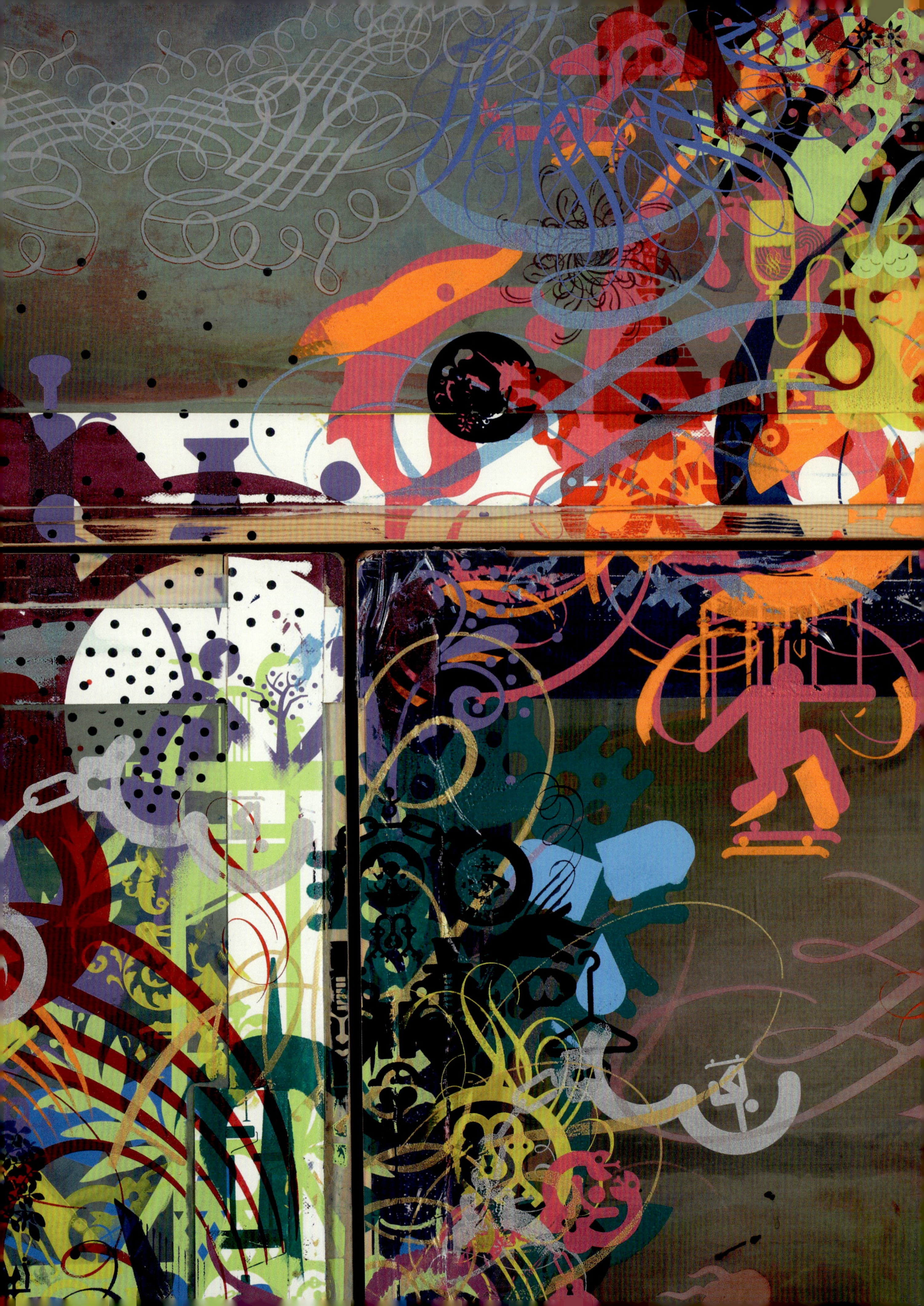

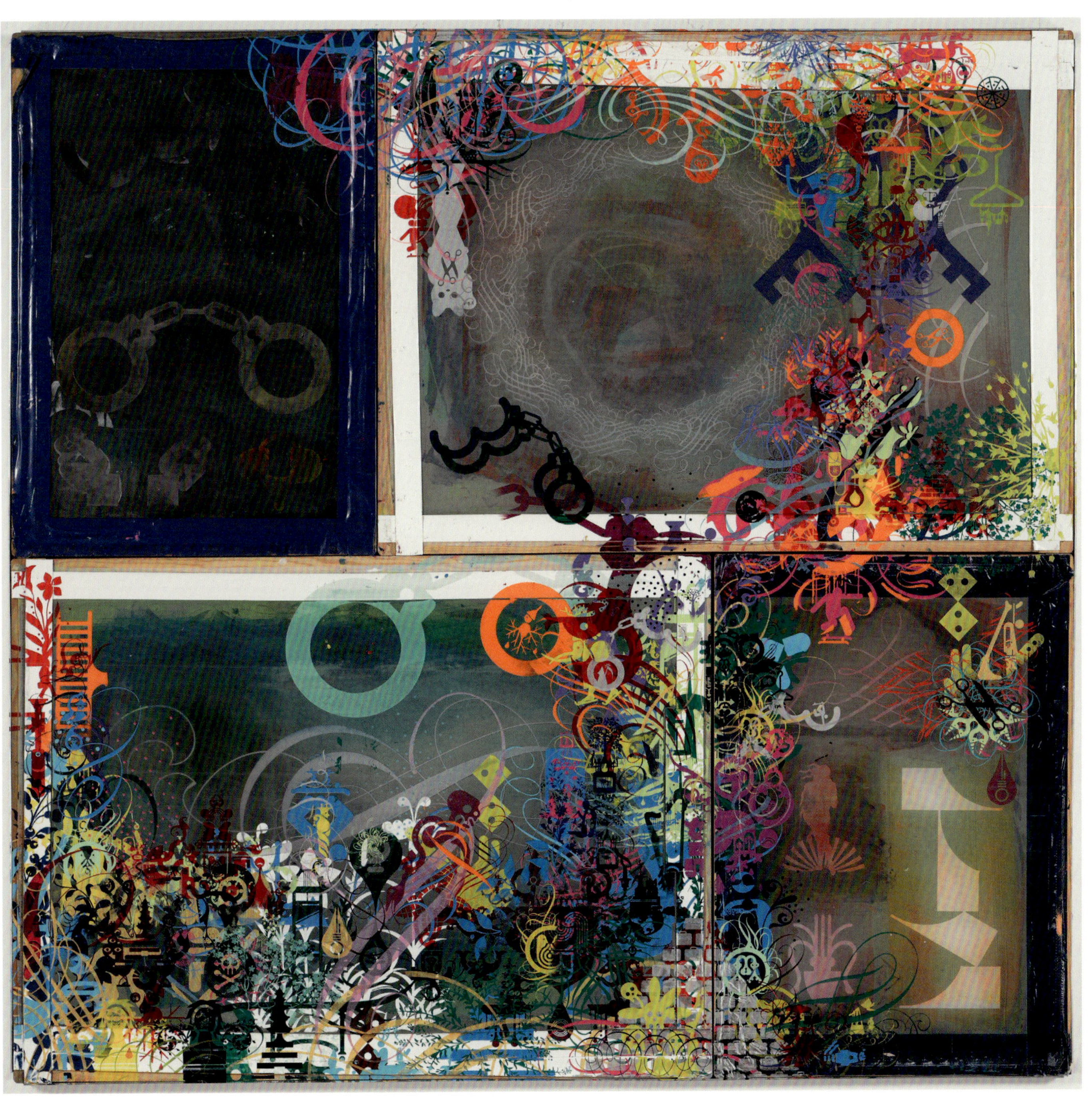

Screen Combine #22, 2016, acrylic and photo emulsion on polyester monofilament screens with polyurethane adhesive and polyethylene tape attached to wood frames with aluminum hardware, 72 x 73.25 in. (182.9 x 186.1 cm); Opposite Page: Detail

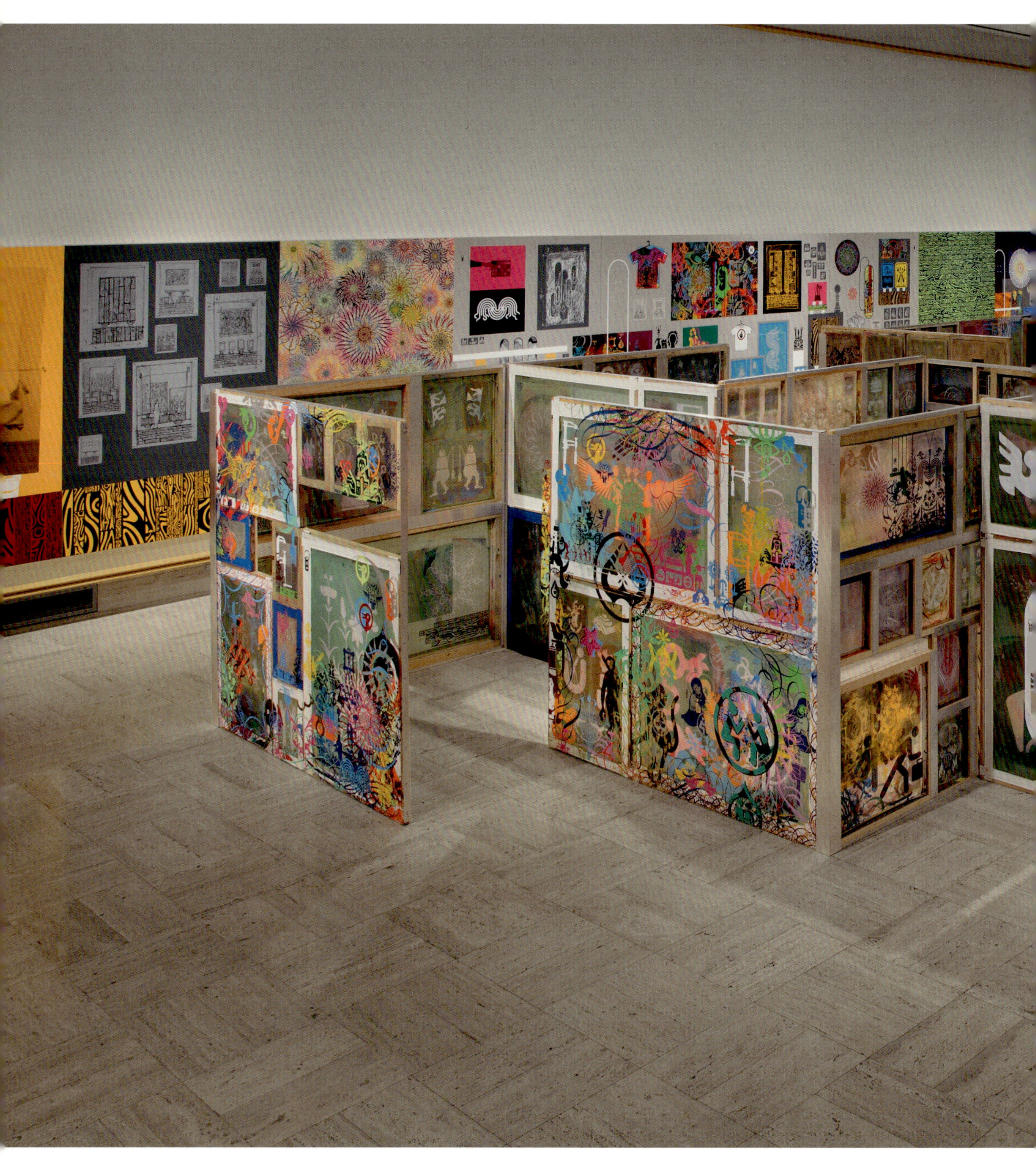

 Studio Views, 2017, installation view, Cranbrook Art Museum, Bloomfield Hills, MI

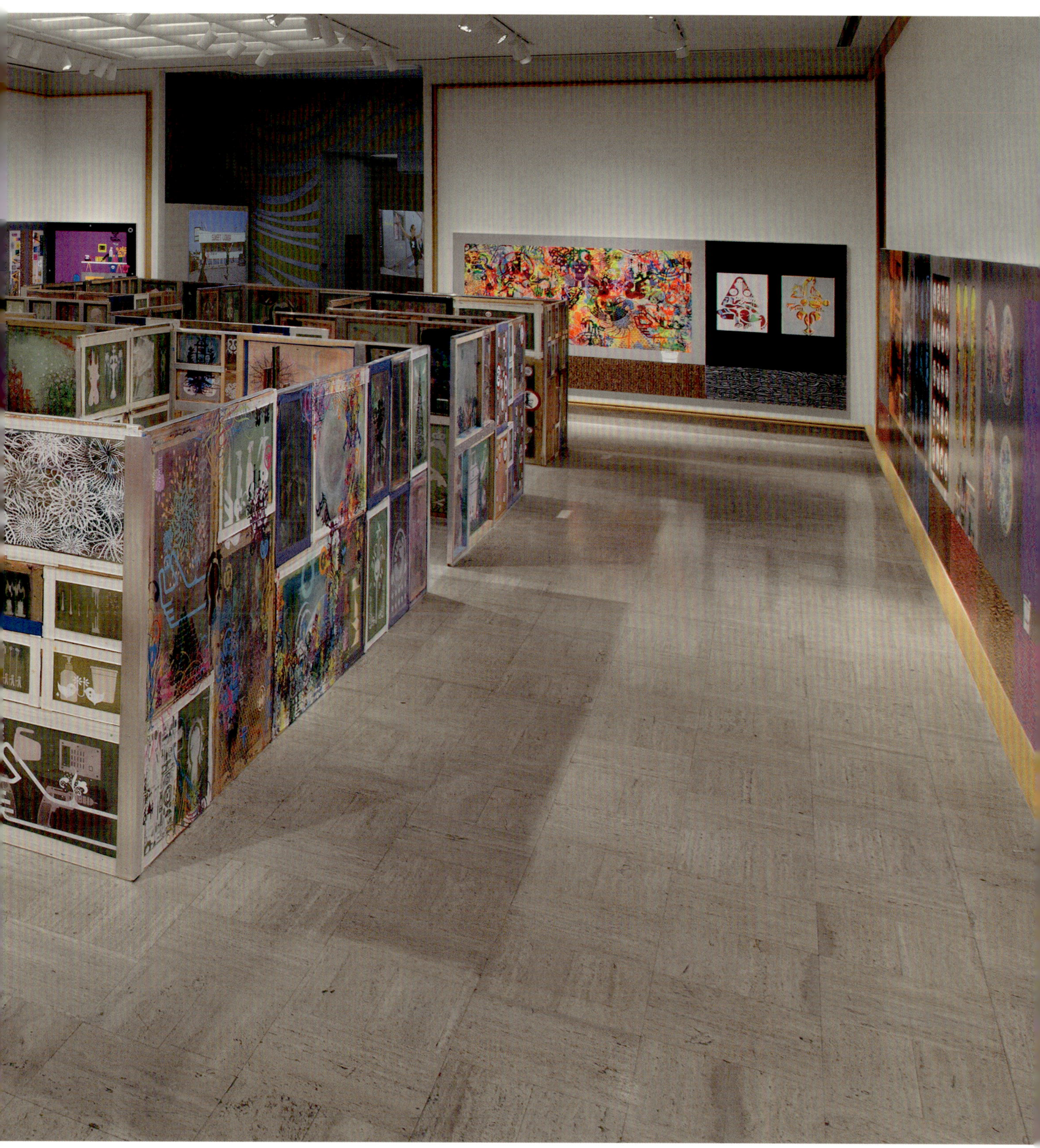

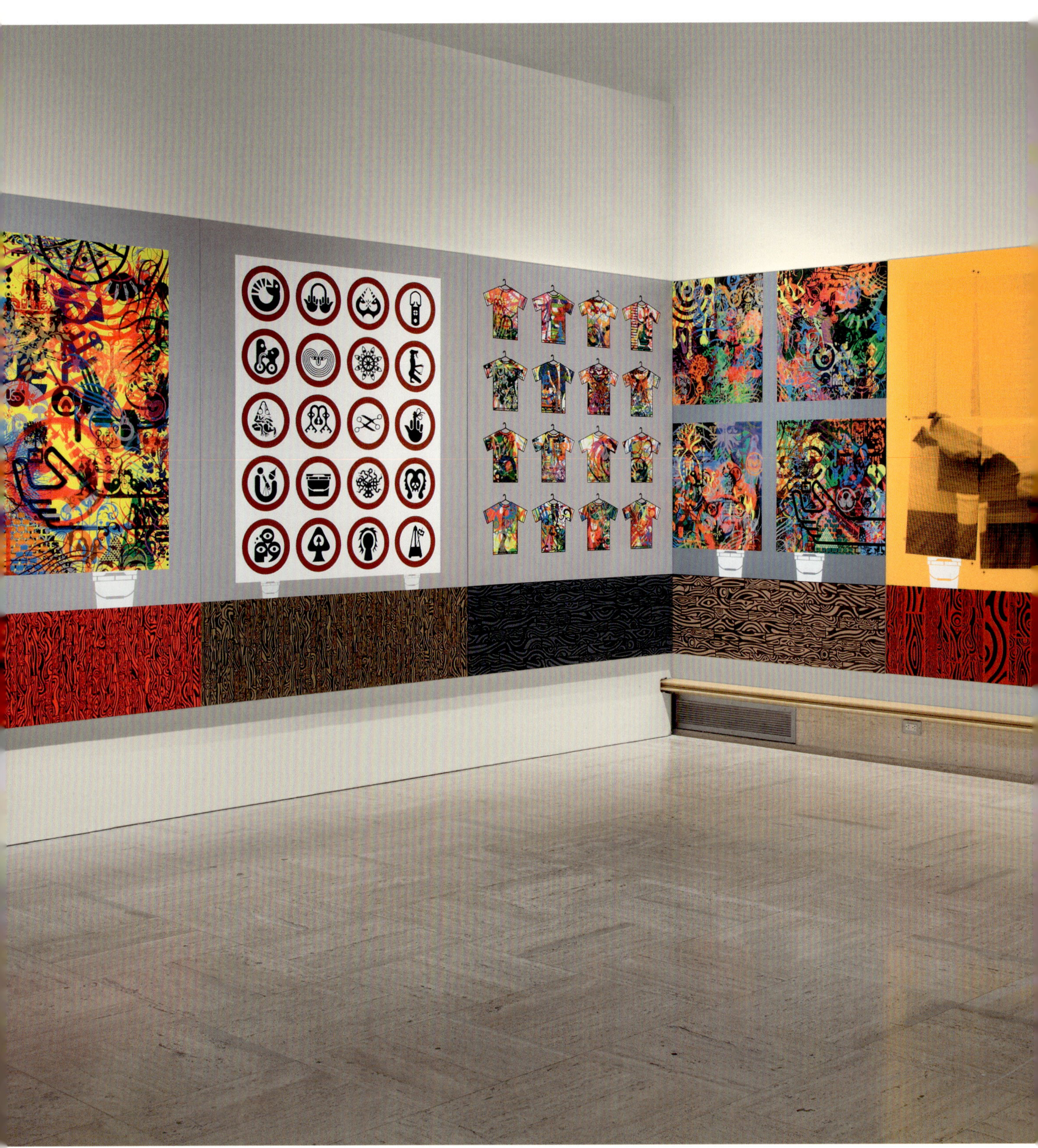

Studio Views, 2017, installation view, Cranbrook Art Museum, Bloomfield Hills, MI

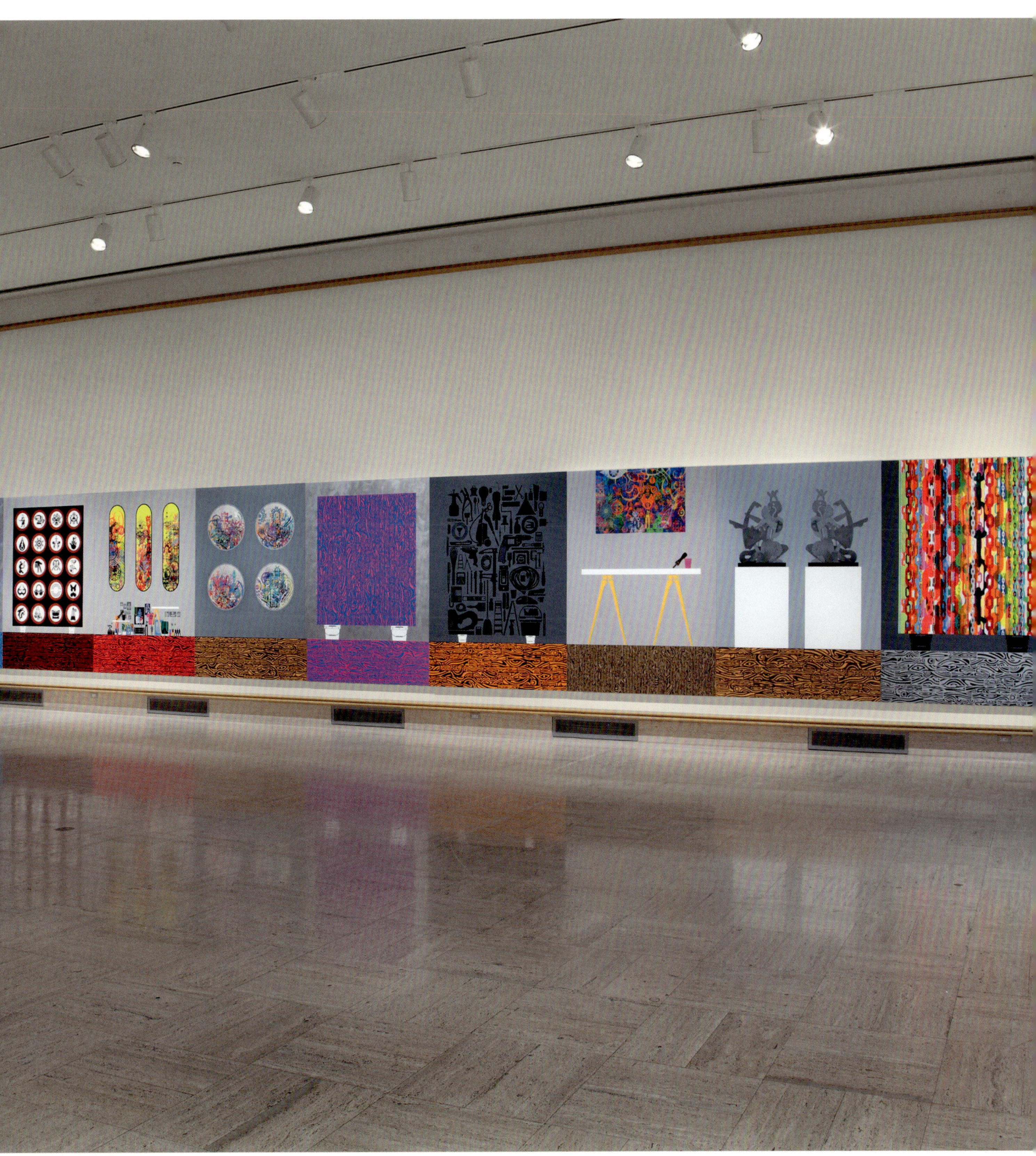

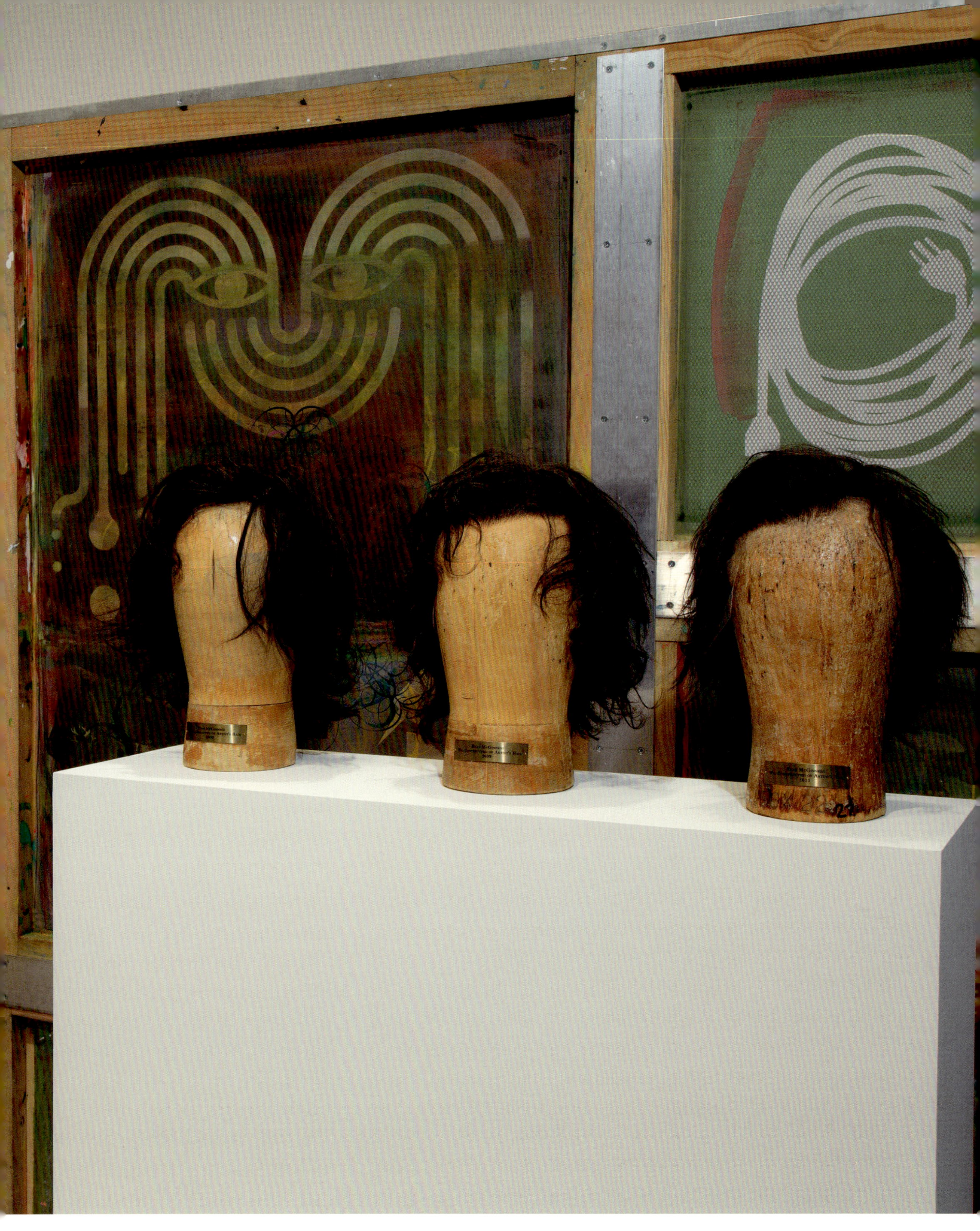

Studio Views, 2017, installation view, Cranbrook Art Museum, Bloomfield Hills, MI

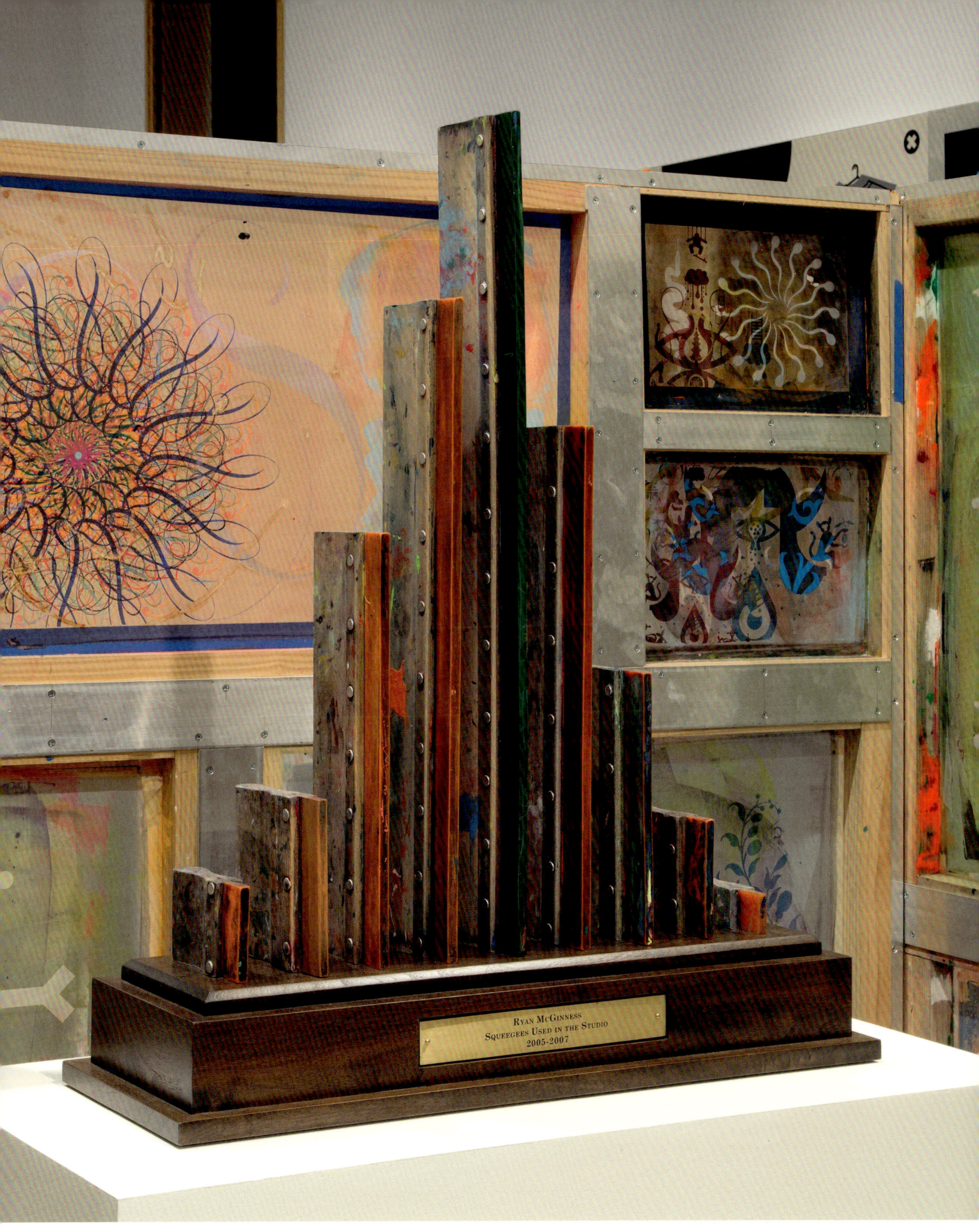

RYAN McGINNESS
SQUEEGEES USED IN THE STUDIO
2005-2007

Chronology

1972

Born Ryan Joseph McGinness on January 9 at 8:02 PM at Virginia Beach General Hospital, Virginia Beach, VA, to Robert and Evelyn McGinness. Robert is a 25-year old computer systems analyst, and Evelyn is a 24-year old dental hygienist who retires to raise her son full-time. She crafts most of her son's toys throughout his childhood. Robert is a surfer, and since the young family is short on furniture, his surfboard also serves as their kitchen table.

1973-1977

The family moves to New Hampshire for Robert's work and for him to attend classes at night. Sister Molly Elizabeth McGinness is born October 2, 1973. The family then moves to Reston, VA, for another job transfer. They remain in Reston, VA, for 3 years where the young McGinness creates a lab in their garage where he spends hours tinkering and paints with his mother on large pieces of cardboard and on the asphalt with buckets of water. "…I can remember pre-school, I guess being very young and being very excited about workshops I had set up for myself… I always liked the idea of a mad scientist laboratory environment, so I had fake tubes made of play-doh going from container to container and fake computer consoles made from cardboard boxes that I had made to look like complicated machines superheroes had." *(Fowler, Brendan. "Interview." Luxurygood, Alife, USA, 2000, pp. 13-18)* The family attends the United States Bicentennial celebration in Washington, DC, in the summer of 1976. In 1977, they move back to New Hampshire for 6 months in order for Robert to complete his MBA. Fondly remembering Virginia Beach and recognizing its good public school system, they move back there and remain where McGinness is raised and attends school, kindergarten through high school.

1977-1984 (Elementary School)

Attends John B. Dey Elementary School, entering kindergarten in 1977. His kindergarten teacher reports, "Ryan is a very good student. His work is very neat and he is a hard worker." Grows up riding dirt bikes, skateboarding, sailing, fishing, playing soccer, in scouts, and going to the beach. Family buys a sailboat and goes sailing on the weekends. Draws on computer paper father brings home from work and builds constructions from computer punch cards. "My mom was a very creative spirit. She was always making things. She was the kind of mother we would give a jigsaw to on Mother's Day, and she'd love it. So we always had activity areas around the house and piles of things in progress. This is actually how my studio is set up today." *(Lecture and Interview with Hugh Davies at the Museum of Contemporary Art San Diego, September 13, 2012)* Is accepted to the Old Donation Center for the Gifted and Talented in Virginia Beach, where art is taught all day one day each week through disciplined lessons. Paints over-sized recreations of masterpieces for the school's cafeteria, including Andy Warhol's Campbell's Soup Cans, Andrew Wyeth's Christina's World, and Picasso's Guernica. "…the program also instilled a very serious, almost intimidating attitude toward art." *Nakamura, Eric. "Ryan's Hope." Giant Robot, USA, Issue 36, 2005, pp. 36-41, 82)* "I sold my first painting when I was in sixth grade. I sold it for $40. An art teacher bought it." *(Wolfe, Duncan. "Ryan McGinness." Human Being Journal, Issue No. 4, Spring 2014, pp. 58-67)* Attends Virginia Beach Boardwalk Art Shows with parents every year and visits the Virginia Museum of Fine Art on school field trips. "When I was in grade school, I was in the mall with some friends. I saw a 'No Farting' button comprised of a buttocks icon, a cartoonish 'poof' symbol, and a universal standard 'no' red diagonal. I thought it was the coolest thing I had ever seen. This is one of my first memories of recognizing and understanding subversion and parody within a situationist product. Needless to say, that moment has informed what I am trying to do in my work today." *(Greenwood, Tom. "The Q&A 500." Ryan McGinness Works., Rizzoli International Publications, Inc., USA,*

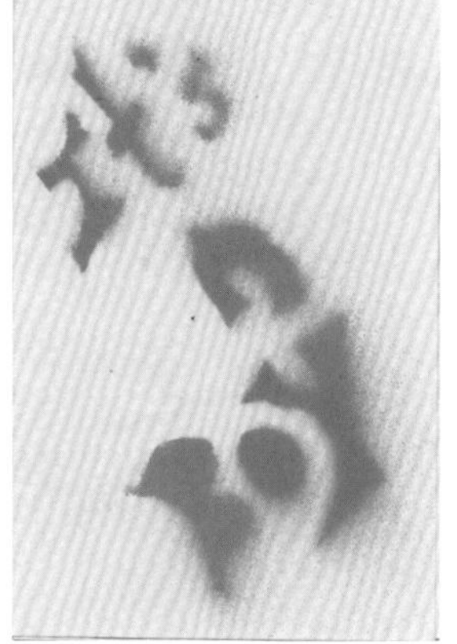
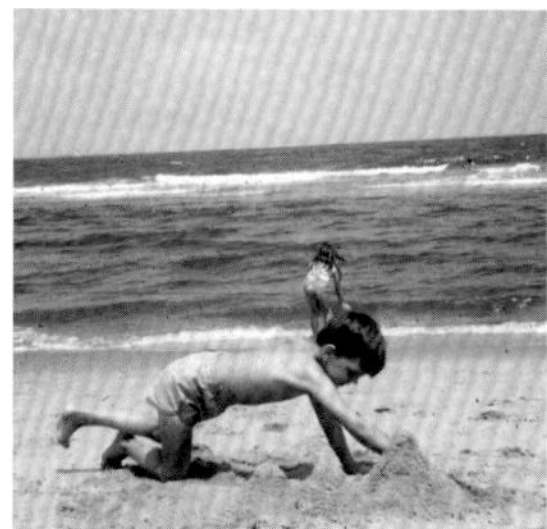

Left: Birth Announcement, 1972, stenciled spray paint by mother, Evelyn McGinness; Right: McGinness and sister in Virginia Beach

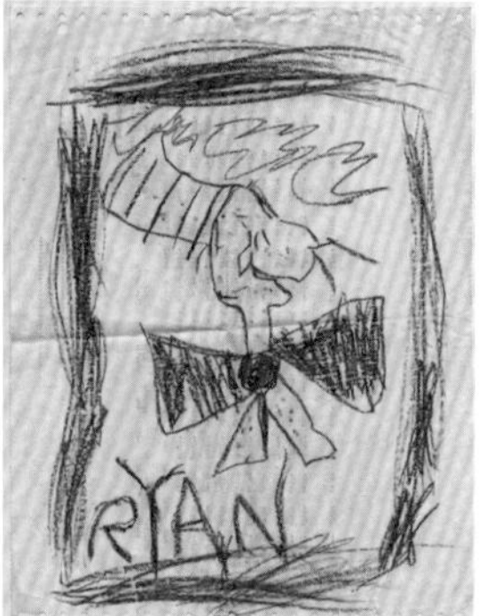

Left: Early childhood drawing of The Cat in The Hat, 1976, crayon on computer paper; Right: Kindergarten report card, 1978

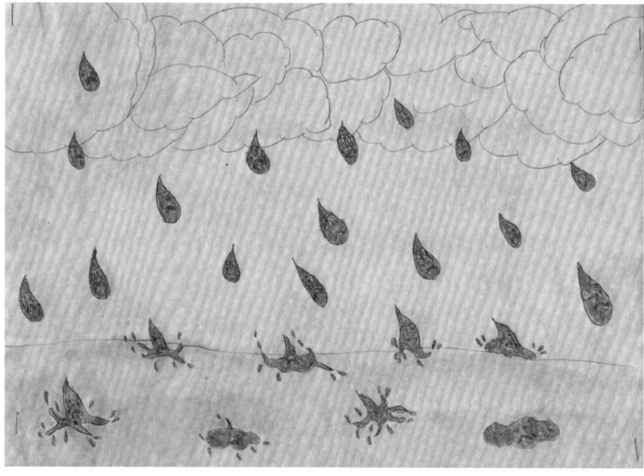

Childhood drawing of anthropomorphised raindrops, c. 1979

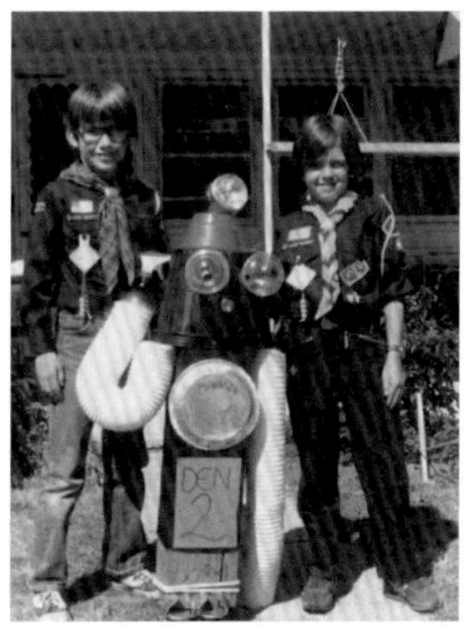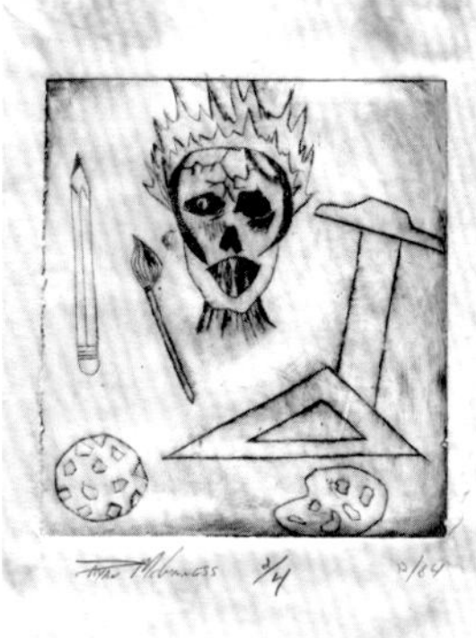

Left: Cub Scouts, c. 1980
Right: Untitled, 1984, etching, ed. 2 of 4

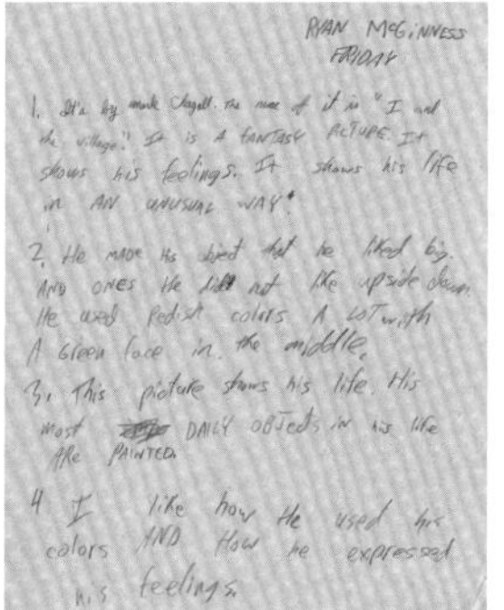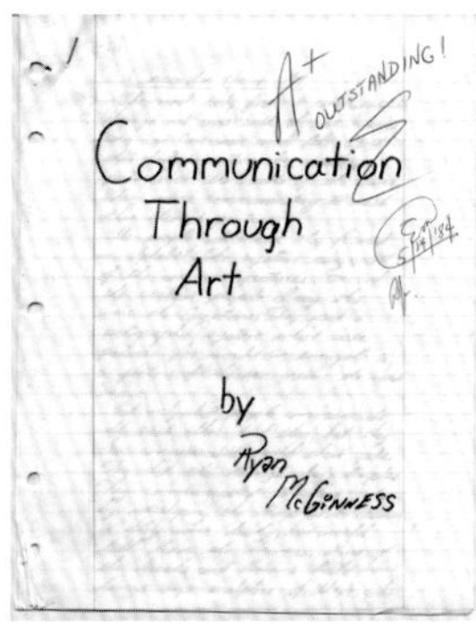

Left: School test answers on Marc Chagall's *I and the Village*, 1983
Right: Cover page for elementary school essay, 1984

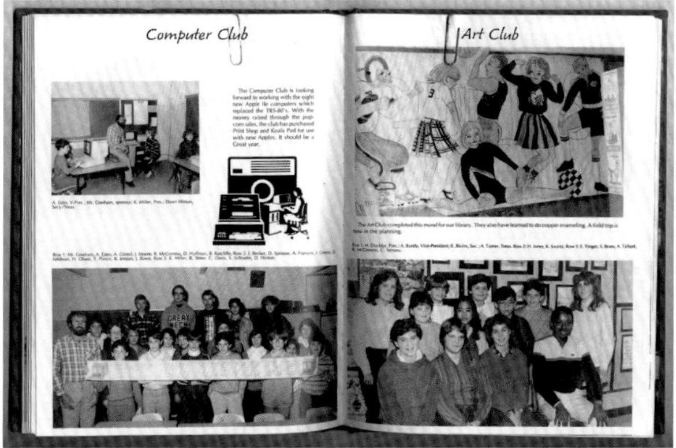

Spread from junior high school yearbook showing McGinness
as a member of both the Computer Club and Art Club, 1985,
Great Neck Junior High School, Virginia Beach, VA

2009, pp. 281-290) Plays community soccer every spring and fall season and is offered a position on the travel league team, representing his city. Plays center forward. By the end of elementary school, travels up and down the East Coast every weekend for soccer. Family sells sailboat. Skates the asphalt Thunder Bowl and the concrete Pipeline at Mt. Trashmore. "This was just as wide plywood boards were starting to be used, and I only had a small wimpy Hobie fiberglass board with deteriorating strips of grip tape. I must have been 10 or 11 years old and apprehensively made my way to the top of the run to wait behind the intimidating big teenagers with their cool gear. They looked at my condition and allowed me to go before all of them while giving me words of encouragement. This small gesture resonated with me for years. It demonstrated the true nature of skateboarding at the time. While it was an individualistic pursuit, we were all in it together regardless of socio-economic background or even ability. All you had to do is show up." *(Stochl, Gerhard. "Talking Skateboarding, Instagram, and Glow-in-the-Dark Art with Ryan McGinness." www.thecreatorsproject.vice.com (July 17, 2015))*

1984-1986 (Junior High School)
Attends Great Neck Junior High School. Continues to play soccer throughout the year, including indoor soccer during the winters. Babysits, mows lawns, and does yard work for neighbors to earn money. Develops interest in computers and learning code. Family buys an Apple IIe in 1984. Buys computer games at the mall, hacks them with personalized messages, and returns them to store repeatedly. Is active in student government and is a member of the National Honor Society, Computer Club, Art Club, and Debate Team. Attends a student government leadership workshop and debate camp during the summers. Continues with Old Donation art program after school and attends private art lessons on Saturday mornings. Reports on local skate contests with photos and articles for skate zines. Attends, most notably, the National Skate Association contest at Mt. Trashmore in June 1986. Continues skateboarding, building ramps, painting skateboard decks, and stenciling t-shirts for friends. "I think my interest in [symbols] comes from growing up in Virginia Beach, which had a surf and skate culture obsessed with branding and saturated with a cult of cool. At an early age, I recognized that the power of a logo—the right kind of logo—can change the value of an otherwise ordinary object like a surfboard or a t-shirt or a skateboard." *(Halley, Peter. "Interview Peter Halley and Ryan McGinness." Ryan McGinness Works., Rizzoli International Publications, Inc., USA, 2009, pp. 8-13)* "So, for example, walking into a skateboard store and looking at, basically, the different oil on wood panels is no different an aesthetic experience than walking into a gallery or walking into a museum and making a value judgement based on the imagery and based on aesthetics." *(Wolfe, Duncan. "Ryan McGinness." Human Being Journal, Issue No. 4, Spring 2014, pp. 58-67)* Takes drum lessons and forms band with friend, Tim McCready. They call themselves Green Suade Filth (sic). Inspired by Dada, Surrealism, and Monty Python, the two friends record cassettes of original songs on a four-track tape recorder and sell them to friends. Writes non-sequitur lyrics, sings lead vocals, and creates the graphics for the band's cassette covers, flyers, posters, and t-shirts. "I could never afford the cool brands or the expensive brands, so I would make my own shirts or paint my own skateboards. And then when those things that I made became valued by my peers, it's then I understood that assuming this power of creating the imagery for myself was intoxicating and just understanding the power of the imagery and the power of the brands from an early age is something that kind of stuck with me, I guess." *(Wolfe, Duncan. "Ryan McGinness." Human Being Journal, Issue No. 4, Spring 2014, pp. 58-67)*

1986-1990 (High School)
Attends Frank W. Cox High School. Meets Trish Goodwin through student government. Although she attends a different high school, the two date

on and off for four years and attend senior prom together. McGinness is active in student government during all four years of high school and is elected his class president, vice president, treasurer, and school vice president. Is also active in numerous other extra-curricular activities as National Honor Society president and debate team captain. In the summer after sophomore year, attends Governor's State School for German Language Study. Also spends summers at a student government leadership workshop and debate camp. Takes Advanced Placement classes and excels in science and calculus. Wins ChemMatters contest by developing a use for polyvinyl alcohol water soluble plastic film and wins the American Society of Engineers' egg drop contest. Develops an interest in Psychology, takes all courses offered, and writes paper on the process of self actualization. Continues with Old Donation art program after school. Continues with band (GSF), recording a total of 9 cassettes, and sells them to local record stores. The band prank calls numerous strangers randomly selected from the phone book and performs over-the-phone focus group concerts. Other high school pranks include recording screams and banging onto the middle of a blank cassette and playing it inside a locker so sounds are heard in the middle of class, posting flyers around school for fictitious band gigs, counterfeiting hall passes and permission slips, performing a Dada poem with trash can on head in a talent show, and securing multiple credit cards by creating fake identities. Continues to silkscreen t-shirts and paint skateboards for friends. "When I was 14 years old, I couldn't afford a new skateboard. So I wrote to all my favorite skateboard companies and told them I was hosting a skate contest in my hometown of Virginia Beach. I asked them to donate prizes for my contest. A few weeks later, I received a huge Powell Peralta skull banner, Bones Brigade t-shirts, Santa Cruz Rob Roskop decks, and numerous stickers. I also received t-shirts from a variety of other companies. I never held the event; I just divided the booty up among my friends." *(Sponsorship, Gingko Press, USA, 2003, p. 11)* Works after school on a country club golf course collecting golf balls and cleaning carts and golf clubs. By senior year, secures an after-school job as an "Artist/Illustrator" for the Oceana Naval Base by designing a logo for its Morale, Welfare, and Recreation department. "I got to work with Kroy lettering machines, copiers, wax machines, etc., doing paste-up layouts and making drawings. This was before computers, so everything was done by hand. I made posters and menus for the Navy base mess halls and flyers for recreational activities." *(Nakamura, Eric. "Ryan's Hope." Giant Robot, USA, Issue 36, 2005, pp. 36-41, 82)* "It was about the same time that I discovered this thing called 'graphic design.' I bought a book called New American Design that I had to special order from my local bookstore…
I really felt a connection with that kind of smart, witty design going on at the time. It was exciting, because it seemed like an opportunity to merge an academic and intellectual pursuit with an artistic pursuit—combining words and images in new ways that I didn't think could be done in any other field." *(Fowler, Brendan. "Interview." Luxurygood, Alife, USA, 2000, pp. 13-18)* Accepted early to Carnegie Mellon University and Rhode Island School of Design. Chooses CMU because mother brings to his attention the fact that Andy Warhol attended. The summer after graduation, goes to New York City with Trish and stays with Trish's sister and brother in-law, an industrial designer who introduces McGinness to the freelance world of being an artist.

1990-1994 (Carnegie Mellon University)
Enters the four-year Bachelor of Fine Arts program at Carnegie Mellon University as an Andrew Carnegie Scholar. Upon enrolling, is given his first email address and takes required computer courses. Continues studies in psychology (which began in high school) and subjects himself to numerous paid psychology experiments during all four years. Attends several theme and costume parties hosted by older art students and is impressed by their creation of total environments and alternative realities. Foundation courses are based on Bauhaus principles with a core curriculum of art

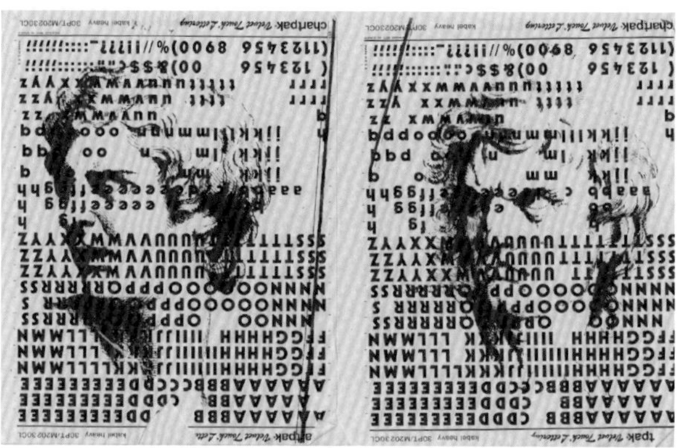

Type transfer photocopy experiments, high school, c. 1988

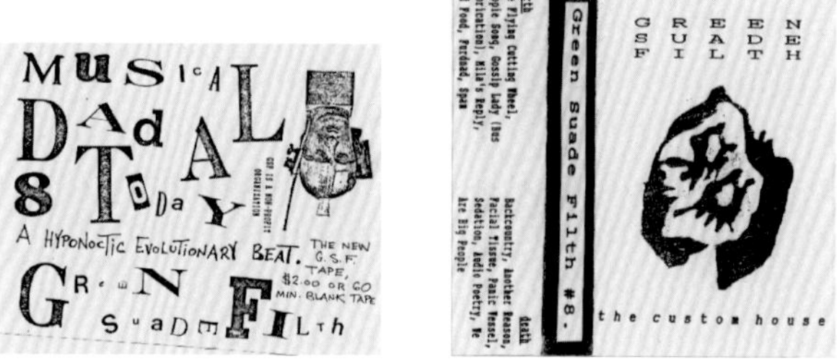

High school band flyer and cassette cover, c. 1988

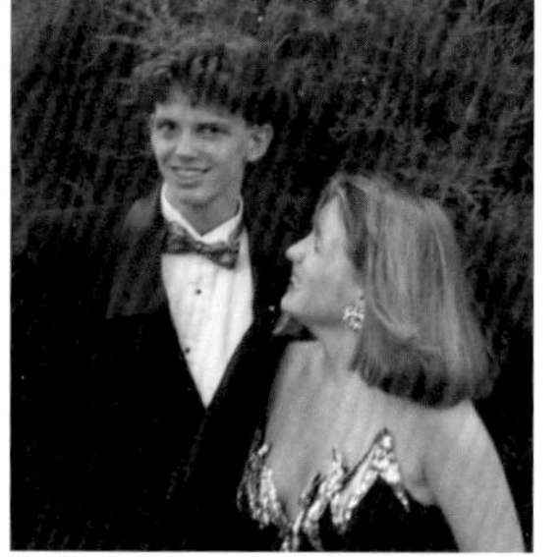

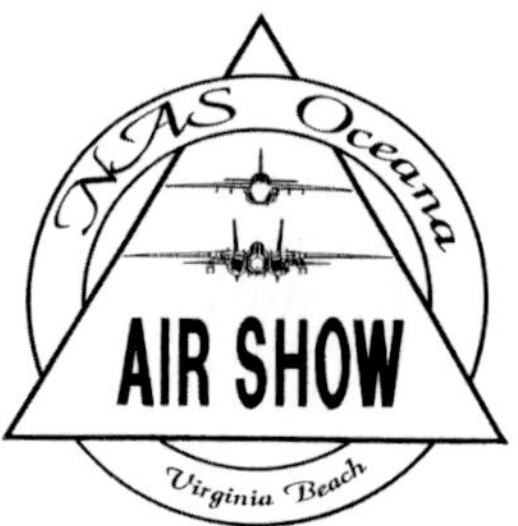

Left: McGinness with prom date, Trish Goodwin, 1990
Right: Logo designed for Naval Air Station, Oceana Air Show, Virginia Beach, 1989

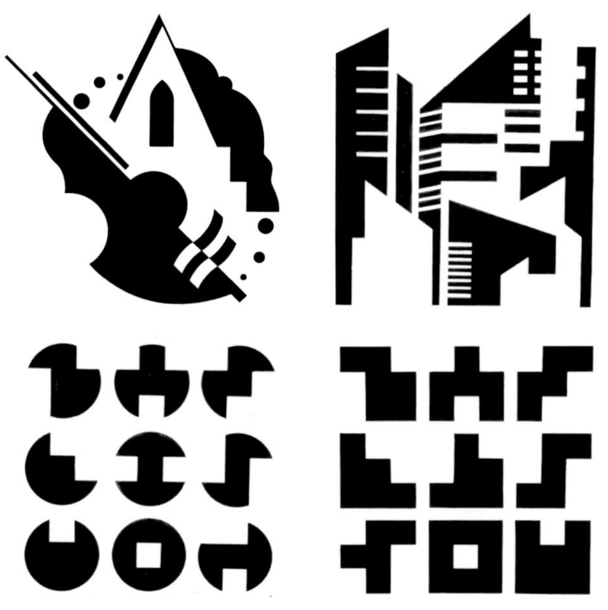

Design foundation studies, Plaka paint with ruling pen on illustration boards, Carnegie Mellon University, 1991

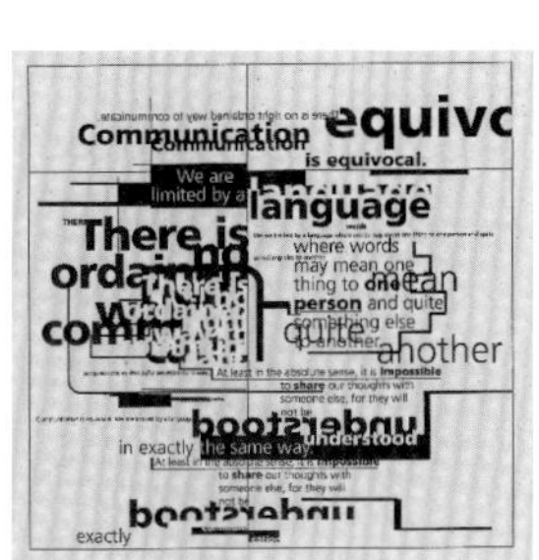
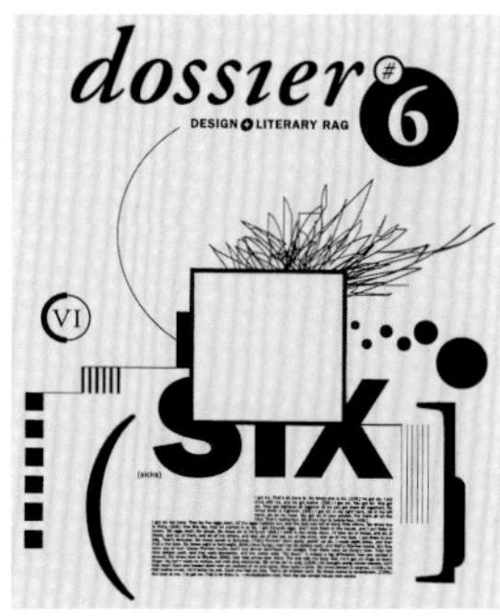

Left: Typography study, Carnegie Mellon University, 1993
Right: Cover for Dossier, student-run design and literary magazine

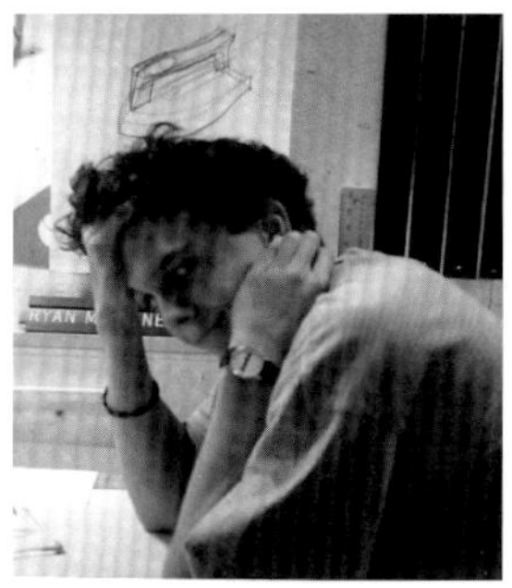
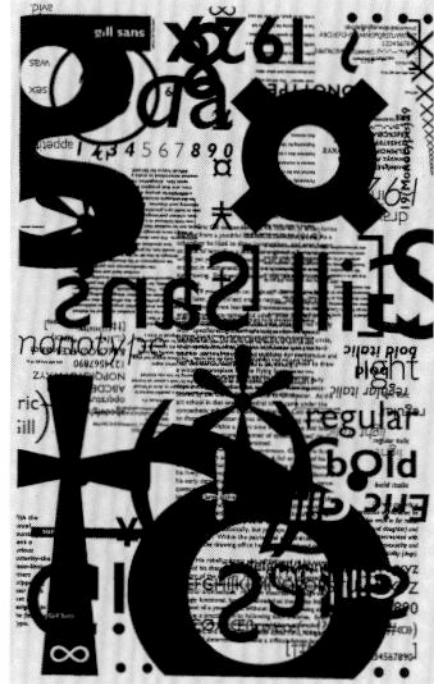

Left: McGinness in studio, Carnegie Mellon University, 1992
Right: Typography study, Carnegie Mellon University, 1993

and design histories taught together. Chooses to major in graphic design and minor in art. His is the last class to be taught traditional design tools and materials before the transition to computers. Learns to cut Rubylith film, operate a photostat machine, develop in the darkroom, and create mechanical boards for reproduction. Sees several bands play in Pittsburgh and hosts a radio show at the college radio station, WRCT. In the summer of 1991, returns to Virginia Beach and works odd jobs at a pizzeria, resort hotel, and silkscreening t-shirts. In the summer of 1992, stays in Pittsburgh to intern at Skutski & Associates, a public relations firm. In the summer of 1993, works as a Junior Designer at The Cantor Group in Pittsburgh and begins internship at The Andy Warhol Museum. Designs invitation and print materials for the soon-to-be-opened museum. "I interned at The Andy Warhol Museum my senior year at CMU. This was the year before the museum opened, so the offices were located in the Carnegie Museum—very close to campus. That was a real treat for me. Of course, I knew about Warhol growing up and when it came time for me to decide on a school, the fact that Andy had gone there, (then called Carnegie Tech), was a contributing factor." *(Lecture and Interview with Hugh Davies at the Museum of Contemporary Art San Diego, September 13, 2012)* Remains in Pittsburgh for most of his holiday breaks choosing to work in the student studios and computer labs. Throughout his four years, works at a deli making sandwiches, as a video editing lab attendant (makes several videos), and does freelance design jobs (designing theater production posters, student magazine covers, posters and album covers for bands). Designs covers for numerous student publications and t-shirts for student organizations. Works as Art Director for *Dossier*, a student design and literary magazine. Works as the Art Director for the Forbes Street Student Gallery designing exhibition invitations and posters and curates an exhibition of fellow design students' work in opposition to the gallery's mission of servicing the art department. Frequents the Carnegie Museum. A class assignment has McGinness creating and installing fake signage in the Carnegie Museum. Visits museums in Washington, DC, on numerous trips to visit girlfriend, Trish Goodwin. Concentrates on typography and icon design starting in junior year. Lives off campus with friends for junior and senior years in houses where he sets up small home painting studios. Throughout his time at CMU, makes his "clip art" paintings using a combination of projecting images and silkscreening. Exhibits paintings in a coffee house and hair salon in Pittsburgh's Oakland neighborhood, near the school's campus. For his senior degree projects, he develops a sign system for Amtrak and creates an independent study, "What Is a Book?"

1994
Attends opening celebration of The Andy Warhol Museum and graduates from Carnegie Mellon University the same weekend, May 14-15. Sells car, loads paintings and supplies into a rental truck and goes to Fairfax, VA, to pick up Trish. The two move to Manhattan into a 350 sq. ft. studio apartment at 295 Park Avenue South at 23rd Street. Furnishes apartment with thrift store and flea market finds. Pounds pavement with multiple copies of portfolio, dropping off to various design firms, magazines, and record labels. Does freelance design work for record labels and concert venues. Printed Matter on Wooster Street sells his pamphlets. Attends gallery openings in SoHo, see bands in the East Village, and goes to museums. By July, he is working at the design firm Pentagram as a Junior Designer. Continues to make his "clip art" paintings in various materials (astroturf, velvet, curtains, and used silkscreens). "When I first moved to New York around 1994, I was trying to make art, which means that you make things that look like other things that already have been defined as art, which is a process that every young artist probably goes through. You learn to develop or recognize your own language and vocabulary; and understand what's really unique. So I started pushing my aesthetic as a result of being more comfortable with who I am." *(Ishikawa, Aiko, "Interview with Ryan McGinness." Plus Eighty-one," JAP, Vol. 47, Spring 2010, pp. 10-19)*

By November, works as a full-time freelancer for record labels, magazines, other various clients. In December, buys first computer for professional work (Power Macintosh 8100/80AV). Attends Thanksgiving dinner at Philip Pearlstein's home.

1995

In February, photographs new series of "clip art" paintings based on line drawings found in the public domain, continuing his fascination with creating reproductions of reproductions. Hosts *Atari Tournament* in Richmond, VA, with friend and previous high school bandmate, Tim McCready. Continues to do design work for record labels and bands and designs numerous logos. Pays off student loans. Brews beer with Trish and the two start to market their "GoGo Juice" at parties and with ads in independent zines. Exhibits paintings in clubs and bars on the Lower East Side. In July, hosts *Liquid Lunch Party* in apartment. Studio apartment gets crowded with beer-making and painting supplies, and in September, sets up his first studio at 580 Broadway, a small interior space in an office building. Meets neighbors Razorfish, a tech start-up company that designs websites. Hosts *Tupperware Party* in studio in November. In December, with the help of Razorfish, sets up first website at ryanmcginness.com.

1996

Begins exhibiting in various group shows and hosting studio visits from curators and dealers. Continues with "clip art" paintings, primarily on stretched plastic. Obsessed with the concept of making paintings of drawings. Makes "shadow paintings" in clear acrylic on clear plastic in which the cast shadow reproduction on the wall dominates over the primary painted image. Writes haiku record reviews for music zines. In May, poses for Spencer Tunick with Trish on Brooklyn Bridge. Sells stickers and t-shirts at Printed Matter. Art directs culture zine, *PopSmear* and meets numerous artists, illustrators, and photographers. Trish and Ryan move into separate apartments, both in the West Village. The two continue to brew GoGo Juice with McGinness concentrating on the labels, hang tags, and ads. In November, mounts first solo exhibition, *Clever Title Goes Here* at a+a Gallery in the Lower East Side. "When I first moved to New York, I was reading a lot of Baudrillard, Foucault, and Wittgenstein as a sort of carry-over or extension from Carnegie Mellon, where Post-Modernism was already being taught as a part of history. The work I was making mimicked a lot of 80s art, but with more of a concern for 'design' (composition, typography, etc.). I think instead of seeing people or work at the time that I admired, I was more inspired to react against all the boring work I was seeing. There wasn't a sense of fun or humor being shared in art that I can remember. However, later, in 1996, I believe it was, I saw Damien Hirst's show at Gagosian, and I was very impressed and inspired. I had one of my first solo shows up at the time where I was trying to create a fun, carnival-like atmosphere. But when I saw Hirst doing what I was trying to do, but 100 times better, I just felt defeated, and that's when I'm usually most inspired." *(Stochl, Gerhard. "A Conversation with Ryan McGinness." Lowdown, Germany, No. 37, Fall 2003, pp. 62-68)*

1997

Continues to explore the collapse of the secondary and primary image within the same picture plane by painting on stretched clear and translucent plastics. Begins to back paintings with mirrors, thus showing the back of the painted surface at the same time as the front. Continues to exhibit in group shows and works out of 580 Broadway. Begins to search for new studio space. In March, marries Trish Goodwin. The two 25-year-olds fly to Las Vegas and get married at the Graceland Chapel with an Elvis impersonator. In May, organizes a *May Day Party* for Razorfish with site-specific installations, including a kissing booth and haircut lounge with one style option: shaved head. Also in May, creates the *No Sweat* exhibition and performance in a gym. In August, starts renovations on loft in Chinatown moving into the space in October. The renovations continue for 5 months, consuming all of McGinness' time.

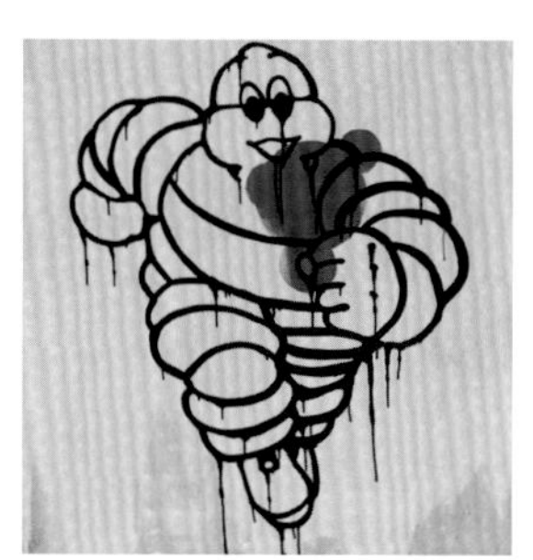
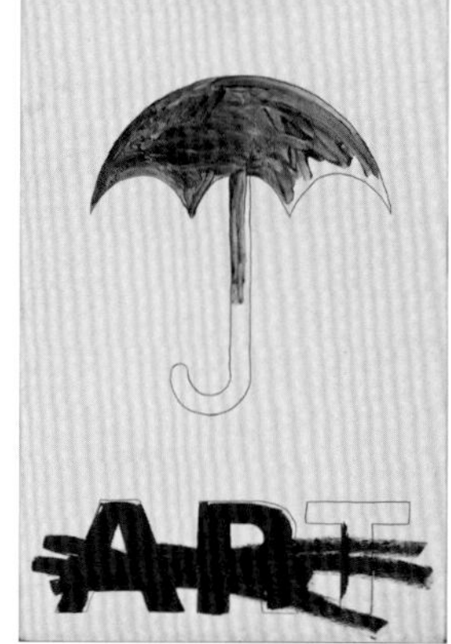

Left: *Michelin Man (Painting of)*, 1994, mixed pigments on canvas, 40 x 40 in. (101.6 x 101.6 cm)
Right: Untitled, 1995, oil on wood, 36 x 24 in. (91.4 x 61 cm)

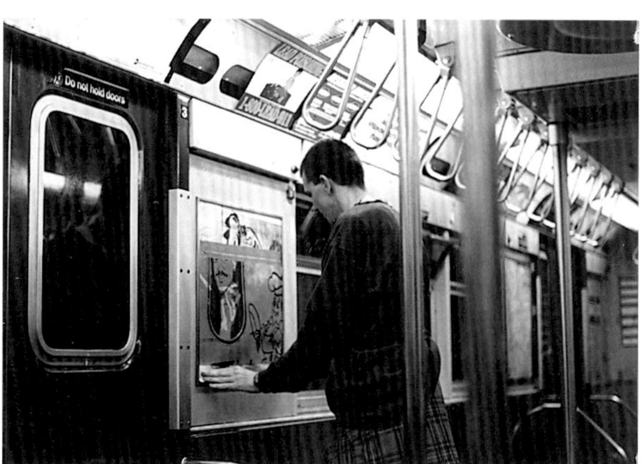

Subway advertising intervention, 1995

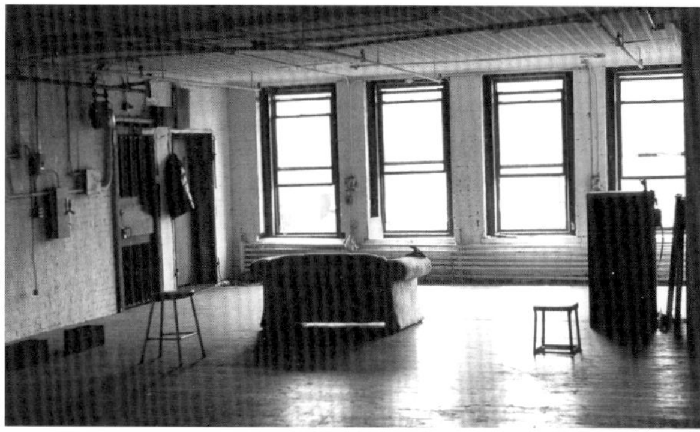

Pre-renovation studio loft, Chinatown, Manhattan, 1997

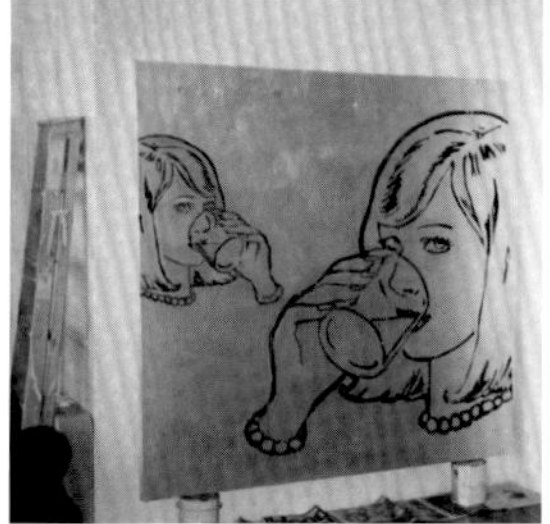

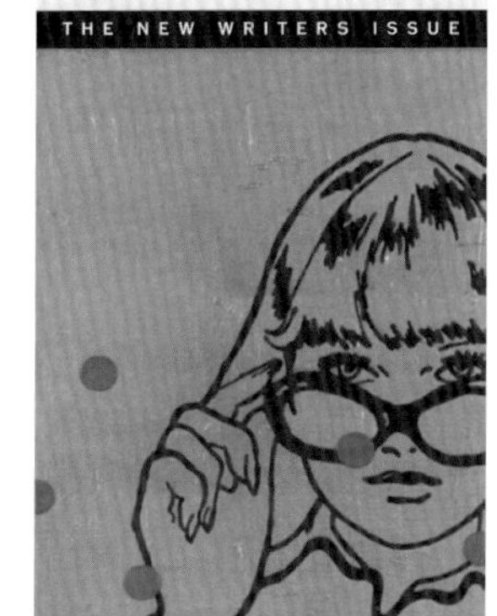

Left: Painting in progress in studio, 1998
Right: *The Paris Review*, Issue 158, Spring/Summer 2001, cover

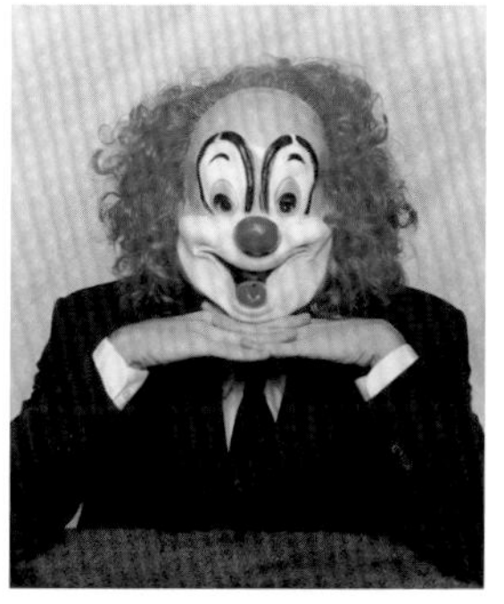

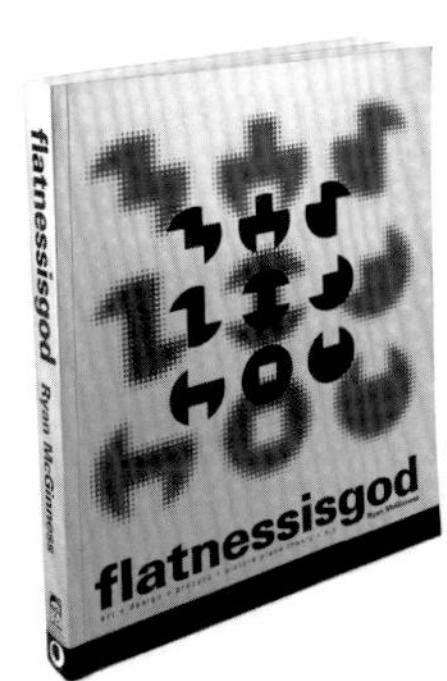

Left: Promotional headshot for launch of *Flatnessisgod* book
Right: First book, *Flatnessisgod*, 1999, 11 x 8.5 in. (27.9 x 21.6 cm),
1C, 256pp., softcover

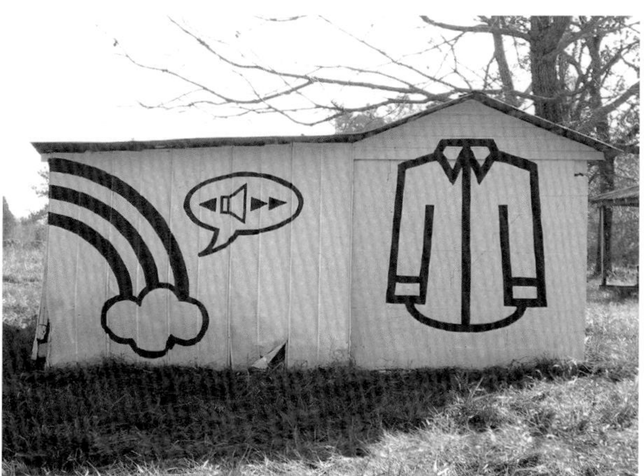

Untitled (Barnstormers), 2000, painted metal barn, Cameron, NC

1998

Paints the first of the icon-based paintings with speech bubbles, UFOs, and icons of other works of art. Begins to subvert the canon of art history by inserting himself into a photo of Andy Warhol, Francesco Clemente, and Jean-Michel Basquiat and flattening Jasper John's Ale Cans sculpture into a painting. Hosts *Networking Is a Skill* event in a club in which attendees map out on a wall chart how they all know each other. Does not attend event but instead sends an imposter as a symbol for the artist host. Continues to show at various galleries in group exhibitions, including Exit Art. Hosts a series of poker nights and parties in studio. In May, hosts a studio roof party featuring 7 bands and raffles off the GoGo Juice beer-making equipment.

1999

In January, installs bootleg postcards of his work in the Museum of Modern Art store in New York. *Time Out* magazine includes McGinness in their "99 to Watch in '99." First book, *Flatnessisgod* is published by Soft Skull Press and Razorfish Studios, New York. First digital collages are materialized as prints on canvas. In May, begins playing soccer in East River Park with what will become the Chinatown Soccer Club. Begins to produce stickers and t-shirts as part of studio practice. Creates first sculptures by balancing his paintings together to create fort-like structures, thus making artworks out of artworks. Begins to grow psilocybin mushrooms in studio. *Emigre* magazine publishes McGinness' project, *Selfsameness*, which includes self-portrait stock photo parodies and "Ryan McGinness logos" designed by numerous designers. Lectures at the American Center for Design Conference, Chicago.

2000

In January, hires first studio assistant. Exhibits in group shows and creates performances at the Limelight, White Box, and Whitney Museum of American Art at Champion. Lectures throughout the year at the AIGA Conference in San Diego, Art Center in Los Angeles, Carnegie Mellon University in Pittsburgh, the AIGA Conference in Chicago, San Diego State University, and Pratt Institute of Art and Design. "I was always pursuing design and art in parallel, and the two just merged for me. Nothing in particular drove me toward being an artist. Making work is not a choice, but rather a default state or way of life. It's not really something I have control over." *(Iwakoshi, Yuka/Noe, Rain. "Ryan McGinness." Educated Community, USA, Issue 5, Spring, 2001, pp. 10-12)* Embraces iconic imagery and hires sign shops in Chinatown to create vinyl on aluminum works. First painted skateboard pieces are exhibited at Alife in New York along with a mural and paintings of his new flat iconic world. Alife publishes McGinness' second book, *Luxurygood*. Is the first artist to collaborate with Supreme, a skateboard and lifestyle brand. Supreme publishes 5 skateboards by McGinness. Creates "grip tape paintings" on wood panels that are exhibited at Houston Gallery in Seattle. In October, accompanies Trish to Singapore and discovers unique sign-making materials. In November, travels to North Carolina to paint barns with the Barnstormers crew. In December, travels to Europe for first time visiting Munich, Berlin, Paris, and London.

2001

Works with industrial and commercial materials to produce picture planes with simple isolated iconic images. Creates first porcelain-baked enamel on steel pieces and vinyl on skateboard editions and exhibits them in Munich. His images are often mistaken for having been appropriated from popular culture commercial sources. "This is the inherent irony in making drawings that are designed to look anonymously made—they are designed to look like they come from somewhere else, so I can't really complain if people make that assumption." *(Byrne, David. "Conversation David Byrne and Ryan McGinness." Ryan McGinness Works., Rizzoli Inter-*

national Publications, Inc., USA, 2009, p. 22-27) Exhibits *How Hyperspace Works* with Exit Art in New York. In May, McGinness' solo exhibition, *Vocabularytest* is praised by the New York Times. His work is used for the cover of *The Paris Review*. In June, travels to Paris for exhibition and book, *Pieceofmind*, at Colette. Hosts several game nights in loft throughout the year. On September 9th, travels to Europe (London, Munich, and Barcelona). Publishes first print, *This Dream Is so Lifelike* with Artomatic in London. In November, travels to Tokyo for exhibition at the Parco Museum, *Evolution Is the Theory of Everything* and is interviewed on Tokyo FM by Takashi Murakami.

2002

In January, exhibits his porcelain-baked enamel on steel pieces at Stux Gallery in New York. Begins to paint his iconic drawings in layers by using the silkscreen process. Begins to experiment with different formulations of acrylic paint for silkscreening, eventually perfecting a process that he will use for years. In April, purchases loft on the corner of Broome and Elizabeth Streets, near the Bowery. The loft is gutted and renovated to McGinness' exacting specifications. In May, travels to Los Angeles for the first time to create an installation at The Standard hotel in downtown Los Angeles. In June, creates two-person exhibition, *Dream Garden* with Julia Chiang at Deitch Projects. By the end of summer, begins working with Deitch Projects in earnest. In August, mother is diagnosed with breast cancer. In November, creates *Products Are the New Art* installation and catalogue at Printed Matter, which includes his *Art History Eraser Shields*. Is asked to present the Adobe Design Achievement Award at Guggenheim Museum and sends imposter instead. In December, curates with Julia Chiang and Cheryl Dunn the group show, *Session the Bowl* at Deitch Projects. The exhibition includes contemporaries Stephen Powers, Barry McGee, KAWS, Shepard Fairey, Todd James, Chris Johanson, Futura, Larry Clark, and Dash Snow. In December, travels to Tokyo for an exhibition and book launch. Takashi Murakami buys several of his paintings. By year's end, signs licensing deal with Sakura in Japan for his RM clothing label.

2003

Paintings become more ambitious in scale and more nuanced in content and composition. Participates in group shows at New Image Art in Los Angeles and the Mori Art Museum in Tokyo. In February, travels to Los Angeles for his *Sponsorship* exhibition at Shepard Fairey's Black Market Gallery. "I did not produce any work for the *Sponsorship* exhibition. Instead, I set up a sponsorship program whereby any company could contribute any amount it wished in cash, products, or services. The sponsors' logos were on display at different sizes and locations (commensurate with their level of contribution), along with product and promotional giveaways." *(Sponsorship, Gingko Press, USA, 2003, p. 13)* In March, participates in the *SK8 on the Wall* exhibition at Rocket Gallery in Tokyo. Completes a series of 100 works on paper titled *Fabricated Cultural Belief Systems*. 20 are acquired by the Museum of Modern Art in New York. In September, speaks at the *Tokion* magazine conference in New York. Travels to Paris for the *A New New York Scene* group show at Agnès B.'s Galerie du Jour. Exhibition includes contemporaries Dan Colen, José Parla, and Dash Snow. In October, creates his *Worlds within Worlds* mirror maze installation at Deitch Projects in New York. Lectures at the Corcoran Gallery in Washington, DC, in November. Completes renovation on Broome Street loft after 19 months. Keeps Centre Street loft and expands studio to take up entire floor.

2004

McGinness begins to embrace the imperfections of the silkscreen process and purposefully incorporates mistakes and misregistered images into his finished paintings. The paintings get more layered and imagery more tangled. "Human organs and plant life. Logos and symbols. Fairy tales

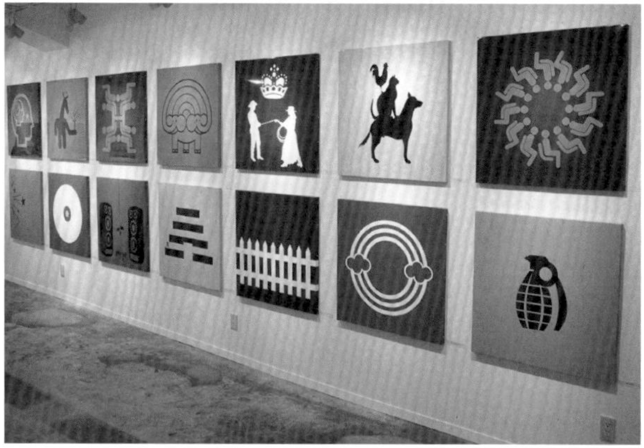

Evolution Is the Theory of Everything, 2001, installation view, Parco Gallery, Tokyo

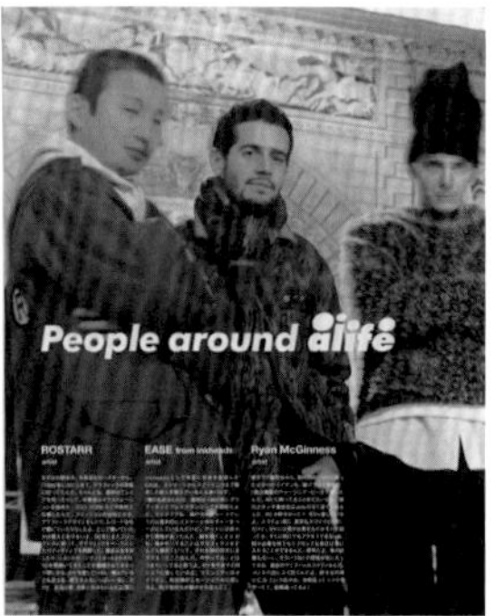

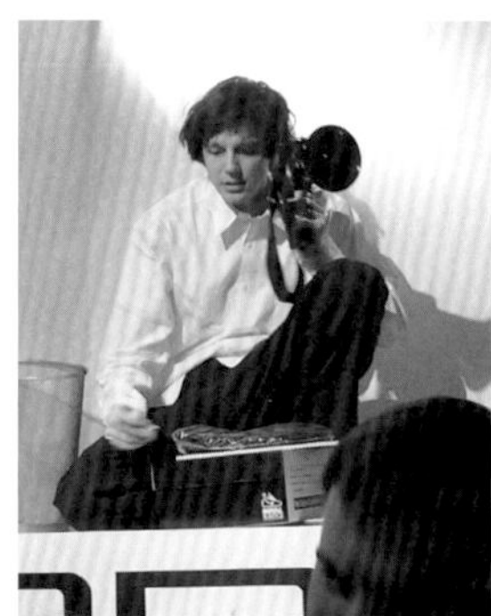

Left: With Romon Yang (Rostarr) and José Parla (Ease) "People around Alife," *Relax Magazine*, Japan, February, 2002, p. 84
Right: McGinness at the *Sponsorship* exhibition giveaway, 2003, Black Market Gallery, Los Angeles

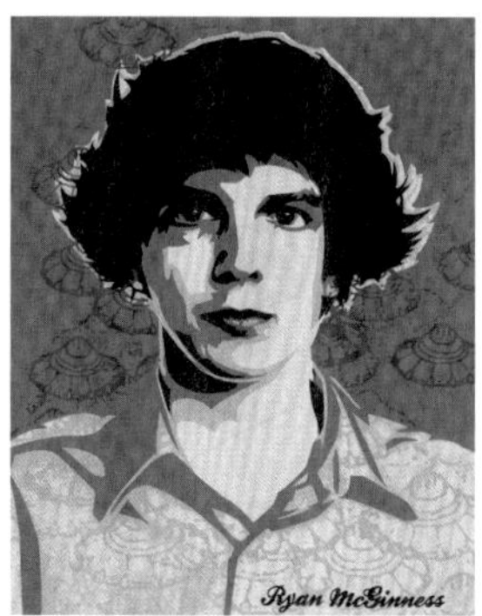

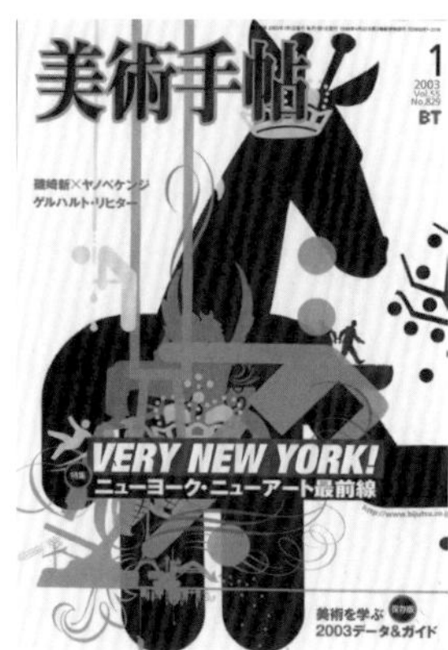

Left: Portrait by Shepard Fairey for *Tokion Magazine*, 2002
Right: *Bijutsu Techo*, Japan, Vol. 55, No. 829, 2003, cover

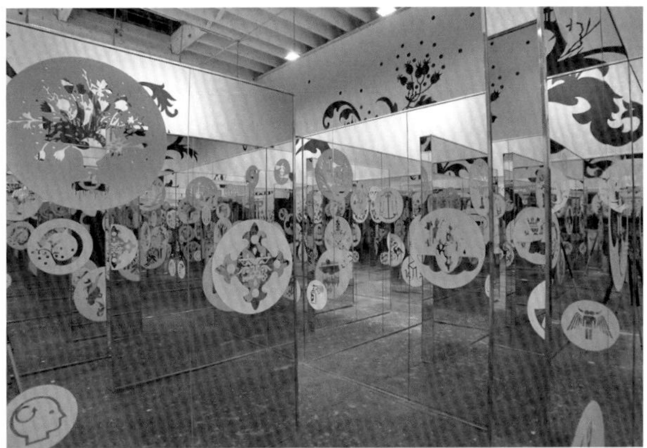

Worlds within Worlds, 2003, installation view, Deitch Projects, New York

Various magazine covers, 2002-2011

and everyday scenes. Family crests and coats of arms. These are a few of the disparate subjects that McGinness fragments, alters, and layers to build his dense networks of brightly colored fantastical imagery. Swathed in ornate, curvaceous lines, McGinness's compositions are a postmodern twist on the eighteenth-century Rococo style, characterized by playful opulence and intricate, coiling forms." *(MoMA Highlights since 1980, The Museum of Modern Art, U.S., 2007, p. 254)* Continues to host parties and game nights in loft. "By 2, only a few close friends remained, and Mr. McGinness finally appeared to relax. He was now free to indulge in his favorite game, one that demanded he draw rather than talk: 'Now,' he said, 'who wants to play Pictionary?'" *(O'Connor, Pauline. "A Night Out with Ryan McGinness." The New York Times, USA, November 21, 2004, p. ST 4)* Throughout the year, travels for exhibitions and projects in Boston, Toronto, Paris, Toulouse, and Madrid. Incorporates studio practice as Ryan McGinness Studios, Inc. Successfully files lawsuit against Burton Snowboards for copyright infringement. *Beautiful Losers* exhibition opens in March at the Contemporary Arts Center, Cincinnati. The exhibition travels internationally for several years and includes contemporaries Barry McGee, KAWS, Shepard Fairey, and Harmony Korine. Builds spray room in studio for spraying backgrounds and perfects technique using water-based metallic car paint. Participates in Creative Time's *Dreamland Artists Club* in Coney Island. Mother passes away from breast cancer in July. In the fall, begins figure drawing in earnest at Will Cotton's studio on Lower East Side. In October, produces commercially available soccer ball for exhibition at Printed Matter. In December, travels to Paris for *Multiverse* exhibition and book launch at Agnès B.'s Galerie du Jour.

2005

Paintings begin to get even larger and more ambitious. Creates first tondos with new *Black Holes* series and exhibits them in Belgium. Creates first letterpress prints. Lectures throughout the year at Museum of Contemporary Art San Diego, School of the Museum of Fine Arts in Boston, Portland Institute of Contemporary Art, University of South Florida Contemporary Art Museum, SFMoMA, Art Academy in Cincinnati, and Columbia University. Appears on *Art Star* TV show filmed at Deitch Projects in March. Creates paintings and installation for the Greater New York group show at MoMA PS1. In April, travels to San Diego for *Pain-free Kittens* exhibition at Quint Gallery. In July, vacations in the south of France. In August, travels to Vancouver and Seattle to work on porcelain-baked enamel on steel pieces. In the fall, travels to Cincinnati for a series of murals and creates his *Universals*, fiberglass two-sided tondos in Massachusetts. *Installationview* exhibit at Deitch Projects opens in October. Rizzoli publishes *Installationview* book.

2006

Begins the year by renovating studio. In February, travels to Madrid to lecture at ARCO Art Fair. Included in numerous international museum shows, including *USA Today from the Saatchi Collection* at the Royal Academy of Art in London and *Printmaking Now* at the Museum of Modern Art in New York. Travels intensively throughout the year for exhibitions and lectures in London, Brussels, Amsterdam, Madrid, Barcelona, and Milan. In spring, creates installation for the Child Study Center at New York University and participates in Deitch Projects' *Garden Party* exhibition. Exhibits with Glenn Horowitz in East Hampton. Creates public art signage installation in New York with the Public Art Fund. In September, separates from Trish. Buys and renovates apartment in the Meatpacking District of Manhattan. Group exhibition at the Baltic Centre for Contemporary Art in Gateshead, England, opens in September and includes contemporaries David Shrigley, Takashi Murakami, Os Gemeos, and Banksy. Successfully files lawsuit against Urban Outfitters for copyright infringement. "There seem to be two reactions people have when they see artwork that they like: they either respectfully support it and want to share it with others, or they attempt to co-opt its ownership and figure out a way to profit from it." *(Sponsorship, Gingko Press, USA, 2003, p. 9)* In November, travels to Copenhagen for print project with Edition Copenhagen. Creates *Never Odd or Even* series of paintings and exhibits them at three galleries in the fall in Milan, Amsterdam, and Madrid.

2007

Explores new materials with new works published by Pace Prints. Works in gold leaf, plastic buttons, laser cutting skateboards, and large welded aluminum sculptures. Also begins working with Lower East Side Printshop on a series of prints. Travels to Netherlands to begin *Art History Is Not Linear* series with Boijmans Museum and Virginia Museum of Fine Arts. In February, travels to Madrid for ARCO Art Fair and creates solo booth with Deitch Projects at the Armory Show in New York. Travels to San Diego for exhibition of new paintings at Quint Gallery in April. In June, travels to Zurich for Art Basel Art Fair where his work is featured at Deitch Projects. In October, opens *Varied Editions* exhibition at Pace Prints. In December, travels to Miami for Art Basel Miami Beach to install Art Positions shipping containers, *Concrete Waves: An Homage to Skate Culture* presented by Art Radio WPS1.org and organized by MoMA PS1.

2008

McGinness creates his *Black-on-Black* series of paintings. Travels to Milan for the exhibition *A Shadow Feeling of Loss*. Experiments with laser cut acrylic sculptures. Continues with *Black Hole* paintings with fluorescent pigments installed with fluorescent adhesive vinyl under black lights. Attends opening in Toronto for exhibition. "The interior room was enveloped in black-lit darkness so the fluorescent visual mash-ups that hung there snapped into sharp focus. Emphasizing the viral aspect of his silk-screened canvases, the artist allowed the imagery to bleed onto the gallery walls via hand-painted extrapolations." *(Ann Jordan, Betty. "Ryan McGinness Artcore." Art News, USA, Vol. 107, No. 11, December, 2008, p. 134)* Artist's book *No Sin/No Future* published by Gingko Press. In October, travels to Cincinnati Art Museum for *Aesthetic Comfort* exhibition, lecture, and book launch.

2009

In February, travels to Aspen for exhibition at Baldwin Gallery. Sets up second, temporary studio in Brooklyn in order to complete the works for Deitch Projects exhibition. In March, *Ryan McGinness Works.* opens at Deitch Projects with a series of large paintings and acrylic sculptures. Book of the same title is published by Rizzoli and includes essays and interviews by Peter Halley and David Byrne. After opening night, travels to St. Lucia for 3 weeks with Trish. The two reunite and move into the apartment on 14th Street. Models for J. Crew clothing campaign. Travels to Milan in May to recover works stolen by gallery in Munich. *50 Parties* project begins in June. McGinness hosts a party with a different theme every week in the studio for a year. Some of the themes include Goth Party, Vogue Ball, Summer Camp, Autopsy, Prom, Party Naked, Fight Club, and Sex, Drugs, and Rock & Roll. In September, travels to Madrid for meetings and Amsterdam to work on Boijmans Museum project. Purchases apartment in Amsterdam in December.

2010

Begins *Women* series of paintings composed of overlapping icons of figures. Continues with *Black Holes*, *Mindscapes*, and *Art History Is Not Linear* series. Perfects process for making cyanotypes. In January, begins renovation of Amsterdam apartment, which takes 20 months to complete. McGinness has several assistants working for him in the studio. "Since the studio has grown, I have less and less time to work on what's at the core of my practice, which is drawing. So I really need to figure out a way to go back to that somehow. The risk that you run in having an art studio

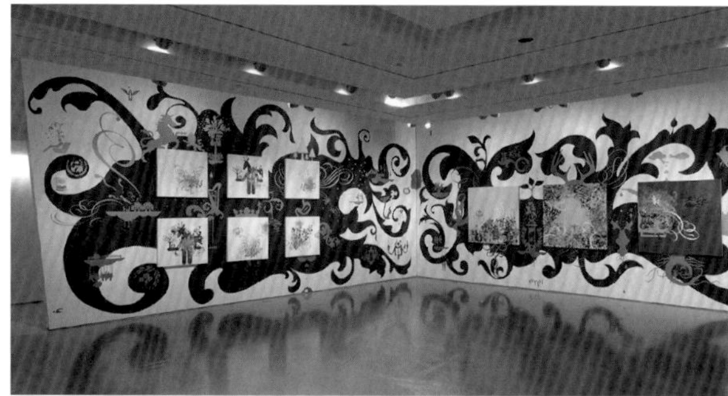

Flocci Non Facio, 2004, installation view, *Beautiful Losers* exhibition, Contemporary Arts Center, Cincinnati

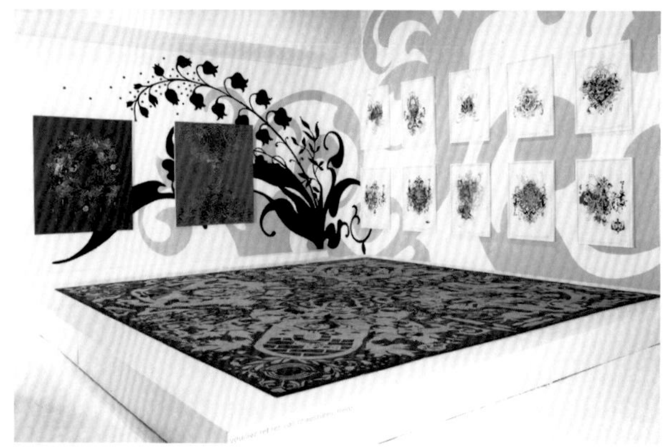

Multiverse, 2004, installation view, Galerie du Jour, Paris

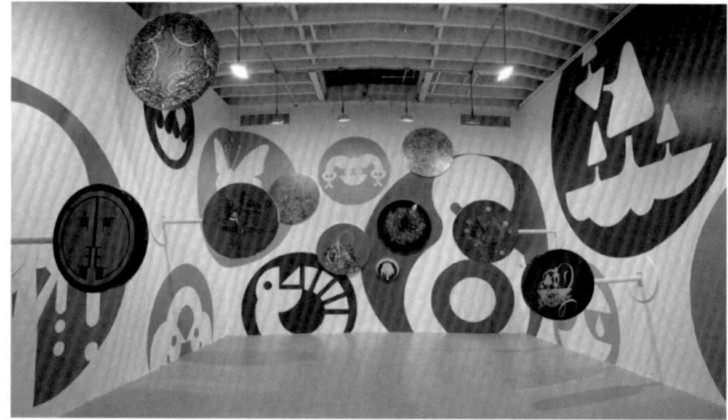

Installationview, 2005, installation view, Deitch Projects, New York

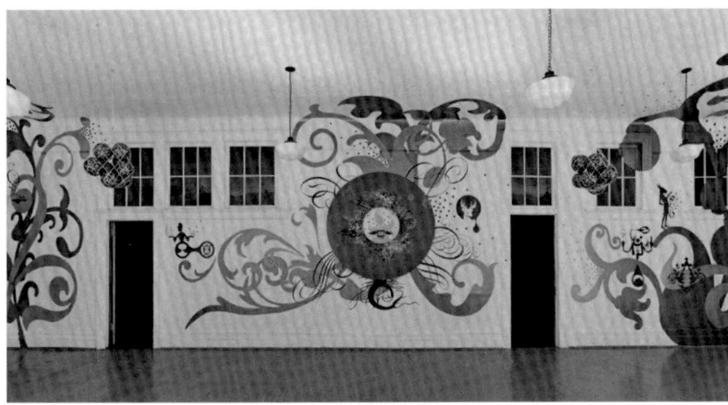

Now Forever, 2005, installation view, *Greater New York* exhibition, MoMA PS1, New York

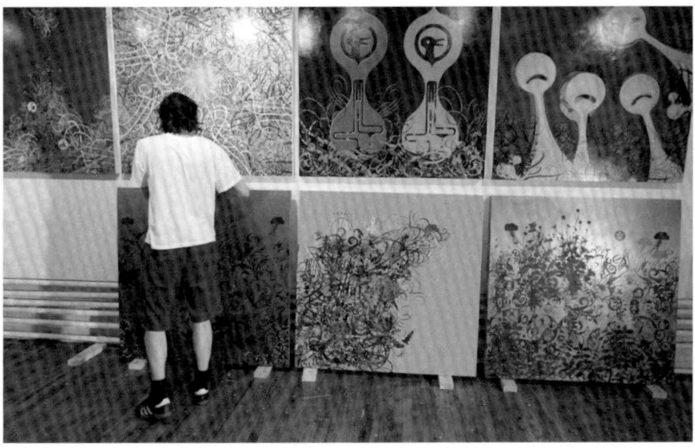

Studio view, 2006

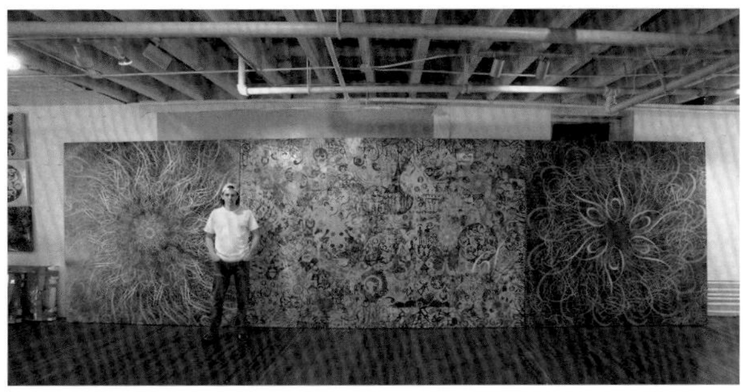

God Cries When I Sleep (in studio), 2007, triptych, acrylic on canvas, 96 x 336 in. (243.8 x 853.4 cm) total

is that you turn into an art director instead of an artist, which is what you wanted to be in the first place." *(Ishikawa, Aiko, "Interview with Ryan McGinness." Plus Eighty-one," JAP, Vol. 47, Spring 2010, pp. 10-19)* In February and March, McGinness spends 6 weeks in Madrid for the S*tudio Franchise* exhibition at La Casa Encendida Museum, where he sets up an operational studio open to the public. The exhibit showcases McGinness' system-based approach to making art and is the first time the artist's real-hair wigs are shown. *Studio Franchise* and *Studio Manual* books are published by the museum. "My battle against chaos and entropy is an on-going struggle that permeates every facet of my life—from how I structure my day, decide what to wear, keep my living and working spaces in order, and keep all my projects under control—to how I build my picture planes, sculptures, and environments." *(Jorquera, Adam. "A Conversation Between Adam Jorquera & Ryan McGinness." Studio Franchise, La Casa Encendida, Spain, 2010, p. 189)* Travels to Helsinki in March for exhibition at Galerie Forsblom. June 26th is the last of the *50 Parties*. Spends the next 6 weeks renovating studio. Lectures at The Virginia Museum of Fine Arts. In December, travels to Miami for Art Basel Miami Beach. "Clearly not one to shy away from subversive acts, he exposed his 'Women' series at Art Basel Miami in December, hanging four fluorescent paintings at a gentleman's club with live dancers daubed in neon paint." *(Clarke, Katherine. "The Graphic Mind of Ryan McGinness." The Wall Street Journal Magazine, USA, Issue No. 16, June, 2011, p. 30)* Spends holidays in Bora Bora.

2011

Continues to develop different bodies of work in parallel. In January, opens *Black Holes* black light exhibition at Phillips de Pury & Company in New York. Travels to Madrid for opening of *Color Obliquo* at Espai Cultural Caja Madrid. Lectures at Virginia Commonwealth University. In May, lives in LA for 4 weeks for multiple exhibitions at Kohn Gallery, Country Club, Subliminal Projects, and Prism Gallery. Lectures at Giant Robot. "Along with planning four different gallery shows here from late May through June—featuring paintings, drawings, works on paper and a high-concept project—he has planned a 'barbecue lecture' for the Giant Robot store on Sawtelle Boulevard, art installations for both Standard hotels in L.A., and a three-night drawing performance at the hotel's Sunset Strip location that begins June 1." *(Finkel, Jori. "For Ryan McGinness, Art is One Big Party." LA Times, USA, Volume CXXX, No. 152, May 4, 2011, p. D8-9)* In June and July, lives in Amsterdam overseeing apartment renovation. First daughter, Evelyn Flower, is born in September. In October, closes on loft on Walker Street in TriBeCa and moves in. In November, purchases screen burner for studio, bringing an integral part of his process in-house.

2012

Lectures throughout the year at Museum of Contemporary Art San Diego, 21c Museum, Hunter College, and Parsons The New School for Design. Is a guest on the *Leonard Lopate Show*, *Artists and the Business of Art*, on WNYC, and speaks at The Drawing Center Symposium, *The State of Drawing*. Starts to incorporate patterns into paintings and continues experimenting with cyanotypes. Develops comprehensive color system for paints in the studio. Begins series of woven silk pieces with Tassinari & Chatel in Paris. In spring, creates the *Geometric Primitives* series and exhibits paintings and cyanotypes at Pace Primitive. Exhibits *Women* paintings and sketch process drawings at Gering & López Gallery in New York in May. In June, travels to Pittsburgh for *Factory Direct* exhibition at The Andy Warhol Museum. "Andy Warhol was the most successful anti-artist of all time. An artist's greatest contribution is in the form of permission. These permissions are given to society, and more impor-tantly, they are passed on to future artists. Artist's barriers are society's expectations based on historical precedence. We prefer our art to look like art and our artists to behave like artists. Andy courageously ignored those expectations." *(Johnson, Catherine. Thank You Andy Warhol. Glitterati Incorporated, USA, 2012, pp. 226-228)* Creates series of prints with Pace Prints to benefit the Africa Foundation. Travels to South Africa. Travels to Aspen for exhibition at Baldwin Gallery. In August, vacations in East Hampton and exhibits *Women* sketch process drawings and cyanotypes at Glenn Horowitz. In September, exhibits *Women: New (Re)Presentations* at Quint Gallery in San Diego. Beginning in November, travels to Barcelona, Copenhagen, Amsterdam, and Helsinki for 6 weeks. Produces editioned prints with Poligrafa in Barcelona and monoprints with Edition Copenhagen.

2013

Experiments with incorporating different materials into paintings, including gold leaf, powder coating, and other sign materials. *Sketchbook Selections 2000-2012* is published by Gingko Press. Spends March in Amsterdam and Helsinki. Exhibits *Women & Mindscapes* at Galerie Forsblom. "Ryan McGinness, the Virginia Beach-bred one-time 'skater-punk' turned 'celebrity artist' who designed boards for Supreme and t-shirts that were sold at Barney's, who covered downtown New York with what some critics called 'zen-snide' sticker art with tag lines like 'A lot of Art is Boring,' and 'I love my Attention Deficit Disorder' in the late 90s is all grown up." *(Codinha, Alessandra. "The Male Gaze Under a Blacklight." Maker, Issue No. 2, Winter 2013, pp. 48-77)* In June, speaks about copyright at the World Creator's Conference in Washington, DC. Creates new image for Human Rights Coalition National Coming Out Day. Travels to Los Angeles for *Women: New (Re)Presentations* book launch in November. In December, attends Art Basel Miami Beach and travels to Tortola for vacation.

2014

Completes the *Art History Is Not Linear (Boijmans)* project. Begins painting on old, retired silkscreens. In January, starts materializing figure drawings in neon. In February, travels to Virginia Museum of Fine Arts for lecture and exhibition, *Studio Visit.* In March, begins renovations on Walker Street loft that take 19 months. Spends 4 weeks in Amsterdam opening two exhibitions and launches artist's book, *Everything Is Everywhere.* Returns to New York in May for *Figure Drawings* opening at Pace Prints. Returns to Amsterdam for 4 weeks. In June is included in the *Beauty Reigns* exhibition at the McNay Art Museum. "The elements are built up as layers of vividly colored images that create a dynamic sense of deep space. The flat application of paint physically contradicts the works' convincing illusion of depth. This flatness, combined with McGinness' high-key palette, produces cool yet seductive visual effects." *(Beauty Reigns: A Baroque Sensibility in Recent Painting, McNay Art Museum, USA, 2014, pp. 76, 84-87, 93, 95, 135, 137)* Completes second print project with Lower East Side Printshop. McGinness' street signs are installed throughout downtown Manhattan by the NYC Department of Transportation, but they are all stolen within days. In August, second daughter, Maxine Violet, is born. In November, travels to San Diego for Quint Gallery exhibition, *Community Identity Stability.* Also travels to Los Angeles, Paris, and Cognac for Hennessy project. Spends December in Amsterdam.

2015

Begins the *Studio View* paintings. "At this point the paintings themselves became the symbols. I experienced a bit of frustration 10-12 years ago when the work became known by the artist's name. So, people wanted a 'Ryan McGinness' painting without really knowing what that means. I became a little distraught about that and thought, well, they just want a symbolic painting, or a representational painting. That's how the *Studio Views* started. But furthermore, these aren't reproductions of paintings that exist. They are primary productions that imply they are reproductions, because the first picture plane that you look at is a space in which something else exists. My hope was that I could collapse that

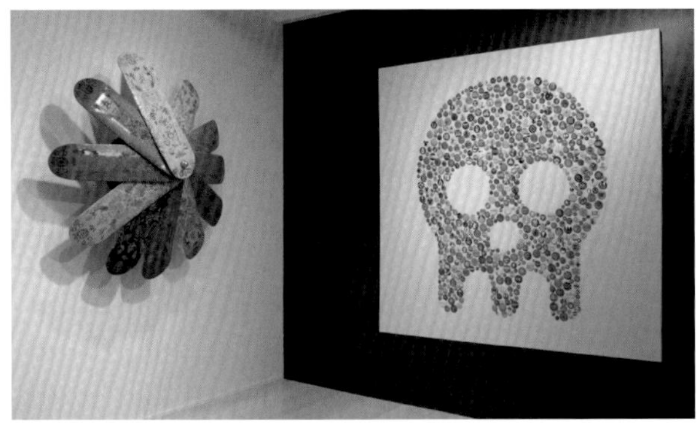

Varied Editions, 2007, installation view, Pace Prints, New York

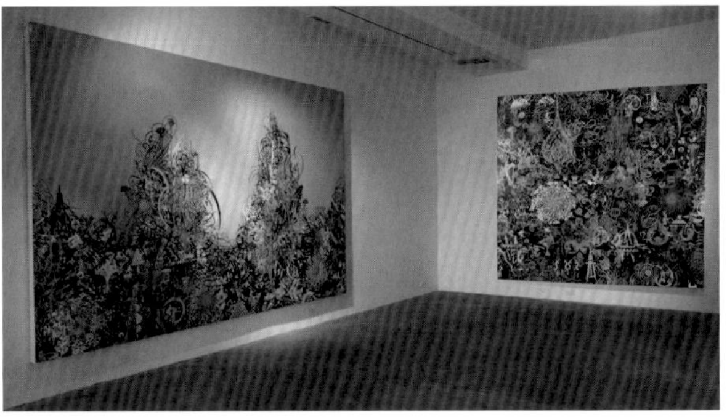

A Rich Fantasy Life, 2007, installation view Quint Gallery, La Jolla

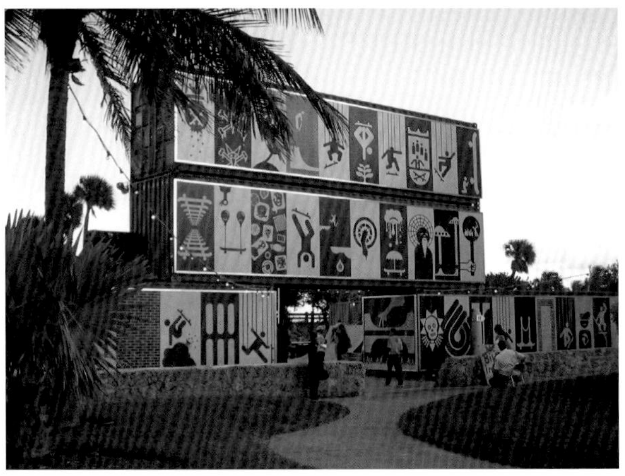

Concrete Waves: An Homage to Skate Culture, 2007, installation view, Art Positions, Art Basel Miami Beach, Miami

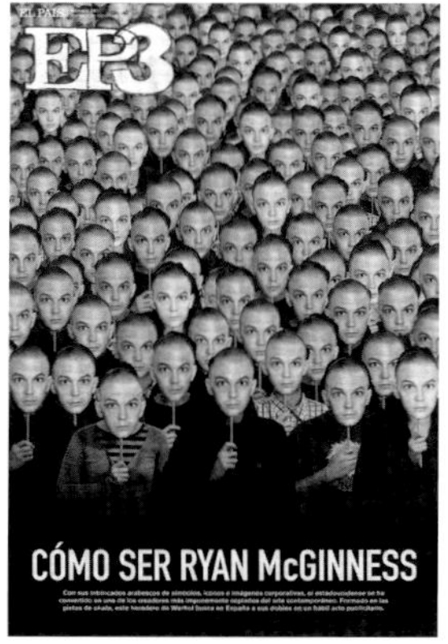
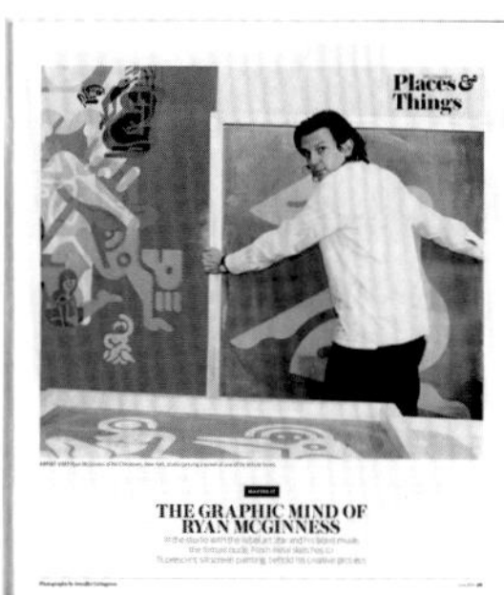

Left: "Cómo ser Ryan McGinness." *El País EP3*, Spain, No. 11.919, February 5, 2010, cover
Right: "The Graphic Mind of Ryan McGinness." *The Wall Street Journal Magazine*, Issue No. 16, June, 2011

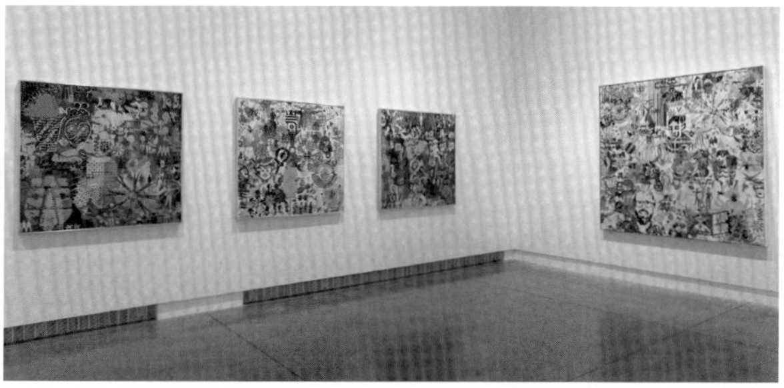

Studio Visit, 2014, installation view, Virginia Museum of Fine Arts, Richmond

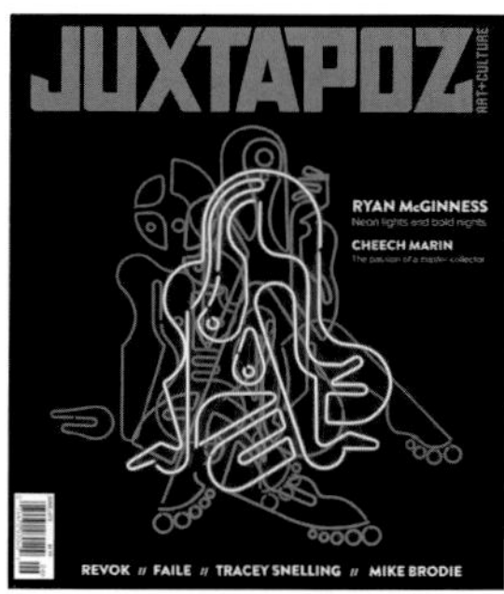
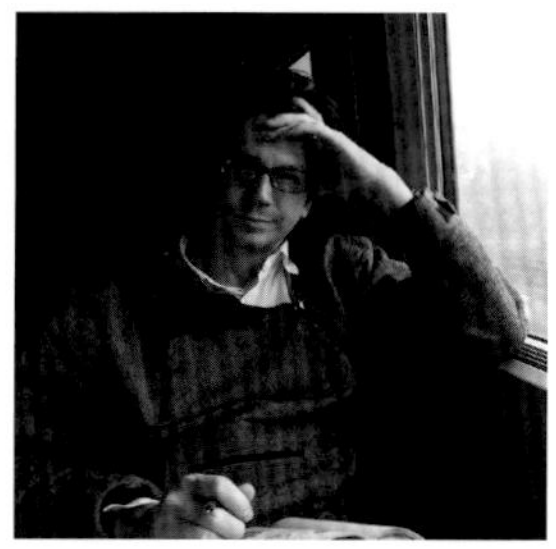

Left: "In the Forest of Signs: Ryan McGinness." *Juxtapoz*, No. 173, Vol. 22, No. 6, June, 2015, cover
Right: McGinness on train from Amsterdam to Paris, 2014

disconnect between the symbol and the referent." *(Lecture at Museum of Fort Worth, TX, October 11, 2016)* In February, family moves back into Walker Street loft while renovations continue. In March, travels to Virginia Beach for exhibition and lecture at Museum of Contemporary Art. In the spring, continues to work with sign materials and creates the *Sign Trees*, which are installed in the Hamptons in the summer. Spends 4 weeks in Gloucester, VA, working on *Mother & Child* drawings. Documentary film, *Ryan McGinness: Studio Process*, directed by Jess Dang, is released in the fall. Begins work on government commissions for the Art in Embassies program in Taiwan and for the US/Mexico border crossing in San Ysidro. Completes *Mother & Child* monoprint series with Lower East Side Print-shop. Publishes *Black Holes (Acid Blotter Tabs)* print edition. In September, travels to Moscow visiting the Kremlin and to St. Petersburg visiting the Winter Palace. In October, 3-year long Instagram project is unveiled at Sotheby's *Take Home a Nude* Benefit for New York Academy of Art. Spends December in Amsterdam.

2016

The *Studio View* paintings get more ambitious in scale and more complicated in their presentation of space. In March, travels to Los Angeles for his *#metadata* exhibition at Kohn Gallery. Galerie du Jour publishes *Signals*, a 500-page book of McGinness' iconic drawings. In August, vacations in Montauk and exhibits new *Signals* paintings at the Surf Lodge. "They use the visual language of universal sign systems and therefore give the illusion that they are communicating blunt pedestrian information, but they undermine that same visual language by evading elucidation." *(Symonds, Alexandria. "One Artist's Very Symbolic New Work, Explained—Sort of." www.nytimes.com (August 10, 2016))* In October, travels to Paris for unveiling of Longchamp headquarters, which had been wrapped for the previous 8 months in details of McGinness' paintings. Lectures at Modern Art Museum of Fort Worth. In December, travels to Miami for launch of *50 Parties* book at Art Basel, where numerous parties are recreated for the night at The Standard.

2017

Continues with *Studio View* paintings. Begins experimenting with halftone paintings. The *Black Holes* morph into the *Dark Energy* series. Continues to work throughout the year on the San Ysidro US/Mexico border project. Begins a regimented microdosing schedule. In February, travels to Turks & Caicos for Father's 70th birthday celebration. In June, travels to Virginia Beach for Children's Hospital of the King's Daughters mural dedication. Creates *Wayfinding*, a skatepark in Detroit with Tony Hawk with his street signs. By October, finishes Art in Embassies commission for American Institute in Taiwan. In November, travels to San Diego for *Ocular Evidence* exhibition at Quint Gallery and to Detroit for *Studio Views* exhibition at the Cranbrook Art Museum.

Selected Bibliography

2017

Morrison, Jim. "Ryan McGinness." www.pilotonline.com (November 14, 2014)
Sharp, Sarah Rose. "Into the Maze-y Mind of Artist Ryan McGinness." www.culturesource.com (December 6, 2017)
Sharp, Sarah Rose. "New Exhibits at Cranbrook Give a Street-eye View of Basquiat, McGinness, Haring." www.freep.com (November 16, 2017)
Carrigan, Margaret. "Where Natalie Frank and Ryan McGinness Go to Practice Their Nude Drawing." www.observer.com (September 13, 2017)
Kailus, Julie. "Tony Hawk Partners with Artist, Community of Detroit to Open Public Art/Skate Park." www.grindtv.com (September 12, 2017)
Roche, Leigh. "Wayfinding- Art Installation & Skatepark in Detroit." www.huffingtonpost.com (September 17, 2017)
Sutton, Benjamin. Editions '17, Lower East Side Print Shop, USA, 2017, pp. 2, 20-27
Cascone, Sarah. "One Model, 10 Nudes: See How Different Artists Treated the Female Form at Will Cotton's Drawing Party." www.artnet.com (October 11, 2017)
Trimpe, Lexi. "Tony Hawk and Artist Ryan McGinness Bring a Contemporary Skate Park to Downtown Detroit." www.hourdetroit.com (August 16, 2017)
Frank, Annalise. "Tony Hawk Test Drives New Wayfinding Skatepark in Detroit." www.crainsdetroit.com (August 15, 2017)
Simpson, Elizabeth. "Encouraging Creativity." *The Virginian Pilot*, USA, June 24, 2017, cover, p. 7
Simpson, Elizabeth. "New York artist returns to hometown of Virginia Beach to present art installation, and nurture creativity of children." www.pilotonline.com (June 23, 2017)

2016

Miller, M.H. "One Artist Threw a Party a Week for an Entire Year." www.nytimes.com (December 7, 2016)
Maurer, Daniel. "Ryan McGinness Combined 50 Parties into a Book and One Big Basel Bash" www.bedfordandbowery.com (December 6, 2016)
Cohen, Alina. "The Art of the Party: "50 Parties" by Ryan McGinness" www.standardculture.com (December 4, 2016)
Mufson, Beckett. "[NSFW] Here's Proof Throwing a Great Party Every Week is Art." www.thecreatorsproject.vice.com (December 2, 2016)
Gavin, Francesca. "Art Events to See if You're in Miami this Month." www.dazeddigital.com (December 1, 2016)
Lasane, Andrew and Eisinger, Dale. "50 Artists You Need to Follow on Instagram" www.complex.com (October 10, 2016)
Bennett, Kim Taylor. "We Talked with Artist Ryan McGinness about His New Project 'Signals'." www.vice.com (September 2, 2016)
Symonds, Alexandria. "One Artist's Very Symbolic New Work, Explained — Sort of." www.nytimes.com (August 10, 2016)
____. "Hauteur de Vue." L'officiel, France, June/July/August, 2016, pp. 46-47
Roche, Delphine. "Oeuvre Éphémère." Numéro, France, June/July, 2016
Flores, Cor "Ryan McGinness Invades Longchamp Paris." www.farenheitmagazine.com (May 13, 2016)
Mufson, Beckett. "Ryan McGinness' Meditations on Motherhood." www.thecreatorsproject.vice.com (May 7, 2016)
Darcella, Aria. "Art and Fashion Meet Again at Ryan McGinness' and Agnès b.'s "Signals'." www.fashionunfiltered.com (May 2, 2016)
Bertrand, Virginie. "Maroquinier Dépliant Sa Toile." Côté Paris, France, April/May, 2016
____. "American Graffiti." L'obs, France, April 28, 2016, p. 116
Mufson, Beckett. "Ryan McGinness Thinks You're Lookin at Art Wrong." www.thecreatorsproject.vice.com (April 22, 2016)
Feitelberg, Rosemary. "Agnès b. Joins Forces with Ryan McGinness." www.wwd.com (April 21, 2016)
Andreas. "New York: Signals." www.superfuture.com (April 20, 2016)
____. "Street Mode" Madame Figaro, France, April 8, 2016, p. 24
____. "Painting: Ryan McGinness Explores #metadata." www.juxtapoz.com (April 6, 2016)
Sleepboy. "Ryan McGinness – '#metadata' @ Kohn Gallery." www.arrestedmotion.com (March 28, 2016)
Wall, Caroline. "Ryan McGinness' 'Mother and Child' Prints for Free Arts NYC." www.whitewallmag.com (March 23, 2016)
Fox, T.S. "Ryan McGinness Opens '#metadata' at Kohn Gallery." www.hypebeast.com (March 23, 2016)
Mufson, Beckett. "Paintings within Paintings Hit Disorienting New Show '#metadata'." www.thecreatorsproject.vice.com (March 17, 2016)
Chung, Alexa. "Street Art." Paris Match, France, March 16, 2016
Vankin, Deborah. "Context for the Data." Los Angeles Times, USA, March 13, 2016, p. F2
Gérard, Violaine. "Ryan McGinness Artiste Contemporain." Air France Magazine, France, March, 2016, p. 80
Smith, J. Travis. "How 10 Influential New Yorkers Take Their Morning Coffee." www.gearpatrol.com (January 15, 2016)

2015

Schmidt, Jason. Artists II, Steidl, Germany, 2015, p. 97
____. "Artist Ryan McGinness and His InstagrAM Self Portrait for Take Home a Nude." www.sothebys.com (October 2015)
Kerwin, Barbara. Drawing from the Inside Out, ATS Art Textbook Society, USA, 2015, pp. 203-204

Randal, Matt. "10 Instagram Accounts You Should Follow." www.widewalls.ch (2015)
Womack, Jessica. "A Visit with Ryan McGinness at Lower East Side Printshop." www.moma.org (October 7, 2015)
Russo, Victor. "Stories in the Sky: Ryan McGinness." www.thescene.whro.org (2015)
Singh, Nidhi Raj. "Judge Liquor by Its Cover." www.newindianexpress.com (September 19, 2015)
Schreffler, Laura. "Artist Ryan McGinness Shares His Haute LA Secrets." www.hauteliving.com (September 3, 2015)
Booker, Briana. "Ryan McGinness, the Man behind the Creative: A Raw & Reflective 1:1 Interview." www.examiner.com (August 29, 2015)
Graver, David. "Interview: Artist Ryan McGinness on Designing for Hennessy." www.coolhunting.com (August 28, 2015)
Landes, Jennifer. "More Is More at Marder." www.easthamptonstar.com (August 13, 2015)
Cavaluzzo, Alexander. "The Indelible Iconography of Ryan McGinness." www.bbook.com (August 10, 2015)
Pham, Rex. "Hennessy VS x Ryan McGinness Limited Bottle." www.uncvr.net (August 10, 2015)
LaSane, Andrew. "Why Ryan McGinness Is the Perfect Fit for Hennessy." www.complex.com (August 10, 2015)
Kirk-Hanley, Sarah. Editions '15, Lower East Side Print Shop, USA, 2015, pp. 21-27
Clark, Trent. "Artist Ryan McGinness Designs Black Light Hennessy V.S Limited Edition Bottle." www.hiphopwired.com (August 3, 2015)
Bowers, Courtney. "Seeing Signs." Hamptons, USA, Vol. 36, Issue 8, July 31-August 6, 2015, p. 82
Restrepo, Javier. "HOMBRE First Look: Hennessy Presents New VS Limited Edition Bottle Design by Ryan McGinness." www.hombre1.com (July 29, 2015)
Witt, Morgan. "Art: Hennessy V.S Limited Edition Artist Bottle by Ryan McGinness." www.strictlysocial.com (July 24, 2015)
Stochl, Gerhard. "Talking Skateboarding, Instagram, and Glow-in-the-Dark Art with Ryan McGinness." www.thecreatorsproject.vice.com (July 17, 2015)
Tay, Michelle. "Artketing: Hennessy Taps Ryan McGinness for Newest Art Label." www.blouinartinfo.com (July 16, 2015)
Pasori, Cedar. "Hennessy Chooses Ryan McGinness For New Artist Bottle Collaboration." www.complex.com (July 13, 2015)
Maleszka, Jamie. "Ryan McGinness Talks His Creative Process for Hennessy's New V.S Limited Edition Bottle." www.massappeal.com (July 13, 2015)
____. "Hennessy Teams Up With Ryan McGinness For New Artist Collaboration'." www.vibe.com (July 12, 2015)
McDermott, Emily. "Signs of Ryan McGinness." www.interviewmagazine.com (July 3, 2015)
Lucy, Martha. The Order of Things. The Barnes Foundation, USA, 2015, p. 31
McCormick, Carlo. "In the Forest of Signs: Ryan McGinness." Juxtapoz, No. 173, Vol. 22, No. 6, June, 2015, cover, pp. 10, 48-59
____. "Guest Designer: Ryan McGinness." Zoetrope: All-Story, Vol. 19, No. 01, Spring 2015, entire issue
____. "Elemental Mugs." Juxtapoz, No. 172, Vol. 22, No. 5, May, 2015, p. 118
Herriman, Kat. "Teamwork: Artist Ryan McGinness collaborates on unisex collection with M. Patmos." www.wmagazine.com (March 31, 2015)
Brask Studio Visits, Brask Publications, DK, 2015, pp. 208-213
"Ryan McGinness: Studio Process." Dir. Jess Dang
Ollison, Rashod. "The Psychedelic Art of Ryan McGinness." The Virginian Pilot, USA, February 7, 2015, cover, p. 6
McIntyre, Niamh. "Instagram Art Is a Joke, and It's on You." www.vice.com (January 27, 2015)
Bengal, Rebecca. "The Fresh Prints of M.Patmos: The Designer Launches a Capsule Collection with Artist Ryan McGinness." www.vogue.com (January 15, 2015)

2014

____. "Ryan McGinness 'Community Identity Stability @ Quint'." www.juxtapoz.com (November 10, 2014)
MacAdam, Alfred. "Ryan McGinness." Art News, Vol. 113, No. 9, October, 2014, p. 118
____. "You Should Know: Artist Ryan McGinness." www.guestofaguest.com (September 30, 2014)
Munro, Cait. "Ryan McGinness Art Inspires Highbrow Street Crime." www.artnet.com (August 9, 2014)
"Thieves Target Cryptic Road Signs Installed For Summer Streets." By Alice Gainer. CBS News. WCBS, New York, 8 Aug. 2014.
Grove, Ánxel. "Cincuenta señales enigmáticas, añadidas a las calles de Nueva York por un artista urbano." www.20minutos.es (August 7, 2014)
Sharp, Sonia. "A Highbrow Street Crime: Stealing Public ArtRyan McGinness's Edgy Signs Were Stolen Almost as Soon as They Were Installed." www.wsj.com (August 7, 2014)
Pasori, Cedar. "Exclusive: Artist Ryan McGinness Details His New York 'Signs' Project and How Almost All of Them Have Been Stolen." www.complex.com (August 6, 2014)
Tinson, Teddy. "Ryan McGinness: Street Art Heist." www.interviewmagazine.com (August 5, 2014)
____. "Signs, 2014 by Ryan McGinness." www.juxtapoz.com (August 5, 2014)
____. "Ryan McGinness: Signs, 2014." www.theworldsbestever.com (August 4, 2014)
Erdos, Elleree. "Ryan McGinness: Fluorescent Body Parts." Art in Print, Vol. 4, No. 2, July-August, 2014, p. 32
Beauty Reigns: A Baroque Sensibility in Recent Painting, McNay Art Museum, USA, 2014, pp. 76, 84-87, 93, 95, 135, 137

____. "Ryan McGinness on his show 'Figure Drawings'." www.paceprints.com
  (June 6, 2014)
Wolfe, Duncan. "Ryan McGinness." *Human Being Journal*, Issue No. 4, Spring 2014,
  pp. 58-67
Munro, Cait. "The 15 Best Artists to Follow on Instagram." www.artnet.com
  (May 21, 2014)
Harris, Anthony. "Ryan McGinness." *RVA*, Issue No. 16, Spring 2014, pp. 30-35
Benrimon, Alexander. "Ryan McGinness on What It Takes to Build a Universe."
  www.artnet.com (May 16, 2014)
Necci. "Trickster Makes the World: Ryan McGinness at the VMFA." www.rvamag.com
  (May 12, 2014)
Szkotak, Molly. "An Interview with Ryan McGinness." www.needsupply.com
  (May 2, 2014)
Ekker, Jan Pieter. "Op Zoek Naar 200 Iconen." *Het Parool*, The Netherlands,
  April 10, 2014, p. PS18
ter Borg, Lucette. "Schilderijen die Oplichten als Lantaarnvissen in Zee." *NRC Handelblad*,
  The Netherlands, April 10, 2014, p. C9
____. "Gallery Ryan McGinness." www.avro.nl (April 8, 2014)
McNamara, Carmel. "Ryan McGinness Takes Over Amsterdam!." www.frameweb.com
  (April 2, 2014)
____. "Ryan McGinness." *de Volkskrant*, The Netherlands, April 1, 2014
Vogel, Wendy. "Ryan McGinness." *Modern Painters*, USA, January, 2014, p. 91

2013
Kulu, Ben. "The Yearbook: 83 Fascinating, Fabulous and Creative New Yorkers
  Who Made the Scene in 2013." *Scene*, Issue No. 21, Winter 2013/2014, p. 29
Colucci, Emily. "Ryan McGinness on His Sketches and His Highly Anticipated Miami
  Art Week Party." www.societeperrier.com (March 11, 2013)
____. "Ryan McGinness x SPiN Standard Glow-in-the-Dark Ping-Pong Table."
  www.arrestedmotion.com (November 4, 2013)
Silver, Leigh. "Ryan McGinness Designs a Dayglo Ping-Pong Table for The Standard
  Los Angeles." www.complex.com (October 31, 2013)
Sutton, Benjamin. "Ryan McGinness Unveils Black Light Ping-Pong Table at
  The Standard in L.A." www.artinfo.com (October 30, 2013)
Rajah. "Ryan McGinness Launches Custom Ping-Pong Table at The Standard."
  www.freshnessmag.com (October 30, 2013)
Standard Staff. "Is This the Coolest Ping-Pong Table Ever Made?"
  www.standardculture.com (October 28, 2013)
Wyrick, Christopher. "Glow-in-the-Dark Ping-Pong Lights Up the SPiN Standard
  Downtown Party." www.hollywoodreporter.com (October 25, 2013)
McCarty, Maureen. "Artist Ryan McGinness on Coming Out as a Straight Ally and
  the Inspiration Behind the NCOD Design." www.hrc.org (October 15, 2013)
Zagaria, Kat. "Finding Infinity: A Ryan McGinness Solo Show at Bridgette Mayer."
  www.paperclips215.com (October 12, 2013)
McCarty, Maureen. "The Votes Are In: Check Out Ryan McGinness's NCOD T-Shirt."
  www.hrc.org (October 11, 2013)
Cheng, Susan. "25 Reasons Ryan McGinness Is the #1 Artist You Should Follow on
  Instagram." www.complex.com (October 10, 2013)
Murg, Stephanie. "Ryan McGinness Creates Artwork for National Coming Out Day."
  www.mediabistro.com (October 7, 2013)
Falkowski, Jamie. "Conversation with Ryan McGinness & José Parlá."
  blog.alldayeveryday.com (September 25, 2013)
Vitrani, Hugo. "Ryan McGinness : L'empire des signes ." www.hugovitrani.com
  (September 3, 2013)
McCarty, Maureen. "The Votes Are In: Check Out Ryan McGinness's NCOD T-Shirt."
  www.hrc.org (October 11, 2013)
Skidmore, Maisie. "Art: Artist Ryan McGinness Allows Viewers a Valuable Glimpse
  into his Creative Process." www.itsnicethat.com (September 16, 2013)
Codinha, Alessandra. "Est Vir Qui Adest." *Sketchbook Selections (2000-2012)*, Gingko Press,
  USA, 2013, pp. 5-9
Zio. "Summer Destinations." www.theworldsbestever.com (July 3, 2013)
Barguirdjian, Delphine. "Life of Ryan." *Scene*, Issue No. 16, June 2013, pp. 88-89
Littman, Brett. "The Making of an Icon." *Women: New (Re)Presentations*, Quint
Contemporary Art, USA, 2013, pp. 48-59
Pincus, Robert L. "Signs of the Nude." *Women: New (Re)Presentations*, Quint Contemporary
  Art, USA, 2013, pp. 15-23
Davies, Hugh M. "Women: New (Re)Presentations Post-Lecture Q&A." *Women: New
  (Re)Presentations*, Quint Contemporary Art, USA, 2013, pp. 154-159
Colucci, Emily. "10 Works of Art We Wish We Could Take Home from the Armory
  Show." www.societeperrier.com (March 11, 2013)
____. *Gold & Silver Metallic Graphics*. Viction: Workshop, Ltd., China, 2013, p. 59
Codinha, Alessandra. "The Male Gaze Under a Blacklight." *Maker*, Issue No. 2,
  Winter 2013, pp. 48-77
Cembalest, Robin. "What I Like About You: Artists to Follow on Instagram."
  www.artnews.com (January 17, 2013)

2012
____. "The Playmate as Fine Art." *Playboy*, USA, Vol. 60, Issue 1,
  January/February 2013, pp. 82-89
Snyder, Drew. "Ryan McGinness: Women: New (Re)Presentations." *Art Ltd.*, USA,
  November/December, 2012, pp. 31-32
Johnson, Catherine. *Thank You Andy Warhol*. Glitterati Incorporated, USA, 2012,
  pp. 226-228

Sleepboy. "Preview: Ryan McGinness – "Women: New (Re)Presentations" @
  Quint Contemporary." www.arrestedmotion.com (September 15, 2012)
____. "Opening: Ryan McGinness 'Women' @ Quint Contemporary Art, San Diego."
  www.juxtapoz.com (September 14, 2012)
Goergen, Stacey. "Inspired Artistry." *Hamptons*, USA, Vol. 34, Issue 8,
  August 3-9, 2012, p. 70
____. "Women: New (Re)Presentations." *Manor House Quarterly*, USA, Summer 2012,
  pp. 38-43
____. "Ryan McGinness Puts His Creative Process on Exhibit." www.artsobserver.com
  (July 3, 2012)
Crow, Kelly. "Ryan McGinness Revives Andy Warhol's Favorite Medium: Silkscreen."
  www.wsj.com (June 29, 2012)
Prickett, Sarah Nicole. "Ryan McGinness' Processed Women." www.bullettmedia.com
  (June 20, 2012)
Baumgardner, Julie. "Editor's Pick: Ryan McGinness at Charles Bank." www.1stdibs.com
  (June 20, 2012)
Laster, Paul. "Ryan McGinness: Women." *Time Out New York*, USA, Issue 864,
  June 14-20, 2012, p. 47
Littman, Brett. "Ryan McGinness." *Flatt*, USA, Issue No. 3, Spring/Summer 2012,
  pp. 16-27
McCormick, Carlo. "The Last Look: Ryan McGinness." *Paper Magazine*, USA, Vol. 28,
  No. 7, May 2012, p. 112
Carneiro, Solange. "Ryan McGinness: Women: Blacklight Paintings & Sculptures."
  mag.weareselecters.com (May 29, 2012)
Dia, Aminata. "Two Timin' Man." *Manhattan*, USA, May 2012, p. 30
Smith, Melissa. "From 'Crappy' to Snappy." www.capitalnewyork.com (May 24, 2012)
Juggernut3. "Openings: Ryan McGinness Women: Blacklight Paintings & Sculptures
  @ Charles Bank." www.arrestedmotion.com (May 21, 2012)
Keane, Erin. "Painter Explores Advertising Influence in 21C Lecture." www.wfpl.org
  (May 17, 2012)
Sleepboy. "Openings: Ryan McGinness Women: Sketches @ Solutions @ Gering López."
  www.arrestedmotion.com (May 15, 2012)
____. "Around the World: Ryan McGinness." www.yoox.com (May 9, 2012)
Brown, Raymond. "Preview: Ryan McGinness Women Series Opens Tonight and
  Tomorrow at Gering & López and Charles Bank." www.12ozprophet.com
  (May 3, 2012)
Juggernut3. "Openings: Ryan McGinness Geometric Primitives at Pace Primitive."
  www.arrestedmotion.com (April 4, 2012)
Enrique, Marcos. "Recap: Ryan McGinness 'Geometric Primitives' at Pace Primitive
  Gallery." www.12ozprophet.com (April 3, 2012)
Standard Staff. "To Do: Ryan McGinness' Show at the Pace Gallery."
  www.standardculture.com (March 29, 2012)

2011
____. "Ryan McGinness Leading Pioneer of the New Semiotics." *Spectrum*, Korea,
  Issue No. 04, Winter 2011, pp. 6-11
Chan, Diane. "Media Shelf: Calendar To-Do List Pad." *Azure Magazine*, USA,
  Vol. 212, November/December 2011, p. 88
Poe. "Incase x Ryan McGinness." www.freshnessmag.com (November 16, 2011)
Karmic Abstraction, Bridgette Mayer Gallery, Philadelphia, UK, 2011, pp. 34-37, 54
Standard Staff. "Ryan McGinness' Studio Manual Unlocks the Secrets to Fine Art
  Success." www.standardculture.com (November 4, 2011)
Myers, Micki. "Ryan McGinness Works (A Lot)." *Maniac Magazine*, USA, October/
  November 2011, pp. 42-44
Colman, David. "In the Art World, No Lack of Ryans." *The New York Times*,
  USA, Vol. CLX, No. 55,518, September 4, 2011, p. 6 ST
McKeough, Tim. "Maybe They'll Study." *The New York Times*, USA, Vol. CLX,
  No. 55,515, September 1, 2011, p. D7
Stephens, Anna Maria. "Life of Ryan." *Riviera*, USA, July/August, 2011, p. 56
____. "Erotisches Händchen." *Architectural Digest*, Germany, July/August 2011, p. 90
Kennedy, Randy. "Not That Kind of Nose Job." *The New York Times*, USA,
  Vol. CLX, No. 55,474, July 22, 2011, pp. C21, 24
Clarke, Katherine. "The Graphic Mind of Ryan McGinness." *The Wall Street Journal
  Magazine*, USA, Issue No. 16, June, 2011, pp. 29-32
Stephanie. "Go See: Ryan McGinness at Michael Kohn Gallery."
  www.platinumcheese.com (June 22, 2011)
Ellison, Victoria. "Warhol's Spawn." *LA Weekly*, USA, Vol. 33, No. 30,
  June 17-23, 2011, p. 46
Daichendt, G. James. "Ryan McGinness Sponsorhip Redux." www.artscenecal.com
  (June 2011)
Brundage, Douglas. "Ryan McGinness Drawing Salon." www.hypebeast.com
  (June 8, 2011)
Evans, Yolanda. "Ryan McGinness Brings Live Nudes to the Standard Hollywood."
  www.refinery29.com (June 6, 2011)
Mozena, Kari. "Ryan McGinness at Michael Kohn Gallery." www.lamag.com
  (June 3, 2011)
Pajer, Nicole and Downing, Dustin. "Ryan McGinness Presents: Women, The Blacklight
  Paintings." www.chinashopmag.com (June 3, 2011)
Saban, Stephen. "Ryan McGinness Invades Los Angeles." www.worldofwonder.net
  (June 2, 2011)
Rolnik, Daniel. "Ryan McGinness Works on Paper/Lecture at Giant Robot."
  www.argotandochre.com (May 24 and June 9, 2011)

Hosie, Evan. "Hautels: The Standard Presents Ryan McGinness Art Installations."
    www.hauteliving.com (May 23, 2011)
Rickert, Lynn. "The Best: Ryan McGinness' Artsy Black-light Playing Cards."
    www.details.com (May 11, 2011)
Gluck, Marissa. "Who Is Ryan McGinness and Why Is He Suddenly Everywhere in
    L.A.?." www.californiahomedesign.com (May 10, 2011)
____. "The Standard x Ryan McGinness Nudie Cards." www.notcot.com (May 7, 2011)
Eckler, Daniel. "Blacklight Nudie Cards by Ryan McGinness." www.definitivetouch.com
    (May 7, 2011)
Finkel, Jori. "For Ryan McGinness, Art is One Big Party." *LA Times*, USA,
    Volume CXXX, No. 152, May 4, 2011, p. D8-9
Standard Staff. "Ryan McGinness' Nudie Cards." www.standardculture.com
    (May 2, 2011)
VanZanten, Virginia. "A New Deck: Blacklight Nudie Cards from Ryan McGinness."
    www.wmagazine.com (May 2, 2011)
Proctor, Roy. "An Info-age Warhol." *Richmond Times Dispatch*, USA, April 10, 2011, p. G8
Berman, Aniko. "Ryan McGinness' "Women: The Blacklight Paintings' at Le Bain,
    New York." www.4x-magazine.com (April, 2011)
Ozols, Victor. "Studio Visit: Meet Joe Blacklight." *Black Book*, USA, Issue 83,
    April, 2011, pp. 32-33
Kollatz Jr., Harry. "The Maker and His Message." *Richmond Magazine*, USA,
    April, 2011, p. 47
Kirk Hanley, Sarah. "Ink: The Lexicon of Tomorrow: Print-Based Installation."
    2010.blog.art21.org (April 8, 2011)
Foster., Richard. "In Living Color." *Style Weekly*, USA, Volume 39, No. 13,
    March 30, 2011, p. 29
Gladman, Randy. "Exhibition: Ryan McGinness at Page Bond Gallery."
    www.ministryofartisticaffairs.com (March 30, 2011)
Litos Graffera, KunstCentret Silkeborg Bad, DEN, 2011, pp. 60-61
Juggernut3. "Openings: Ryan McGinness Women the Blacklight Paintings at Standard
    NY's Le Bain." www.arrestedmotion.com (March 11, 2011)
Siegler, Mara. "Last Night's Parties." www.guestofaguest.com (March 7, 2011)
Wallin, Yasha. "Lady Havoc! Ryan McGinness Brings 'Women: The Blacklight Paintings'
    to Le Bain." www.papermag.com (March 5, 2011)
Kamenoff, Corey. "The Standard Ryan McGinness 'Women: The Blacklight Paintings'
    Installation." www.cultureshoq.com (March 4, 2011)
Scott-Richards, Victoria. "Ryan McGinness' Black Light Paintings."
    www.privilegedclub.com (March 4, 2011)
Woollard, Deidre. "Ryan McGinness' Black Light Paintings at The Standard."
    www.luxist.com (March 3, 2011)
Standard Staff. "Ryan McGinness New Blacklight Women." www.standardculture.com
    (March 3, 2011)
Christiansen, Dan. "Ryan McGinness." *Living Proof*, USA, No. 6, 2011, cover, pp. 56-65
____. "Art Parties + Openings." *Art + Auction*, Vol. 34. No. 7, March 2011, p.26
Lowpro. "Teaser: Armory Week '11 Ryan McGinness Women the Blacklight Paintings
    at Country Club." www.arrestedmotion.com (February 22, 2011)
Corbett, Rachel. "Lost in the 'Art Machine'." www.observer.com (February 22, 2011)
Harrington, Steven. "Ryan McGinness Black Holes Draw You Inside and Outside."
    www.brooklynstreetart.com (February 8, 2011)
____. "In the Air: Naked Ambition." *Art + Auction*, Vol. 34. No. 6, February 2011, p.15
Juggernut3. "Ryan McGinness Black Holes Party at Phillips de Pury."
    www.arrestedmotion.com (January 27, 2011)
Siegler, Mara. "Last Night's Parties." www.guestofaguest.com (January 24, 2011)
Juggernut3. "Indoors: Ryan McGinness Black Holes Party at Phillips de Pury."
    www.arrestedmotion.com (January 11, 2011)
Standard Staff. "The Black Hole Series." www.standardculture.com (January 5, 2011)
Oliver, James. "Ryan McGinness 'Black Holes' at Phillips de Pury."
    www.slamxhype.com (January 4, 2011)
Juggernut3. "Openings: Ryan McGinness Black Holes Party at Phillips de Pury."
    www.arrestedmotion.com (January 3, 2011)

2010
____. "Ryan McGinness." *Muscle Up*, AUS, No. 1, 2010, p.128-131
Viva la Revolución, Museum of Contemporary Art San Diego, USA, 2010, pp. 88-91
Orden, Erica, "Local Buyers Wrap Teeming Art Basel." *The Wall Street Journal*, USA,
    December 6, 2010, p. A28
Juggernut3. "Ryan McGinness Black Holes Party at Phillips de Pury."
    www.arrestedmotion.com (December 22, 2010)
DC. "Ryan McGinness 'Black Holes' at Phillips de Pury & Company."
    www.livingproof.com (December 21, 2010)
Oliver, James. "Ryan McGinness 'Women: The Blacklight Paintings' at Club Madonna."
    www.slamxhype.com (December 21, 2010)
Morrison, Jim. "The Escape Artists: Ryan McGinness." *Distinction*, USA, Vol. 8,
    Fall, 2010, cover, pp. 73-81
Juggernut3. "Basel Week Miami '10: Ryan McGinness 'Women: The Blacklight Paintings'
    at Club Madonna." www.arrestedmotion.com (December 20, 2010)
Donoghue, Katy. "Miami Tribute to Andy Warhol." www.whitewallmag.com
    (December 9, 2010)
Lala, Kisa. "Inside Out Galleries at Wynwood." www.spreadartculture.com
    (December 7, 2010)
Laster, Paul. "Ryan McGinness Brings the Art Crowd to a Strip Club."
    www.artbasel.aol.com (December 4, 2010)

Saizarbitoria, Jauretsi. "The Fader Goes to Art Basel, Part 2." www.thefader.com
    (December 4, 2010)
Standard Staff. "Ryan McGinness' New Inspiration." www.standardculture.com
    (December 3, 2010)
Artinfo Staff. "Look Out Hustler, Here Comes Ryan McGinness." www.artinfo.com
    (December 3, 2010)
Oñate, Curro. "Ryan McGinness." *Staf*, Spain, No. 45, October, 2010, cover, pp. 34-37
Stochl, Gerhard. "Ryan McGinness." *Arkitip*, USA, No. 55, Fall, 2010, pp. 80-83
"Work of Art." *Bravo*, Dir. Pretty Matches Productions and Magical Elves Productions,
    TV Program, Episode 8, Air Date: July 28, 2010
Heller, Steven. "The Message Is the Message." The New York Times, USA,
    June 6, 2010, Book Review, pp. 40-41
____. "Old Meets New at the Virginia MFA." *Art in America*, No. 6, June/July 2010, p.198
Global New Art, Taguchi Art Collection, Bijutsu Shuppan-Sha Co. Ltd., JAP, 2010,
    pp. 63, 103, 115
Nakamura, Eric. "Book Collector: Studio Manual." *Giant Robot*, USA, Issue 65,
    May, p. 14
Annas, Teresa, "Beach-bred Art Star Hits Richmond." *The Virginian-Pilot, The Daily Break*,
    USA, April 30, 2010
Robertson, Rebecca. "Logo Motive." *Art News*, USA, Vol. 109, No. 4, April, 2010, p. 25
Laster, Paul. "Finding Ryan McGinness." *Studio Franchise*, La Casa Encendida, Spain,
    2010, pp. 7-26
Costa, Jordi. "The Real McGinness." *Studio Franchise*, La Casa Encendida, Spain,
    2010, pp. 117-123
Jorquera, Adam. "A Conversation Between Adam Jorquera & Ryan McGinness."
    Studio Franchise, La Casa Encendida, Spain, 2010, pp. 175-190
Molina, Óscar Alonso. "Ser o no ser Ryan McGinness." *ABCD*, Suplemento Sección,
    Spain, March 20, 2010, pp. 32-33
Salaices, David. "Interview with Ryan McGinness." www.glltn.com (March 29, 2010)
Burgos, Pilar Heranz, "Ryan McGinness." *Vanidad*, Revista Sección, Spain,
    March 1, 2010, p. 50
____. "El Estudio Franquicia de McGinness." *Publico*, Hoy Sección, Spain,
    February 22, 2010, p. 40
Fajardo, José, "Artista por Cinco Días." *Metropoli*, Ocio Sección, Spain,
    February 12, 2010, p. 48
de Llano, Pablo. "Taller McGinness, pase sin llamer." *El País*, Spain, No. 11.924,
    February 10, 2010, p.7
Pulido, Beatriz, "Cuarenta Ryan McGinness Originales." *El Mundo*, Madrid Sección,
    Spain, February 5, 2010, p. 8
____. "Universos Transplantados." *Tiempo*, Spain, February 5, 2010, p. 73
Costa, Jordi, "Cómo ser Ryan McGinness." *El País EP3*, Spain, No. 11.919,
    February 5, 2010, cover, p. 5
Garrán, Elena, "Ryan McGinness Se Muda A Madrid." *DT*, Revista Sección, Spain,
    February 1, 2010, pp. 66-67
Bodin, Claudia, "Die Galeristen haben uns sehr unterstützt." *Art Das Kunstmagazin*,
    DEU, February, 2010, p. 110
Ishikawa, Aiko, "Interview with Ryan McGinness." *Plus Eighty-one*," JAP, Vol. 47,
    Spring 2010, pp. 10-19

2009
Wolff, Rachel. "Art Talk: He Shrunk Andy Warhol." *Art News*, USA, Vol. 108, No. 9,
    October, 2009, p. 33
Galligan, Gregory. "Exhibtion Reviews: Ryan McGinness." *Art in America*, USA, No. 8,
    September, 2009, p. 145
Fig, Joe. *Inside the Painter's Studio*, Princeton Architectural Press, USA, 2009, pp. 120-127
____. "Big Think Interviews with Ryan McGinness." www.bigthink.com (2009)
Leffler, Laura. "Ryan McGinness, New York." *Art Papers*, USA, Issue 33/03,
    May/June 2009, pp. 63-64
McCormick, Carlo. "System Overload." *Paper Magazine*, USA, Vol. 25, Issue 8,
    March, 2009, p. 35
____. "Printing Press: Ryan McGinness Works." *Elle Decor*, USA, Vol. 20, No. 2,
    March, 2009, p. 52
Gavin, Francesca. *Creative Space: Urban Homes of Artists and Innovators*, Laurence King
    Publishing, UK, 2009, pp. 118-123
____. "Book Collector: Ryan McGinness Works." *Giant Robot*, USA, Issue 59, 2009, p. 14
____. "…crit…books." *I.D. Magazine*, USA, Vol. 56, No. 2, March/April 2009, p. 85
Guarnieri, Anne-Marie. "Culture Watch." *Gotham*, USA, March, 2009, p. 142
Halley, Peter. "Interview Peter Halley and Ryan McGinness." *Ryan McGinness Works.*,
    Rizzoli International Publications, Inc., USA, 2009, pp. 8-13
Lindquist, Greg. "Inside the Studio: Notes from a Former Assistant." *Ryan McGinness
    Works.*, Rizzoli International Publications, Inc., USA, 2009, pp. 14-21
Byrne, David. "Conversation David Byrne and Ryan McGinness." *Ryan McGinness Works.*,
    Rizzoli International Publications, Inc., USA, 2009, pp. 22-27
Neil, Jonathan T. D. "The Looks of Looks, or, Ryan McGinness's Ontology of Color."
    Ryan McGinness Works., Rizzoli International Publications, Inc., USA, 2009,
    pp. 28-35
Greenwood, Tom. "The Q&A 500." *Ryan McGinness Works.*, Rizzoli International
    Publications, Inc., USA, 2009, pp. 281-290
Powers, Bill. "Art: Ryan McGinness." *Purple Fashion Magazine*, USA, Vol. 3, Issue 11,
    Spring/Summer, 2009, pp. 56
____. "Book Collector: No Sin/No Future." *Giant Robot*, USA, Issue 58, 2009, p. 14
Rodríguez, Begoña. "Toy Art." *Lapiz*, Spain, Vol. 28, No. 250-251, March, 2009,
    pp. 151-167

Montejo Navas, Adolfo. "Another Aesthetic Mainstream." *Lápiz*, Spain, Vol. 28,
    No. 250-251, March, 2009, pp. 113-131
Carson, Andrea. "Blind Spot." *Azure*, CAN, January/February, 2009, pp. 94-95
Rosen, Steven. "My Favorite Art Shows of 2008." *City Beat*, USA,
    December 31, 2008 - January 6, 2009, p. 25

2008
Ann Jordan, Betty. "Ryan McGinness Artcore." *Art News*, USA, Vol. 107, No. 11,
    December, 2008, p. 134
Collection Agnés B., JRP/Ringier, Zurich, CH, 2008, p. 217
Abstract America: New Painting, The Saatchi Gallery, Jonathan Cape, UK, 2008, pp. 240-247
Harkavay, Tamara. "Aesthetic Comfort." *Cincinnati Art Museum Member Magazine*, USA,
    Fall 2008, pp. 10-11
Jager, David. "Cool Aesthetic Comfort." *Now Magazine*, CAN, Vol. 28, No. 11,
    November 11, 2008
Cammisuli, Alice. "Ryan McGinness." *Exibart.on Paper*, Italy, No. 53, Anno VII,
    November, 2008, p. 65
____. "Favorite Things." *Giant Robot*, USA, Issue 57, 2008, p. 15
Sandals, Leah. "A Study in Contrasts." *National Post*, CAN, October 11, 2008, Toronto,
    At the Galleries, p. 21
____. "Ryan McGinness: Art by Design." *Canadian Art*,
    www.canadianart.ca/online/see-it/2008/10/09/ryan-mcginness, October 9, 2008
Dault, Gary Michael. "Silk-screens of a Pop Culture's Wreckage." *The Globe & Mail*,
    CAN, October 4, 2008, p. R19
____. "Ryan McGinness: A Shadow Feeling of Loss." *Vedere a Milano*, Italy, No. 280,
    October, 2008, p. 7
Bradbury, Leonie. "Transgressive Beaurty." *Arkitip*, USA, No. 48, Fall, 2008, pp. 2-47
Lindquist, Greg. "Inside the Studio: Notes from a Former Assistant." *Arkitip*, USA,
    No. 48, Fall, 2008, pp. 48-59
Quaroni, Ivan. "McGinness. Graffiti Urbani Minimal Chic." *Arte*, Italy, No. 421,
    September, 2008, p. 75
Royal Academy Illustrated 2008, Royal Academy of Arts, U.K., 2008, pp. 34, 42
The Future Must be Sweet—Lower East Side Print Shop Celebrates 40 Years, Marilyn S. Kushner,
    USA, 2008, pp. 22, 81-81
Bryant, Eric. "Ryan McGinness, Pace Prints." *Art News*, USA, Vol. 107, No. 2,
    February, 2008, p. 124
Deem, Megan. "The Art of Revenge." *Elle*, USA, No. 270, February, 2008, p. 138
Sharkey, Alix. "Art Basel 2007." *Ocean Drive*, USA, Vol. 16, No. 1, January, 2008,
    pp. 262-274

2007
MoMA Highlights since 1980, The Museum of Modern Art, U.S., 2007, p. 254
Hamersly, Michael. "For Jet Set or Skate Set." *The Miami Herald*, USA,
    December 5, 2007, pp. cover, 21A
Miller, Ken. *Revisionaries: A Decade of Art in Tokion*, Abrams Image, USA, 2007, pp. 56-57
Merrill, Kenneth. "Art Projects: Art in Public Spaces." *Home Miami*, USA,
    December 2007, p.18
Doctor Roncero, Rafael. *MUSAC Collection. Volume II*, MUSAC, Spain, 2007, pp. 326-329
Lindquist, Greg. "Ryan McGinness: Varied Editions." www.artcritical.com
    (November 9, 2007)
Cembalest, Robin. "Famous in 2012." *Art News*, USA, Vol. 106, No. 10,
    November, 2007, pp. 200-209
Allsop, Laura. "Dispatches Consumed." *Art Review*, UK, Issue 16, November, 2007, p. 39
Rubino, Abdrés. "León de dos Cabezas." *El País Semanal*, Spain, No. 1.621,
    October 21, 2007, p. 58
Stiff, Burl. "New Works Added at MCASD." *The San Diego Union-Tribune*, USA,
    July 10, 2007, p. E9
Lorent, Claude. "Knokke Art Estival." *La Libre Belgique*, Belgium, August 11, 2007, p. 17
Landscape: Form & Thought, Ingrao Gallery, USA, 2007, pp. 4, 30-33
Pincus, Robert. "Fantastic Planet." *The San Diego Union-Tribune*, USA, April 26, 2007,
    p. 25
Goddard, Dan. "Works Start Small and Then Grow." *San Antonio Express-News*, USA,
    April 25, 2007, S.A. Life
Salkin, Allen. "Selling Himself, And Prints, Too." *The New York Times*, USA, April 8, 2007,
    Sunday Styles, pp. 1, 11
Sheets, Hilarie M. "Ballerinas, Unicorns, and Boom Boxes." *Art News*, USA, Vol. 106,
    No. 4, April, 2007, pp. cover, 118-121
Martin, Penny. "Dress Art." *Another Magazine*, UK, No. 12, Spring/Summer 2007,
    pp.161-168
____. "Kunst: Galeries aan de Gracht." *Eigen Huis & Interieus*, The Netherlands,
    January 2007, p.53

2006
____. "Under the Influence." *Elle Decor*, USA, No. 132, December, 2006, p.56
Navarro, Mariano. "Ryan McGinness." *El Cultural, El Mundo*, Spain,
    November 30-December 6, 2006, pp. 30-31
____. Cover, *Art on Paper*, USA, Vol. 11, No. 2, USA, November/December, 2006
Branded and On Display, Krannert Art Museum and Kinkead Pavillion,
    University of Illinois, USA, 2006, p. 48
Mora, Tachy. "Ryan McGinness." *Neo 2*, Spain, November, 2006, p. 155
Beatrice, Luca. "I Trionfi Baracchi di Ryan McGinness." *Arte*, Italy, October, 2006, p. 83
"Start Milano." *Non Solo Moda*, Television Program, Italy, October 21, 2006
USA Today: New American Art from the Saatchi Gallery, Royal Academy of Art, U.K.,
    2006, pp. 236-243

Lamoree, Jhim. "Schilderijen Als Draaimolens." *Het Parool*, The Netherlands,
    October 14, 2006
Freeborn, John. *Big Kids Little Kids*, USA, 2006, pp. 100-101
Smallenburg, Sandra. "Logo's Die Niet Helpen Maar Ontregelen." *NRC Handelblad*,
    The Netherlands, October 13, 2006
Neil, Jonathan. "A Bit of What You Fancy: Ryan McGinness." *Art Review*, UK, Issue 4,
    October, 2006, p. 38
Powers, Bill. "Re-Elect Skull & Bones." *Black Book*, USA, No. 47, October, 2006, p. 42
van der Beek, Wim. "Ryan McGinness."*Kunstbeeld*, The Netherlands, No. 10, 2006
Spank The Monkey, Baltic Center for Contemporary Art, Die Gestalten Verlag,
    Germany, 2006, pp. 130-137
"The Run Up." Dir. Shaun Roberts & Joey Garfield, Upper Playground &
    Fifty24SF Gallery
Fox, Killian. "Spraypainting by Numbers." *The Observer*, UK, October 1, 2006,
    Art 2, Review, Critics 21
Powers, Bill. "Biting Ryan (The Plot Thickens)." *Black Book*, USA, No. 46,
    September, 2006, p. 67
Plummer, D'Lynne. "Sign Language: Ryan McGinness." *Art New England*, USA,
    August/September, 2006, pp. 18-19
van Cauwelaert de Wyels, Karolien. "Fraffiti In Huis?." *Elle Belgïe*, Belgium,
    June, 2006, pp. 70-72
Murg, Stephanie. "Scents and Sensibility." *Art News*, USA, Vol. 105, No. 4,
    April, 2006, p. 40
"Great Museums: MoMA." *Great Museums*, Dir. Chesney Doyle, Narr. Debby Wye,
    Channel 13, WNET April 9, 2006
Edgar, Heather. "Someone Write Ryan McGinness a Song." *Off the Wookie*, USA,
    April, 2006, pp. 39-48
Palmer, Valerie. "Art Smart." *Anthem*, USA, No. 21, March/April, 2006, pp. 40-41
Hares, Amber. "Noted: Installationview." *Afterimage*, USA, March/April, 2006, p. 54
Cook, Greg. "A Galaxy Far, Far Away." *The Boston Phoenix*, USA, March 24, 2006, p. 23
Alverson, Brigid. "Worlds within Worlds." *North Shore Sunday*, USA, March 5, 2006,
    pp. 11-12
McQuaid, Cate. "Brand Identity." *The Boston Globe*, USA, March 3, 2006, pp. D5, D20
Spence, Rebecca. "How Street It Is." *Art News*, USA, Vol. 105, No. 2, February, 2006,
    pp. 110-111
Mac Alpine, Dan. "Prepare to be Subverted—Mildly." *Beverly Citizen*, USA,
    February 16, 2006, p. 7
Bebermeyer, Mary. "Beautiful Losers: Street to the Museum." *Review*, USA,
    February, 2006, pp. 40-43
____. "Installationview: Ryan McGinness." *Reference and Research Book News*, USA,
    Vol. 24, No. 1, February, 2006
____. "Free Wrapping Paper." *Art on Paper*, USA, Vol. 10, No. 3, January/February, 2006,
    p. 16
Kuspit, Donald. "Reviews: Ryan McGinness." *Art Forum*, USA, XLIV, No. 5,
    January, 2006, p. 222-223

2005
Biesenbach, Klaus. *Greater New York 2005*, Museum of Modern Art, USA, 2005,
    pp. 40, 246-247
Nakamura, Eric. "Book Collector: Installationview." *Giant Robot*, USA, Issue 39, 2005,
    p. 18
Klanten, Robert. *Hidden Track: How Visual Culture is Going Places*, Die Gestalten Verlag,
    Germany, 2005, pp. 180-183
Miller, Jeffrey. "Things We Love." *House & Garden*, USA, December, 2005, p. 106-107
Outland, Michele. "Installationview." *Domino*, USA, December, 2005, p. 145
Berry, Colin. "Installationview." *Print*, USA, November/December, 2005, p. 324
____. "Ryan McGinness: Installationview." *Juxtapoz*, USA, No. 59,
    November/December, 2005, p. 76
Bourgais, Étienne. "Galerie Art Multiplicatif." *B. Story*, France, No. 1, 2005, pp. 10, 22-23
Valdez, Sarah. "Ryan McGinness." *Paper*, USA, Vol. 22, No. 5, November, 2005, p. 124
Ollman, Leah. "Ryan McGinness at Quint." *Art in America*, USA, No. 10,
    November, 2005, p.189
Tanner, Dylan. "Ryan McGinness Has Nothing to Hide." *Portland State University Vanguard*,
    USA, November 2, 2005
____. "Goings on About Town: Ryan McGinness." *The New Yorker*, USA,
    November 7, 2005, p. 23
Lappin, Criswell. "McGinness is God." *Metropolis*, USA, October, 2005, pp. 40, 42
____. "Vu Pour Vous." *Beaux Arts*, France, October 2005, p. 78
Motley, John. "Ryan McGinness." *The Portland Mercury*, USA,
    October 27-November 2, 2005
Tanner, Dylan. "The Evelution of Intellegent Design." *Portland State University Vanguard*,
    USA, October 26,
Roberts, Todd C. "McGinness' Goal." *Res*, USA, Vol. 8, No. 4, pp. 39
____. "Hot List: Graphology." *Harper's Bazaar*, USA, October 2005, p. 211
____. "Education Is in Fashion." *Vanity Fair*, USA, No. 542, October 2005, p. 74
Deitch, Jeffrey. "Ryan's Forest of Signs." *Installationview*, Rizzoli International Publications,
    Inc., USA, 2005, pp. 13-15
Bronson, AA. "From Low to High and Back Again." *Installationview*, Rizzoli International
    Publications, Inc., USA, 2005, pp. 77-80
McCormick, Carlo. "Hybrid States." *Installationview*, Rizzoli International Publications,
    Inc., USA, 2005, pp. 201-204
Gladman, Randy. "Art and Entertainment." *Installationview*, Rizzoli International
    Publications, Inc., USA, 2005, pp. 211-215
Briggs, Newt. "Culture Watch: Punk Art." *Departures*, USA, July/August, 2005, p. 78

Schmidt, Jason. "Work in Progress: Ryan McGinness." *V Magazine*, USA, Fall Preview, 2005, p. 42
Trebay, Guy. "Keeping T-Shirts In the Moment." *The New York Times*, USA, July 21, 2005, p. G1, G5
Yesilada, Merve. "Art That Is Just Wallpaper." *UCSA Guardian*, USA, Vol. 115, July 8, 2005
Nuckols, Ben. "Exhibit Brings Together Artists from Youth Subcultures." *Newsday*, USA, July 1, 2005
Heartney, Eleanor. "Return to the Real?." *Art in America*, USA, No. 6, June/July, 2005, pp. 85-89
Freeman Gill, John. "Urban History to Go: Black, No Sugar." *The New York Times*, USA, June 26, 2005, p. CY 4
Jones, Matt. "Art." *Exit*, UK, Issue 10, Spring/Summer, 2005, p. 24
Nakamura, Eric. "Book Collector." *Giant Robot*, USA, Issue 37, 2005, p. 18
Moore, Thurston. *Mix Tape: The Art of Cassette Culture*, Universe Publishing, USA, 2005, pp. 46-49
Boardman, Mickey. "Home Is Where the Art Is." *Paper*, USA, May, 2005, pp. 106-109
Pincus, Robert. "A Win for 'Loser'." *San Diego Union-Tribune*, USA, April 28, 2005, p. 34
Nakamura, Eric. "Ryan's Hope." *Giant Robot*, USA, Issue 36, 2005, pp. 36-41, 82
Boatwright, Angela. "Inside Look: Ryan McGinness." *The Drama*, USA, Spring, 2005, p. 12
____. "Culture Shock: In the Mix," *Gotham*, USA, Vol. 5, Issue 3, March, 2005, p. 298
McGee, Celia. "PS 1's Study in Cutting-Edge." *Daily News*, USA, March 11, 2005
____. "Diary of an Overworked Artist." *Black Book*, USA, No. 37, February/March, 2005, pp. 101-102
Graff, Philippe. "McGinness chez agnès b." *Spray*, France, No. 9, 2005, pp. 6, 45, 80
Lameignère, E., "Ryan McGinness." *Redux Magazine*, France, No. 4, 2005, p. 16
____. "30 Global Visionaries." *Planet*, USA, No. 9, 2005, pp. 6, 45, 80
Pagel, David. "Fight the System: Search for Beauty." *Los Angeles Times*, USA, February 15, 2005, p. E1, E4
____. "Color My World." *The New York Times Style Magazine*, USA, Winter 2005
Twemlow, Alice. "Well Hung." *Grafik*, UK, No. 126, February, 2005, pp. 42-45
____. "Crazy in Love." *Paper*, USA, February, 2005, p. 48

2004
Boatwright, Angela. "Extra Curricular." *Anthem*, USA, No. 15, 2004, p. 94
Kawachi, Taka. "Ryan McGinness." *Luca*, Japan, No. 8, Special Issue, 2004, pp. 30-31
James, Todd. "REAS Presents: Ryan McGinness." *Mass Appeal*, USA, Issue 31, December, 2004, pp. 74-75
Nakamura, Eric. "Book Collector: Living Signs." *Giant Robot*, USA, Issue 35, 2004, p. 24
____. "Black Book Gift Guide." *Black Book*, USA, No. 36, December, 2004, p. 50
Earthly Delights, exhibition catalogue, Massachustts College of Art, USA, 2004
O'Connor, Pauline. "A Night Out with Ryan McGinness." *The New York Times*, USA, November 21, 2004, p. ST 4
____. "The Man-Child Gift Guide." *Time Out*, USA, Issue 477, November 18-24, 2004, p. 36
Coleman, Michael. "Beautiful Losers." *Bail*, USA, No. 3, Fall 2004, p. 46
Witkin, Christian. "Big Night (Esquire Style)." *Esquire*, USA, Vol. 142, No. 5, November 2004, pp. 160-169
Epler, Matt and Krauss, Peter. "Touring the Studios: Ryan McGinness." *Res*, USA, Vol. 7, No. 5, pp. 54-55
Iwakoshi, Yuka. "In New York City." *Quest Magazine*, Japan, No. 18, 2004, pp. 18-19
Rose, Aaron. "Beautiful Losers." *Monster Children*, Australia, No. 6, Winter, 2004, pp. 70-83
Von Poggensee, Amanda. "Reconstructing Reality." *Zink Magazine*, USA, October, 2004, pp. 216-217
____. "The New Collectibles." *The New York Times*, USA, Style Magazine, September 19, 2004, p. 88
Kawachi, Taka. "Beautiful Losers." *Luca*, Japan, No. 6, 2004, pp. 68-79
Beautiful Losers: Contemporary Art and Street Culture, Iconoclast/D.A.P., USA, 2004, pp. 97, 118, 119, 231, 254
Petronio, Ezra. "Styles and Styles." *Self Service*, USA, No. 21, Fall/Winter, 2004, p. 132
Baker, Kenneth. "Bubbling Over in Talent." *Art News*, USA, Vol. 103, No. 8, September, 2004, p. 102
Dougherty, Michael. "The Art of the Mix Tape." *Black Book*, USA, No. 34, Fall, 2004, p. 58
Sasnaitis, Jurate. "Ryan McGinness: Project Rainbow." *Poster*, Australia, Issue 5, Autumn, 2004, p. 14
Stricker, Eric. "Beautiful Losers." *Transworld Skateboarding*, USA, Vol. 22, No. 9, September, 2004, pp. 200-213
____. "Ryan McGinness Soccer Ball." *Cargo*, USA, September, 2004, p. 71
Gibb, Brian. "Ryan McGinness." *Art Prostitute*, USA, Issue 4, Summer, 2004, pp. 69-79
____. "Ryan McGinness." *i-D*, UK, No. 246, August, 2004, p. 94
Newton, Matthew. "Style: Beautiful Losers." *XLR8R*, USA, Issue 79, August, 2004, pp. 72-73
Nelson, Katherine. "Signs of the Times." *ReadyMade*, USA, Issue 12, July/August, 2004, pp. 42-43
____. "Ven a Mi Expo." *Neo2*, Spain, No. 35, July/August, 2004, p. 135
Sastre, Leticia. "Ryan McGinness." *Vanidad*, Spain, No. 107, July/August, 2004, p. 45
Jacobs, Kate. "The Dream Team." *Paper Magazine*, USA, June/July, 2004, p. 32
____. "Expo: Ryan McGinness." *H*, Spain, No. 54, June, 2004, p. 10
García Yelo, María. "Ryan McGinness: Living Signs." *Blanco Negro Cultural*, Spain, No. 645, June, 2004, p. 30

Vozmediano, Elena. "McGinness y la Superabundancia Icónica." *El Cultural*, Spain, May 20-26, 2004, p. 28
Kawachi, Taka. "We Are Beautiful Losers." *Relax*, Japan, May, 2004, pp. 82-89
Powers, Bill. "Wearable Art." *The New York Times*, USA, Sunday Styles, April 18, 2004, p. 3
Mendelsohn, Meredith. "Ryan McGinness: Deitch Projects." *Art News*, USA, Vol. 103, No. 4, April, 2004, p. 117
Temin, Christine. "Weird Science." *The Boston Globe*, USA, February 27, 2004, pp. C15, C20
Bruley, Abigale. "Ryan McGinness: Project Rainbow Connection." *Rockpile*, USA, No. 100, 2004, pp. 56-59
Khemsurov, Monica. "Profile: Ryan McGinness." *Surface*, USA, No. 45, 2004, pp. 113-115
____. "Neuerscheinungen: Ryan McGinness, Project Rainbow."*Page*, Germany, February, 2004, p. 112
____. "The Commodificaton of Street Art." *Tokion*, USA, January/February, 2004, pp. 42-47

2003
Nakamura, Eric. "Book Collector: Project Rainbow." *Giant Robot*, USA, Issue 31, Winter, 2003/2004, p. 24
____. "New York: Ryan McGinness." *Elle*, Japan, No. 230, December, 2003, p. 109
Heavy, Alife/Neverstop, USA, 2003, p. 16
Amoral, A.D. "Rainbow Connections." *Philadelphia City Paper*, USA, No. 960, October 9-13, 2003
Chen, Aric. "Graphic Language." *hint.com*, USA, October, 2003
Stochl, Gerhard. "A Conversation with Ryan McGinness." *Lodown*, Germany, No. 37, Fall 2003, pp. 62-68
Switzer, Ken. "Pop Culture Gurus." *The Village Voice*, USA, Vol. XLVIII, September 3-9, 2003, p. 52
____. "Facsimile Template." *Arkitip*, USA, Issue 18, Fall 2003, p. 96
Swanson, Carl. "Punk Soul Brother." *Black Book*, USA, No. 29, Fall 2003, pp. 74-76
King, James. "Design for Kids." *Eye*, UK, Number 48, Vol. 12, Summer 2003, p. 86
____. "Anytime Life-Like: Ryan McGinness." *Studio Voice*, Japan, Vol. 326, February, 2003, p. 11
"Hot Apple Pie." *Metropolis*, Dir. Monica Blas & Luis Cerveró, Spanish TV Program, 2003
____. "Book Collector: Ryan McGinness (Gas Book 09)." *Giant Robot*, USA, Issue 28, Summer, 2003, p. 20
McCormick, Carlo. "Ver-The-Counter Culture." *Paper Magazine*, USA, May 2003, pp. 86-91
Design for Kids, Viction Workshop, China, 2003, pp. 158-167
Nadel, Dan. "Y'Know, Cool Stuff…." *Eye*, UK, No. 47, Vol. 12, Spring 2003, pp. 18-29
Fujimori, Manami. "Very New York." *Bijutsu Techo*, Japan, Vol. 55, No. 829, 2003, pp. 37, 54-55, 278
Akasaka, Eijin. "Who's Who: Ryan McGinness." *Pen*, Japan, No. 100, February, 2003, p. 120
____. "Julia Chiang/Ryan McGinness." *Sherman*, USA, No. 1, Winter 2002/2003, p. 15
____. "The Great Escape." *Boiler*, Italy, January-March, 2003, pp. 74-77
Beatty, Dustin. "Ryan McGinness." *Anthem*, USA, No. 8, Spring 2003, pp. 62-69
____. "Player's Choice." *Vogue*, Japan, No. 43, March, 2003, insert, p. 277
Low, Tad. "Stop Signs: Ryan McGinness Reinvents Your World." *Made Magazine*, Canada, Spring 2003, pp. 61-83
____. "What the World Needs Now: Ryan McGinness." *Relax*, Japan, February, 2003, pp. 30-33
Hung Yan Wing, Tom. "Ryan McGinness: This Dream Is So Life-Like." *Milk*, China, Issue 78, January, 2003, insert

2002
Nishimura, Daisuke. "Ryan McGinness." *Atmosphere*, Japan, Issue 01, Fall 2002, pp. 2-3
Damura, Haruka. "Portraits: The Creators." *Flux*, Canada, Fall 2002, pp. 13-15
Nakamura, Eric. "Dream Gardeners." *Giant Robot*, USA, Issue 26, Fall 2002, pp. 62-63
Farrelly, Liz. "Space Invaders." *The Independent Magazine*, UK, August 3, 2002, pp. 41-42
Farrell, Aimée. "Vital Signs." *Vogue*, UK, August, 2002, p. 40
Zepher. "Royal Elastic Streetwise One." *While You Were Sleeping*, USA, Issue 19, 2002, p. 30
Towhindn, Mandana. "Import of the Month." *Dazed & Confused*, UK, August, 2002, p. 140
____. "Julia Chiang and Ryan McGinness." *The New Yorker*, USA, July 29, 2002, p. 17
ONOX. "Ryan McGinness, Earth Music Artist T Series." *Relax*, Japan, August, 2002, pp. 124-125
____. "Ryan McGinness." *Co.S, Contents Supreme*, Japan, Vol. 5, June/July, 2002, p. 6
Inspiration = Ideas, Rockport Publishers, USA, 2002, pp. 90-95
Glickman, Adam. "The Disobedients: Ryan McGinness Interview." *Tokion*, USA, May/June, 2002, pp. 32-34
____. "Favorite Disks." *Ryoko Tsushin*, Japan, Vol. 467, May, 2002, p. 113
Mulvihill, Kieth. "Kitsch and Caboodle." *Time Out*, USA, Issue 336, March 7-14, 2002, pp. 14-15
____. "Hot Off The Presses!." *Strength*, USA, April, 2002, p. 48
Glickman, Adam. "Dalek vs. Ryan McGinness vs. Ease vs. Ro Starr." *Tokion*, USA, March/April, 2002, pp. 40-43
____. "Sunday People." *Relax*, Japan, March, 2002, p. 134
Gladman, Randy. "Ryan McGinness: Art & Entertainment." *Strength*, USA, January/February, 2002, pp. 95-102

____. "Ryan McGinness." *Art Investor*, Germany, January/February, 2002, p. 50
____. "People Around Alife." *Relax*, Japan, February, 2002, p. 84
Kawachi, Taka. "Art: Ryan McGinness." *Ryoko Tsushin*, Japan, Vol. 462, January, 2002, p. 137
____. "Ryan McGinness." *Advertising Criticism*, Japan, No. 256, January, 2002, pp. 120-124
Dougherty, Emily. "Board Game." *Nylon*, USA, December/January, 2002, p. 46

2001
____. "Ninety-nine A-List." *Strength*, USA, December, 2001, p. 72
Zines, Booth-Clibborn Editions, UK, 2001, p. 17
____. "Pieceofmind." *Umbrella Magazine*, USA, Vol. 24, No. 3/4, December, 2001
Te-ton. "Best Must Hit Shit: A.R.O." *Relax*, Japan, December, 2001, p. 126
Dank, Roy. "Anti-Art: Ryan McGinness." *XLR8R*, USA, No. 54, November, 2001, p. 19
Kawachi, Taka. "New York & Duchamp: Ryan McGinness." *GQ Japan*, Japan, No. 104, October, 2001, pp. 112-113
____. "Spunky." *The New Yorker*, USA, October 22, 2001, p. 14
Johnson, Ken. "Spunky." *The New York Times*, USA, October 19, 2001, p. E39
Bergmans, Jeroen. "The Agenda." *Wallpaper*, USA, October, 2001, p. 286
Wright, Jeffrey. "Space: The Final Frontier." *NY Arts*, USA, Vol. 6, No. 10, October, 2001, p. 76
Sato, Eko. "Colette Seen By Ryan McGinness." *Studio Voice*, Japan, Vol. 310, October, 2001, pp. 44-45
Lewis, Terry. "Graphic Guerrilla." *Jalouse*, France, November, 2001, pp. 36-37
Hatakeyama, Hiroyiki. "Art for All: Ryan McGinness." *Relax*, Japan, October, 2001, pp. 30-35
____. "Ryan McGinness: Le Livre Or & Noir." *Depeche Mode*, France, September, 2001, p. 10
Scrawl: More Dirt, Booth-Clibborn Editions, UK, 2001, pp. 72-77
____. "Q&A." *Gasbook*, Japan, No. 11, Fall, 2001
Maekawa, Akane. "Denim to Mode: Ryan McGinness." *Ryoko Tsushin*, Japan, Vol. 458, September, 2001, p. 85
____. "Luxurygood." *Umbrella Magazine*, USA, Vol. 24, No. 2, August, 2001, p. 52
Hatakeyama, Hiroyiki. "Man Watching." *Relax*, Japan, August, 2001, p. 20
de Bure, Gilles. "Ryan McGinness: Portrait." *L'oeil*, France, July/August, 2001, p. 16
____. "Fusion." *Sportswear International*, USA, Summer, 2001, p. 35
____. "Pure Genius." *i-D*, UK, Issue 211, July, 2001, p. 36
____. *The Paris Review*, USA, Issue 158, Spring/Summer 2001, cover
Perruche, Céline. "Ryan McGinness: Fun Art." *Perso*, France, July/August, 2001, p. 18
____. "Rawhide!." *Strength*, USA, July/August, 2001, p. 42
Smith, Roberta. "Ryan McGinness: Vocabularytest." *The New York Times*, USA, June 8, 2001, p. E31
____. "Birth (Ryan McGinness)." *Fidget*, USA, Spring, Issue 4, 2001, p. 12
____. "Colette." *The Style*, Japan, June, 2001, p. 150
Wolff, Zoë. "Ryan McGinness Beer Cozies." *Time Out*, Issue 296, USA, May 24-31, 2001, p. 27
____. "Ryan McGinness: Vocabularytest." *The New Yorker*, USA, May 28, 2001, p. 26
Turchin, Dr. Valentin. "Language, Metalanguage, and the Metasystem Transition." *Vocabularytest*, Joseph Silvestro Gallery, USA, 2001, pp. 8-13
Russell, Peter. "The Global Brain." *Vocabularytest*, Joseph Silvestro Gallery, USA, 2001, pp. 16-23
Hunt, David. "Signal Density." *Vocabularytest*, Joseph Silvestro Gallery, USA, 2001, pp. 26-28
Cotter, Holland. "Mixed Greens at Space 101." *The New York Times*, USA, May 18, 2001, p. E29
Kawachi, Taka. "Poetic Horizons: Ryan McGinness." *Studio Voice*, Japan, Vol. 306, June, 2001, p. 28
Waterman, Lauren. "Mixed Greens." *Vogue*, USA, May, 2001, p. 188
Iwakoshi, Yuka/Noe, Rain. "Ryan McGinness." *Educated Community*, USA, Issue 5, Spring, 2001, pp. 10-12
Turner, Grady. "Portnoy's Complaint: A Memo to Fellow Art Critics." *Flash Art*, USA, March-April, 2001, pp. 43, 51
Saizarbitoria, Jauretsi. "Try Not to Graffiti the Chickens." *Jane*, USA, April, 2001, p. 56
Hunt, David. "Honcho Featured Artist: Ryan McGinness." *Honcho*, USA, March, 2001, pp. 75-76
____. "Tough Enough." *Nylon*, USA, March, 2001, p. 86
____. "Art Page." *Flux*, Canada, Issue 11, 2001, p. 8
Logo World, P.I.E. Books, Japan, 2001
____. "No Shtick." *Strength*, USA, March, 2001, p. 36
Donalds, Ariana. "Full Volume: Ryan McGinness." *Print*, USA, Issue LV:I, January/February, 2001, pp. 131-133
Kamijyo, Masahiro. "90s Design Overview: Flatnessisgod." *Design Plex*, Japan, January, 2001, pp. 35-65
____. "Ryan McGinness, Luxurygood." *Giant Robot*, USA, Issue 20, Spring 2001, p. 14
Hataketyama, Hiroyuki. "Ryan McGinness." *Ryoko Tsushin*, Japan, Vol. 451, February, 2001, pp. 32-33
____. "Alife." *Paper Magazine*, USA, January, 2001, p. 96
Velez, Ben. "Welcome to Flavor Country." *Flyer*, USA, January, 2001, pp. 24-27
____. "Ryan McGinness." *Sense*, Japan, Issue 1, 2001, p. 20
____. "Jesus Beer Koozies." *Vice*, Canada, Vol. 7, No. 9, 2001, p. 31
____. "Sound Icons." *Sandbox*, USA, Winter 2001, p. 11

2000
Search for Art, Italy, Mandarina Duck, 2000, pp. 132-133
Floridis, Tad. "Pop Smear Guerilla Artist." *Gear*, USA, November, 2000, pp. 36-37

____. "Board Games." *Details*, USA, Fall 2000, p. 164
McGuinness, Mary. "Nuance of (non) sense." *Luxurygood*, Alife, USA, 2000, pp. 9-10
Fowler, Brendan. "Interview." *Luxurygood*, Alife, USA, 2000, pp. 13-18
Burnham, Helen. "Uncanny Insites." *Interior Spaces in Contemporary Art*, exhibition catalog, USA, Whitney Museum of American Art at Champion, 2000, p. 17
____. "The Face of Change: 100 Years of Self Portraits." *List*, USA, Summer 2000, p. 128
____. "Postcards from the Edge." *V Magazine*, USA, Issue 6, Summer 2000, p. 56
Snyder, Scott. "Ryan McGinness." *Arkitip*, USA, Issue 5, 2000, pp. 9-13
Hunt, David. "Tomorrow." *Tomorrow*, exhibition catalog, USA, Rare, New York, 2000, pp. 8, 32-35
____. "Hot Graphic Artist: Ryan McGinness." *Details*, USA, April 2000, p. 87
Ivinski, Pamela A. "Begin the Begets." *Print*, USA, Issue LIII:VI, 2000, p. 20
Grant, Angelynn. "Book Reviews: flatnessisgod." *Communication Arts*, USA, January/February 2000, p. 178

1999
Royce, Roger. "Ryan McGinness." *Copper Press*, USA, Issue 2, Winter 1999, pp. 76-78
VanderLans, Rudy. "Selfsameness." *Emigre*, USA, Issue 52, Winter 1999, pp. 49-59
____. "Samplers: 10 Hot Items." *Gear*, USA, December, 1999, p. 28
____. "Ryan McGinness." *Fidget*, USA, Issue 1, October, 1999, p. 16
Chaplin, Julia. "Pulse: Lafayette Street." *The New York Times*, USA, October 3, 1999, p. ST3
____. "Ryan McGinness." *Search for Art Magazine*, Italy, No. 2, September 1999, pp. 16-21
____. "Words About Pictures." *Feed Magazine*, USA, feedmag.com, 1999
Blackburn, Mary Walling. "flatnessisgod." *Weekly Alibi*, USA, September 27, 1999
Hoyt, Mathew. "Who Uses Who: Flatnessisgod." *Zing Magazine*, USA, Vol. 3, Fall 1999, p. 271
____. "Eye Candy: flatnessisgod." *Pop Culture 1999*, USA, Fall 1999, pp. 4, 14
G. Dave. "Flatness is God." *Vice*, Canada, Vol. 6, No.7, 1999, p. 81
____. "Flatnessisgod Review." *Umbrella*, USA, Vol. 22, September, 1999, p. 83
Bruton, Clive. "Ryan McGinness: Is it design? Is it art? It is Life!." *DZ3.com*, UK, 1999
McCarthy, Jackie. "Sight Gag: Ryan McGinness Makes Artistic Virtue out of Design Necessity." *Resonance*, USA, Issue 22, 1999, pp. 12-13
Reid, Calvin. "Small Press New York." *Publishers Weekly*, USA, August 16, 1999, p. 25
Holland, Taylor. "Off the Bookshelf." *The Austin Chronicle*, USA, August 2, 1999
Ferguson, Sarah. "The Punks of Publishing." *The Village Voice*, USA, June 30, 1999, villagevoice.com
Turner, Grady. "Museum as Muse." *Flash Art*, USA, May/June 1999, p. 48
Gute, Charles. "Book Report from L.A." *artnet.com*, USA, June, 1999
Stewart, Mathew. "Ryan McGinness Line Art." *Surface*, USA, Issue #45, 1999, p. 130
____. "99 to Watch in 99." *Time Out*, USA, Jan/Feb 1999, p. 24
1 & 2 Color Graphics Volume 2, P.I.E. Books, Japan, 1999, pp. 47, 103, 213

1997
New Typographics 2, P.I.E. Books, Japan, 1997, pp. 75, 77, 187
____. "The Early Word." *Microsoft's Sidewalk.com*, USA, 1997
Morel, James. "McGinness, Ryan J." *Popsmear Magazine*, USA, No. 10, 1997, pp. 8-9

1996
Stacey, Dave. "Tupperware!." *Mommy & I Are One*, USA, 1996, pp. 50-51
____. "Opening to End All Openings." *Resident Publications*, USA, Fall 1996
Hammond, Bryce. "Art Haiku." *Hero Ragazine*, USA, 1996, pp. 34-35

1995
Creative Flyer Graphics 2, P.I.E. Books, Japan, 1995, pp. 80-81
____. "Typographic." *Razorfish's BlueDot*, USA, 1995
Morel, James. "Live at Ryan McGinness' Studio." *Popsmear Magazine*, USA, No. 6, 1995, p. 50

Acknowledgments & Credits

Contributors

Dieter Buchhart

Dieter Buchhart is a curator and art theorist. After completing doctorates in both art history and the science of restoration, he has curated many exhibitions at renowned museums and art spaces around the world. From 2007 to 2009, he served as director of the Kunsthalle Krems near Vienna. As an art critic, he has published many articles and interviews in prominent art journals like *Kunstforum International* and several monographs. The author of many catalogue essays, magazine articles, and lectures dealing with art theory, his research foci include art around 1900 and expressionism, 1980s art, and contemporary art.

Translation of Dieter Buchhart's essay from German to English by **Dr. Brian Currid**.

Andrew Blauvelt

Andrew Blauvelt is a curator, designer, and educator. He is Director of Cranbrook Art Museum in Bloomfield Hills, Michigan. Prior to Cranbrook, Blauvelt was Senior Curator of Architecture and Design at the Walker Art Center in Minneapolis, where he also served in a number of capacities, including Design Director and Chief of Communications and Audience Engagement. His most recent exhibitions include *Hippie Modernism: The Struggle for Utopia* (2015) and *Too Fast to Live, Too Young to Die: Punk Graphics* (2018).

Ben Sutton

Benjamin Sutton is an art critic, journalist, and curator living in Brooklyn. He is the news editor at *Hyperallergic*, and his articles on public art, artist documentaries, the tedium of art fairs, and other divisive issues have appeared there and in *Modern Painters*, *Brooklyn Magazine*, *artnet News*, among others. He has curated exhibitions at the Lower East Side Printshop, Field Projects, the Spring Break Art Show, and the Gowanus Loft. *Mother & Child* originally appeared in *Editions '17* published by The Lower East Side Printshop in 2017.

Carlo McCormick

Carlo McCormick is a critic and curator based in New York City. *In the Forest of Signs* originally appeared in *Juxtapoz*, No. 173, Vol. 22, No. 6, June, 2015, cover, pp. 10, 48-59.

Bill Powers

Bill Powers owns Half Gallery in New York. He is editor-at-large for *Purple Fashion Magazine*. His work has also appeared in *The New York Times*, *ARTnews*, and *GQ Style*. A previous version of *Shock & Aww* appeard in *Purple Magazine*, Vol. 3, Issue 11, Spring/Summer, 2009, pp. 56.

Photographers & Image Credits

Courtesy **Agnès B., Paris** p. 20

Austin Kennedy, Courtesy Pace Prints, New York pp. 95, 96, 97

Courtesy **Cincinnati Art Museum, Cincinnati** pp. 66, 67

Claire Schneider, Courtesy **Quint Gallery, San Diego** p. 156

Cormac Regan, Courtesy **La Casa Encendida, Madrid** pp. 110, 111

David Stover, Courtesy **Virginia Museum of Fine Arts, Richmond** pp. 126, 128, 129, 157

EPW Studio pp. 19, 22, 26, 28, 30, 31, 74, 75, 112, 113

Farzad Owrang Front Cover, Back Cover, pp. 2, 7, 8, 9, 14, 17, 18, 25, 28, 33, 41, 42, 44, 47, 48, 49, 53, 56, 57, 60, 61, 62, 63, 72, 73, 76, 77, 78, 79, 81, 82, 83, 84, 85, 86, 88, 89, 90, 91, 92, 93, 98, 102, 103, 106, 108, 109, 114, 115, 120, 121, 122, 123, 124, 125, 130, 131, 132, 133, 134, 138, 139, 155, 166

Courtesy **Galerie du Jour, Paris** p. 154

Hans Wilchut pp. 50, 51, 100, 101

Jenny Gorman p. 34

Courtesy **Kohn Gallery, Los Angeles** pp. 54, 55, 58, 104, 105, 135, 136, 137

Courtesy **Library Street Collective, Detroit** p. 37

Michael Halsband p. 45

Oren Eckhaus, Courtesy **Pace Prints, New York** p. 156

Courtesy **Parco Gallery, Tokyo** p. 152

PD Rearick, Courtesy **Cranbrook Art Museum** pp. 140, 141, 142, 143, 144, 145

Philipp Scholz Rittermann, Courtesy **Quint Gallery, San Diego** pp. 68, 69, 70, 71

Shepard Fairey, Courtesy **Black Market Gallery, Los Angeles** p. 152

Tim Darwish pp. 36, 151

Tom Powel Imaging, Inc. pp. 10, 116, 117, 118, 119, 150, 153, 154, 155

Tony Walsh, Courtesy **Contemporary Arts Center, Cincinnati** p. 154

Many of the pigments used in the paintings reproduced in this book reflect different sections of the light spectrum based on their physical properties. These unique attributes are further amplified with the artist's layering techniques. Therefore, in-person observation of the artworks is required for full appreciation. While it is obviously next to impossible to achieve by machine offset printing in four process inks the exact effects of these paints, the greatest possible care was taken to prevent loss of value and detail.

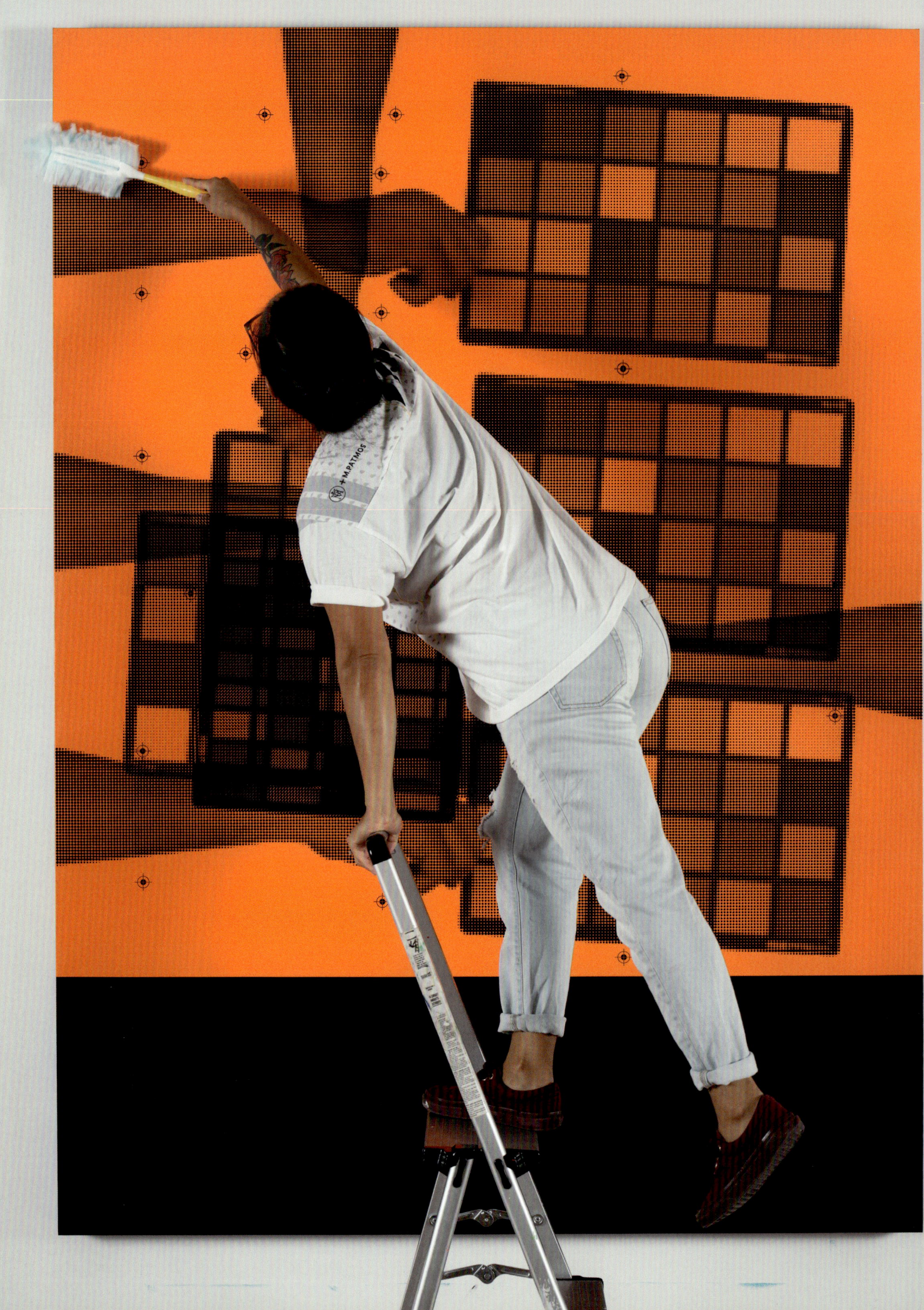

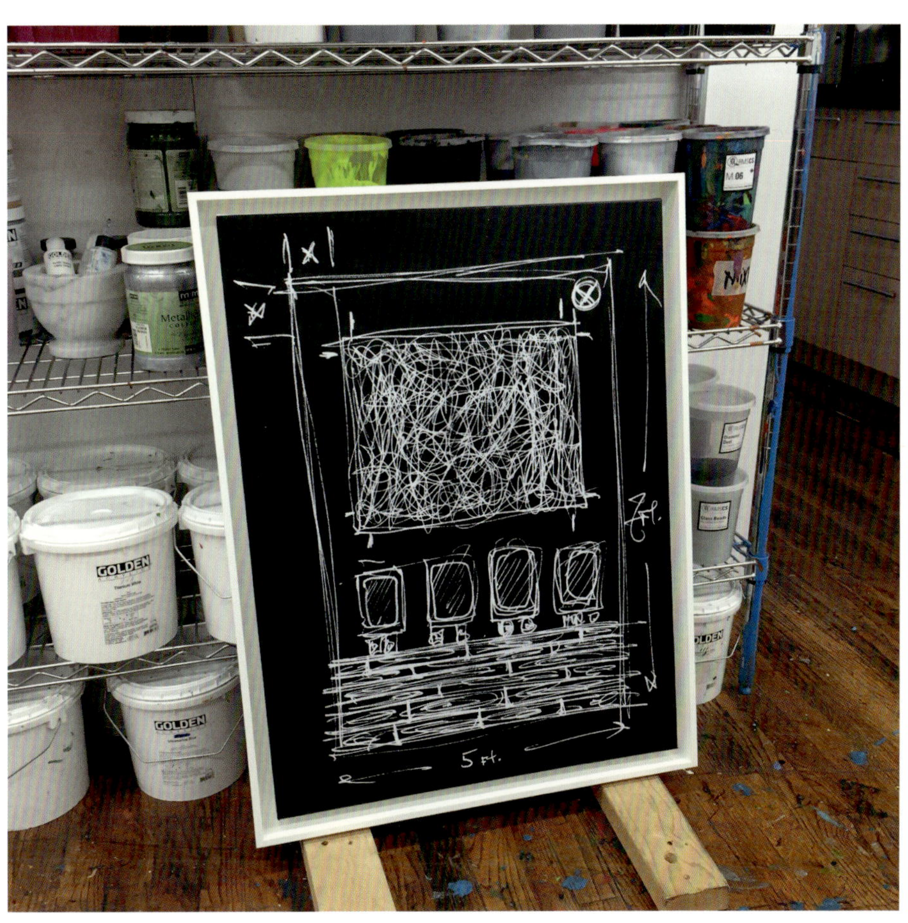

Opposite Page: Gina Kim in studio cleaning painting
Above: *Painting of a Sketch for a Painting* (in studio), 2016,
acrylic on linen, 30 x 22 in. (76.2 x 55.9 in.)